# THE BIBLE:
## A Reader's Guide

**Parting the Red Sea**
*Miracle is one theme of Exodus 14 when
Moses parts the Red Sea, allowing
God's people to leave Egypt and begin their
journey to the Promised Land (see page 28).*

# THE BIBLE:
# A Reader's Guide

R. P. Nettelhorst

METRO BOOKS

New York

**METRO BOOKS**
New York

An Imprint of Sterling Publishing
387 Park Avenue South
New York, NY 10016

**Editor** Liz Jones
**Art Director** Caroline Guest
**Designer** Tanya Goldsmith
**Picture Research** Sarah Bell
**Indexer** Diana LeCore
**Creative Director** Moira Clinch
**Publisher** Paul Carslake

ISBN 978-1-4351-3264-1

For information about custom editions, special
sales, and premium and corporate purchases,
please contact:

Sterling Special Sales at 800-805-5489 or
specialsales@sterlingpublishing.com.

Manufactured in China

10 9 8 7 6 5 4 3 2 1

www.sterlingpublishing.com

# Contents

# Foreword

The Bible was written thousands of years ago, in different languages, by people living in pre-industrial, mostly agricultural societies. The following pages are designed to serve as your roadmap to the foreign land that is the Bible. It is designed to become your travel guide, pointing out the significant sights while explaining their significance and putting them into context as you explore.

The Bible contains a range of literature: stories, poetry, wisdom, and letters composed by dozens of people over hundreds of years. It has comforted and challenged human beings around the world for thousands of years. The rich and poor, the famous and infamous, the farmer and scientist, the poet and laborer have all found benefit in reading it. The stories and poetry have affected our language and the message of the book has changed the lives of individuals and civilizations. Our modern concepts of justice, tolerance, love, and human rights all grow out of how this book has been read and put into practice.

Is the Bible simply a random assembly of ancient texts? Not at all. In fact, there are overall themes to its chapters. Jesus argued that the entire Bible could be summarized by two commands: to "love God" and to "love your neighbor as yourself."

Seeing the patterns that Jesus recognized in a book as large and complicated as the Bible isn't easy. During the first century, an Ethiopian treasury official was returning home after a visit to Jerusalem. As he traveled by chariot, he was struggling with a difficult section of the Bible. An early Christian named Philip ran up alongside him and asked, "Do you understand what you are reading?"

"How can I," said the Ethiopian, "unless someone explains it to me?"

R. P. Nettelhorst's book is designed to explain the Bible to those, like that ancient Ethiopian, who want to understand it better.

**History begins**
*History is the theme in the Bible's first chapter,*
*when God created the heavens, the earth, and*
*humanity, and history begins (see page 16).*

# About this book

This book is designed to come alongside the modern reader. Would you like to find all the moral teachings in the Bible? Would you like to follow all the passages that deal with worship? Do you want to know everything the Bible has to teach on prayer? Or know which sections are prophecies about the future—or history lessons from the past?

The key to this book is that every chapter of the Bible is summarized briefly and then color coded according to theme. It acts like a knowledgeable friend to guide you through the cultural and historical contexts, making it easy to grasp the meaning and purpose of any section, while seeing how it all fits into the bigger picture.

Those reading the Bible can use this book as introduction and guide. It will help them see the forest for the trees, granting an overall sense of where they are and where they are going. It will help keep travelers in this foreign land from getting lost and, in fact, will help them feel at home.

## Notes on the translation of the Bible

The New International Version (NIV) is the translation selected for the biblical quotations. It also served as the basis for the commentaries and introductions. The NIV was originally published in 1978 and was most recently updated in 2010. More than 100 scholars participated in both the original NIV and this latest revision. In order to avoid sectarian bias, the translators were selected from many denominations, from many different English-speaking nations including Australia, Canada, Great Britain, New Zealand, and the United States. Responsibility for the translation is held by a self-governing body, the Committee on Bible Translation, composed of scholars from many seminaries, colleges, and universities. The NIV translators made use of the best ancient texts currently available. Their translation also reflects recent changes in the English language. For instance, they adopted gender-neutral terms where gender is unspecified in the original text or where both genders were intended.

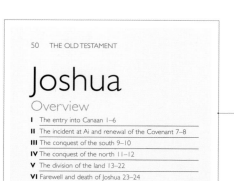

**Introductions**
*Each of the 66 books of the Bible is given a general introduction, including an overview of the book's structure.*

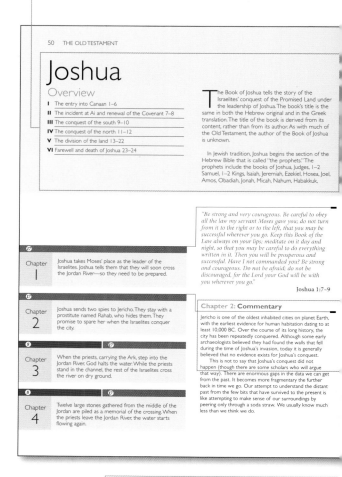

**Commentaries**
*Short commentaries discuss significant or difficult portions of the text, explaining the historical or cultural background, or significant theological issues.*

## Chapter 2: **Commentary**

Jericho is one of the oldest inhabited cities on planet Earth, with the earliest evidence for human habitation dating to at least 10,000 BC. Over the course of its long history, the city has been repeatedly conquered. Although some early archaeologists believed they had found the walls that fell during the time of Joshua's invasion, today it is generally believed that no evidence exists for Joshua's conquest.

This is not to say that Joshua's conquest did not happen (though there are some scholars who will argue that way).

**Theme finder**
*Each of the chapters
is assigned between
one and three
themes, coded by
color and number.*

| 8 | 17 |
|---|---|

The Israelites march around Jericho once a day for six days, and then seven times on the seventh day. Then the walls of Jericho fall down. The Israelites conquer Jericho.

Chapter
6

**Chapter
summaries**
*Each of the 1189
chapters that
make up the Bible
is summarized.*

| 9 | 17 |
|---|---|

Achin steals some of the spoils from Jericho, rather than destroying it. As a consequence, the Israelites lose a battle at Ai. Achin and his family are stoned to death for his theft.

Chapter
7

ephaniah, Haggai, Zechariah, and Malachi. The ophets are divided into two parts, the earlier, or rmer, and the later. The books of Joshua through Kings are referred to as "the earlier prophets" with e rest getting the designation "later prophets."
    Most scholars today see Joshua as part of a series writings that includes the books of Deuteronomy, dges, 1–2 Samuel, and 1–2 Kings that appear to ve been assembled during the time of Josiah or en later, during the Babylonian exile. These mbined works are sometimes referred to as the Deuteronomistic History" of Israel.

**Rahab**
*When Joshua sent spies to Jericho, they visited a brothel run by Rahab. She protected the spies, and so when the Israelites conquered Jericho and slaughtered its populace, they spared both her and her family.*

ow when Joshua was near Jericho, he looked up
d saw a man standing in front of him with a
awn sword in his hand. Joshua went up to him
d asked, "Are you for us or for our enemies?"
    "Neither," he replied, "but as commander of the
my of the Lord I have now come."
                                          Joshua 5:13–14

hapter 6: **Commentary**

shua's interaction with the angel of the Lord is puzzling.
ow could God not be on the Israelites' side?
    It is hard to miss the theological point of this exchange:
od is on his own side. The question for Joshua and the
her freed slaves is the question for all of us: are we
oosing to be on His side? God is not for or against
yone. If he's not even on his chosen people's side, then
hat hope does anyone else have? God isn't on our side,
hether it's a basketball game, a legal battle, or a war.

hapter 8: **Commentary**

me scholars propose that the story of the conquest of
is an etiological tale designed to explain the existence of
as a ruin. W.F. Albright suggested that the biblical story
tually describes the conquest of Bethel. Callaway
oposed that the story in Joshua describes the destruction
the small, unwalled village around 1125 BC. Others have
ggested that the Ai in Joshua has yet to be excavated and
s nothing to do with et-Tell at all.

| 8 | 17 |
|---|---|

The Israelites then circumcise all the men and celebrate Passover. For the first time, the Israelites eat some Canaanite food. The manna stops coming.

Chapter
5

| 8 | 17 |
|---|---|

The Israelites march around Jericho once a day for six days, and then seven times on the seventh day. Then the walls of Jericho fall down. The Israelites conquer Jericho.

Chapter
6

| 9 | 17 |
|---|---|

Achin steals some of the spoils from Jericho, rather than destroying it. As a consequence, the Israelites lose a battle at Ai. Achin and his family are stoned to death for his theft.

Chapter
7

| 11 | 17 |
|---|---|

The Israelites successfully conquer the small city of Ai. Joshua builds an altar on Mount Ebal, offers sacrifices, and the blessings and cursings of the covenant are read aloud.

Chapter
8

## Key to themes

Every chapter of the Bible is summarized briefly and color-coded according to theme. The 18 themes that have been applied to the texts will provide the reader with an overall sense of the primary point or points of each chapter. For more information about each of the themes, see pages 10–13.

| Praise | 1 |
|---|---|
| Forgiveness | 2 |
| Moral teaching | 3 |
| Mourning | 4 |
| Poetry | 5 |
| Parables | 6 |
| Prophecy | 7 |
| Miracles | 8 |
| Judgment | 9 |
| Love | 10 |
| Worship | 11 |
| Prayer | 12 |
| Apocalypse | 13 |
| Contract | 14 |
| Angels and Demons | 15 |
| Inventory | 16 |
| History | 17 |
| Wisdom Literature | 18 |

**Fold-out page: key
to the themes**
*Opposite page 255,
you'll find a fold-out
page containing an
at-a-glance key to the
color and number
system used to identify
the themes. Keep this
page open as you use
this book, or until you
become familiar with
the key.*

*Now when Joshua was near Jericho, he looked up
and saw a man standing in front of him with a
drawn sword in his hand. Joshua went up to him
and asked, "Are you for us or for our enemies?"*
    *"Neither," he replied, "but as commander of the
army of the Lord I have now come."*
                                          **Joshua 5:13–14**

**Selected
quotations**
*There are important
quotations from each of
the biblical books.*

# About the themes

**Prophet in peril**
*When Daniel refused to pray to anyone but God, Darius threw him to the lions in Daniel 6. Miracle and Prayer become that chapter's dominant themes (see page 175).*

**An angel appears**
*Gabriel reveals the future to the prophet Daniel in Daniel 9. That chapter's themes include Prophecy, Apocalypse, and Angels and Demons (see page 175).*

The division of the Bible into chapters was done somewhat haphazardly for reference purposes, long after the Bible was written. The chapter divisions were not made on the basis of content. So, chapters can sometimes contain multiple ideas or themes.

Of the hundreds of ideas and motifs to be found in the Bible, it is possible to reduce them to 18 broad themes. So, for example, the theme of "Parables" also includes fables. "Inventory" includes all the genealogies, the lists of materials used for building the Temple, the census records, the lists of priests or musicians, soldiers, military conquests, and the arrangement of territory distributed among the tribes. "Moral Teaching" includes the laws of Moses, the words of Jesus, and Paul's instructions to local churches and words of encouragement.

The 18 themes that have been applied to the texts will provide the reader with an overall sense of the primary point or points of each chapter. It is one thing to use an index or concordance to locate a given phrase or word. But if the reader wishes to locate all the passages in the Bible that focus on poetry, or to discover all the parables, the 18 broad themes will make that task much easier.

**Following is a key to the colored tabs and the themes they relate to, with a little contextual information about each one.**

## Praise

People praise God by describing his wonderful characteristics, and by recounting all the great things he had done for them, their loved ones, or their nation. Praise is commonly offered to God in response to his actions: because he delivered an individual or a group from some trouble, or simply in general recognition of God as creator and daily benefactor. Praise serves to help people avoid taking life and its joys for granted.

## Mourning

Mourning is an outward expression of sorrow in the face of personal or national suffering, loss, and disaster. It is often linked with hope for a better future. Mourning is often expressed in poetry and it is often ritualized. It is commonly directed to God as a complaint, with the request and hope, stated or unstated, that God will respond and alleviate the cause of the mourning, and restore prosperity, peace, and joy.

## Forgiveness

Throughout the Bible, the guilty regularly beg God for mercy when they realize they are being punished for a crime. God is willing to grant them relief. In response, the guilty turn from their wickedness, begin living righteously, and apologize. But God grants his forgiveness first. God's forgiveness is an undeserved kindness that he graciously bestows on those who are still his enemies. God even forgives those who continue to return to the same sin, every time they ask.

## Poetry

Poetry is an expression of emotions in a memorable and ornately structured way. While many cultures rhyme sounds in their poetry, the poetry of the Bible rhymes concepts instead. Poetry impacts the heart more than the head, and so will be most common in prayers, in praise, and in lamentation. It is found throughout the Bible, both in the Old and New Testaments. The Psalms, the Proverbs, and most of the prophecies of the Bible are poetry.

## Moral teaching

The moral teaching in the Bible explains how people should treat one another and includes, among other things, all the commandments and legal texts of the Bible. It also includes Jesus' words to his disciples, instructions about prayer, and the qualifications of deacons and pastors. It includes the beatitudes and the comforting words of encouragement offered to those going through difficult times. The moral teachings are summed up in the single command to love one another.

## Parables

Parables and fables are short, memorable stories. They appear throughout the Bible. Fables use animals and plants as the main characters, while parables use people. Parables and fables have a moral. They are not designed just for entertainment, but to teach and to bring about a change in behavior. In most instances, parables and fables have but a single point to make. Jesus regularly taught by using parables and in fact, most of the parables in the Bible came from him.

# Prophecy

A prophecy is usually a warning that God's judgment is coming. It describes future events. Most, though not all, prophecies in the Bible are poetic. The descriptions are often cryptic and make more sense following the predicted events than before them. Prophecies are rarely heeded. Prophecy comes from God through his spokespeople, the prophets. Prophecy shows up throughout the Bible, both in the Old and New Testaments, and not just in the books traditionally labeled as "prophets."

# Love

According to Jesus, loving God and loving people summarizes all the Commandments. People do not harm those they love. Love, therefore, is the overall point of the Bible. Ideally, love means desiring what is best for others, regardless of their behavior. Love describes emotions ranging from sexual desire to the feelings of parents, children, siblings, and friends for one another. It also refers to the obligations that exist within covenant relationships, such as the one between God and Israel.

# Miracles

Although it is common to think of miracles as a violation of natural law, modern theologians generally reject that as a definition. God seems no more willing to violate the natural laws than he is to violate the moral laws. Miracles are actually simply the intervention of the divine in human affairs in ways that are spectacular and noticeable, as when God parted the Red Sea, Jesus turned water into wine, or an outnumbered Israelite army defeated its enemies.

# Worship

Worship is about focusing on God through ritual. In a general sense, every aspect of life may be counted as part of worship. However, worship is usually more specifically about the sacrifices, the offering of prayers, public assemblies for praise or thanks, and the celebration of the feast days. It includes the Temple, the altars, the equipment, and even the clothing of the priests. Worship includes fasting, circumcision, abstaining from certain foods, and keeping the Sabbath.

# Judgment

Judgment is the deserved punishment rendered to those guilty of violating contracts, relationships, laws, regulations, and customs. God judges his people when they violate the agreements they have made with him, just as governments judge those who break the laws of the land, and just as parents punish their children who misbehave. Judgment is always in the context of a relationship with God, governments, or individuals. God's judgments have a corrective and redemptive purpose.

# Prayer

Prayer happens when people talk to God. It happens when people let him know how they feel and what they want and need. Sometimes it is formal and public; other times it is informal and private. Human beings seek God's counsel and aid, they offer thanks for personal and national deliverance, and they beg forgiveness for personal and corporate sins. Prayers move and influence God and move and influence the one who is praying.

# Apocalypse

During times of suffering and oppression, apocalyptic literature expressed the desire for judgment against those responsible. Apocalypse expresses the hope that God will establish a kingdom of righteousness and justice. It was a style of literature common in the last century BC and the first century AD. Apocalypse appears in the Old Testament prophets, including sections of Daniel, Ezekiel, and Isaiah. In the New Testament, the Book of Revelation stands as the primary example of apocalypse.

# Inventory

Inventory includes all the lists in the Bible, whether of genealogies, names and numbers of people, their property, the land allotments of tribes, tax records, donations, building materials for the Temple, ceremonies, soldiers, or exiles. The lists demonstrated for the Bible's original readers that the Bible's stories were about their relatives. That the stories included mundane details demonstrated God's concern, not just for nations and empires, but for individuals and the affairs of everyday life.

# Contract

Contracts are formal, legally binding agreements or promises made between individuals, between nations, and between God and his people. An older term used by theologians for the contracts of the Bible is "covenant" or "testament." Thus, the entire Bible is divided into two contracts, called the Old and New Testaments. The contractual nature of God's relationships explains how people in the Bible related to God and why God acted toward them the way that he did.

# History

History is the story of what happened in the lives of people and nations, arranged more or less chronologically. In the Bible, history explains the significance of past events in the lives of God's people, with both corporate and individual implications. As Paul would write in the New Testament, "These things happened to them as examples and were written down as warnings for us, on whom the culmination of the ages has come." (1 Corinthians 10:11).

# Angels and Demons

The good supernatural beings who serve as God's emissaries are called angels. The demons and Satan are apparently angels who turned evil and rebelled against God. The angels, the demons, and Satan are minor characters in the Bible. Only two angels—Michael and Gabriel—are even given names. The words "Satan" and "Devil" are designations, not names. Only once do female angels appear in the Bible (Zechariah 5:9), and many angels do not have wings.

# Wisdom Literature

Wisdom literature explains how to live well. It is generally intensely practical, explaining how to conduct oneself, or how to face the inevitable dilemmas and trials of life. It consists of stories that illustrate the importance of good choices, essays about the meaning of life, and proverbial sayings. In the Bible, wisdom literature includes the books of Proverbs and Job, some of the Psalms, Ecclesiastes, James, and the Joseph story in Genesis.

**Tower of Babel**
Israel in Bondage and the Tower of Babel,
*nineteenth-century painting by Caimi.*

# The Old Testament

The Old Testament is a collection of works composed mostly by anonymous Jewish writers over multiple centuries. They were then edited and collected by equally anonymous editors. The order of the books and the number of books varies according to religious tradition. Protestants and Jews accept 39 books but arrange them in different ways. Roman Catholics and the various Eastern Orthodox communities include additional books that Protestants and Jews label as apocryphal.

The contents of the Old Testament works include genealogies, census data, detailed regulations and rules, and poetry: all within the context of stories designed to tell about ordinary human beings living in extraordinary times and how they interacted with God. The characters of the stories are portrayed with both their virtues and flaws: good and evil are usually clearly visible in every person. The purpose of the stories, related as history or biography, is largely theological.

In addition to stories, there are also collections of poems, the prayers and songs of the ancient Israelites. They contain praise and complaint, thanksgiving, joy and sorrow, with calls for vengeance or justice. There are essays on the purpose of life, guidelines for living well, love poems, and discussions about why the righteous suffer and the wicked prosper.

Then, the prophets call the people to repentance from sin, warn of impending judgment, encourage faithfulness to God, and offer hope in the midst of suffering.

# Genesis

## Overview

The English title of Genesis comes from the ancient Greek translation of the Old Testament (the Septuagint) and means "origin." In Hebrew, the book's title is taken from the first word in the book, *berashit*, which means "in the beginning." Although Moses is traditionally assumed to be the author of the Book of Genesis, nowhere in the Bible is he specifically identified as its author. As with most of the books in the Old Testament, Genesis is actually an anonymous work. Most scholars assume that Genesis was put together in its current form between 500 and 400 BC. In contrast, traditionalists insist that it was composed during the time of Moses, between the thirteenth and fifteenth centuries BC.

The Book of Genesis has at least three obvious purposes. First, it is a reaction against the prevailing mythology and polytheism that dominated the world of the Ancient Near East. The Babylonian creation epic, known as *Enuma Elish*, described a battle between the gods and their ultimate decision to

---

**17**

**Chapter 1**

God creates the universe over the course of six days, then rests on the seventh.

**17**

**Chapter 2**

God creates Adam and Eve and puts them in the Garden of Eden, warning them that they can eat from every tree but one: the Tree of the Knowledge of Good and Evil.

**9**    **15**    **17**

**Chapter 3**

Adam and Eve eat fruit from the only forbidden tree, become mortal, and God expels them from the Garden of Eden to keep them away from the Tree of Life.

**9**    **16**    **17**

**Chapter 4**

God sends Cain, one of Adam and Eve's sons, into exile after Cain murders Abel, one of his brothers; Cain then marries, builds a city, and has many descendants.

---

## Chapters 1–2: **Commentary**

The first two chapters of Genesis are arranged thematically, in two parallel sections. The first three days describe the creation of "stages": light and dark, water above and below, and dry land. On the last three days, the "actors" appear: sun, moon, and stars; birds and fish; and animals and people. The second chapter looks at the sixth day, expanding on it and describing in greater detail how God made Adam from the dirt, and Eve from his rib, and how he gave them the Garden of Eden to tend.

*Then the Lord said to Cain, "Where is your brother Abel?"*

*"I don't know," he replied. "Am I my brother's keeper?"*

*The Lord said, "What have you done? Listen! Your brother's blood cries out to me from the ground. Now you are under a curse and driven from the ground, which opened its mouth to receive your brother's blood from your hand. When you work the ground, it will no longer yield its crops for you. You will be a restless wanderer on the earth."*

**Genesis 4:9–11**

create human beings to serve them as slaves. However, the Book of Genesis has but one God, who created human beings not as slaves, but as the masters of the world.

Second, the story of Genesis is designed to demonstrate that the one God worshiped by Israel does not belong to them exclusively. Although the gods of the nations around Israel were usually perceived as national deities, the God of Genesis is the God not just of one nation, but of all human beings everywhere. And all human beings everywhere are also shown to make up one big family with a common ancestor.

Third, and finally, the Book of Genesis reveals how God decided to take a special interest in a group of people—one piece of that larger human family—who would later become the Israelites.

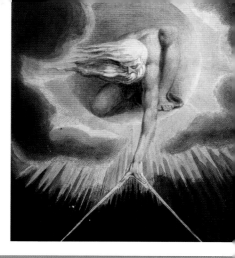

**Creation of the universe**
*The Bible begins with God creating the universe. In contrast to the Babylonian myths of the day, the Bible is unconcerned with explaining the origin of God.*

| 16 | | | Chapter 5 |
|---|---|---|---|
| A genealogy from Adam to Noah, including Methuselah, who is said to live longer than anyone else in the Bible: a remarkable 969 years. | | | |

| 9 | | 17 | Chapter 6 |
|---|---|---|---|
| God is dismayed by the behavior of the human race and decides to drown everyone except Noah, whom he orders to build a large ship for himself, his family, and all the animals. | | | |

| 9 | | 17 | Chapter 7 |
|---|---|---|---|
| After Noah, his family, and the animals enter the large ship he built, 40 days of rain cover the world with water, drowning everyone except for those on the ship. | | | |

| 17 | Chapter 8 |
|---|---|
| After nearly a year spent aboard ship, Noah and his family, with the animals, disembark and Noah thanks God for their survival by offering him a sacrifice. | |

| 14 | 17 | Chapter 9 |
|---|---|---|
| God makes a contract with the human race, sealed with a rainbow, that he will never destroy the world with a flood again; then Noah gets drunk and curses his grandson, Canaan. | | |

| 16 | Chapter 10 |
|---|---|
| A genealogy of the descendants of Noah's three sons, Shem, Ham, and Japheth. | |

## Chapters 5–6: Commentary

Chapter 6 begins with a description of how "the sons of God" married "the daughters of men." Many have speculated about who those sons might be. Some point out that the phrase is later used for angels, and so imagine that angels—or demons—married human women. Others suggest affairs between royalty and commoners, or between the descendants of Seth (another son of Adam and Eve) and those of Cain. The real answer probably describes how the human race propagated after the time of Adam and Eve. Therefore Adam and his male descendants are the "sons of God" (see Luke 3:37).

## Chapter 9: Commentary

Why did Noah curse his grandson, Canaan? According to the story, Ham "saw his father's nakedness." When Noah learned what had happened, he cursed Ham's son, Canaan. Noah's reaction seems extreme. But if we look at some of the laws regulating sexual behavior in the later Mosaic legislation (see for instance, Leviticus 18:8), we discover that the phrase is used as an idiom for sexual relation: "seeing his nakedness" meant having intercourse with his wife. Canaan is the offspring of an affair between Ham and Noah's wife, which is why Noah reacts as he does.

**Chapter 11**
⑨ ⑯
Noah's descendants construct the city and tower of Babel: God confuses their language, so that they scatter across the world. Shem's genealogy ends with Abram.

**Chapter 12**
⑦ ⑰
God sends Abram to the land of Canaan, promising him future blessings. After a famine in Canaan, Abram and his wife have an adventure in Egypt.

**Chapter 13**
⑦ ⑰
Abram settles west of the Jordan River, while his nephew Lot moves east, near Sodom. God promises Abram descendants as numerous as "the stars in the sky."

**Chapter 14**
⑭ ⑰
Abram gathers an army and attacks the Mesopotamian conquerors of Sodom, rescuing his nephew Lot. In thanks, Abram gives Melchizedek, king and priest of Salem, a tenth of the spoils.

**Chapter 15**
⑭
God makes a contract with Abram, assuring him that he will have a child who will become his heir, rather than his servant, Eliezer of Damascus.

**Chapter 16**
⑰
Unable to bear children, Abram takes Sarai's servant Hagar as a second wife. Hagar gives birth to a son, Ishmael, creating conflict between Hagar and Sarai.

**Chapter 17**
⑦ ⑭
God establishes circumcision as the sign of the covenant between Abram and God and changes Abram's name to Abraham and Sarai's name to Sarah.

**Chapter 18**
⑦ ⑮ ⑰
God and two angels arrive at Abraham's home and he invites them to dinner. God reveals his intention to destroy Sodom for its wickedness.

*But the Lord came down to see the city and the tower they were building. The Lord said, "If as one people speaking the same language they have begun to do this, then nothing they plan to do will be impossible for them. Come, let us go down and confuse their language so they will not understand each other."*

**Genesis 11:5–7**

*"I will make you into a great nation,
and I will bless you;
I will make your name great,
and you will be a blessing.
I will bless those who bless you,
and whoever curses you I will curse;
and all peoples on earth
will be blessed through you."*

**Genesis 12:2–3**

## Chapter 14: **Commentary**

Salem is traditionally thought to be an alternative name for Jerusalem. Melchizedek, whose name in Hebrew means "king of righteousness," appears out of nowhere in the story of Abram. The New Testament author of the Book of Hebrews writes that he has no "father or mother" or descendants. That is, unlike most people in the Bible, he receives no genealogical listing, not even so much as a "son of," nor is anyone else in the Bible listed as his descendant. The New Testament, playing off on his mention in Psalm 110:4, takes him as a picture of Jesus, who, like Jesus, though not obviously connected to Levi, the priestly tribe, acts as a priest of God (Hebrews 6:20, 7:1–17). Much is also made of the payment of a tithe—a ten percent tax—to Melchizedek as an indication of his superiority to Abram and, as Abram was his father, Levi (see Hebrews 7:15–17).

## Chapters 16–17: **Commentary**

Circumcision was not unique to the Jewish people. The Ancient Egyptians, for instance, practiced circumcision. God took a familiar action and endowed it with new significance, making it the sign of his covenant with Abram. The name Abram meant "exalted father." It was changed to Abraham, "father of a multitude." His wife went from Sarai to Sarah, but both names mean "princess." The name changes signified the fulfillment of God's promise that they would have a child born to them.

Some scholars have argued that the different names, Abraham and Abram, Sarah and Sarai, indicate multiple versions of the Patriarch stories that an editor combined to create the final form of the Book of Genesis.

*Then the Lord rained down burning sulfur on Sodom and Gomorrah—from the Lord out of the heavens. Thus he overthrew those cities and the entire plain, destroying all those living in the cities—and also the vegetation in the land. But Lot's wife looked back, and she became a pillar of salt.*
**Genesis 19:24–26**

## Chapters 20–21: **Commentary**

Abraham sends Hagar and Ishmael away after Abraham's wife Sarah saw Ishmael "mocking" on the day that Isaac was weaned. Although the word translated "mocking" can mean precisely that, it is intriguing that the same word appears later in Genesis 26:8–9 where it describes the conjugal caresses of Isaac and his wife Rebecca. It also shows up in Genesis 39:14 when Potiphar's wife accuses Joseph of attempted rape. Given Sarah's extreme reaction to Ishmael's behavior, and the other uses of the term elsewhere in Genesis, it may be that something worse than mere "mocking" occurred.

*And said, "I swear by myself, declares the Lord, that because you have done this and have not withheld your son, your only son, I will surely bless you and make your descendants as numerous as the stars in the sky and as the sand on the seashore. Your descendants will take possession of the cities of their enemies, and through your offspring all nations on earth will be blessed, because you have obeyed me."*
**Genesis 22:16–18**

## Chapters 23–24: **Commentary**

The meaning of "put your hand under my thigh" is not obvious to most modern readers. In the Ancient Near East, when people made solemn promises, it was common to place one's hand on a sacred object associated with the god that one worshiped. Often, this meant holding a small image of the god. The custom continues today, when the President of the United States places his hand on a Bible as he takes his oath of office.

Abraham was a monotheist who did not make images of his God. The only sacred object associated with his worship of Yahweh was his circumcision. The word "thigh" is a common euphemism for the genitals. Therefore this peculiar phrase means that Abraham's servant had to grasp an intimate part of Abraham when he took his solemn oath.

---

**9**  **15**  **17**

Lot and two of his daughters leave Sodom before it is destroyed, but his wife doesn't make it. Then Lot's two daughters get him drunk so he'll impregnate them.

Chapter **19**

---

**17**

Abraham lies to King Abimelek about his relationship to Sarah. But in a dream, God reveals the truth, so Abimelek sends Abraham and Sarah away, with gifts of sheep, cattle, and slaves.

Chapter **20**

---

**14**  **17**

Sarah finally gives birth to a son, Isaac. After he is weaned, she forces Abraham to send Hagar and Ishmael into exile. Meanwhile, Abraham makes a treaty of peace with Abimelek.

Chapter **21**

---

**11**  **17**

God tests Abraham by ordering him to sacrifice Isaac as a burnt offering on a mountain, but at the very last minute, God makes Abraham substitute a ram in Isaac's place.

Chapter **22**

---

**4**  **14**  **17**

After Sarah dies at the age of 127, Abraham purchases some land and a cave in Hebron from Ephron the Hittite and buries her there.

Chapter **23**

---

**17**

Abraham sends one of his servants to the village of Nahor to find a wife for his son Isaac. The servant returns with Rebecca, the sister of Laban.

Chapter **24**

---

**16**  **17**

Abraham remarries and has many more children before finally dying at the age of 175. Esau, Isaac's firstborn son, sells his birthright to his brother Jacob in exchange for a bowl of stew.

Chapter **25**

**⑭    ⑰**

Chapter

**26**

When a famine arises where Isaac lives, God makes a covenant with him and tells him not to go to Egypt. So Isaac goes to Garar and lies to Abimelek about his relationship with Rebecca.

**⑰**

Chapter

**27**

Esau is murderously angry after Jacob tricks his father Isaac into giving him, rather than Esau, his blessing. So Rebecca sends Jacob off to live with her brother Laban.

**⑦    ⑭    ⑰**

Chapter

**28**

On the way to Laban, Jacob dreams of a ladder to heaven and God promises him future blessings. Jacob vows to worship God and give him a tenth of his future earnings.

*Stay in this land for a while, and I will be with you and will bless you. For to you and your descendants I will give all these lands and will confirm the oath I swore to your father Abraham. I will make your descendants as numerous as the stars in the sky and will give them all these lands, and through your offspring all nations on earth will be blessed...*

**Genesis 26:3–4**

## Chapter 28: **Commentary**

Following his dream, Jacob set up a stone—the one he'd used to rest his head on while he slept—as a pillar and poured oil on it. In establishing formal treaties between two parties, it was common for a rock to serve as a symbol of the new relationship. The pouring of the oil on the rock signifies that it has been set apart for this new and special purpose of serving as a memorial for the covenant that was being made. This "anointing" was also performed on people when they took on new and special roles in their lives: when a man became king or a priest, he was anointed with oil. Just as stones were set up to mark the boundaries between nations or landowners, so the rock represents a dividing marker between two periods in Jacob's life.

*Then Jacob made a vow, saying, "If God will be with me and will watch over me on this journey I am taking and will give me food to eat and clothes to wear so that I return safely to my father's household, then the Lord will be my God and this stone that I have set up as a pillar will be God's house, and of all that you give me I will give you a tenth."*

**Genesis 28:20–22**

**Jacob's ladder**
*Jacob dreamed that he saw angels going up and down a ladder into heaven when God promised to take care of him while he was away from his homeland.*

## Chapter 31: **Commentary**

The Hebrew language is a dialect of Canaanite, the language the inhabitants of Palestine used. It was the language Jacob had grown up with. The region of Haran, where Laban lived, used a different language: Aramaic. Hebrew and Aramaic are both members of the Semitic family of languages, but they have many differences. Jacob and Laban set up rocks to symbolize their treaty, but they each used their own language to designate the name of the memorial. Laban's phrase, *Jegar Sahadutha* is Aramaic and means "witness heap." Jacob's phrase *Galeed* is Hebrew and means the same thing: "witness heap."

*So Jacob took a stone and set it up as a pillar. He said to his relatives, "Gather some stones." So they took stones and piled them in a heap, and they ate there by the heap. Laban called it Jegar Sahadutha, and Jacob called it Galeed.*

*Laban said, "This heap is a witness between you and me today." That is why it was called Galeed.*

**Genesis 31:45–48**

## Chapter 32: **Commentary**

Jacob's nighttime wrestling match is an odd episode, made odder when his opponent reveals himself to be God. God tells Jacob that he will have a new name, "Israel" which means "he struggles with God." Jacob named the location of his struggle "Peniel," a Hebrew phrase which means "face of God," since he had seen God face to face. In the New Testament, the apostle John explains that no one has ever seen God (John 1:18 and 6:46). Christian scholars reconcile the apparent contradiction by arguing that the God of the Old Testament whom Abraham, Jacob, Moses, and the later Hebrew prophets heard, saw, and spoke with—Yahweh—is not the Father, but rather the Son of God, who became the man Jesus Christ in the New Testament.

## Chapter 36: **Commentary**

The phrase "before any Israelite king reigned" is anachronistic if one assumes Moses to be the author of Genesis. Although a belief in Mosaic authorship is "traditional," it is in fact improbable given the occurrence of this and other statements unlikely to have come from Moses (see for instance Numbers 12:3).

---

**10** | **17**

Jacob works seven years for his uncle Laban in order to marry Rachel. But Laban tricks him into marrying her sister Leah, too. Leah bears him four sons, but Rachel remains childless.

Chapter
**29**

**17**

Rachel's servant Bilhah and Leah's servant Zilpah also marry Jacob. Leah, Bilhah, and Zilpah give birth to six more sons and a daughter before Rachel finally bears Joseph.

Chapter
**30**

**14** | **17**

After working for about 20 years for Laban, Jacob and his family sneak off to Canaan. An angry Laban pursues them, but finally makes a peace treaty with Jacob.

Chapter
**31**

**17**

A worried Jacob sends messengers bearing gifts to his brother Esau to let him know that he's coming. Jacob spends a night wrestling God, who changes Jacob's name to Israel.

Chapter
**32**

**17**

When Jacob finally meets up with his brother Esau, he discovers that Esau has forgiven him. Jacob and his family then settle down near the city of Shechem.

Chapter
**33**

**9** | **14** | **17**

The prince of Shechem kidnaps Jacob's daughter Dinah and rapes her. Jacob's sons Simeon and Levi rescue their sister and kill everyone in Shechem.

Chapter
**34**

**4** | **14** | **16**

Rachel dies giving birth to her second son, Benjamin. She is buried in Bethlehem. Altogether, Jacob has 12 sons. Jacob's father Isaac dies at the age of 180.

Chapter
**35**

**16**

A genealogy lists all of Esau's children, along with their descendants. Esau is also called Edom, and his nation, formed of his descendants, has many kings.

Chapter
**36**

| 4 | 17 | 18 |

## Chapter 37

Jacob shows obvious favoritism to his son Joseph. So his brothers sell him into slavery in Egypt, but pretend that he has been killed by wild animals.

| 10 | 17 | 18 |

## Chapter 38

Two of Judah's sons marry Tamar, then die. Judah refuses to let another son marry her, so Tamar disguises herself as a prostitute, sleeps with Judah, and has twins.

| 17 | 18 |

## Chapter 39

In Egypt, the wife of Potiphar, Joseph's master, tries to seduce him. Infuriated by his rejection, she accuses him of attempted rape, so Potiphar throws him into prison.

| 7 | 17 | 18 |

## Chapter 40

In prison, Joseph interprets the disturbing dreams of Pharaoh's cupbearer and baker: the cupbearer will return to his position; the baker will be executed.

| 7 | 17 | 18 |

## Chapter 41

Joseph interprets the Pharaoh's dreams: seven years of plenty and seven years of famine. So the Pharaoh puts Joseph in charge of preparing for the famine.

| 17 | 18 |

## Chapter 42

Because of the famine, Jacob sends Joseph's brothers to buy grain in Egypt. Joseph imprisons his brother Simeon, promising to free him only if they bring back Benjamin.

| 17 | 18 |

## Chapter 43

Jacob sends the brothers back a second time to Egypt, reluctantly allowing Benjamin to go along. Back in Egypt, Joseph releases Simeon and gives them a banquet.

| 17 | 18 |

## Chapter 44

Joseph has one of his servants secretly sneak a valuable cup into Benjamin's bag, then accuses them of theft. His brother Judah pleads to take Benjamin's punishment.

## Chapter 37: Commentary

Joseph is the firstborn son of the woman that Jacob loved. If Laban hadn't tricked him into marrying his daughter Leah instead of Rachael, Rachael would have been the only woman Jacob married. Instead, he wound up with four wives, who produced ten other children before Rachael finally became pregnant and gave birth to Joseph. Rachael then died giving birth to her second-born, Benjamin.

Despite the fact that Reuben was Jacob's firstborn son, Jacob treated Joseph as if he were the firstborn. His "richly ornamented robe" and his supervisory role over his brothers indicated his preeminence in the family—and created enormous resentment.

This is why his brothers ultimately plotted against him and sold him into slavery.

## Chapter 38: Commentary

When a man died without having children, it was the duty of the man's brother to marry his widow and get her pregnant, so that the first son she bore could carry on the name and inherit the property of the dead brother. Onan married the woman, but refused to get her pregnant because he wanted his brother's inheritance for himself.

If there were no brothers able to fulfill the law, then the next nearest relative was required to fulfill it. Tamar's actions, therefore, forced Judah—the next nearest relative—to simply do his duty.

## Chapter 42: Commentary

From his perspective, and from the perspective of his sons standing around him, Jacob's complaint appears fully reasonable, perfectly understandable, and self-evidently true (Genesis 42:36).

And yet, from the perspective of the readers of the story, his words couldn't be more wrong! The readers of this episode know some things that Jacob didn't know. They know that Joseph was not only not dead, but that he was second in command in Egypt, the most powerful and wealthy nation on the planet at that time.

The reality of Jacob's existence is that everything could hardly be better. But poor Jacob simply doesn't know this yet.

*Their father Jacob said to them, "You have deprived me of my children. Joseph is no more and Simeon is no more, and now you want to take Benjamin. Everything is against me!"*

**Genesis 42:36**

*And he wept so loudly that the Egyptians heard
him, and Pharaoh's household heard about it.
   Joseph said to his brothers, "I am Joseph! Is
my father still living?" But his brothers were not
able to answer him, because they were terrified at
his presence.*

**Genesis 45:2–3**

*Then he blessed Joseph and said,
   "May the God before whom my fathers
Abraham and Isaac walked faithfully,
the God who has been my shepherd
all my life to this day,
the Angel who has delivered me from all harm
—may he bless these boys.
May they be called by my name
and the names of my fathers Abraham and Isaac,
and may they increase greatly
on the earth."*

**Genesis 48:15–16**

## Chapters 49–50: **Commentary**

Upon the death of Jacob his body was "embalmed"
(Genesis 50:1–3). Likewise, when Joseph died, the text
informs us that he was embalmed (Genesis 50:26). What
this means, given that they were in Egypt, is that both
Jacob and Joseph were mummified.

   The brain was extracted through the nostrils with an
iron hook, the contents of the abdomen were removed,
and the cavity was then washed out with palm wine. Then
the cavity was filled with a variety of spices. Then the
entire body was dunked in a vat of natrum for 70 days.
Afterward, it was washed and wrapped from head to foot
in linen strips smeared with gum and finally placed in a
wooden case shaped like a human being.

*But Joseph said to them, "Don't be afraid. Am I in
the place of God? You intended to harm me, but
God intended it for good to accomplish what is now
being done, the saving of many lives. So then, don't
be afraid. I will provide for you and your children."
And he reassured them and spoke kindly to them.*

**Genesis 50:19–21**

**Joseph reveals his identity**
*Joseph finally revealed his identity to his brothers. They were
not entirely happy to learn that he was alive and well.*

**17** **18**
Joseph finally reveals his true identity to his brothers,
then sends for Jacob and their families to be brought
back to Egypt to live in prosperity with him.

Chapter **45**

**16** **17** **18**
Jacob and his whole family travel to Goshen in Egypt,
where Joseph and his father Jacob are finally reunited.

Chapter **46**

**17** **18**
Joseph presents his father to Pharaoh, who
guarantees their safety and prosperity. Meanwhile,
Joseph reduces most of the Egyptians to
permanent serfdom.

Chapter **47**

**17** **18**
Jacob's father adopts Joseph's sons, Manasseh and
Ephraim, granting the rights of the firstborn to the
second-born Ephraim instead of Manasseh.

Chapter **48**

**16** **17** **18**
Jacob then pronounces a blessing on each of his 12
sons. Just before his death, he asks to be buried in
Abraham's tomb in Hebron.

Chapter **49**

**4** **17** **18**
After 70 days of official mourning, Joseph, his
brothers, and representatives of Pharaoh take Jacob's
body to Hebron and bury it. Joseph dies at the
age of 110.

Chapter **50**

# Exodus

## Overview

**I** Salvation 1:1–18:27

   **a** Liberation 1:1–15:21

   **b** Journey to Sinai 15:22–18:27

**II** Covenant: the result of salvation 19:1–40:38

   **a** The giving of the Ten Commandments 19:1–20:21

   **b** Expansion on the theme of the Ten Commandments 20:22–40:38

The English title of Exodus comes from the Greek translation of the Old Testament (the Septuagint) and means "departure." In Hebrew, the book's title is taken from the first words in the book, *eleh shemot*, which mean "these are the names." Some scholars believe Moses wrote Exodus between the fifteenth and thirteenth centuries BC. But most scholars now assume it is a composite work produced between 600 and 400 BC.

Since the Book of Exodus nowhere identifies the Pharaoh by name, and since there is, as yet, no unambiguous archaeological evidence for the Exodus, the precise date for the Israelites' escape from bondage remains uncertain. A few scholars even doubt that the Exodus ever happened. But most scholars assume that the Exodus occurred during the reign of Pharaoh Ramses II, in the thirteenth century BC.

**Moses in a basket**
*Moses' mother placed him in a basket and then sent him into the Nile near where Pharaoh's daughter regularly bathed.*

*But when she could hide him no longer, she got a papyrus basket for him and coated it with tar and pitch. Then she placed the child in it and put it among the reeds along the bank of the Nile. His sister stood at a distance to see what would happen to him.*

*Then Pharaoh's daughter went down to the Nile to bathe, and her attendants were walking along the riverbank. She saw the basket among the reeds and sent her female slave to get it. She opened it and saw the baby. He was crying, and she felt sorry for him. "This is one of the Hebrew babies," she said.*

**Exodus 2:3–6**

**17**

**Chapter 1**

After Joseph and all his brothers die, the Israelite population grows rapidly. To control the Israelite population growth, the Pharaoh decrees the death of all male Israelite babies.

**17**

**Chapter 2**

After rescuing him from a reed basket, Pharaoh's daughter raises Moses as her own. Moses later kills an Egyptian, flees to Midian, marries, and lives as a shepherd.

The Pharaoh of Egypt was believed to be an incarnation of Ra. Therefore, God's plagues attacked not just the power, health, and livelihood of the Egyptians, but the gods that they believed in, the protectors of the Nile River, the cattle, and the weather.

For the Ancient Israelites, the book of Exodus was a very practical instruction book that told them how to live as God's people. It explained how they should treat each other and how they should treat, think about, and worship God. It contains God's Ten Commandments along with other regulations.

The Book of Exodus can also be described as "salvation history." It demonstrated for the Israelites that just as God had the power to rescue them from the most powerful nation on Earth, so he also had the power to save them from their sins.

## Chapter 3: **Commentary**

Moses had a question for the voice of the God: which god are you? He is not yet thinking monotheistically. The reason people have names is because there are a lot of them. But if there was only one person, there would be no need for names. So God responded to Moses by telling him, "I am that I am." His point was, there wasn't anyone else. There are no other gods. God said "I am." So when Moses went back to the people of Israel in Egypt, he told them that "He is" was the God that had sent him. The Hebrew word for "He is" thus became God's name: "Yahweh," sometimes rendered in English as "Jehovah."

**Moses meets God**
*Forty years after he had left Egypt, God appeared to Moses in a bush that burned but was not consumed by the flames and told him to return to lead the Israelites.*

*God said to Moses, "I AM WHO I AM. This is what you are to say to the Israelites: 'I AM has sent me to you.'"*

*God also said to Moses, "Say to the Israelites, 'The Lord, the God of your fathers—the God of Abraham, the God of Isaac and the God of Jacob— has sent me to you.'*

*"This is my name forever,
the name you shall call me
from generation to generation."*

**Exodus 3:14–15**

8

17

God speaks to Moses from a burning bush and sends him to Egypt to rescue the Israelites from slavery. God identifies himself as Yahweh, the God of Abraham, Isaac, and Jacob.

Chapter
3

**Chapter 4**

(8) (17)

Moses returns to Egypt able to perform three miracles. God tries to kill Moses' uncircumcised son, forcing his wife to circumcise him in order to save his life.

**Chapter 5**

(8) (12) (17)

Moses and Aaron asks Pharaoh to let the people take a three-day journey into the wilderness in order to sacrifice to Yahweh. Pharaoh refuses and oppressed the slaves even more.

**Chapter 6**

(8) (16)

God reassures Moses that eventually Pharaoh will let the Israelites go, despite Moses' serious doubts. A genealogy of Moses' family follows.

**Chapter 7**

(8) (9)

An 80-year-old Moses turns his staff into a snake, then brings the First Plague: all the water in Egypt turns into blood. Pharaoh refuses to let the people go.

**Chapter 8**

(8) (9)

The Second Plague: frogs. The Third Plague: gnats. The Fourth Plague: flies. And still, the Pharaoh refuses to let the people go.

**Chapter 9**

(8) (9)

The Fifth Plague: the livestock all die. The Sixth Plague: boils on everyone. The Seventh Plague: hail. But Pharaoh repeatedly refuses to let the Israelites go.

## Chapters 4–5:

What constitutes lying? The Bible tells us that God does not lie (Numbers 23:19). But God has Moses tell the Pharaoh that the Israelites want to go worship God somewhere in the wilderness, away from the Egyptians, for three days. He doesn't tell Pharaoh the real plan: that God is rescuing the Israelites from Egyptian bondage.

The prohibitions in the Bible against lying are about bearing false witness in legal settings. But God—and the Israelites—are at war with Egypt now. When a general misleads his opponent, when a spy hides his identity, or when a chess player leads his opponent into making a bad move, that is not "lying." Likewise, when God misleads Pharaoh, it is not a lie in the biblical sense. It is a tactic of war—or game play.

*God also said to Moses, "I am the Lord. I appeared to Abraham, to Isaac and to Jacob as God Almighty, but by my name the Lord I did not make myself fully known to them. I also established my covenant with them to give them the land of Canaan, where they resided as foreigners. Moreover, I have heard the groaning of the Israelites, whom the Egyptians are enslaving, and I have remembered my covenant.*

*"Therefore, say to the Israelites: 'I am the Lord, and I will bring you out from under the yoke of the Egyptians. I will free you from being slaves to them, and I will redeem you with an outstretched arm and with mighty acts of judgment."*

**Exodus 6:2–6**

*After Moses and Aaron left Pharaoh, Moses cried out to the Lord about the frogs he had brought on Pharaoh. And the Lord did what Moses asked. The frogs died in the houses, in the courtyards and in the fields. They were piled into heaps, and the land reeked of them. But when Pharaoh saw that there was relief, he hardened his heart and would not listen to Moses and Aaron, just as the Lord had said.*

**Exodus 8:12–15**

**The Plagues of Egypt**
*God sent a series of ten plagues against the Pharaoh of Egypt, creating both human and financial disaster.*

*So Moses stretched out his staff over Egypt, and the Lord made an east wind blow across the land all that day and all that night. By morning the wind had brought the locusts; they invaded all Egypt and settled down in every area of the country in great numbers. Never before had there been such a plague of locusts, nor will there ever be again. They covered all the ground until it was black. They devoured all that was left after the hail—everything growing in the fields and the fruit on the trees. Nothing green remained on tree or plant in all the land of Egypt.*

**Exodus 10:13–15**

## Chapter 12: **Commentary**

The dating of the Exodus is controversial. Traditionally, it was assumed that the Exodus occurred around 1440 BC, based on the mention in 1 Kings 6:1 of when Solomon built the Temple in Jerusalem. The date of Solomon's reign is relatively well established, so 480 years earlier gives the 1440 date. However, scholars noticed that the 480 is an unusual number: 40 years, the traditional length of a generation multiplied by 12, a significant number in Jewish history given the number of tribes. Was the number to be understood literally, or as something more symbolic? Today, most scholars assume a date for the Exodus of around 1290 BC, based on archaeological evidence, though a significant minority doubt that there was an Exodus at all and argue that the Jewish people arose gradually from among the existing Canaanite inhabitants of Palestine, perhaps from several migrations of nomads into the region.

The failure of Exodus to give the identity of the Pharaoh of the Exodus, along with any external written documentation about the Exodus, makes the dating of the event problematic for the foreseeable future.

*By day the Lord went ahead of them in a pillar of cloud to guide them on their way and by night in a pillar of fire to give them light, so that they could travel by day or night. Neither the pillar of cloud by day nor the pillar of fire by night left its place in front of the people.*

**Exodus 13:21–22**

**Meeting before Pharaoh**
*Moses and Aaron stood before Pharaoh and demanded that he let the Israelites leave Egypt to worship Yahweh.*

| 8 | 9 | Chapter 10 |
|---|---|---|
| The Eighth Plague: locusts. Pharaoh agrees to let the men go, but God is not satisfied. The Ninth Plague brings darkness, and once again the Pharaoh tells Moses no. | | |

| 8 | 9 | Chapter 11 |
|---|---|---|
| For the Tenth Plague Moses warns Pharaoh that all the firstborn of Egypt will die at midnight, while all the Israelites will be spared. Pharaoh refuses to listen. | | |

| 4 | 8 | 11 | Chapter 12 |
|---|---|---|---|
| God establishes the Passover ceremony to remind his people of the Exodus from Egypt. After the firstborn die, Pharaoh tells them to go and worship their God. | | | |

| 8 | 17 | Chapter 13 |
|---|---|---|
| The Israelites leave Egypt, with God moving ahead of them, appearing as a pillar of cloud by day and a pillar of fire by night. | | |

**Crossing the sea**
*After the winds blew all night long, a passage
through the sea opened, allowing the Israelites
to escape from the pursuing Egyptian army.*

## Chapter 14: Commentary

The traditional name for the body of water through which the Israelites fled from Egypt is the Red Sea. However, the Hebrew actually translates as "sea of reeds." As with so much of the Exodus story, there are more questions than certainty. The precise route of the Exodus remains unknown, since none of the places mentioned have been definitively identified. Thus, the body of water crossed by the Israelites remains unknown; speculation ranges from northern routes along the coast, to crossings of the bitter lakes, to treks across what we today call the Red Sea.

**8**      **17**

**Chapter 14**

When Pharaoh realizes the Israelites are not returning, he sends his army after them. God parts the Red Sea so the Israelites can escape, then drowns the pursuing Egyptian army.

**1**      **5**      **8**

**Chapter 15**

Moses and the Israelites sing to Yahweh. Then Miriam, Moses' sister, sings and dances. Three days later Moses tosses a piece of wood into a bitter spring to make it drinkable.

**8**

**Chapter 16**

In the Desert of Sin the people wish for food like they'd enjoyed in Egypt. So God sends them quails for meat and provides manna each morning for bread.

*"I will sing to the Lord,
for he is highly exalted.
Both horse and driver
he has hurled into the sea.*
    *"The Lord is my strength and my defense;
he has become my salvation.
He is my God, and I will praise him,
my father's God, and I will exalt him.
The Lord is a warrior;
the Lord is his name."*

**Exodus 15:1–3**

## Chapter 20: **Commentary**

The rules and regulations that make up the rest of the books of Exodus, Numbers, and Deuteronomy are all based upon these ten commandments as listed here in Exodus 20. Although the Jewish people and the various Christian churches all refer to these commandments as the Ten Commandments, how they divide them up varies.

*The traditional Jewish arrangement of the Ten Commandments is as follows:*

1. I am the Lord your God
2. You shall have no other gods before me; make no idols
3. Do not misuse God's name
4. Remember the Sabbath and sanctify it
5. Honor your father and mother
6. Do not murder
7. Do not commit adultery
8. Do not steal
9. Do not bear false witness
10. Do not covet

## Chapter 21: **Commentary**

The principle of "eye for eye" and "tooth for tooth" is in fact a profound step forward in the limitation of retribution. The point of the "eye for eye"—what is called the *lex talionis*—was to establish a limit to punishment. Where before, a man might suffer the death penalty for theft, the *lex talionis* restricts retribution to nothing harsher than the crime that was committed. In practice, the penalties stipulated were rarely as severe as the crimes.

## Chapters 22–23: **Commentary**

The law prohibiting cooking a young goat in its mother's milk (verse 19) is the basis of modern Jewish kosher regulations prohibiting the mixing of milk and meat products under any circumstances.

*Moses and Aaron, Nadab and Abihu, and the seventy elders of Israel went up and saw the God of Israel. Under his feet was something like a pavement made of lapis lazuli, as bright blue as the sky. But God did not raise his hand against these leaders of the Israelites; they saw God, and they ate and drank.*

*The Lord said to Moses, "Come up to me on the mountain and stay here, and I will give you the tablets of stone with the law and commandments I have written for their instruction."*

**Exodus 24:9–12**

---

**8** **17**

When Moses strikes the rock at Horeb, water gushes out despite the Israelites' worries. The Israelites defeat the Amalekites as long as Moses holds his staff over his head.

Chapter
**17**

**8** **17**

Moses' father-in-law Jethro visits, bringing Moses' wife Zipporah and his sons with him. He also helps Moses set up an organization for governing the Israelites.

Chapter
**18**

**14** **17**

Moses and the people travel into the desert and camp in front of Mount Sinai. God calls Moses up to the mountain top, but warns the people of Israel to wait below.

Chapter
**19**

**3** **14**

On top of the mountain, God speaks the Ten Commandments to Moses and makes a point to prohibit idol-making; God also explains how to properly construct altars.

Chapter
**20**

**3** **14**

God regulates the treatment of Hebrew servants, explains how to handle personal injuries, and establishes the principle of eye for eye, limiting the harshness of penalties.

Chapter
**21**

**3** **14**

God gives Moses laws regarding property, compensation for losses, regulated sexual behavior, and establishes protection for foreigners, widows, and orphans.

Chapter
**22**

**3** **14**

God demands impartial justice. He establishes the six-day work week and three annual festivals: Unleavened Bread, Harvest, and Ingathering. God prohibits treaties with the Canaanites.

Chapter
**23**

**8** **14** **17**

Moses, Aaron, Nadab, Abihu, and 70 elders of Israel go up on Mount Sinai to have a meal with God and confirm their covenant with him.

Chapter
**24**

*11*

**Chapter 25**

God asks the Israelites to bring Moses the materials to build a Tabernacle. God explains how to make the Ark of the Covenant, the Table, and the Lampstand.

*11*

**Chapter 26**

God instructs the Israelites on how to make his Tabernacle, which will serve as portable Temple for worshiping God.

*11*

**Chapter 27**

God tells the Israelites to build an altar for the burnt offerings and explains all the utensils that it will need; he also describes how to make the Lampstand oil.

*11*

**Chapter 28**

God explains how to make the priestly clothing: the *ephod*, a breastpiece of gold with its 12 gems, the robes, the tunics, and even the undergarments.

*11*

**Chapter 29**

God specifies how the priests have to be consecrated over seven days: the clothing, the anointing, the sacrifices, the blood, the special bread, and the drink offerings.

*11*

**Chapter 30**

God specifies the design of the incense altar, the incense, the anointing oil, and the bronze washbasin. Every Israelite has to pay a half-shekel tax for the Tabernacle.

*11*

**Chapter 31**

God picks Bezalel and Oholiab to manufacture of all the materials needed for worshiping God. Then God gives Moses two tablets of stone bearing the Ten Commandments.

*9*    *17*

**Chapter 32**

Moses discovers the Israelites worshiping a calf idol and partying. He smashes the tablets and the idol. Then the Levites slaughter 3,000 and God sends a plague.

*"Command the Israelites to bring you clear oil of pressed olives for the light so that the lamps may be kept burning. In the tent of meeting, outside the curtain that shields the ark of the covenant law, Aaron and his sons are to keep the lamps burning before the Lord from evening till morning. This is to be a lasting ordinance among the Israelites for the generations to come."*

**Exodus 27:20–21**

## Chapter 32: **Commentary**

While Moses was on Mount Sinai receiving the Ten Commandments from God, the people of Israel convinced Aaron to make a golden calf idol. Baal, the god worshiped in Canaan, and the Egyptian deity Amon-Re were both commonly represented by bulls. Idolatry and the worship of multiple gods was normal throughout the Near East. As a result, for most of their history, the Ancient Israelites tended to follow the practices of the societies around them, building idols and worshiping the local gods in addition to their worship of Yahweh, despite the prohibitions in the Law of Moses and the constant reminders by the prophets. The imagery of Exodus 32 resembles the imagery of the calf idols that Jeroboam made following his successful rebellion against Rehoboam (1 Kings 25–33).

*When Joshua heard the noise of the people shouting, he said to Moses, "There is the sound of war in the camp."*
*   Moses replied:*
*   "It is not the sound of victory,*
*it is not the sound of defeat;*
*it is the sound of singing that I hear."*
*   When Moses approached the camp and saw the calf and the dancing, his anger burned and he threw the tablets out of his hands, breaking them to pieces at the foot of the mountain. And he took the calf the people had made and burned it in the fire; then he ground it to powder, scattered it on the water and made the Israelites drink it.*

**Exodus 32:17–20**

*The Lord said to Moses, "Chisel out two stone tablets like the first ones, and I will write on them the words that were on the first tablets, which you broke. Be ready in the morning, and then come up on Mount Sinai. Present yourself to me there on top of the mountain."*

**Exodus 34:1–2**

**Breaking the law**
*While Moses was with God on Mount Sinai for 40 days, the Israelites turned to idolatry. In fury upon his return, Moses smashes the tablets with the Ten Commandments.*

*The Israelites had done all the work just as the Lord had commanded Moses. Moses inspected the work and saw that they had done it just as the Lord had commanded. So Moses blessed them.*

**Exodus 39:42–43**

| 2 | | 12 |
| --- | --- | --- |

Moses begs God to forgive the Israelites, which he does. Then Moses asks to see God's glory, but God only lets him see his back.

Chapter **33**

| 3 | 8 | 17 |
| --- | --- | --- |

God tells Moses to make replacements for the two smashed stone tablets and then to meet him back on Mount Sinai so he can rewrite the Ten Commandments for him.

Chapter **34**

| 11 |
| --- |

The people bring the materials that they need for building the Tabernacle and associated items. Then Bezalel, Oholiab, and other skilled people set to work.

Chapter **35**

| 11 | 16 |
| --- | --- |

The Israelites donate more material than the workers need. The building and design of the Tabernacle is given in great detail.

Chapter **36**

| 11 | 16 |
| --- | --- |

Bezalel makes the Ark of the Covenant; the details of its materials, shape, and size are given. Others construct the Table, Lampstand, and the Altar of Incense.

Chapter **37**

| 11 | 16 |
| --- | --- |

The other workers build the Altar of Burnt Offering, the Basin for Washing, and the Courtyard. There is a detailed listing of the materials used.

Chapter **38**

| 11 | 16 |
| --- | --- |

Skilled workers at last make all the priestly garments. Once everything has been manufactured, Moses inspects it, then blesses the people for their hard work.

Chapter **39**

| 8 | 11 |
| --- | --- |

God tells Moses to set up the Tabernacle, consecrate the priests, and place the tablets of the law inside the Ark of the Covenant. Then the glory of God fills the Tabernacle.

Chapter **40**

# Leviticus

## Overview

The English title for Leviticus comes from the Greek translation of the Old Testament and is a reference to the tribe of Levi. In Hebrew, the book's title is taken from the first word in the book, *vayiqra*—which means "and he called." Although Moses is traditionally assumed to be the author of the Book of Leviticus, nowhere in the Bible is he specifically identified as its author. Leviticus is actually an anonymous work and most modern scholars believe the book was composed sometime between 600 and 400 BC.

In Leviticus, God explains how the Israelites are to worship him. It includes rituals of sacrifice, priestly

---

**Chapter 1**

God explains to Moses how they are to sacrifice a burnt offering: the sort of animal to be burned is based on how much the one sacrificing can afford.

**Chapter 2**

God explains the requirements for a grain offering.

**Chapter 3**

God explains the requirements for a fellowship offering.

**Chapter 4**

God explains the requirements for a sin offering. The animal to be sacrificed varies depending upon who has sinned: priest, community, or citizen.

**Chapter 5**

God explains that anyone who does not bear witness when asked has to make a sin offering. Those who sin unintentionally have to make a guilt offering.

---

*"If the offering is a burnt offering from the herd, you are to offer a male without defect. You must present it at the entrance to the tent of meeting so that it will be acceptable to the Lord. You are to lay your hand on the head of the burnt offering, and it will be accepted on your behalf to make atonement for you. You are to slaughter the young bull before the Lord, and then Aaron's sons the priests shall bring the blood and splash it against the sides of the altar at the entrance to the tent of meeting. You are to skin the burnt offering and cut it into pieces."*

**Leviticus 1:3–6**

## Chapter 5: **Commentary**

Sacrifice comes from a recognition that in order to live, something else must die. This is true regardless of whether one is a vegetarian or a meat eater. In order to stay alive, a biological organism must consume other living things, whether it is a potato, or the flesh of another animal. Plants grow in soil enriched by the decay of previously living plants and animals. Life grows from death.

Thus, the sacrifice of an animal was a recognition that spiritual life also grew from death. The shedding of blood served as a graphic picture. But flour could take the place of a blood sacrifice. Flour, from which bread was made, was a clear picture of life as well. Not all sacrifices had to be bloody.

clothing, and the design and layout of the Tabernacle. Leviticus was a "how to" guide that told the Israelites, and especially their priests, how to worship their God, Yahweh.

The idea for sacrifice was derived from basic biology. In order to stay alive, something else must die. Likewise, sacrifice represented spiritual death and spiritual life, the exchange of guilt for innocence.

The first 16 chapters, with chapter 27, are sometimes called the Priestly Code because of their emphasis on the duties and activities of the priests. Chapters 17 through 26 are sometimes referred to as the Holiness Code because those chapters detail various laws and regulations.

*Anyone who eats the fat of an animal from which a food offering may be presented to the Lord must be cut off from their people. And wherever you live, you must not eat the blood of any bird or animal. Anyone who eats blood must be cut off from their people.*

**Leviticus 7:25–27**

*Moses then said to Aaron, "This is what the Lord spoke of when he said:*
*"Among those who approach me*
*I will be proved holy;*
*in the sight of all the people*
*I will be honored."'*
*Aaron remained silent.*

**Leviticus 10:3**

## Chapters 11–12: **Commentary**

Why all these regulations about what kind of animals could be eaten, acceptable clothing materials, how to cut hair, how to behave after childbirth, and the like? By forcing them to think about God's regulations during the course of their normal daily activities, as well as the significant milestones of their lives, God was ensuring that his people would always be conscious of God's presence and concern for them. It demonstrated that God cared about even their smallest problems, and that they would never be separated from God's presence and love.

**Chapter 6** — The guilt offering also applies for someone who deceives a neighbor. God then gives detailed regulations regarding burnt offerings, grain offerings, and sin offerings.

**Chapter 7** — God explains the guilt offering and fellowship offering. He prohibits eating fat and blood, and decides what sacrificed portions belonged to the priests.

**Chapter 8** — God has Moses ordain Aaron and his sons as God's priests; the ceremony of ordination is described in detail.

**Chapter 9** — Aaron and his sons perform a series of sin offerings, burnt offerings, fellowship offerings, and grain offerings. Then fire comes from God and consumes the burnt offerings.

**Chapter 10** — Nadab and Abihu offer the wrong incense, so God kills them. Then Moses warns Aaron and his sons not to drink alcohol while serving in the Tabernacle.

**Chapter 11** — God lists the animals that the Israelites can eat, such as cows and grasshoppers, as well as those they can't eat, such as pigs and reptiles.

**Chapter 12** — Women were ceremonially unclean for 40 or 80 days after giving birth, depending on the child's gender. Sons have to be circumcised on the eighth day after birth.

**Chapter 13**

God explains how to handle someone who comes down with a skin disease like leprosy. God also explains what to do about mold that might appear on fabric.

*"A man who has lost his hair and is bald is clean. If he has lost his hair from the front of his scalp and has a bald forehead, he is clean."*

**Leviticus 13:40–41**

**Chapter 14**

After someone has been cleansed from a skin disease or fabric mold, the priest certifies it and then offers sacrifices.

*"Aaron is to offer the bull for his own sin offering to make atonement for himself and his household. Then he is to take the two goats and present them before the Lord at the entrance to the tent of meeting. He is to cast lots for the two goats—one lot for the Lord and the other for the scapegoat. Aaron shall bring the goat whose lot falls to the Lord and sacrifice it for a sin offering. But the goat chosen by lot as the scapegoat shall be presented alive before the Lord to be used for making atonement by sending it into the wilderness as a scapegoat."*

**Leviticus 16:6–10**

**Chapter 15**

God explains what to do about bodily discharges of various sorts—such as blood, pus, or semen— and the sacrifices to be offered as part of the cleansing ritual.

**Chapter 16**

Once a year on the Day of Atonement, the high priest enters the Most Holy place to offer a sacrifice for the collective sins of the Israelite people.

## Chapter 19: **Commentary**

When Jesus was asked what the most important commandments in the Bible might be, he quoted two, one of which appears here, in Leviticus 19:18: "love your neighbor as yourself." Jesus explained that all the words of the Bible could be summarized by that commandment.

**Chapter 17**

Sacrifices are to be performed only by the official priests and only at the Tabernacle. Eating blood or animals found dead is prohibited.

*"Stand up in the presence of the aged, show respect for the elderly and revere your God. I am the Lord.*
   *"When a foreigner resides among you in your land, do not mistreat them. The foreigner residing among you must be treated as your native-born. Love them as yourself, for you were foreigners in Egypt. I am the Lord your God."*

**Leviticus 19:32–34**

**Chapter 18**

The Israelites must not act like the Egyptians or Canaanites, and various sexual practices are forbidden. The Israelites must not sacrifice their children to the god Molek.

**Chapter 19**

God reiterates and expands upon the Ten Commandments, adding prohibitions against various occult practices. He tells them to love others, respect the aged, and treat foreigners well.

**The Tabernacle**
*God gave the Israelites detailed instructions for how to build a tent for worship and sacrifice, and explained the details of how to dress the priests.*

## Chapter 21: **Commentary**

Does God have a thing against the handicapped? No; the sacrifice was a picture—a parable—of God's relationship with them. Sacrifices and those performing the sacrifices were to be perfect, because they represented God's perfection.

*"There are six days when you may work, but the seventh day is a day of sabbath rest, a day of sacred assembly. You are not to do any work; wherever you live, it is a sabbath to the Lord."*

**Leviticus 23:3**

## Chapter 25: **Commentary**

Every seventh year the Israelites were to leave their fields unplanted, their vineyards unpruned, and their crops ungathered. However, they failed to abide by this requirement. Part of the reason that the Israelites were sent into Babylonian exile for 70 years was to make up for all the years that the Israelites had failed to let the land rest (see 2 Chronicles 36:21). Besides condemning the Israelites for their idolatry, the prophets repeatedly criticized the Israelites for their oppression of the poor. Just as they failed to let the land rest every seventh year, so they failed to abide by the concept of the year of Jubilee. Every 50 years all debts were canceled and purchased lands reverted to their original owners. The year of Jubilee was designed to prevent the utter ruin of those who fell into debt, essentially filling the role that modern bankruptcy laws serve today.

*"'If you follow my decrees and are careful to obey my commands, I will send you rain in its season, and the ground will yield its crops and the trees their fruit. Your threshing will continue until grape harvest and the grape harvest will continue until planting, and you will eat all the food you want and live in safety in your land.*

*"I will grant peace in the land, and you will lie down and no one will make you afraid. I will remove wild beasts from the land, and the sword will not pass through your country."*

**Leviticus 26:3–6**

---

**3**

God explains the penalties that must be exacted for the violations of any of God's laws, repeating many of the prohibitions previously listed.

**Chapter 20**

---

**3** | **11**

Priestly behavior is constrained: they are limited in whom they can marry and how they can behave when someone dies. The handicapped cannot become priests.

**Chapter 21**

---

**11**

Ceremonially unclean priests are excluded from sacrificial services. Food dedicated to God can only be consumed by priests and their families. Certain sacrifices are forbidden.

**Chapter 22**

---

**11**

The appointed Israelite holy days: the Sabbath, the Passover and Unleavened Bread, First Fruits, Festival of Weeks, Festival of Trumpets, Day of Atonement, and the Festival of Tabernacles.

**Chapter 23**

---

**3** | **9** | **11**

Twelve loaves of bread sit on a table in the Tabernacle. God orders the execution of a man guilty of blasphemy and reiterates several other laws.

**Chapter 24**

---

**3**

Every seventh year the fields must not to be plowed or harvested. Every fiftieth year debts must be canceled, land returned to its original owners, and slaves freed.

**Chapter 25**

---

**3** | **14**

God promises blessing and prosperity for the Israelites if they keep his laws, punishments for disobedience, and forgiveness for confession of sin and repentance.

**Chapter 26**

---

**3**

God explains the regulations about dedicating something to God and the cost of redeeming it. He also explains what cannot be redeemed.

**Chapter 27**

# Numbers

## Overview

The English title of Numbers comes from the Greek translation of the Old Testament. In Hebrew, the book's title is taken from the first word in the book, *bemidbar*—which means "in the wilderness." Traditionally, Numbers was assumed to have been written by Moses sometime between 1400 and 1290 BC (depending upon the date of the Exodus from Egypt). Today, most scholars assume the date of composition for the Book of Numbers is somewhere between 600 and 400 BC.

The Book of Numbers describes the events of the Israelite wanderings in the wilderness for the 40 years after they had left Egypt. Several times Moses counts the people of Israel and the people of various tribes. Among the stories told in Numbers is that of

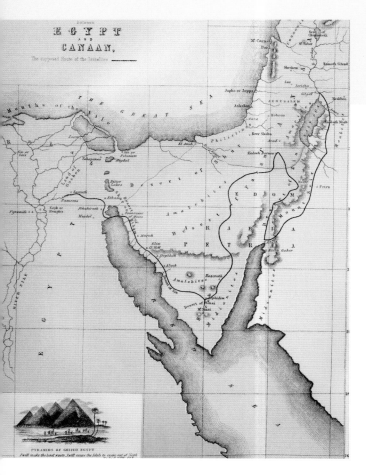

**The wandering**
*The Israelites left the region of Goshen in Egypt and wandered in what is today called the Sinai Peninsula for 40 years. The black line on the map shows the route taken by the tribe.*

## Chapter 1: **Commentary**

There is some variation in listing the 12 tribes. Usually, Joseph is split into two, while Levi is excluded. Fourteen names can potentially be called tribes, as follows:

*Reuben*
*Simeon*
*Levi*
*Judah*
*Dan*
*Naphtali*
*Gad*
*Asher*
*Issachar*
*Zebulun*
*Joseph*
*Manasseh*
*Ephraim*
*Benjamin*

Commonly, Ephraim and Manasseh are referred to as "half-tribes" in order to make clear that combined, they form a single tribe called Joseph. But in one list in the New Testament (Revelation 7:5–8), both Levi and Joseph are included, along with Manasseh—while Dan is inexplicably excluded. Regardless of the names used in listing the tribes, their number is always the same: 12.

Chapter

1

Moses takes a census of the Israelite men 20 years old and older by tribes, for a total of 603,550, excluding the tribe of Levi.

Balaam, son of Beor, whose donkey is said to have spoken to him in chapter 22.

Beginning in 1960, there were a series of Dutch archaeological excavations at a site known as Deir Alla in Jordan. The excavations were sponsored by the Netherlands Organization for the Advancement of Pure Research, under the auspices of the Department of Theology, University of Leiden. In 1967 the archaeologists unearthed what is called the Deir Alla Inscription, a fragmentary inscription written in a Semitic dialect with Canaanite and Aramaic elements. Dating between 840 and 760 BC, it seems to contain the words of Balaam, son of Beor— apparently the same Balaam described in the Book of Numbers. In the Deir Alla inscription he is referred to as a "seer" and he predicts a coming destruction.

**Miriam, the sister of Moses**
*Miriam, Moses' sister who helped hide him while he was a baby, led the Israelites in celebratory song, and also challenged his leadership of the Israelites (Numbers 12).*

*"I have taken the Levites from among the Israelites in place of the first male offspring of every Israelite woman. The Levites are mine, for all the firstborn are mine. When I struck down all the firstborn in Egypt, I set apart for myself every firstborn in Israel, whether human or animal. They are to be mine. I am the Lord."*

**Numbers 3:12–13**

*"Say to the Israelites: 'Any man or woman who wrongs another in any way and so is unfaithful to the Lord is guilty and must confess the sin they have committed. They must make full restitution for the wrong they have done, add a fifth of the value to it and give it all to the person they have wronged."*

**Numbers 5:6–7**

*16*

Whenever the Israelites pause in their travels toward the Promised Land, the 12 tribes set up camp surrounding the Tabernacle, three to a side.

Chapter
2

*16*

Moses counts the Levites and the firstborn male Israelites. There are 273 more firstborn Israelites than there are Levite males; the excess have to pay five shekels each.

Chapter
3

*16*

Moses counts the Kohathite branch of the Levites and assigns them their duties. The same is then done for the Gershonite and Merarite Levitical branches.

Chapter
4

*3*

The ceremonially unclean sit outside the Israelite camp. Restitution must be made to those who have been wronged. A husband suspecting his wife of infidelity has certain options.

Chapter
5

| | |
|---|---|
| **3** **5** **11** | |
| Chapter **6** | An Israelite can take a Nazarite vow to abstain from fermented beverages, grapes, raisins, and haircuts. They must avoid dead bodies. The priests offer a blessing. |
| **11** **16** | |
| Chapter **7** | During the 12 days it takes for the Tabernacle to be dedicated and opened for worship, each of the tribes bring gifts of silver, gold, and animals for sacrifice. |
| **11** | |
| Chapter **8** | The Levites are consecrated to God's service in a public ceremony. Only Levites between the ages of 25 and 50 are allowed to serve in the Tabernacle. |
| **8** **11** | |
| Chapter **9** | During the second year out from Egypt, the people celebrate Passover. Then God's cloud covers the newly dedicated Tabernacle. The Israelites resume their travels only when the cloud lifts. |
| **16** | |
| Chapter **10** | Two silver trumpets are made to call the community together and to break camp. After God's cloud lifts, the Israelites leave the Sinai and travel for three days. |
| **7** **9** | |
| Chapter **11** | The people complained about the food, so God kills some of them. God puts his Spirit upon 70 of the Israelite elders to help Moses. |

*"The Lord bless you
and keep you;
the Lord make his face shine on you
and be gracious to you;
the Lord turn his face toward you
and give you peace."*

**Numbers 6:24–27**

## Chapter 6: **Commentary**

The Nazirite vow was usually made voluntarily, for a set period of time, during which the individual would abstain from wine and grapes, let his or her hair grow, and avoid dead bodies. The word "Nazirite" means "consecrated." The vow was similar to the limitations placed upon a priest while he was on duty: he was not to drink alcohol or come in contact with dead bodies except if a very close relative died (Leviticus 10:9 and Leviticus 21:1–12). Thus, the idea of the Nazirite vow was that an ordinary Israelite could choose to devote himself entirely to God for a while, most commonly for about 30 days; the actual time would be specified by the individual. Three individuals in the Bible were made Nazirites, at the command of God, from birth: Samson (Judges 13:5), Samuel (1 Samuel 1:11), and John the Baptist (Luke 1:13–15).

*On the day the tabernacle, the tent of the covenant law, was set up, the cloud covered it. From evening till morning the cloud above the tabernacle looked like fire. That is how it continued to be; the cloud covered it, and at night it looked like fire. Whenever the cloud lifted from above the tent, the Israelites set out; wherever the cloud settled, the Israelites encamped.*

**Numbers 9:15–17**

*"Why have you brought this trouble on your servant? What have I done to displease you that you put the burden of all these people on me? Did I conceive all these people? Did I give them birth? Why do you tell me to carry them in my arms, as a nurse carries an infant, to the land you promised on oath to their ancestors? Where can I get meat for all these people? They keep wailing to me, 'Give us meat to eat!' I cannot carry all these people by myself; the burden is too heavy for me. If this is how you are going to treat me, please go ahead and kill me—if I have found favor in your eyes—and do not let me face my own ruin."*

**Numbers 11:11–15**

## Chapter 12: **Commentary**

Although Moses was already married to Zipporah (see Exodus 2:21–22) some have speculated that he had divorced her, based on the fact that in Exodus 18:2 it says he had "sent her away." It is a phrase often idiomatically used for divorce (Deuteronomy 24:4 and Matthew 19:7). On the other hand, polygamy was never prohibited, so perhaps the Cushite Moses married was a second wife in addition to Zipporah. In any case, his brother and sister used his marriage to her to challenge his position of leadership.

When they reached the Valley of Eshkol, they cut off a branch bearing a single cluster of grapes. Two of them carried it on a pole between them, along with some pomegranates and figs. That place was called the Valley of Eshkol because of the cluster of grapes the Israelites cut off there. At the end of forty days they returned from exploring the land.

**Numbers 13:23–25**

## Chapter 15: **Commentary**

In Numbers 15:32–36 the narrative explains how an unnamed man was stoned for picking up sticks on the Sabbath. It seems odd that he should suffer the death penalty merely for gathering wood on the wrong day, especially when the story follows a passage (15:22–31) that explains offering sacrifices for unintentional sins.

That context is what helps to explain the reaction. This is not the story of an individual who forgot what day it was, or even someone who decided that his need for wood overcame the prohibition. Instead, the context indicates that the man was engaged in an act of conscious rebellion against the community and against God.

This passage helps to explain the anger that the religious establishment had for Jesus when he appeared to violate the Sabbath day restrictions (Matthew 12:1–12).

## Chapter 16: **Commentary**

As with the man who violated the Sabbath, so Korah and his followers were guilty of attempting to rebel against the community, and against the leadership of Moses (Numbers 16:1). As with the man caught violating the Sabbath, Korah and his followers were executed. Unlike the Sabbath breaker, who died at the hands of the community, Korah and his followers were executed directly by God. Why? To demonstrate to the rest of the community that God wanted Moses to lead the people of Israel, and that it was not merely Moses attempting to cling to power.

---

**2**   **9**   **17**

Moses marries a Cushite, so Miriam and Aaron complain about Moses' leadership. God tells them that Moses is rightfully in charge and gives Miriam leprosy for a week.

Chapter **12**

**17**

Moses sends 12 men to explore Canaan, one from each tribe. Ten say it is impossible to conquer Canaan, but Joshua and Caleb disagree.

Chapter **13**

**The grapes of Canaan**
*They cut off a branch bearing a single cluster of grapes. Two of them carried it on a pole between them. (Numbers 13:23)*

**2**   **9**   **12**

The Israelites want to give up and return to Egypt. Therefore God tells them that those more than 20 years old will die in the wilderness.

Chapter **14**

**3**   **9**

God lists several extra offerings and sacrifices, then orders that a man gathering wood on the Sabbath be stoned. Everyone must wear blue tassels as a reminder of the rules.

Chapter **15**

**9**

When Korah and some other community leaders challenge Moses' authority, God kills them. When the Israelites react with outrage, a plague kills another 14,700.

Chapter **16**

**8** | **17**

Chapter **17**

God puts an end to the grumbling against Moses and Aaron once and for all when, out of 12 labeled staffs, only Aaron's sprouts, buds, and produces almonds.

**11**

Chapter **18**

Only Aaron and his descendants can be priests. The other Levites serve as support staff. No priests or Levites are allowed to own any land.

**11**

Chapter **19**

A red heifer is sacrificed. Its ashes are put in a ceremonially clean place, to be mixed, as needed, in water to "cleanse" those who have touched the dead.

**4** | **17**

Chapter **20**

Moses' sister Miriam dies. After the Edomites forbid the Israelites passage through their land, Moses' brother Aaron dies.

**9** | **17**

Chapter **21**

The Israelites defeat Arad. God sends snakes because of Israelite grumbling, so Moses sets up a bronze snake to save them. Then the Israelites defeat the kings Sihon and Og.

**8** | **17**

Chapter **22**

On his way to curse the Israelites for Moab's King Balak, Balaam's donkey talks to him. Then an angel warns Balaam to speak only God's words.

**5** | **7** | **17**

Chapter **23**

Balaam pronounces two blessings on the Israelites instead of curses. An angry Balak takes Balaam to a different spot and orders him to curse them.

**5** | **7** | **17**

Chapter **24**

Instead of a curse, once again, Balaam offers a blessing. An angry Balak sends Balaam away unpaid, so Balaam pronounces four more blessings upon the Israelites.

---

*So Moses spoke to the Israelites, and their leaders gave him twelve staffs, one for the leader of each of their ancestral tribes, and Aaron's staff was among them. Moses placed the staffs before the Lord in the tent of the covenant law.*

*The next day Moses entered the tent and saw that Aaron's staff, which represented the tribe of Levi, had not only sprouted but had budded, blossomed and produced almonds.*

**Numbers 17:6–8**

*So Moses took the staff from the Lord's presence, just as he commanded him. He and Aaron gathered the assembly together in front of the rock and Moses said to them, "Listen, you rebels, must we bring you water out of this rock?" Then Moses raised his arm and struck the rock twice with his staff. Water gushed out, and the community and their livestock drank.*

*But the Lord said to Moses and Aaron, "Because you did not trust in me enough to honor me as holy in the sight of the Israelites, you will not bring this community into the land I give them."*

**Numbers 20:9–12**

## Chapter 21: **Commentary**

The emblem of a snake on a pole is now known as the Rod of Asclepius, an ancient symbol associated with the Greek god Asclepius, the son of Apollo, who practiced medicine in Ancient Greek mythology. His attributes were the snake and the staff. The well-known Greek physician, Hippocrates, of the Hippocratic Oath, was a worshiper of Asclepius. Asclepius was supposedly so skilled as a healer, that he had even brought the dead back to life. For raising the dead, he was punished and placed in the sky as the constellation Ophiuhus (the "serpent bearer").

Today, the emblem of a snake on a staff continues to be used by the medical community as a symbol of healing.

*God is not human, that he should lie,*
*not a human being, that he should change his mind.*
*Does he speak and then not act?*
*Does he promise and not fulfill?*
*I have received a command to bless;*
*he has blessed, and I cannot change it.*

**Numbers 23:19–20**

## Chapter 25: **Commentary**

The Israelites traveled through Moab on their way to their Promised Land. Balak, its king, feared what the Israelites might do to him and his nation. Therefore, he asked the prophet Balaam to curse the Israelites who had camped along the Jordan River. For a price, Balaam was happy to comply, but God stopped him. Balaam came up with a plan to get around God's prohibition. He made Balak send his women to the Israelites to seduce them into worshiping other gods (Numbers 31:16). God did judge the Israelites for this, but he also judged Balaam. The Israelites killed him when they conquered the allies of Moab, the Midianites (Numbers 31:8).

## Chapter 27: **Commentary**

Women in the Ancient Near East generally had limited rights. They were often treated as little more than property. Those without a father, husband, or brother were often reduced to begging (see Ruth 1:20–2:3). Zelophehad, of the tribe of Manesseh, died with no sons. His daughters asked Moses to do something about their father's plight. Not only would his property be distributed among his clan, his name would disappear and it would be as if he had never existed. They asked Moses to give them the property, so that Zelophehad's name would be preserved. God told Moses to grant their request.

**9** **17**

God sends a plague against the Israelites for worshiping the Moabite gods. When Phineas, a grandson of Aaron the priest, kills an Israelite and a Midianite, the plague stops.

Chapter
**25**

**16**

After the plague, Moses takes a second census of the Israelites. Everyone counted in the first census had died during the 40 years of wandering.

Chapter
**26**

**3** **17**

Since their father Zelophehad dies without sons, his daughters will inherit their father's property. Joshua is then chosen as Moses' successor.

Chapter
**27**

**3** **17**

God summarizes the regular offerings and sacrifices: the daily, weekly, and monthly, along with those for Passover and the Festival of Weeks.

Chapter
**28**

**Aaron's staff that blossomed**
*After Korah's rebellion against Moses and Aaron, God had Moses collect 12 staffs, one each from the leader of every Israelite tribe. Only the staff of Aaron blossomed.*

**11**

Chapter
**29**

God summarizes the offerings and sacrifices to be made during the Festival of Trumpets, the Day of Atonement, and the Festival of Tabernacles.

**3**

Chapter
**30**

Vows are usually unbreakable, but the father of an unmarried woman, or the husband of a married woman, can disavow any vow she makes when he first learns about it.

**9**        **17**

Chapter
**31**

The Israelites kill every male Moabite and Midianite, including King Balak and the prophet Balaam and take their women, children, and livestock as spoils.

**17**

Chapter
**32**

The tribes of Reuben, Gad, and Manasseh are allowed to settle east of the Jordan when their men agree to fight alongside the other tribes until all Canaan is conquered.

*When a man makes a vow to the Lord or takes an oath to obligate himself by a pledge, he must not break his word but must do everything he said.*
**Numbers 30:2**

## Chapter 30: Commentary

Vows were treated very seriously in ancient Israel. According to Numbers 30:2, when a man made a vow to Yahweh, or obligated himself by a pledge, he had to keep his word. Deuteronomy 23:23 specifies that "Whatever your lips utter you must be sure to do, because you made your vow freely to the Lord your God with your own mouth." Sometimes, such vows were taken too seriously, as when Jephthah sacrificed his daughter as a burnt offering (Judges 11:30–39). Women could make vows the same as men. However, their vows became binding only if the men in their lives—their fathers or husbands—agreed with them and confirmed them.

**Passover Seder**
*Every year the Israelites were to remember how God rescued them from Egyptian slavery and brought them to their Promised Land.*

| Hebrew holidays<br>Names (English, Hebrew) | Dates<br>(Hebrew and Modern) |
| --- | --- |
| Sabbath, Shabbat | every seven days |
| Passover, Pesach | 15–16 Nisan (March–April) |
| Festival of Weeks, Pentecost, Shavuot | 6–7 Sivan (May–June) |
| Festival of Trumpets, Rosh Hashana | 1 Tisri (September–October) |
| Day of Atonement, Yom Kippur | 9 Tisri (September–October) |
| Festival of Tabernacles, Booths, Succot | 15–21 Tishri (September–October) |

*The Jewish calendar is a lunar calendar. Therefore, the dates of the holidays vary from year to year on our common Gregorian calendar, which is a solar calendar.*

**Balaam and his donkey**
*Balaam's donkey stopped in its tracks because it saw an angel blocking the path. Balaam beat the donkey, who then explained why he was refusing to budge.*

*"Take possession of the land and settle in it, for I have given you the land to possess. Distribute the land by lot, according to your clans. To a larger group give a larger inheritance, and to a smaller group a smaller one. Whatever falls to them by lot will be theirs. Distribute it according to your ancestral tribes.*

*"But if you do not drive out the inhabitants of the land, those you allow to remain will become barbs in your eyes and thorns in your sides. They will give you trouble in the land where you will live. And then I will do to you what I plan to do to them."*

**Numbers 33:53–56**

*"Six of the towns you give the Levites will be cities of refuge, to which a person who has killed someone may flee. In addition, give them forty-two other towns."*

**Numbers 35:6**

**16** | **17**

A summary of the Israelites' journeys from the time they left Egypt until they stand on the plains of Moab across from Jericho.

Chapter
**33**

**16**

God establishes the outer boundaries of the Promised Land and assigns one leader from each tribe, excluding Levi, to determine which tribe gets which portion.

Chapter
**34**

**16**

The Levites grant certain towns scattered throughout the nation. Six of those towns became Cities of Refuge for those guilty of involuntary manslaughter.

Chapter
**35**

**3**

The daughters of Zelophehad are required to marry only members of their own tribe, so that their father's property does not wind up being transferred to another tribe.

Chapter
**36**

# Deuteronomy

## Overview

Although Moses is traditionally assumed to be the author of the Book of Deuteronomy, Deuteronomy is actually an anonymous work. The English title comes from the Greek translation of the Old Testament (the Septuagint), meaning "second law" because the book repeats what has appeared in Exodus, Leviticus, and Numbers. In Hebrew, the book's title is taken from the first words in the book, *eleh devarim*—which mean "these are the words."

The format of Deuteronomy follows the structure of Ancient Near Eastern suzerain treaties, which were made between greater and lesser powers. Israel, the lesser power, had been freed from bondage as Egypt's vassal and was now voluntarily becoming the vassal of Yahweh. Therefore, the Book of Deuteronomy is a treaty between God and Israel. Such treaties began with historical prologue, to explain the need for the treaty, followed by its regulations, and the benefits that came from keeping

---

**Chapter 1**

Forty years after leaving Egypt, Moses explains how the Israelites wound up wandering in the wilderness until only Joshua and Caleb remained of the original group.

*The Lord your God has increased your numbers so that today you are as numerous as the stars in the sky. May the Lord, the God of your ancestors, increase you a thousand times and bless you as he has promised!*

**Deuteronomy 1:10–11**

**Chapter 2**

Moses summarizes their history from leaving Kadesh Barnea until they defeated Sihon, king of Heshbon.

*The Lord your God has blessed you in all the work of your hands. He has watched over your journey through this vast wilderness. These forty years the Lord your God has been with you, and you have not lacked anything.*

**Deuteronomy 2:7**

**Chapter 3**

Og is also defeated. So the lands of Sihon and Og are given to the tribes of Reuben and Gad. Moses cannot enter the Promised Land. Joshua will take his place.

**Chapter 4**

God will judge the Israelites if they disobey, but they could be forgiven. God is great and loves them. Bezer, Ramoth, and Golan become Cities of Refuge.

*What other nation is so great as to have their gods near them the way the Lord our God is near us whenever we pray to him? And what other nation is so great as to have such righteous decrees and laws as this body of laws I am setting before you today?*

**Deuteronomy 4:7–8**

it versus the problems from breaking it. Gods and goddesses were then called upon to bear witness to the treaty. In Deuteronomy, since the Israelites only believed in one God, the heavens and earth were called upon to bear witness to the treaty. Compare the outline of a standard Ancient Near Eastern treaty below, with the outline of Deuteronomy above:

Outline of a typical Ancient Near Eastern suzerain treaty:

I. Preamble—"These are the words..."
II. Historical prologue—the events which led to and now form the basis of the treaty
III. General stipulations—statements about the future relationship, summarizing the purpose of the specific stipulations that follow
IV. Specific stipulations
V. Divine witnesses
VI. Blessings and cursings

## Chapter 6: **Commentary**

This chapter contains the commandment quoted by Jesus in the New Testament. Leviticus 19:18 says to love people. Deuteronomy 6:5 tells us to love God. On these two commandments, Jesus taught, hangs the entire Bible. Everything else is merely commentary.

God says that "you" are to teach his commandments to "your" children. In Hebrew, there are four forms of the word "you." In this passage, it is the masculine singular form that is used. Therefore, the responsibility for training children falls primarily on the father. As a result, the high priest Eli, the prophet Samuel, and King David are criticized for the behavior of their children.

*Hear, O Israel: The Lord our God, the Lord is one. Love the Lord your God with all your heart and with all your soul and with all your strength. These commandments that I give you today are to be on your hearts. Impress them on your children. Talk about them when you sit at home and when you walk along the road, when you lie down and when you get up. Tie them as symbols on your hands and bind them on your foreheads. Write them on the doorframes of your houses and on your gates.*

**Deuteronomy 6:4–9**

**Moses and the Covenant**
*The Book of Deuteronomy was the formal contract that transferred ownership of Israel from Egypt to God.*

③  ⑭

After repeating the Ten Commandments, Moses reminds them that he has become their mediator with God because they didn't want to hear God's voice any more.

Chapter
5

③  ⑭

Moses tells the people to love God and to keep his commandments, teaching them to their children and future generations.

Chapter
6

**3** **14**

Chapter

**7**

Moses orders the Israelites to destroy both the Canaanites and their religion. God chooses the Israelites because he loves them; he will bless their obedience and punish their disobedience.

**3** **14**

Chapter

**8**

The Israelites must not forget about God after they become prosperous in their new land. Moses warns that if they forget God, God will punish them.

**3** **14**

Chapter

**9**

God does not give Canaan to the Israelites because they are righteous, but because the Canaanites were wicked. In fact, the Israelites have a history of disobedience, too.

**3** **14** **17**

Chapter

**10**

Moses reminds the Israelites how he replaced the Ten Commandments after smashing them. God is powerful. The people must love him and love each other.

## Chapter 7: **Commentary**

Many commentators have been harsh in their criticism of the commandments to exterminate the Canaanites. However, it is intriguing to compare the commandment with the reality of what happened. The Canaanites were not, in fact, exterminated. Some of them—Rahab the harlot and her family (Joshua 6:25), for instance, and the Gibeonites (Joshua 9), were made part of the Israelite community. The word translated as "destroy" actually means to devote something entirely to God. Often, that meant that the object was burned as an offering. But it could also mean that the object was converted to God's use.

In actual practice, God's intention for the Israelites and the Canaanites (and other enemies of his people) was along the lines of the words attributed to Abraham Lincoln: "the best way to destroy your enemies is to make them your friends."

*If you ever forget the Lord your God and follow other gods and worship and bow down to them, I testify against you today that you will surely be destroyed. Like the nations the Lord destroyed before you, so you will be destroyed for not obeying the Lord your God.*

**Deuteronomy 8:19–20**

*For the Lord your God is God of gods and Lord of lords, the great God, mighty and awesome, who shows no partiality and accepts no bribes. He defends the cause of the fatherless and the widow, and loves the foreigner residing among you, giving them food and clothing. And you are to love those who are foreigners, for you yourselves were foreigners in Egypt. Fear the Lord your God and serve him. Hold fast to him and take your oaths in his name. He is the one you praise; he is your God, who performed for you those great and awesome wonders you saw with your own eyes. Your ancestors who went down into Egypt were seventy in all, and now the Lord your God has made you as numerous as the stars in the sky.*

**Deuteronomy 10:17–22**

**Restoring the law**
*After Moses smashed the Ten Commandments, God called him back to Mount Sinai so he could make a replacement copy.*

*Love the Lord your God and keep his requirements, his decrees, his laws and his commands always.*

**Deuteronomy 11:1**

| 3 | 14 | 11 |
|---|---|---|

God blesses obedience and curses disobedience. When they enter the land, they must proclaim those blessings from Mount Gerizim and the curses from Mount Ebal.

Chapter

11

---

*See that you do all I command you; do not add to it or take away from it.*

**Deuteronomy 12:32**

| 3 | 14 |
|---|---|

The Israelites must worship only Yahweh, only in the prescribed way, and only at the prescribed place. They must never add to or subtract from God's laws.

Chapter

12

---

## Chapter 15: **Commentary**

Together with Leviticus 25:8–38, God established as a principle that both debts and slavery were only temporary conditions. Every seven years, debts were canceled. The same was true of slaves. In the seventh year of servitude—usually entered into as a consequence of poverty—the slave was supposed to be set free. Not only that, but the freed slave was not to be released empty-handed. Instead, he or she was to be well provisioned. The Israelites were supposed to remember how they had suffered as slaves in Egypt and to be careful to never treat people so badly themselves.

| 3 | 14 |
|---|---|

If a prophet predicts the future and performs miracles, but encourages the worship of other gods, then he should be ignored and all who worship other gods must be destroyed.

Chapter

13

| 3 | 14 |
|---|---|

Only certain animals, birds, and fish can be eaten. The Israelites must give one tenth of their income for the support of Levites, foreigners, orphans, and widows.

Chapter

14

---

## Chapter 16: **Commentary**

Asherah poles were a phallic symbol representing the Canaanite fertility goddess, Asherah (equivalent to the Persian Ishtar, the Greek Aphrodite, and the Roman Venus). Asherah was worshiped by men paying money and engaging in intercourse with temple prostitutes. It was a form of sympathetic magic designed to guarantee fertile fields, farm animals, and wives.

| 3 | 14 |
|---|---|

Every seven years all debts must be canceled and all slaves must be freed. Slaves cannot be sent away empty-handed. Firstborn male animals are to be sacrificed.

Chapter

15

| 3 | 14 |
|---|---|

They must celebrate the holy days, they must appoint honest judges and officials in every town; and they must never set up Asherah poles or sacred stones.

Chapter

16

---

## Chapter 17: **Commentary**

The king was forbidden to acquire large numbers of horses. He was forbidden to have a large number of wives and he was not allowed to accumulate large amounts of silver or gold. Upon becoming king, he was to make a copy of God's law for himself and to read it regularly so that he would obey it. He was also not to think of himself as better than the other Israelites who were not king. That way, Moses said, he and his descendants would reign a long time. At a time when most kings considered themselves to be gods, whose whim was law and who could do as they pleased, the Israelite king was considered the equal of all other citizens, limited by and subject to the same laws, and forbidden to enrich himself.

| 3 | 14 |
|---|---|

Defective animals must not be sacrificed. Worshipers of other gods must die. The Tabernacle priests are the highest court. The Israelite king must be subject to the laws.

Chapter

17

| 3 | 14 |
|---|---|

The Levites receive no land. God forbids occult practices. Instead, God will send prophets, recognizable when what they say happens. Otherwise, they could be ignored.

Chapter

18

**3** | **15**

Chapter
**19**

At least three Cities of Refuge are to be established west of the Jordan. Boundary stones must not be moved. One witness is not enough to convict anyone of a crime. False witnesses are to receive punishment.

**3** | **15**

Chapter
**20**

Only those willing and unafraid, without entanglements, are allowed to fight in war. Peace treaties can be arranged with distant nations, but not with the Canaanites.

**3** | **15**

Chapter
**21**

Unsolved murders require the sacrifice of an animal. Firstborn rights are established. Israelites can marry women they capture in war. Rebellious sons can be executed.

**3** | **15**

Chapter
**22**

There are laws regarding the care of lost animals, rooftops, seeds, animal husbandry, clothing, adultery, rape, and false accusations of infidelity.

**3** | **15**

Chapter
**23**

Some can be excluded from the Israelites' assembly for defect of birth. Escaped slaves seeking refuge must be protected, vows kept, the poor protected and gleaning (collecting leftover crops) permitted.

**3** | **15**

Chapter
**24**

Remarriage after divorce is regulated. Those recently married must not go to war for a year. Kidnappers are to be executed. Foreigners, orphans, and widows must be protected.

**3** | **15**

Chapter
**25**

No more than 40 lashes. Widows without sons must marry their husband's brother. A woman loses her hand if she grabs a man's genitals during a fight. Amalekites must die.

**3** | **15**

Chapter
**26**

Offerings of first fruits and tithes must be given to God in gratitude for his provision. The Israelites must carefully obey God's commands, since they voluntarily agreed to them.

---

*The officers shall say to the army: "Has anyone built a new house and not yet begun to live in it? Let him go home, or he may die in battle and someone else may begin to live in it. Has anyone planted a vineyard and not begun to enjoy it? Let him go home, or he may die in battle and someone else enjoy it. Has anyone become pledged to a woman and not married her? Let him go home, or he may die in battle and someone else marry her." Then the officers shall add, "Is anyone afraid or fainthearted? Let him go home so that his fellow soldiers will not become disheartened too."*
**Deuteronomy 20:5–8**

*If you see your fellow Israelite's donkey or ox fallen on the road, do not ignore it. Help the owner get it to its feet.*
**Deuteronomy 22:4**

**The death of Moses**
*Because he disobeyed God's command, God did not let Moses live to see the Israelites enter the Promised Land.*

*If a slave has taken refuge with you, do not hand them over to their master. Let them live among you wherever they like and in whatever town they choose. Do not oppress them.*
**Deuteronomy 23:15–16**

*You have declared this day that the Lord is your God and that you will walk in obedience to him, that you will keep his decrees, commands and laws—that you will listen to him. And the Lord has declared this day that you are his people, his treasured possession as he promised, and that you are to keep all his commands. He has declared that he will set you in praise, fame and honor high above all the nations he has made and that you will be a people holy to the Lord your God, as he promised.*
**Deuteronomy 26:17–19**

*The Lord will make you the head, not the tail. If you pay attention to the commands of the Lord your God that I give you this day and carefully follow them, you will always be at the top, never at the bottom. Do not turn aside from any of the commands I give you today, to the right or to the left, following other gods and serving them.*

**Deuteronomy 28:13–14**

## Chapter 28: **Commentary**

The Book of Deuteronomy is a formal contract, or treaty, between God and his people Israel. If the Israelites fulfilled the contract as laid out in the first 27 chapters of the book, then they would receive the blessings described in Deuteronomy 28:1–14. However, if they failed to keep the requirements, then God was obligated to bring a series of curses upon them, as described in Deuteronomy 28:15–68. The list of curses for disobedience is far more detailed and extensive than the list of potential blessings for obedience. This disparity is normal. Those treaties from the ancient world that have survived spend more time on the consequence for failing to abide by treaties than the consequences for keeping them.

*When all these blessings and curses I have set before you come on you and you take them to heart wherever the Lord your God disperses you among the nations, and when you and your children return to the Lord your God and obey him with all your heart and with all your soul according to everything I command you today, then the Lord your God will restore your fortunes and have compassion on you and gather you again from all the nations where he scattered you.*

**Deuteronomy 30:1–3**

## Chapters 33–34: **Commentary**

At the conclusion of the Book of Deuteronomy, Moses is given a chance to view the Promised Land before he dies, and his body is buried by God. Some traditionalists will argue that Deuteronomy was written by Moses himself, suggesting that this last chapter describing his death was perhaps penned by Joshua. Most scholars, however, assume that Moses did not write it, with his death at the end of the book as one of the primary bits of evidence against this. Most scholars assume that Genesis– Deuteronomy, Joshua, Judges, Ruth, and 1 Samuel–2 Kings were all assembled and edited after the Babylonian exile from earlier source materials. Together, they form what is sometimes referred to as a "salvation history."

**3 | 14**

Upon crossing the Jordan, the Israelites must go to Mount Ebal, write the law on plaster-coated stones, build an altar, curse lawbreakers, and sacrifice fellowship offerings.

**Chapter 27**

**3 | 9 | 14**

Blessings come upon the Israelites for obedience and curses for disobedience. Continued disobedience would ultimately result in the Israelites being exiled from their land.

**Chapter 28**

**3 | 14 | 17**

Because of all the wonders that they had seen since leaving Egypt, the Israelites must obey God's commands. Otherwise, God will send them into exile.

**Chapter 29**

**2 | 14**

If the curses come, the Israelites can always beg God's forgiveness. Moses calls upon the heavens and earth to bear witness to this treaty between Israel and God.

**Chapter 30**

**3 | 14 | 17**

Since Moses is about to die, Joshua will take his place. Every seven years, when debts are forgiven, the Law of God must be read to the Israelites.

**Chapter 31**

**5 | 7 | 14**

Moses recites a song that calls on the heavens to bear witness that God is great, but that the Israelites are wicked and will suffer punishment before repenting.

**Chapter 32**

**5 | 7 | 14**

Moses pronounces a blessing, in the form of a poem, upon each of the 12 tribes of Israel.

**Chapter 33**

**17**

Moses climbs Mount Nebo, sees the Promised Land, and dies. God himself buries Moses. Then the Israelites mourn his death for 30 days.

**Chapter 34**

# Joshua

## Overview

The Book of Joshua tells the story of the Israelites' conquest of the Promised Land under the leadership of Joshua. The book's title is the same in both the Hebrew original and in the Greek translation. The title of the book is derived from its content, rather than from its author. As with much of the Old Testament, the author of the Book of Joshua is unknown.

In Jewish tradition, Joshua begins the section of the Hebrew Bible that is called "the prophets." The prophets include the books of Joshua, Judges, 1–2 Samuel, 1–2 Kings, Isaiah, Jeremiah, Ezekiel, Hosea, Joel, Amos, Obadiah, Jonah, Micah, Nahum, Habakkuk,

| | |
|---|---|
| **17** | |
| Chapter **1** | Joshua takes Moses' place as the leader of the Israelites. Joshua tells them that they will soon cross the Jordan River—so they need to be prepared. |

*"Be strong and very courageous. Be careful to obey all the law my servant Moses gave you; do not turn from it to the right or to the left, that you may be successful wherever you go. Keep this Book of the Law always on your lips; meditate on it day and night, so that you may be careful to do everything written in it. Then you will be prosperous and successful. Have I not commanded you? Be strong and courageous. Do not be afraid; do not be discouraged, for the Lord your God will be with you wherever you go."*

**Joshua 1:7–9**

| | |
|---|---|
| **17** | |
| Chapter **2** | Joshua sends two spies to Jericho. They stay with a prostitute named Rahab, who hides them. They promise to spare her when the Israelites conquer the city. |

## Chapter 2: **Commentary**

Jericho is one of the oldest inhabited cities on planet Earth, with the earliest evidence for human habitation dating to at least 10,000 BC. Over the course of its long history, the city has been repeatedly conquered. Although some early archaeologists believed they had found the walls that fell during the time of Joshua's invasion, today it is generally believed that no evidence exists for Joshua's conquest.

This is not to say that Joshua's conquest did not happen (though there are some scholars who will argue that way). There are enormous gaps in the data we can get from the past. It becomes more fragmentary the further back in time we go. Our attempt to understand the distant past from the few bits that have survived to the present is like attempting to make sense of our surroundings by peering only through a soda straw. We usually know much less than we think we do.

| | | |
|---|---|---|
| **8** | | **17** |
| Chapter **3** | When the priests, carrying the Ark, step into the Jordan River, God halts the water. While the priests stand in the channel, the rest of the Israelites cross the river on dry ground. | |

| | | |
|---|---|---|
| **8** | | **17** |
| Chapter **4** | Twelve large stones gathered from the middle of the Jordan are piled as a memorial of the crossing. When the priests leave the Jordan River, the water starts flowing again. | |

Zephaniah, Haggai, Zechariah, and Malachi. The prophets are divided into two parts, the earlier, or former, and the later. The books of Joshua through 2 Kings are referred to as "the earlier prophets" with the rest getting the designation "later prophets."

Most scholars today see Joshua as part of a series of writings that includes the books of Deuteronomy, Judges, 1–2 Samuel, and 1–2 Kings that appear to have been assembled during the time of Josiah or even later, during the Babylonian exile. These combined works are sometimes referred to as the "Deuteronomistic History" of Israel.

**Rahab**
*When Joshua sent spies to Jericho, they visited a brothel run by Rahab. She protected the spies, and so when the Israelites conquered Jericho and slaughtered its populace, they spared both her and her family.*

*Now when Joshua was near Jericho, he looked up and saw a man standing in front of him with a drawn sword in his hand. Joshua went up to him and asked, "Are you for us or for our enemies?"*

*"Neither," he replied, "but as commander of the army of the Lord I have now come."*

**Joshua 5:13–14**

## Chapter 6: **Commentary**

Joshua's interaction with the angel of the Lord is puzzling. How could God not be on the Israelites' side?

It is hard to miss the theological point of this exchange: God is on his own side. The question for Joshua and the other freed slaves is the question for all of us: are we choosing to be on His side? God is not for or against anyone. If he's not even on his chosen people's side, then what hope does anyone else have? God isn't on our side, whether it's a basketball game, a legal battle, or a war.

## Chapter 8: **Commentary**

Some scholars propose that the story of the conquest of Ai is an etiological tale designed to explain the existence of Ai as a ruin. W.F. Albright suggested that the biblical story actually describes the conquest of Bethel. Callaway proposed that the story in Joshua describes the destruction of the small, unwalled village around 1125 BC. Others have suggested that the Ai in Joshua has yet to be excavated and has nothing to do with et-Tell at all.

---

**8**     **17**

The Israelites then circumcise all the men and celebrate Passover. For the first time, the Israelites eat some Canaanite food. The manna stops coming.

Chapter
**5**

---

**8**     **17**

The Israelites march around Jericho once a day for six days, and then seven times on the seventh day. Then the walls of Jericho fall down. The Israelites conquer Jericho.

Chapter
**6**

---

**9**     **17**

Achin steals some of the spoils from Jericho, rather than destroying it. As a consequence, the Israelites lose a battle at Ai. Achin and his family are stoned to death for his theft.

Chapter
**7**

---

**11**     **17**

The Israelites successfully conquer the small city of Ai. Joshua builds an altar on Mount Ebal, offers sacrifices, and the blessings and cursings of the covenant are read aloud.

Chapter
**8**

**Chapter 9** *(14)* *(17)*

Canaanites from Gibeon trick the Israelites into making a peace treaty. When the Israelites learn of their deception, they enslave the Gibeonites.

**Chapter 10** *(5)* *(8)* *(17)*

Joshua and the Israelites rescue the Gibeonites from an attack by five kings. God makes the sun and moon stand still in the sky. The Israelites conquer most of southern Canaan.

**Chapter 11** *(17)*

Joshua and the Israelites defeat most of the kings and cities of the northern part of Canaan.

**Chapter 12** *(16)* *(17)*

A list of all the kings and their cities that the Israelites defeated and conquered.

**Chapter 13** *(16)* *(17)*

For an elderly Joshua God lists the land still remaining to be conquered in Canaan. The land east of the Jordan is apportioned between Reuben, Gad, and half of Manasseh.

**Chapter 14** *(16)* *(17)*

The land west of the Jordan River is apportioned by lot between the remaining nine and a half tribes. An 85-year-old Caleb receives the city of Hebron as his personal inheritance.

**Chapter 15** *(16)* *(17)*

The land allotted to Judah is outlined, with its borders.

**Chapter 16** *(16)* *(17)*

The land allotted to Ephraim is outlined, with its borders.

## Chapter 10: **Commentary**

Among the few spectacular, impossible-to-explain miracles that are related in the Bible, the one that happened during a battle against the Amorites stands out: Joshua prayed that the sun and moon would stand still so they would have the added daylight necessary to defeat their foes.

A bit of poetry, the words that Joshua spoke to God in his request for intervention, are said to have been written in "the Book of Jashar" a source mentioned once more in the Bible, in 2 Samuel 1:18. The Book of Jashar, whatever it might have been, no longer exists. Most scholars assume that it was a collection of archaic poetry. *Jashar* is a Hebrew word that means "upright" or "righteous."

On the day the Lord gave the Amorites over to Israel, Joshua said to the Lord in the presence of Israel:
"Sun, stand still over Gibeon,
and you, moon, over the Valley of Aijalon."
So the sun stood still,
and the moon stopped,
till the nation avenged itself on its enemies,
as it is written in the Book of Jashar.
The sun stopped in the middle of the sky and delayed going down about a full day. There has never been a day like it before or since, a day when the Lord listened to a human being. Surely the Lord was fighting for Israel!

**Joshua 10:12–14**

So Joshua took the entire land, just as the Lord had directed Moses, and he gave it as an inheritance to Israel according to their tribal divisions. Then the land had rest from war.

**Joshua 11:23**

When Joshua had grown old, the Lord said to him, "You are now very old, and there are still very large areas of land to be taken over."

**Joshua 13:1**

And Caleb said, "I will give my daughter Aksah in marriage to the man who attacks and captures Kiriath Sepher." Othniel son of Kenaz, Caleb's brother, took it; so Caleb gave his daughter Aksah to him in marriage.

**Joshua 15:16–17**

*The whole assembly of the Israelites gathered at Shiloh and set up the tent of meeting there. The country was brought under their control, but there were still seven Israelite tribes who had not yet received their inheritance.*

*So Joshua said to the Israelites: "How long will you wait before you begin to take possession of the land that the Lord, the God of your ancestors, has given you?"*

**Joshua 18:1–3**

## Chapter 20: **Commentary**

In the ancient world, there were no police officers to hunt down criminals. Instead, the task was left to those who witnessed the crime, to soldiers, and to the family members of the victim. It was primarily the duty of a relative of a murder victim to see to it that the murderer was captured and executed. This relative was referred to as "the avenger of blood." To prevent vigilantism, cities of refuge were established for the accused to flee to, where he or she could be protected until after a trial established guilt or innocence. Since a verdict of innocent would not necessarily satisfy a wrathful family member, those accused could stay in a city of refuge so they would remain protected from vengeful relatives.

*"That is why we said, 'Let us get ready and build an altar—but not for burnt offerings or sacrifices.' On the contrary, it is to be a witness between us and you and the generations that follow, that we will worship the Lord at his sanctuary with our burnt offerings, sacrifices and fellowship offerings. Then in the future your descendants will not be able to say to ours, 'You have no share in the Lord.'"*

**Joshua 22:26–27**

## Chapters 23–24: **Commentary**

Although we think of the Israelites as monotheists, in practice they were not until they returned from Babylonian exile during the fifth century BC. As is clear in Joshua's charge to the Israelites who had just spent 40 years wandering in the wilderness and who had now conquered the land of Canaan, they were still worshiping other gods. Therefore, he calls upon them to choose whether they will continue worshiping those other gods, or whether they will turn to Yahweh. Though the Israelites that day chose Yahweh, their choice didn't stick and within a generation they began worshiping the gods of Canaan in addition.

---

| 16 | 17 |
|---|---|
The land allotted to Manasseh is outlined, with its borders.

**Chapter 17**

| 16 | 17 |
|---|---|
The Tabernacle is erected in Shiloh. The remaining seven tribes divide the land by lot and survey it. The land allotted to Benjamin is outlined, with its borders.

**Chapter 18**

| 16 | 17 |
|---|---|
The land allotted to Simeon, Zebulun, Issachar, Asher, Naphtali, and Dan is outlined, with its borders. Joshua is granted the town of Timnath Serah as his personal inheritance.

**Chapter 19**

| 3 | 16 | 17 |
|---|---|---|
The cities of refuge are established so that those who kill accidentally will have a place to run from the avenger of blood.

**Chapter 20**

| 16 | 17 |
|---|---|
The Levites are given towns among the other tribal possessions to inhabit, since the Levites receive no territory of their own.

**Chapter 21**

| 17 |
|---|
The men of Reuben, Gad, and half the tribe of Manasseh finally return to their lands east of the Jordan. They build an altar on the border as a memorial to their union with Israel.

**Chapter 22**

| 3 | 17 |
|---|---|
Near the end of his life, Joshua reminds the Israelites to obey the laws of Yahweh and to worship no other gods.

**Chapter 23**

| 3 | 17 |
|---|---|
Joshua renews the covenant between God and the Israelites. Then, at the age of 110, Joshua dies and is buried.

**Chapter 24**

# Judges
## Overview

The Book of Judges tells the story of those individuals who led Israel between the death of Joshua and the rise of Israel's first king. The title of the book is the same in both the Hebrew original and in the Greek translation. It was derived from the content of the book, rather than its author.

The stories that make up the book were probably collected during the early monarchy and were then edited into a national history, perhaps by the seventh century BC. The purpose of the book seems to have been as an apology for the existence of the monarchy. Within Israel, one finds two conflicting concepts: the idea that the monarchy was

## Chapter 1: **Commentary**

While chronology is not lacking in Hebrew literature, it is not the only, most important, or overriding sequencer of the material. Rather, other things can become more important, thereby skewing the chronology in unexpected ways.

Joshua 15 is devoted to the distribution of the land among the tribes. The story of Caleb and his daughter appears in 15:13–19. This same story is repeated here near the beginning of Judges (1:1–15), which informs us that Joshua died before the incident with Caleb occurred. Yet in Joshua, we do not see the death of Joshua until the end of the book (Joshua 24:28–30).

There is no difficulty, however, if it is understood that theme will override chronology in the arranging of a narrative, even a story, because the incident with Caleb is described in a section of the Book of Joshua devoted to the theme of the conquest. The author of Judges uses the same story in a different context, for a different purpose.

**17**

Chapter
1

After Joshua's death, the Israelites renew their fight against the remaining Canaanites and conquer more territory, but they fail to get rid of all of the Canaanites.

**3**    **15**    **17**

Chapter
2

At Bokim, the angel of Yahweh warns the Israelites that because of their idolatry, God will not drive out all the Canaanites and so they will repeatedly face oppression.

**9**    **17**

Chapter
3

Othniel rescues the Israelites from Aram Nahariam. Then Ehud assassinates Eglon, the king of Moab, by stabbing him in the belly. Shamgar kills 600 Philistines with an ox goad.

**9**    **17**

Chapter
4

Deborah leads the Israelites in a successful battle against Jabin, defeating his general Sisera in battle. Jael kills a sleeping Sisera when she drives a tent peg through his head.

*But Jael, Heber's wife, picked up a tent peg and a hammer and went quietly to him while he lay fast asleep, exhausted. She drove the peg through his temple into the ground, and he died.*

*Just then Barak came by in pursuit of Sisera, and Jael went out to meet him. "Come," she said, "I will show you the man you're looking for." So he went in with her, and there lay Sisera with the tent peg through his temple—dead.*

**Judges 4:21–22**

a bad thing, contrary to God's original intentions for the nation (see 1 Samuel 8, 12), and the idea that God selected Saul and then David to rule them (see 1 Samuel 9–10, 16:1–13). The Book of Judges argues that, prior to the existence of the monarchy, Israel existed in constant turmoil where people behaved badly because there was no king to impose order on the chaos.

The author of the Book of Judges is unknown. The book covers events from Joshua's death, around 1380 BC or 1150 BC (depending on the date for the Exodus) until close to the time of Samuel (around 1075 BC), who can be considered the last judge before the beginning of the monarchal period.

## Chapter 5: **Commentary**

Judges chapter 4 tells the story of Deborah's victory over Sisera, and how Sisera was killed by Jael. Chapter 5 tells the same story. The difference between the two accounts has to do with their structure. Chapter 4 relates the events as a prose narrative, while chapter 5 relates the events as a poem. The purposes of narrative and poetry are not the same. Narrative relates facts. Poetry aims at the emotions. The differences between chapters 4 and 5 are not contradictions; instead, they are complementary.

Hebrew poetry does not rhyme the sounds at the ends of the lines. Instead, Hebrew poetry, like all the other poetry of the Ancient Near East, rhymes ideas. The technical term for this is parallelism: the lines repeat the same concept in different words, sometimes synonymously, sometimes giving the opposite, and sometimes merely building and expanding upon what went in the line before. To modern ears, Hebrew poetry can sound very repetitious.

*No sooner had Gideon died than the Israelites again prostituted themselves to the Baals. They set up Baal-Berith as their god and did not remember the Lord their God, who had rescued them from the hands of all their enemies on every side. They also failed to show any loyalty to the family of Jerub-Baal (that is, Gideon) in spite of all the good things he had done for them.*

**Judges 8:33–35**

**Barak and Deborah**
*Deborah, the judge of Israel, with her general Barak, lead the Israelites to victory in battle against Jabin, king of Canaan in Hazor.*

**5** | **17**

Deborah and Barak sing a song celebrating their victory over Jabin and his general, Sisera.

Chapter
**5**

**8** | **9** | **17**

Gideon destroys his father's gods, raises an army against the oppressive Midianites, then begs Yahweh to give him a sign of his favor, using fleece.

Chapter
**6**

**8** | **17**

Gideon miraculously defeats the Midianites with only 300 men after the bulk of the assembled Israelite army abandons him.

Chapter
**7**

**17**

After Gideon's 300 defeat the Midianites, he makes a gold *ephod*. After 40 years of peace, Gideon dies and the Israelites revert to worshiping Canaanite gods.

Chapter
**8**

**6**  **9**  **17**

**Chapter 9**

Gideon's son Abimelek sets himself up as the king of Shechem after killing all but one of his brothers. With a fable, the surviving brother warns Shechem of a coming disaster.

**9**  **17**

**Chapter 10**

Tola leads Israel as a judge for 23 years, followed by Jair who rules for 22. After returning to idolatry, the Philistines and Amonites oppress Israel. Israel repents and seeks a leader.

**9**  **17**

**Chapter 11**

The people of Gilead chose Jephtha to lead them. Jephtha promises God he will sacrifice the first thing he meets after his victory. He is victorious and sacrifices his daughter.

**9**  **17**

**Chapter 12**

Jepthah and his fellow Gileadites fight against the tribe of Ehpraim. After he dies, Ibzan, Elon, and Abdon follow him as the leaders of Israel.

**15**  **17**

**Chapter 13**

Manoah's wife can't get pregnant. An angel promises them a son who will be a Nazirite from birth. He will deliver Israel from the Philistines. His name is Samson.

**8**  **9**  **17**

**Chapter 14**

Samson marries a Philistine and tells a riddle. His threatened wife reveals the answer. Samson kills 30 Philistines to pay off a bet. Meanwhile, his wife is given to another man.

**8**  **9**  **17**

**Chapter 15**

When Samson discovers that his wife has been given to another, he burns down the Philistines' fields. Samson kills the Philistines who murder his wife and father-in-law.

*Again the Israelites did evil in the eyes of the Lord. They served the Baals and the Ashtoreths, and the gods of Aram, the gods of Sidon, the gods of Moab, the gods of the Ammonites and the gods of the Philistines. And because the Israelites forsook the Lord and no longer served him, he became angry with them. He sold them into the hands of the Philistines and the Ammonites...*

**Judges 10:6–7**

## Chapter 11: Commentary

Jephtha, like most Israelites of the time, was not a monotheist. He may have worshiped Yahweh exclusively as his God, but he recognized the existence of other deities, as his letter to the Ammonite king indicates. Monotheism does not become the universal and sole belief of the Jewish people until they suffer the Babylonian conquest, exile, and return in the years between 605 and 535 BC. Until then, the prophets will harp on this issue as they attempt to call the people to an understanding of Yahweh as not just the only God that they should worship, but as the only God that actually exists. Given that the Israelites came from and were surrounded by a polytheistic cultural setting, monotheism was a very difficult concept for them to accept.

*"We are doomed to die!" he said to his wife. "We have seen God!"*

*But his wife answered, "If the Lord had meant to kill us, he would not have accepted a burnt offering and grain offering from our hands, nor shown us all these things or now told us this."*

*The woman gave birth to a boy and named him Samson. He grew and the Lord blessed him...*

**Judges 13:22–24**

*Finding a fresh jawbone of a donkey, he grabbed it and struck down a thousand men.*

*Then Samson said,*
*"With a donkey's jawbone*
*I have made donkeys of them.*
*With a donkey's jawbone*
*I have killed a thousand men."*

*When he finished speaking, he threw away the jawbone; and the place was called Ramath Lehi.*

**Judges 15:15–17**

*After putting him to sleep on her lap, she called for someone to shave off the seven braids of his hair, and so began to subdue him. And his strength left him.*

*Then she called, "Samson, the Philistines are upon you!"*

*He awoke from his sleep and thought, "I'll go out as before and shake myself free." But he did not know that the Lord had left him.*

*Then the Philistines seized him, gouged out his eyes and took him down to Gaza. Binding him with bronze shackles, they set him to grinding grain in the prison. But the hair on his head began to grow again after it had been shaved.*

**Judges 16:19–22**

## Chapter 16: **Commentary**

Samson comes across as a flawed superhero: impulsive and often out of control. His value to God and the Israelites lay exclusively in his ability to cause problems for the Philistines. Although his parents raised him as a Nazirite from birth, in practice Samson frequently fails to abide by the Nazirite restrictions.

Why did Samson lose his strength when Delilah cut his hair? According to the rules of the Nazirite vow, cutting the hair ended the vow. With the cutting of his hair, he was no longer a Nazirite and thus no longer specially devoted to God—and so his special power went away as well (see Numbers 6:18–20). But a vow can be restarted. When his hair started to grow, he returned to being what he had been before: a Nazirite (see Numbers 6:12).

## Chapters 17–21: **Commentary**

Judges 17, 18, 19, and 21 all contain the phrase "In those days Israel had no king." Both 17 and 21 add to it the phrase "everyone did as they saw fit." Judges 17–21 is designed to demonstrate what Israelite society had become during the period of the judges—the time from the death of Joshua until Saul became the first king over the nation. The author's point is clearly demonstrated by these words: the nation was in a sorry state. Not only were they adrift politically and militarily, but also morally and spiritually. Without a king, the author argues, the nation is without hope and in desperate straits.

*In those days Israel had no king; everyone did as they saw fit.*

**Judges 21:25**

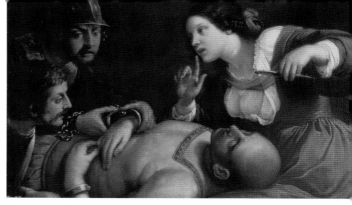

**Samson and Delilah**
*Samson fell in love with Delilah, but she betrayed him, tricked him, and turned him over to his enemies, the Philistines.*

**8** **12** **17**

After a night with a prostitute, Samson demolishes the city gates. Later, Delilah cuts off Samson's hair. The Philistines capture and blind him. His hair grows back and he gets his revenge.

Chapter **16**

**11** **17**

Micah steals silver from his mother. When he returns it, she makes an idol from some of it. Micah hires a Levite from Bethlehem to serve as a priest for the idol.

Chapter **17**

**17**

As the tribe of Dan heads off to conquer Laish, they steal the idol from Micah and ask his priest, the Levite, to join them. The priest happily goes with them to Laish.

Chapter **18**

**17**

A Levite spends the night in Gibeah of Benjamin, where his concubine is raped and murdered. He cuts her into 12 pieces that he distributes to each of the 12 tribes.

Chapter **19**

**9** **17**

The tribe of Benjamin refuses to bring the murderers to justice, so the other tribes go to war against them. They kill nearly everyone in the tribe of Benjamin.

Chapter **20**

**17**

The Israelites had sworn never to give their daughters in marriage to Benjaminites, so they tell the surviving Benjaminites to kidnap their daughters for marriage, instead.

Chapter **21**

# Ruth

## Overview

The English title of the Book of Ruth is the same as the title of the book in Hebrew. It is the story of a Moabite convert to Judaism who becomes the ancestor of King David.

The author of the Book of Ruth is unknown. From the genealogy at the end (4:18–22) the book obviously could have been composed no earlier than the time of David. Two periods have generally been proposed, one during the post-exilic period of Ezra and Nehemiah, and the second during the reign of either David or Solomon. The basis for the later date of composition is as follows. First, there are linguistic clues, such as the apparent use of Aramaic, which would point to a time when Hebrew was being replaced by Aramaic. Second, there are theological clues: the purpose of the book seems to be to remind the Israelites David's ancestry was foreign, perhaps as a reaction to the anti-foreign sentiment that was growing during the post-exilic period when the Israelites returned from captivity in Mesopotamia.

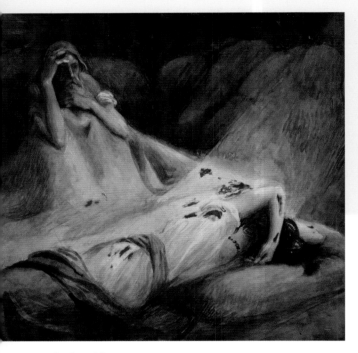

**Ruth and Boaz**
*After the harvest festival, when Boaz found Ruth in bed with him, he knew that he had to make things right and marry her.*

*"Look," said Naomi, "your sister-in-law is going back to her people and her gods. Go back with her."*
*But Ruth replied, "Don't urge me to leave you or to turn back from you. Where you go I will go, and where you stay I will stay. Your people will be my people and your God my God. Where you die I will die, and there I will be buried. May the Lord deal with me, be it ever so severely, if even death separates you and me."*

**Ruth 1:15–17**

**17**

| Chapter I | Naomi's husband and sons die while they are living in Moab. Naomi decides to return to her home in Bethlehem and her widowed daughter-in-law, Ruth, decides to go with her. |
|---|---|

## Chapter 2: **Commentary**

In the ancient world, even in Israel, the status of women was low. Without a father, brother, son, or husband to protect them, women were reduced to poverty.
Their only way of staying alive was by begging, gleaning, or prostitution.

**17**

| Chapter 2 | Ruth begins gleaning in the fields of Boaz, a relative of Naomi's husband. Boaz notices Ruth and makes certain that she is protected and that she receives extra grain. |
|---|---|

Naomi, because she was left without a husband or sons, was placed in a difficult situation. She had no way of providing for herself except by either begging or becoming a prostitute. Her daughter-in-law Ruth was in a similar situation. A provision in the Mosaic legislation, however, offered them hope. According to Deuteronomy 25:5–10, the brother or closest relative of a childless widow was supposed to marry her and her firstborn child from such a union was to carry on the name of the dead husband. In the story of the Book of Ruth, Boaz is a near relative who takes an interest in Ruth. Therefore, Naomi and Ruth conspire to force his hand. During the harvest celebration, after he'd partied, Ruth went to where he was sleeping, uncovered him, and lay down beside him. When he found her in bed with him, he assumed he'd had intercourse with her and set out then to make things right by marrying her, which of course was Naomi and Ruth's goal. Their desperate circumstance was thereby relieved, and Ruth became the great-grandmother of King David.

## Chapter 3: **Commentary**

Deuteronomy 25:5–6 obliges a brother to marry the widow of his childless brother; if a brother is not available, then the duty transfers to the next closest relative. The firstborn child is then considered to be both the heir of the dead brother and the child of the dead brother. Other examples of this occur in the Bible, for instance in Genesis 36:8–10 where Onan marries the widow of his brother.

**17**

Naomi and Ruth conspire to force Boaz to marry Ruth. On the night of the big harvest celebration, after Boaz has gotten drunk, he awakens to find Ruth in bed with him.

Chapter
3

**16**     **18**

Boaz quickly makes the necessary arrangements and marries Ruth. Their son, Obed, becomes the grandfather of King David.

Chapter
4

***Ruth and Naomi***
*Ruth was a Moabite, but when her husband died, she converted to Judaism and returned to Bethlehem with her mother-in-law Naomi.*

# I Samuel

## Overview

The title, Samuel, is the same in both the Hebrew original and in the Greek translation. It was derived from the principle character in the early part of the book, the last judge, Samuel.

Though separated into two books in our translations, they were originally one. The book tells the story of the prophet Samuel, the first King of Israel, Saul, and his replacement by his successor, David. The purpose of the Book of 1 Samuel is to explain how David, rather than a descendant of Saul, became king over Israel. The Book of 1 Samuel has as part of its purpose an apology for David's rule.

An additional purpose of the Book of 1 Samuel, which carries forward through 2 Samuel and into 1 and 2 Kings, is to illustrate the cause for God's

---

*"I prayed for this child, and the Lord has granted me what I asked of him. So now I give him to the Lord. For his whole life he will be given over to the Lord." And he worshiped the Lord there.*

**1 Samuel 1:27–28**

## Chapter 2: **Commentary**

Hannah's prayer is anachronistic and probably dates from a time much later in Israelite history. She is quoted as saying, "He will give strength to his king and exalt the horn of his anointed." This, despite the fact that Saul would not become Israel's first king until several decades later. Although her words can be taken as a prophecy, most scholars believe the poem was put into her mouth by the later author as it expressed her emotional state. It's also possible that it was modified by an editor at a later date.

---

**12**                    **17**

**Chapter 1**  Having problems getting pregnant, Hannah promises God that her firstborn son will be a Nazirite raised by the high priest. She becomes pregnant and fulfills her vow.

**1**            **5**            **17**

**Chapter 2**  Hannah praises and thanks God. The high priest Eli has wicked sons who steal sacrifices and sleep with Temple prostitutes. God warns of coming judgment.

**7**                    **17**

**Chapter 3**  God calls Samuel to become his prophet and tells him that Eli and his family are going to be judged by God.

**9**                    **17**

**Chapter 4**  The Philistines capture the Ark and kill Eli's sons. Eli tumbles in shock from his chair and breaks his neck, while one of his daughters-in-law goes into labor and dies giving birth.

---

*A third time the Lord called, "Samuel!" And Samuel got up and went to Eli and said, "Here I am; you called me."*

*Then Eli realized that the Lord was calling the boy. So Eli told Samuel, "Go and lie down, and if he calls you, say, 'Speak, Lord, for your servant is listening.'" So Samuel went and lay down in his place.*

*The Lord came and stood there, calling as at the other times, "Samuel! Samuel!"*

*Then Samuel said, "Speak, for your servant is listening."*

**1 Samuel 3:8–10**

judgment on the nation of Israel which will result in its destruction and captivity in Babylon. The story in 1 Samuel demonstrates that even during the imagined golden age of Saul and then David, both the kings of Israel and the people of Israel failed to remain faithful to God. The books argue then that the Babylonian captivity was both just and inevitable given the pattern of disobedience throughout Israelite history.

The author and date of composition of the Book of 1 Samuel is unknown, though it seems probable that it dates to a relatively late period in the history of Israel, probably after the time of the Babylonian captivity given that the narrative style continues unbroken through the end of 2 Kings, which ends with the nation being carried off to Babylon following the destruction of Jerusalem and its Temple.

**Samuel in the Tabernacle**
*Samuel's mother Hannah promised God that she would devote her firstborn son to God. So when Samuel was weaned, she turned him over to be adopted by the High Priest, Eli.*

*The Lord's hand was heavy on the people of Ashdod and its vicinity; he brought devastation on them and afflicted them with tumors. When the people of Ashdod saw what was happening, they said, "The ark of the god of Israel must not stay here with us, because his hand is heavy on us and on Dagon our god." So they called together all the rulers of the Philistines and asked them, "What shall we do with the ark of the god of Israel?"*

**1 Samuel 5:6–8**

## Chapters 6–8: **Commentary**

Within Israelite thinking, there is a dualism regarding kingship: Judges as a whole argues for the need of a king, while the experience of the Israelites from the time of Saul until the end of the monarchy with the Babylonian captivity demonstrates that kings were hardly a panacea. In fact, within the biblical documents there is a recognition that human government of any sort is necessarily flawed. Even the great David and Solomon were less than ideal. Under the best of circumstances, the king takes your crops, your money, and your children and uses them for his purposes. Having no king is bad—but having a king is bad, too. The biblical portrayal of the king is reminiscent of what Winston Churchill said about democracy in a speech before the House of Commons in 1947: "Many forms of Government have been tried and will be tried in this world of sin and woe. No one pretends that democracy is perfect or all-wise. Indeed, it has been said that democracy is the worst form of government except all those other forms that have been tried from time to time."

| 9 | 17 | |
|---|---|---|
| The Philistines place the Ark in the Temple of Dagon. Dagon repeatedly falls on his face before the Ark. After an outbreak of tumors they decide to return the ark to the Israelites. | | Chapter 5 |

| 9 | 17 | |
|---|---|---|
| The Philistines send the Ark back, pulled by cows. The Israelites at Beth Shemesh peek into the Ark, so God kills them. The unhappy survivors send the Ark to Kiriath Jearim. | | Chapter 6 |

| 11 | 17 | |
|---|---|---|
| The Ark stays in Kiriath Jearim for 20 years. Samuel grows up, leads Israel, and calls the people to Mizpah to recommit themselves to Yahweh. Then they defeat the Philistines. | | Chapter 7 |

| 17 | |
|---|---|
| When Samuel is old, the Israelites ask him for a king. Samuel warns that the king will tax them and conscript their children as servants and warriors, but they still demand a king. | Chapter 8 |

**⑰**

**Chapter 9**

One day Saul from Benjamin is looking for his father's lost donkeys. He meets Samuel, who invites him to dinner.

**⑰**

**Chapter 10**

Samuel informs Saul that the donkeys are safe, that he will become the king of Israel, and that he will prophesy. Then Samuel arranges a meeting in Gilgal, where he proclaims Saul king.

**⑰**

**Chapter 11**

The Ammonites threaten Jabesh Gilead. Saul leads an army against the Ammonites and defeats them. The people of Israel reaffirm Saul's kingship.

**⑨**    **⑰**

**Chapter 12**

Samuel tells the Israelites that they have displeased God by asking for a king. So rain falls during the wheat harvest. He encourages obedience to God's commands.

**⑨**    **⑰**

**Chapter 13**

The Philistines assemble for an all-out war after Jonathan attacks Geba. Because Saul is afraid and disobeys Samuel and God, God decided to replace Saul with a new king.

**⑭**    **⑰**

**Chapter 14**

Unaware of Saul's vow, Jonathan eats honey. Thanks to Jonathan, the Israelites rout the Philistines. Saul's soldiers prevent Saul from executing Jonathan for violating the vow.

*As Saul turned to leave Samuel, God changed Saul's heart, and all these signs were fulfilled that day. When he and his servant arrived at Gibeah, a procession of prophets met him; the Spirit of God came powerfully upon him, and he joined in their prophesying. When all those who had formerly known him saw him prophesying with the prophets, they asked each other, "What is this that has happened to the son of Kish? Is Saul also among the prophets?"*

**1 Samuel 10:9–11**

## Chapter 13: Commentary

The Ancient Near East is divided broadly into three eras: Stone Age, Bronze Age, and Iron Age, with subdivisions within each. These names refer to the sorts of tools that were predominantly used during these periods. The dates for these ages vary from people group to people group and from one part of the world to another, but the periods work for most parts of the world. In the Near East as a whole, the time periods are as follows: Stone Age is from about 2,000,000–3300 BC, the Bronze Age 3300–1200 BC, and the Iron Age from about 1200–586 BC.

From the time of Samson through Saul, the Israelites were transitioning from a Bronze Age civilization to an Iron Age civilization. The Philistines had a monopoly on iron-making technology that allowed them to dominate the Israelites economically and militarily.

*Saul's sons were Jonathan, Ishvi and Malki-Shua. The name of his older daughter was Merab, and that of the younger was Michal. His wife's name was Ahinoam daughter of Ahimaaz. The name of the commander of Saul's army was Abner son of Ner, and Ner was Saul's uncle. Saul's father Kish and Abner's father Ner were sons of Abiel.*

*All the days of Saul there was bitter war with the Philistines, and whenever Saul saw a mighty or brave man, he took him into his service.*

**1 Samuel 14:49–52**

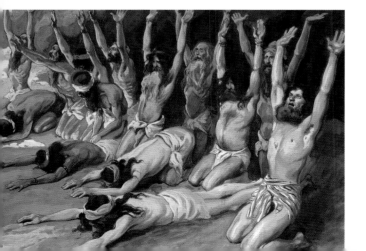

**Saul among the prophets**
After his first meeting with Samuel, the Spirit of God comes upon Saul and he starts prophesying.

*When they arrived, Samuel saw Eliab and thought, "Surely the Lord's anointed stands here before the Lord."*

*But the Lord said to Samuel, "Do not consider his appearance or his height, for I have rejected him. The Lord does not look at the things people look at. People look at the outward appearance, but the Lord looks at the heart."*

**1 Samuel 16:6–7**

## Chapter 17: **Commentary**

In 13:7–15 Samuel tells Saul that his kingdom will not endure, but will be given to another. In 15:7–34, Samuel tells Saul that God has rejected him and given the kingdom to another. In 16:14–23 David enters Saul's service, playing the harp for him in order to make him feel better. Yet, come 17:55–18:2, after slaying Goliath, Saul seems not to have previously met David—and David then enters Saul's service.

If a topical/thematic arrangement of the narrative is recognized, these apparent problems are relatively easily dealt with. The key to the link between these apparently separate incidents is the mention of animals for sacrifice in 13:7–9 and 15:20–21. The perspective of the two descriptions is somewhat different, but notice that the passage in 13 is much shorter and much more condensed than the account of 15, which can therefore be taken as an expansion of the earlier account.

Both narratives (16:14–23 and 17:1–18:2) end at the same point, with David entering Saul's service. The difference is that 16:14–23 is a summary account, while 17:1–18:2 is an expanded account of the same time frame, but with the emphasis somewhat different, as the former (16:14–23) narrative ends on Saul's emotional problems resulting from his rejection by God, and the latter (17:1–18:2) on military problems associated with the Philistines. In both cases, David is involved, but the Hebrew approach to relating the story separates thematic elements and concentrates on them one at a time.

*After David had finished talking with Saul, Jonathan became one in spirit with David, and he loved him as himself. From that day Saul kept David with him and did not let him return home to his family. And Jonathan made a covenant with David because he loved him as himself. Jonathan took off the robe he was wearing and gave it to David, along with his tunic, and even his sword, his bow and his belt.*

*Whatever mission Saul sent him on, David was so successful that Saul gave him a high rank in the army. This pleased all the troops, and Saul's officers as well.*

**1 Samuel 18:1–5**

---

**⑨** | **⑰**

Saul spares Agag, the king of the Amalekites, along with some animals. Samuel tells Saul that God will replace Saul with a new king. Then Samuel executes Agag.

Chapter **15**

---

**⑰**

In Bethlehem, Saul anoints David as the next king, to replace Saul. David enters Saul's service as his musician and armor bearer. David's lyre playing eases Saul's mental anguish.

Chapter **16**

---

**⑰**

David visits his brothers in Saul's army, accepts the challenge of Goliath, and kills him with a sling. The Philistine army flees in panic with the Israelites in pursuit.

Chapter **17**

---

**⑩** | **⑰**

David and Jonathan become best friends. David joins Saul's army, advances quickly, and wins victories. Saul becomes paranoid. David becomes Saul's son-in-law after delivering 200 Philistine foreskins.

Chapter **18**

---

**David the musician**
*After Saul was rejected by God, he was despondent. He hired David to play music in the hope that it would make him feel better.*

**Chapter 19** ⑩ ⑰

Saul decides to execute David. David's wife Michal helps him escape the palace when she puts an idol into his bed and tells Saul's servants that David is sick.

**Chapter 20** ⑩ ⑭ ⑰

Jonathan confirms to David that his father is out to kill him. They promise undying friendship and Jonathan admits that he expects David to become king some day.

**Chapter 21** ⑰

David flees to Nob where the priest Ahimelek gives him bread and Goliath's sword. David seeks refuge with Achish, the king of Gath, but must fake insanity to avoid execution.

**Chapter 22** ⑰

David, his brothers, and 400 others hide in a cave in Adullam. David's parents hide in Moab. Meanwhile, Saul kills Ahimelek and the priests who helped David at Nob.

**Chapter 23** ⑰

David and his men defeat the Philistines attacking Keilah, but its citizens want to turn him over to Saul. David must flee and hide from Saul in the Desert of Ziph.

**Chapter 24** ⑰

When Saul goes into a cave near En Gedi to relieve himself, a hidden David cuts off a corner of his garment. David shows Saul how easily he could have killed him if he'd wanted.

**Saul's suicide**
The Philistines defeat the Israelite army and mortally wound Saul, who then chooses to kill himself.

## Chapter 19: **Commentary**

In her attempt to protect her husband David from her father Saul, Michal had an idol that she could stick in David's bed.

How is it that the daughter of Saul, the king of Israel, the wife of David, the future king of Israel, had an idol? Despite the prohibition on idols and the worship of other gods in the first two of the Ten Commandments, the practice of the Israelites, even in the royal household, was far from ideal.

This is a consequence of three things: first, the simple fact that all the other nations around them, their whole culture and outlook on life, was one filled with multiple gods and goddesses. Polytheism—the worship of many gods—and idolatry—were simply a part of daily life, the air that they breathed. Second, though in the modern world, most people have at least one copy of the Bible in their homes, in the Ancient world, it was rare for people to have any books of any sort. Third, the synagogue system of weekly teaching of the contents of the sacred writings did not exist. There were no weekly worship services, no sermons, no Sabbath schools.

*David took these words to heart and was very much afraid of Achish king of Gath. So he pretended to be insane in their presence; and while he was in their hands he acted like a madman, making marks on the doors of the gate and letting saliva run down his beard.*

*Achish said to his servants, "Look at the man! He is insane! Why bring him to me? Am I so short of madmen that you have to bring this fellow here to carry on like this in front of me? Must this man come into my house?"*

**1 Samuel 21:12–15**

*I know that you will surely be king and that the kingdom of Israel will be established in your hands. Now swear to me by the Lord that you will not kill off my descendants or wipe out my name from my father's family."*

*So David gave his oath to Saul. Then Saul returned home, but David and his men went up to the stronghold.*

**1 Samuel 24:20–22**

## Chapter 25: **Commentary**

In reading the Bible one should expect to experience some culture shock. An example of this comes with David's marriage to Abigail when he is still married to Michal, Saul's daughter. It is not the first time we have seen polygamy in the Bible, however. Samuel's mother was one of the two wives that his father Elkanah had (1 Samuel 1:2). In fact, there are no prohibitions in the Bible against having multiple wives or multiple husbands. Instead, the Bible merely regulates it: prohibiting one man from marrying sisters (Leviticus 18:18) or marrying a mother and daughter (Leviticus 18:17). And it stipulates that the firstborn son, even if born to the wife he doesn't love, must still receive the rights and privileges of the firstborn son (Deuteronomy 21:15–17).

*Now David and his men went up and raided the Geshurites, the Girzites and the Amalekites. (From ancient times these peoples had lived in the land extending to Shur and Egypt.) Whenever David attacked an area, he did not leave a man or woman alive, but took sheep and cattle, donkeys and camels, and clothes. Then he returned to Achish.*

**1 Samuel 27:8–9**

## Chapter 28: **Commentary**

What does the Bible have to say about ghosts? After Samuel's death, Saul visits a medium and has her contact the dead Samuel. He appears as a "ghostly figure coming out of the earth" (1 Samuel 28:13) who then goes on to tell Saul that he too will soon be dead, killed by the Philistines he was going off to fight. In the New Testament, the disciples believed in ghosts (see Matthew 14:26, Mark 6:49). In Luke 24:37–39, after Jesus' resurrection, the disciples imagined he was a ghost when they first saw him. In reaction to their fear, Jesus did not tell them "ghosts do not exist." Rather, he told them to touch him, because "a ghost does not have flesh and bones, as you see I have."

*The fighting grew fierce around Saul, and when the archers overtook him, they wounded him critically.*

*Saul said to his armor-bearer, "Draw your sword and run me through, or these uncircumcised fellows will come and run me through and abuse me."*

*But his armor-bearer was terrified and would not do it; so Saul took his own sword and fell on it. When the armor-bearer saw that Saul was dead, he too fell on his sword and died with him.*

**1 Samuel 31:3–5**

---

**17** Samuel dies. In Carmel, Nabal refuses to give David food, so Nabal's wife Abigail secretly feeds him. After Nabal dies, David marries her, while David's wife Michal marries another man.

Chapter **25**

**17** David has the opportunity to kill a poorly guarded Saul while he sleeps. Later, from a safe distance, he lets Saul know what he could have done. Saul stops hunting David.

Chapter **26**

**17** David and his men move into Philistine territory. They join the army of Achish, king of Gath, who gives them Ziklag. David claims to kill Israelites while really killing Philistines.

Chapter **27**

**7** **17** The Philistines, with David and his men, prepare for battle against Israel. A medium at Endor contacts the dead Samuel for Saul. Samuel reveals that the Philistines will kill him.

Chapter **28**

**17** Achish sends David and his men back to Ziklag when the other Philistine kings refuse to let David join them in their battle against the Israelites.

Chapter **29**

**17** The Amalekites have torched Ziklag and taken their wives, children, and belongings. David and his men rescue their families and property. David sends gifts to the elders of Judah.

Chapter **30**

**9** **17** The Philistines defeat Israel in battle and kill Saul and his son Jonathan. The Philistines strip them of their armor, cut off Saul's head, and pin their bodies to the wall of Beth Shan.

Chapter **31**

# 2 Samuel

## Overview

The title, Samuel, is the same in both the Hebrew original and in the Greek translation. It was derived from the principle character in the early part of the book, the last judge, Samuel. Calling the book Samuel, however, is a misnomer, especially for 2 Samuel, since Samuel himself never appears in 2 Samuel at all. Though separated into two books in our translations, they were originally one book.

2 Samuel tells the story of King David. Though he had been selected by David from his brothers and is described as a "man after" God's "own heart" (1 Samuel 13:14), 2 Samuel does not flinch from

| 4 | 5 | 17 |
|---|---|---|

**Chapter 1**

David learns of Saul's death and the death of Jonathan. David then takes up a lament for them.

*"Daughters of Israel,*
*weep for Saul,*
*who clothed you in scarlet and finery,*
*who adorned your garments with ornaments of gold.*
    *"How the mighty have fallen in battle!*
*Jonathan lies slain on your heights.*
*I grieve for you, Jonathan my brother;*
*you were very dear to me.*
*Your love for me was wonderful,*
*more wonderful than that of women.*
    *"How the mighty have fallen!*
    *The weapons of war have perished!"*

**2 Samuel 1:24–27**

## Chapter 2: **Commentary**

**17**

**Chapter 2**

David becomes king over Judah in Hebron, while Abner, the commander of Saul's army, makes Saul's son Ish-Bosheth king over Israel. Civil war breaks out between them.

Names often included the names of the gods. For instance, the name Elijah includes both the word *El*, meaning God, and "Yah," God's name. One of Saul's sons is named Ishbosheth and another is named Mephibosheth. The word *bosheth* in Hebrew means "shame" which would seem an odd thing to call one's children—until we discover he is also called "Eshbaal" in 1 Chronicles 8:33 and 9:39. *Baal* is a Hebrew word that means "Lord" or "Master" and was often used as an epithet for God. But Baal was also the name of a major Canaanite deity and the Israelites often worshiped Baal instead of Yahweh. Exodus 23:13 states "Do not invoke the names of other gods; do not let them be heard on your lips." After the Israelites had returned from the Babylonian captivity, they were very conscious of the fact that they had suffered that captivity for failing to keep God's commandments.

**17**

**Chapter 3**

David grows stronger, while Ish-Bosheth grows weaker. David has several sons by his many wives in Hebron. Abner defects to David, but Joab is distrustful and murders him.

The Israelites eventually became very uncomfortable with ever hearing or using the word *Baal* because of its idolatrous connotations, so scribes purposely corrupted the names of Saul's children to avoid using it.

**17**

**Chapter 4**

Rekab and Baanah murder the king of Israel, Ish-Bosheth, son of Saul in his bed, cut off his head, and bring it to David. David executes Rekab and Baanah.

revealing many moral lapses on David's part. The most famous, of course, was his adulterous affair with Bathsheba, which led him to murder her husband Uriah (2 Samuel 11–12). David was also a very poor father. He failed to properly raise, discipline, or care for his children (following in the footsteps of Eli and Samuel; see 1 Samuel 2:29, 8:1–4), so that his son Amnon raped his sister Tamar, while another son, Absalom, killed his brother Amnon and later led a rebellion against his father David.

David is portrayed as a very flawed man that God still loved and worked through, despite his many mistakes and crimes.

## Chapter 6: **Commentary**

Why the harsh judgment on Uzzah for merely touching the Ark of the Covenant, especially when one considers how the Philistines had treated it while it had been in their possession? Because the Israelites had been given specific instructions on how to handle it in the Books of Moses (Exodus 25:14). God expected them to follow those regulations; by putting it into a cart and trying to move it like the Philistines, they were choosing to act in a way contrary to the instructions God had given them. To whom much is given, much is required (Luke 12:48).

*Your house and your kingdom will endure forever before me; your throne will be established forever.*
**2 Samuel 7:16**

## Chapter 12: **Commentary**

According to Deuteronomy 17:18–19, the king of Israel was to make a copy of the Law of Moses for himself and to read it on a regular basis. The story of David's response to Nathan's story about a man who steals a sheep serves as evidence that David must have done this. In 2 Samuel 12:6 David exclaims to Nathan that "he must pay for that lamb four times over..." Why four times over? Because of one obscure verse in Exodus 22:1, the only place in the Bible which gives the penalty for stealing sheep: "Whoever steals an ox or a sheep and slaughters it or sells it must pay back five head of cattle for the ox and four sheep for the sheep." Only a man who copied the text for himself and read it regularly could have remembered such an obscure fact.

**17**

David becomes king over a united Israel. David then conquers Jerusalem, builds his palace, takes more wives, and has more children. David defeats the Philistines.

Chapter **5**

**11**    **17**

On the first attempt to move the Ark of the Covenant from Shiloh to Jerusalem, Uzzah dies. The second attempt succeeds, but his wife Michal criticizes David for dancing.

Chapter **6**

**7**    **12**    **17**

David wants to build a temple for Yahweh, but God tells him his son will build it instead. God promises that David's kingdom will endure forever. David thanks God in prayer.

Chapter **7**

**17**

David conquers the Philistines, the Arameans, Edom, Moab, the Ammonites, and Amalek. His control over Israel is firmly established.

Chapter **8**

**14**    **17**

David takes in Saul's handicapped son, Mephibosheth, and provides well for him and his family.

Chapter **9**

**17**

David sends a delegation to express sympathy when the king of Ammon dies. The delegation is mistreated, so David conquers Ammon and their allies, the Arameans.

Chapter **10**

**17**

While David's army is off fighting Ammon, David stays home and has an affair with Uriah's wife, Bathsheba. After she gets pregnant, he has her husband killed and marries her.

Chapter **11**

**2**    **9**    **17**

The prophet Nathan rebukes David for his affair and murder. He warns him that trouble will plague him the rest of his life. The child born to Bathsheba dies.

Chapter **12**

## Chapter 13: **Commentary**

The Bible never prohibits polygamy. Thus, several of the kings of Israel had multiple wives. King David had at least seven wives, plus concubines (1 Chronicles 3:1–9) and Solomon is noted as having 300 concubines and 700 wives (1 Kings 11:3). Deuteronomy 17:17 states that kings should not "take many wives" to themselves. How many is too many is not specified. Having multiple wives meant that there were larger numbers of children, thereby improving the chances that the king would be able to produce an heir. Unfortunately, multiplied sons also meant multiplied sibling rivalry, with the younger sons sometimes resorting to murder in order to gain the throne. And kings had to fear not only that a younger son might murder his older sons, but that he might attempt to murder the father himself.

Amnon was David's firstborn son and therefore the heir to the throne. Absalom was the third-born son (see 1 Chronicles 3:1–2). Although Amnon's rape of Absalom's sister may have caused Absalom to murder Amnon, it also improved his chances of gaining the throne.

---

| 9 | | 17 | |
|---|---|---|---|

**Chapter 13**

Amnon rapes his half-sister Tamar. Two years later her brother Absalom kills Amnon, then flees from his father David to Talmai, the king of Geshur, where he stays for three years.

| 2 | | 17 | |
|---|---|---|---|

**Chapter 14**

Absalom finally arranges, through David's general Joab, to return home to Jerusalem. He reconciles with his father David.

*In all Israel there was not a man so highly praised for his handsome appearance as Absalom. From the top of his head to the sole of his foot there was no blemish in him. Whenever he cut the hair of his head—he used to cut his hair once a year because it became too heavy for him—he would weigh it, and its weight was two hundred shekels by the royal standard.*
**2 Samuel 14:25–26**

| 9 | | 17 | |
|---|---|---|---|

**Chapter 15**

Absalom conspires to overthrow David. David flees Jerusalem, taking loyalists with him, but he leaves some priests, ten concubines, and his advisor Hushai to undermine Absalom.

| 9 | | 17 | |
|---|---|---|---|

**Chapter 16**

Mephibosheth's servant Ziba claims that Mephibosheth has turned against David. Shimei, a relative of Saul's, curses David. Absalom sleeps with David's ten concubines.

| 17 | |
|---|---|

**Chapter 17**

Ahithophel advises Absalom to immediately pursue David and kill him. But Hushai tells him to wait and gather an army. Absalom agrees, so Ahithophel hangs himself.

*The battle spread out over the whole countryside, and the forest swallowed up more men that day than the sword.*

*Now Absalom happened to meet David's men. He was riding his mule, and as the mule went under the thick branches of a large oak, Absalom's hair got caught in the tree. He was left hanging in midair, while the mule he was riding kept on going.*

*When one of the men saw what had happened, he told Joab, "I just saw Absalom hanging in an oak tree..." And ten of Joab's armor-bearers surrounded Absalom, struck him and killed him.*
**2 Samuel 18:8–10, 15**

| 4 | | 9 | | 17 | |
|---|---|---|---|---|---|

**Chapter 18**

David's army routs Absalom's army. Absalom gets tangled in tree branches by his long hair. David's general, Joab, kills him. David mourns his death.

| 2 | | 17 | |
|---|---|---|---|

**Chapter 19**

David returns to Jerusalem in triumph. Mephibosheth claims Ziba lied about him, so David splits the property between them. Shimei begs forgiveness for his curses.

*Then the woman went to all the people with her wise advice, and they cut off the head of Sheba son of Bikri and threw it to Joab. So he sounded the trumpet, and his men dispersed from the city, each returning to his home. And Joab went back to the king in Jerusalem.*
**2 Samuel 20:22**

| 9 | | 17 | |
|---|---|---|---|

**Chapter 20**

Sheba leads a rebellion against David. Joab leads the army against Sheba, who takes refuge in Abel Beth Maakah. The town's elders cut off his head, ending the rebellion.

## Chapter 21: **Commentary**

According to Joshua 9, the Canaanite people of Gibea tricked the Israelites into entering into a peace treaty with them, despite the fact that God had told the Israelites to make no treaties at all with the Canaanites (Exodus 34:12–16). Years later, Saul had attempted to exterminate the Gibeonites, in violation of the treaty, though in apparent agreement with God's original order that Canaanites should all be exterminated (Exodus 23:31–3, Deuteronomy 20:16–18).

Instead of being pleased, God punishes the Israelites for violating the treaty. In fact, the Canaanites were never exterminated, and given God's reaction to Saul's genocidal activity, perhaps genocide was never God's intent.

What about the prohibition on sons suffering for the misdeeds of parents (Deuteronomy 24:16 and Ezekiel 18)? Given that Saul's sons fought with him, and given the prohibition on punishing the innocent, these sons, like Saul, were probably guilty of the attempted genocide.

*The cords of the grave coiled around me;*
*the snares of death confronted me.*
*"In my distress I called to the Lord;*
*I called out to my God.*
*From his temple he heard my voice;*
*my cry came to his ears."*

**2 Samuel 22:6–7**

*The God of Israel spoke,*
*the Rock of Israel said to me:*
*"When one rules over people in righteousness,*
*when he rules in the fear of God,*
*he is like the light of morning at sunrise*
*on a cloudless morning,*
*like the brightness after rain*
*that brings grass from the earth."*

**2 Samuel 23:3–4**

## Chapter 24: **Commentary**

In 2 Samuel 24:1 the author explains that God was angry with the Israelites and incited David to take a census. In 1 Chronicles 21:1, the same incident is described, but the author of 1 Chronicles informs us that Satan was the one who incited David to take the census.

Why the difference? By the time Chronicles was written, the Jewish people were uncomfortable with the idea of God being directly and immediately to blame for suffering and pain; therefore the change was made for theological sensibilities and to distance God from immediate responsibility.

**10** | **18**

To stop a famine, David lets the Gibeonite survivors of Saul's attempted genocide execute seven of Saul's descendants. David's wars against the Philistines succeed.

Chapter
**21**

**1** | **6**

David offers up a song of praise to Yahweh for his deliverance from his enemies.

Chapter
**22**

**The murder of Amnon**
*Absalom, King David's third-eldest son, murdered Amnon, David's eldest son and heir to the throne, because Amnon had raped Absalom's sister and had suffered no punishment.*

**1** | **5** | **16**

David's last words, a poem in praise of God, are followed by a list of the names and deeds of David's most famous soldiers.

Chapter
**23**

**9** | **15** | **17**

David sins by taking a census. God sends a plague, which stops at Jerusalem when David builds an altar and makes sacrifices on the threshing floor of Araunah, the Jebusite.

Chapter
**24**

# I Kings

## Overview

The title "Kings" is the same in both the Hebrew original and in the Greek translation. It was derived from the content of the book. Though separated into two books in our translations, they were originally one book. The author of 1 Kings is unknown. It is clear that the materials contained in the books of 1–2 Kings are derived from other sources.

It tells the unvarnished story of David's son, Solomon, the division of the nation into two parts (north and south), and the kings of those two kingdoms—Israel, and Judah, who ruled after him. The Book of 1 Kings covers the time from the reign of King Solomon, David's successor, through the division of the nation into two parts, north and south, at the beginning of Rehoboam's reign. During the time of Solomon's son Rehoboam, the nation of Israel split into two. The southern kingdom consisted of the tribes of Judah, Simeon, and Levi and came to be called Judah. The northern kingdom, made up of the remaining ten tribes, continued to go by the name of Israel. While the southern kingdom remained under

---

## Chapter 2: **Commentary**

Near the end of his life, David was given Abishag as a wife to care for him as a nurse. Adonijah, his son, then attempted to set himself up as king, but David intervened and made Solomon king instead. Some while later, Adonijah asked if he could marry Abishag. Solomon's response to the request was fury; he had Adonijah executed.

Why did Solomon respond so harshly? Because Adonijah was his older brother and therefore had a legitimate claim to the throne; by taking one of David's wives as his own, he was thereby establishing an even stronger claim to the throne. Given time, he might have rallied enough support to overthrow Solomon. Therefore, Solomon killed him in order to remove that potential threat to his power.

---

**17**

Chapter

**1**

David's son Adonijah tries to claim the throne of Israel for himself but fails in the attempt. David sets up his son Solomon as the next king instead.

**9**     **17**

Chapter

**2**

David tells Solomon to obey God's laws and take vengeance on those who wronged him. After David dies, Solomon kills Adonijah, deposes Abiathar, and executes Joab and Shimei.

**12**     **17**     **18**

Chapter

**3**

Solomon asks God for wisdom, which he grants. When two prostitutes both claim to be the mother of a baby, Solomon tells them to cut the baby in two.

*Then the king said, "Bring me a sword." So they brought a sword for the king. He then gave an order: "Cut the living child in two and give half to one and half to the other."*

**1 Kings 3:24–25**

the control of kings descended from David, the northern kingdom suffered under a series of dynasties, with succession commonly occurring by assassination. No one family ever remained dominant in the north.

The northern kingdom is also shown to be more syncretistic in its religious practices than the south, with its first king guilty of officially establishing idolatry in his attempt to separate the northern tribes from the religious domination of the Temple in Jerusalem out of fear that if his people continued to see Jerusalem as the center of their religious life, it might inevitably lead them to view it as the center of their political life as well.

Besides covering the political and military history of the time from Solomon through Jehoshaphat in the south and Jereoboam I through Ahaziah in the north, I Kings also tells the story of the prophets who attempted to keep the people faithfully worshiping Yahweh. Prophets mentioned by name include Nathan (1 Kings 1:38), Ahijah (1 Kings 11:29), Jehu (1 Kings 16), and Elijah, who dominates the second half of I Kings, from 1 Kings 17–22 and on into 2 Kings.

## Chapter 4: **Commentary**

Solomon asked for wisdom so that he would be a better king. His wisdom is not described in religious terms, despite the later proverb that states that the "beginning of wisdom" is the fear of the Lord (Proverbs 9:10). Instead, Solomon's wisdom is described in conventional, Ancient Near Eastern terms: human relations, poetry, song, proverbs, and an understanding of nature.

*"But will God really dwell on earth? The heavens, even the highest heaven, cannot contain you. How much less this temple I have built! Yet give attention to your servant's prayer and his plea for mercy, Lord my God. Hear the cry and the prayer that your servant is praying in your presence this day. May your eyes be open toward this temple night and day, this place of which you said, 'My Name shall be there,' so that you will hear the prayer your servant prays toward this place. Hear the supplication of your servant and of your people Israel when they pray toward this place. Hear from heaven, your dwelling place, and when you hear, forgive."*

**1 Kings 8:27–30**

**Jeroboam and the golden calves**
*Jeroboam led a successful rebellion against Rehoboam and established a new kingdom made up of the ten northern tribes.*

| 16 | | |
|---|---|---|
| A list of Solomon's officials, daily food rations, and the prosperity of Israel during his rule. Solomon writes proverbs, composes songs, and demonstrates a knowledge of nature. | Chapter **4** | |

| 17 | | |
|---|---|---|
| From Hiram, the king of Tyre, Solomon hires workers and supplies to build the Temple for God in Jerusalem. | Chapter **5** | |

| 17 | | |
|---|---|---|
| Solomon spends seven years building the Temple for Yahweh, using large amounts of cedar and gold. | Chapter **6** | |

| 16 | 17 | |
|---|---|---|
| Solomon spends 13 years building a palace for himself. A description of the Temple's furnishings is given. | Chapter **7** | |

| 11 | 12 | 17 |
|---|---|---|
| The Ark of the Covenant is placed in the Temple. Solomon formally dedicates the Temple with a prayer, many sacrifices, and a festival that lasts 14 days. | Chapter **8** | |

| 14 | 16 | 17 |
|---|---|---|

**Chapter 9**

Yahweh tells Solomon that his throne will endure forever if his descendants are obedient to God. Solomon conquers enemies, builds ships, and marries Pharaoh's daughter.

| 16 | 17 |
|---|---|

**Chapter 10**

The Queen of Sheba visits Solomon after hearing about his wisdom. Solomon acquires great wealth through his extensive trade with neighboring countries.

| 17 | |
|---|---|

**Chapter 11**

Solomon marries foreign women, builds temples for their gods, and sacrifices to them. As a judgment against Solomon, Jeroboam will take ten tribes of Israel from Rehoboam.

| 9 | 17 |
|---|---|

**Chapter 12**

Solomon dies. His son Rehoboam becomes king. Ten of the tribes rebel, making Jeroboam their king. Jeroboam establishes temples in Bethel and Dan, with golden calf idols.

| 7 | 17 |
|---|---|

**Chapter 13**

A prophet tells Jeroboam that someday Josiah will burn human bones on the altar he'd built in Bethel. The prophet then dies on his way home because he believes a lie.

| 7 | 17 |
|---|---|

**Chapter 14**

Ahijah predicts the death of Jeroboam's son and the destruction of his kingdom. Pharoah invades Jerusalem and plunders it. Nadab succeeds Jeroboam. Abijah succeeds Rehoboam.

## Chapters 10–11: **Commentary**

God promises Solomon an everlasting kingdom if he worships Yahweh and obeys him (chapter 9), but promises Israel exile and the destruction of the Temple for disobedience (1 Kings 9). The lists of Solomon's many wives, great wealth, and trips to Egypt to procure horses may appear to be in praise of Solomon. But when compared to the list of requirements that the king was to fulfill in Deuteronomy 17, it becomes obvious that instead of praising Solomon, the author is criticizing him for having broken Yahweh's commands. Chapter 10 explains how Solomon also turned away from Yahweh and started worshiping other gods. Thus, chapters 9 through 11 set up the theme and point of 1–2 Kings: the reason that Israel was divided and then taken into first Assyrian and then Babylonian captivity. Their downfall began at the height of Israel's power and glory, during the reign of Israel's wisest, richest, and most powerful king.

## Chapter 12: **Commentary**

When the Israelites left Egypt and Moses was up on Mount Sinai getting the Ten Commandments, the Israelites built golden calves and worshiped them, announcing "these are your gods" that brought you from Egypt. That choice on the part of the Israelites turned out badly, with an angry God and an angry Moses killing quite a large number of Israelites for it. So why did Jeroboam set up golden calf idols after things had gone so badly before? And after the Ten Commandments themselves forbid the making of such idols?

The Canaanite god Baal was often portrayed as a bull or calf. Therefore, portraying Yahweh with such an image was not a big step to make, given the natural syncretism of people. Given the centrality of Jerusalem to the religious life of the Israelites, to allow people to continue worshiping in Jerusalem would have been political suicide on Jeroboam's part. Without also separating religiously from the south, his kingdom had no chance of successfully separating politically from it. His rebellion would have been stillborn.

*By the word of the Lord a man of God came from Judah to Bethel, as Jeroboam was standing by the altar to make an offering. By the word of the Lord he cried out against the altar: "Altar, altar! This is what the Lord says: 'A son named Josiah will be born to the house of David. On you he will sacrifice the priests of the high places who make offerings here, and human bones will be burned on you.'"*
**1 Kings 13:1–2**

**Solomon and the Queen of Sheba**
*The Queen of Sheba visited Solomon and was impressed by his wealth and wisdom.*

*Ahab son of Omri did more evil in the eyes of the Lord than any of those before him... He set up an altar for Baal in the temple of Baal that he built in Samaria. Ahab also made an Asherah pole and did more to arouse the anger of the Lord, the God of Israel, than did all the kings of Israel before him.*

**1 Kings 16:30–33**

## Chapters 17–18: **Commentary**

The contest that Elijah sets up between Yahweh and Baal must be understood in a polytheistic framework. For the people of Israel, the question was not, "which god exists?" Rather, the question was simply, "which one should be the God of Israel?"

When Baal lost, and his priests and worshipers were slaughtered, Jezebel's reaction is not to conclude she had been wrong to worship Baal. Instead, she was angry that Elijah had killed all those people and she was determined to see justice done. None of those who saw the events of the day suffered a crisis of faith. They did not doubt the existence of Baal. For Jezebel, Baal had merely been bested by Yahweh on that day. If Elijah had died, that might have changed the winner.

*When Elijah heard it, he pulled his cloak over his face and went out and stood at the mouth of the cave.*

*Then a voice said to him, "What are you doing here, Elijah?"*

*He replied, "I have been very zealous for the Lord God Almighty. The Israelites have rejected your covenant, torn down your altars, and put your prophets to death with the sword. I am the only one left, and now they are trying to kill me too."*

**1 Kings 19:13–14**

## Chapter 21: **Commentary**

The king of Israel was "not to consider himself better than his fellow Israelites" (Deuteronomy 17:20). Israelite kings were subject to the laws and were to think of their fellow Israelites as their equals. This was a radical notion, completely alien to the thinking of most kings in the Ancient world who believed themselves to be divine beings, above the law, and able to do as they pleased. The difference in attitude is revealed in Ahab's and Jezebel's reaction to Naboth's refusal to sell his vineyard to Ahab. Ahab accepts Naboth's refusal and is disappointed. His wife Jezebel, the daughter of the king of Sidon, reacts with incredulity at her husband's quiet acceptance. She, in contrast, behaves as a ruler would in Sidon: she simply has Naboth killed and takes the vineyard.

---

**17**

Abijah, king of Judah, rules briefly and is succeeded by Asa who worships Yahweh faithfully, allies with Ben-Hadad, and fights wars with Baasha, king of Israel.

Chapter **15**

---

**17**

After two years, Baasha assassinates Nadab. Zimri assassinates his son Elah. Omri assassinates Zimri and establishes Samaria as his capital. His son Ahab marries Jezebel.

Chapter **16**

---

**7**    **8**    **17**

Elijah the prophet predicts drought, then hides from Ahab, first near a brook, then with a widow in Zarephath near Sidon who is miraculously fed. Elijah resurrects her dead son.

Chapter **17**

---

**7**    **9**    **17**

After three years, Elijah has a contest on Mount Carmel to see who should be worshiped: Yahweh or Baal. Baal loses, so Elijah has Baal's prophets killed. Then the drought ends.

Chapter **18**

---

**7**    **17**

Jezebel threatens to kill Elijah, so he runs away. God reassures Elijah and tells him to pick Elisha to become Israel's next prophet. Elisha becomes Elijah's disciple and servant.

Chapter **19**

---

**7**    **17**

Ahab defeats Ben-Hadad, the king of Aram, when he attacks Samaria, but Ahab lets him live and grants a favorable treaty. A prophet condemns Ahab for his leniency.

Chapter **20**

---

**7**    **17**

Ahab's wife Jezebel arranges to have Naboth killed so Ahab can steal his vineyard. Elijah foretells that Ahab's descendants will die and that dogs will eat Jezebel.

Chapter **21**

---

**7**    **9**    **17**

Jehoshaphat joins Ahab in an alliance against Aram to attack Ramoth Gilead. The prophet Micaiah predicts Ahab's death. Jehoshaphat and Ahab go to war anyway and Ahab dies.

Chapter **22**

# 2 Kings

## Overview

The title "Kings" is the same in both the Hebrew original and in the Greek translation. It was derived from the content of the book. Though separated into two books in our translations, 1 and 2 Kings were originally one book. As with 1 Kings, the author of 2 Kings is unknown. It is clear that the materials contained in the books of 1–2 Kings are derived from other sources. (cf. 1 Kings 11:41 and 2 Kings 8:23, for example.)

2 Kings tells the story of the kings of Israel and Judah until their conquest by the Assyrian and Babylonian empires when their people are taken away to exile. Both the author and date of composition for the Book of 2 Kings is unknown, though given that it ends after the destruction of Jerusalem and its Temple, the book seems clearly to date from sometime either during, or more likely, following the Babylonian exile. The purpose of the Book of 2 Kings, along with the preceding 1 Kings, is therefore to demonstrate the cause of the captivity in Babylon for Judah and Assyria for Israel, which the author concludes was due to both north and south becoming unfaithful to Yahweh by worship of other gods. The author blames the religious failure on the kings of Israel and the kings of Judah who are responsible for leading the people of Judah and Israel astray. Thus, the author of Kings interprets the events of Israel's history and explains them theologically as God's judgment. The role of prophets, in Israel's history, therefore, is to give God's point of view on matters. Without the prophet explaining what was happening, one could not conclude that God was involved in the events; such a conclusion, without the prophets, would be nothing more than speculation.

The author of Kings argues that the revivals under Hezekiah and Josiah were insufficient to stave off God's judgment.

---

7     9     17

Chapter
1

Ahab's son Ahaziah injures himself. He sends messengers to consult Baal-Zeub, the god of Ekron, about recovering. Elijah intercepts them and tells them Ahaziah will die.

*At this the king sent to Elijah another captain with his fifty men. The captain said to him, "Man of God, this is what the king says, 'Come down at once!'"*

*"If I am a man of God," Elijah replied, "may fire come down from heaven and consume you and your fifty men!" Then the fire of God fell from heaven and consumed him and his fifty men.*

**2 Kings 1:11–12**

*As they were walking along and talking together, suddenly a chariot of fire and horses of fire appeared and separated the two of them, and Elijah went up to heaven in a whirlwind. Elisha saw this and cried out, "My father! My father! The chariots and horsemen of Israel!" And Elisha saw him no more. Then he took hold of his garment and tore it in two.*

**2 Kings 2:11–12**

## Chapter 4: **Commentary**

Obvious comparisons may be made between Elijah, Elisha, and Jesus. Elisha multiplies and feeds bread to a large group, just as Jesus would later feed thousands with a handful of bread (Matthew 16:8–12). Elisha, like Elijah, raises a dead boy to life (1 Kings 17 and 2 Kings 4). Jesus raised several people back to life (Mark 5:35–43, Luke 7:12–15, John 11). Elisha cured a man of leprosy (2 Kings 5). Jesus, too, cured people of leprosy (Mark 1:40–42 and Luke 17:12–19). After Elisha died, when a dead man was buried next to him and touched his bones, he sprang back to life (2 Kings 13:21). After Jesus died, according to Matthew's account, many dead people came back to life (Matthew 27:51–54).

| 7 | 8 | 9 | |
|---|---|---|---|
| After Elijah is taken away by a fiery chariot, Elisha crosses the Jordan, purifies a bad spring, and calls out bears to maul boys who made fun of his baldness. | | | Chapter **2** |

| 17 | | |
|---|---|---|
| Ahab's son, Joram, succeeds Ahaziah as king. He reigns 12 years. During his reign, Moab successfully revolts against Israel and gains its independence. | | Chapter **3** |

| 7 | 8 | 17 | |
|---|---|---|---|
| Elisha miraculously helps a widow pay off her husband's creditors. Then Elisha raises a dead boy back to life, fixes a poisoned stew, and multiplies loaves of bread to feed a crowd. | | | Chapter **4** |

**Elijah's chariot**
*The prophet Elijah ascends into the sky riding a chariot lofted by a whirlwind. His servant Elisha witnesses the event and becomes a prophet to replace him.*

| ⑦ | ⑨ | ⑰ |
|---|---|---|

### Chapter 5

Elisha heals Naaman, the commander of the king of Aram, of leprosy. Elisha refuses payment, but Gehazi secretly makes him pay. So Elisha curses Gehazi with leprosy.

| ⑧ | ⑰ |
|---|---|

### Chapter 6

Elisha makes an ax head float. He blinds an army and leads them captive to Samaria. The king of Samaria wants Elisha dead when a siege against Samaria leads to cannibalism.

| ⑦ | ⑧ | ⑰ |
|---|---|---|

### Chapter 7

Elisha announces that the siege-induced famine will end. The Aramean army inexplicably retreats, leaving piles of food, which lepers discover and report to the king.

| ⑰ |
|---|

### Chapter 8

The mother of the resurrected boy has her land restored after Gehazi tells her story to the king. Hazael murders Ben-Hadad. Jehoram, king of Judah, is succeeded by his son Ahaziah.

| ⑦ | ⑨ | ⑰ |
|---|---|---|

### Chapter 9

Elisha sends a prophet to anoint Jehu king of Israel. So Jehu kills Joram king of Israel and Ahaziah king of Judah. Then he kills Jezebel, who is eaten by dogs.

## Chapter 5: **Commentary**

Elisha had been Elijah's servant (1 Kings 19:21). After Elijah's disappearance, Elisha took Elijah's place as the most important prophet in Israel. Gehazi served Elisha in the same way that Elisha had served Elijah.

The disease that Naaman suffered from is identified as leprosy. There is some question among scholars as to whether it is the same illness that we today call Hansen's Disease. Elisha did not believe that serving God or healing people was a way to gain wealth or power. Therefore, when Elisha cured Naaman, he refused his offer for payment.

One of the apostle Paul's criticisms of false teachers was that they "think that godliness is a means to financial gain." (1 Timothy 6:5). Perhaps Paul had Gehazi in mind. Gehazi lied in order to gain wealth from Naaman, so Elisha cursed him with the leprosy that had afflicted Naaman. Gehazi would therefore never become a prophet. Years later Israel's king asked Gehazi to tell stories about Elisha's deeds. Just then, the mother of a boy Elisha had brought back to life (2 Kings 4:8–37) arrived seeking the king's help (2 Kings 8:4–5).

*The officer had said to the man of God, "Look, even if the Lord should open the floodgates of the heavens, could this happen?" The man of God had replied, "You will see it with your own eyes, but you will not eat any of it!" And that is exactly what happened to him, for the people trampled him in the gateway, and he died.*

**2 Kings 7:19–20**

*Jehu went in and ate and drank. "Take care of that cursed woman," he said, "and bury her, for she was a king's daughter." But when they went out to bury her, they found nothing except her skull, her feet and her hands. They went back and told Jehu, who said, "This is the word of the Lord that he spoke through his servant Elijah the Tishbite: On the plot of ground at Jezreel dogs will devour Jezebel's flesh. Jezebel's body will be like dung on the ground in the plot at Jezreel, so that no one will be able to say, 'This is Jezebel.'"*

**2 Kings 9:34–37**

**Painted Jezebel**
*Jezebel, the mother of Joram, king of Israel, is tossed out a window and dies on the orders of his general, Jehu, who had already killed the king and taken his place on the throne.*

*As soon as Jehu had finished making the burnt offering, he ordered the guards and officers: "Go in and kill them; let no one escape." So they cut them down with the sword. The guards and officers threw the bodies out and then entered the inner shrine of the temple of Baal. They brought the sacred stone out of the temple of Baal and burned it. They demolished the sacred stone of Baal and tore down the temple of Baal, and people have used it for a latrine to this day.*

*So Jehu destroyed Baal worship in Israel.*

**2 Kings 10:25–28**

## Chapter 11: **Commentary**

Athaliah is the only ruling queen that Judah ever had. She was the daughter of King Ahab of Israel and his wife, the notorious Jezebel, who was the daughter of the king of Sidon. Athaliah was the wife of Jehoram, the king of Judah, who had ruled from about 849 to 843 BC. After he was killed by Jehu, who also killed Jezebel and Jezebel's son, the king of Israel, she took the throne of Judah. Her first act was to attempt to murder all the male heirs to the throne of Judah. However, six years later, Jehoiada, one of the priests, staged a successful coup when he produced Joash, a male heir who had survived her attempted purge.

*Elisha died and was buried.*

*Now Moabite raiders used to enter the country every spring. Once while some Israelites were burying a man, suddenly they saw a band of raiders; so they threw the man's body into Elisha's tomb. When the body touched Elisha's bones, the man came to life and stood up on his feet.*

**2 Kings 13:20–21**

*He did evil in the eyes of the Lord. He did not turn away from the sins of Jeroboam son of Nebat, which he had caused Israel to commit.*

*In the time of Pekah king of Israel, Tiglath-Pileser king of Assyria came and took Ijon, Abel Beth Maakah, Janoah, Kedesh and Hazor. He took Gilead and Galilee, including all the land of Naphtali, and deported the people to Assyria.*

**2 Kings 15:28–29**

**Athaliah**
*Judah's sole queen came to the throne by mass murder and ended her reign by herself being murdered.*

**9** **17**

Jehu slaughters the remainder of Ahab's family, kills the worshipers of Baal, demolishes Baal's temple, and turns Baal's altar and sacred stones into a latrine.

Chapter **10**

**17**

In Judah, Ahaziah's mother Athaliah kills all but one of the royal sons and makes herself queen. Seven years later, Joash becomes king after a successful rebellion against Athaliah.

Chapter **11**

**17**

Joash rules 40 years. He refurbishes the temple in Jerusalem, then strips its gold to pay Hazael to stop his attack on Jerusalem. After Joash's murder, his son Amaziah becomes king.

Chapter **12**

**7** **17**

Jehoahaz rebels against Hazael, king of Aram. During the reign of his son Jehoash, Elisha dies after predicting Jehoash will defeat Aram three times. Ben-Hadad succeeds Hazael.

Chapter **13**

**17**

Amaziah king of Judah unsuccessfully fights against Israel. He is assassinated. His son Azariah becomes king. Jeroboam II becomes king of Israel and restores its borders.

Chapter **14**

**9** **17**

Azariah has leprosy, so his son Jotham rules. Ahaz follows Jotham. In Israel, Shallum assassinates Zechariah. Menahem assassinates Shallum. Pekah assassinates Pekahiah. Hoshea assassinates Pekah.

Chapter **15**

| Chapter 16 | Ahaz worships idols and sacrifices a son. When Rezin king of Aram and Pekah king of Israel march against him, he pays Tiglath-Pileser king of the Assyrians to fight them. |
| Chapter 17 | As God's judgment against their idolatry, Shalmaneser king of Assyria attacks and conquers Samaria, capital of Israel, and deports king Hoshea and the upper class to Assyria. |
| Chapter 18 | Hezekiah king of Judah restores the worship of Yahweh. Judah celebrates Passover for the first time in centuries. Sennacherib king of Assyria threatens Jerusalem and lays siege to it. |
| Chapter 19 | Hezekiah prays for help and the prophet Isaiah predicts deliverance. Sennacherib's army dies of a plague and he leaves. Back home, two of Sennacherib's sons assassinate him. |
| Chapter 20 | Hezekiah becomes ill and miraculously recovers. Hezekiah shows Babylonian envoys his wealth. Isaiah predicts the Babylonian conquest. Hezekiah dies. His son Manasseh succeeds him. |
| Chapter 21 | Manasseh worships false gods, sacrifices a son, practices divination, consults mediums, and murders. His son Amon is assassinated. Amon's son Josiah replaces him. |

**Sennacherib's army dies**
*Hezekiah and Judah survive thanks to a plague that devastates the Assyrian king's army, forcing an end to Jerusalem's siege.*

## Chapters 16–17: **Commentary**

Some, upon reading that all Israel was taken captive in 2 Kings 17:18, with none left "but the tribe of Judah only" assume that the ten tribes that made up the northern kingdom of Israel all went into exile, never to be heard from again. Upon that reading is built the myth of the ten lost tribes of Israel. However, it must be remembered that Levi and Benjamin were also left behind, as clearly indicated by such passages as 2 Chronicles 34:30, 32. Therefore, 2 Kings 17:18 must be interpreted as referring to Judah as a kingdom and to the end of the northern kingdom as a separate entity.

*Hezekiah received the letter from the messengers and read it. Then he went up to the temple of the Lord and spread it out before the Lord. And Hezekiah prayed to the Lord: "Lord, the God of Israel, enthroned between the cherubim, you alone are God over all the kingdoms of the earth. You have made heaven and earth. Give ear, Lord, and hear; open your eyes, Lord, and see; listen to the words Sennacherib has sent to ridicule the living God.*
**2 Kings 19:14–16**

## Chapter 21: **Commentary**

Manasseh, the son of Hezekiah, was born during the extra 15 years of life that God had given Hezekiah after he had prayed for recovery from a severe illness (2 Kings 20:4–6). Manasseh is described as a vile king, guilty not only of idolatry and the worship of gods other than Yahweh, but even of human sacrifice (2 Kings 21:6). The author of 2 Kings has nothing good to say about him. He argues that Manasseh was the immediate cause of Judah being conquered by Babylon.

However, the author of 2 Chronicles adds a positive note to Manasseh's biography. He reports that Manasseh was taken into temporary exile by the Assyrians. In Assyria, he repented of his sins and prayed for deliverance which God granted (2 Chronicles 33:15–17). The apocryphal book, The Prayer of Manasseh, purports to be a copy of this prayer that he offered up to God. However, the prayer is not regarded as authentic by most scholars and is not accepted as scripture by Judaism, Roman Catholicism, or Protestantism.

## Chapter 22: **Commentary**

During the renovations of the Temple under King Josiah, the priests found the "Book of the Law." Most scholars believe this is a reference to the Book of Deuteronomy, though some have suggested that it refers to the entire Pentateuch. Many scholars also suggest that the priests didn't exactly "find" the Book of Deuteronomy. Instead, they argue that it was during this period of time that the priests in fact wrote the Book of Deuteronomy to help promote the religious reform movement that Josiah and the priests had instituted. More traditional scholars, however, reject such an interpretation of the situation.

*Furthermore, Josiah got rid of the mediums and spiritists, the household gods, the idols and all the other detestable things seen in Judah and Jerusalem. This he did to fulfill the requirements of the law written in the book that Hilkiah the priest had discovered in the temple of the Lord. Neither before nor after Josiah was there a king like him who turned to the Lord as he did—with all his heart and with all his soul and with all his strength, in accordance with all the Law of Moses.*

*Nevertheless, the Lord did not turn away from the heat of his fierce anger, which burned against Judah because of all that Manasseh had done to arouse his anger.*

**2 Kings 23:24–26**

*On the seventh day of the fifth month, in the nineteenth year of Nebuchadnezzar king of Babylon, Nebuzaradan commander of the imperial guard, an official of the king of Babylon, came to Jerusalem. He set fire to the temple of the Lord, the royal palace and all the houses of Jerusalem. Every important building he burned down. The whole Babylonian army under the commander of the imperial guard broke down the walls around Jerusalem. Nebuzaradan the commander of the guard carried into exile the people who remained in the city, along with the rest of the populace and those who had deserted to the king of Babylon. But the commander left behind some of the poorest people of the land to work the vineyards and fields.*

**2 Kings 25:8–12**

**Josiah dies in battle**
*King Josiah renovated the Temple in Jerusalem and restored the worship of Yahweh. But he dies during his futile battle with Necho, the Pharoah of Egypt.*

**7** | **17**

During Josiah's renovations of the Temple, the priests find "the Book of the Law." The female prophet Huldah warns that Judah will be judged, but not during Josiah's lifetime.

Chapter
**22**

**11** | **17**

Josiah removes all the idols and once again celebrates Passover. He dies when he goes to war with Pharaoh Necho at Megiddo. Jehoiakim becomes king and pays Necho tribute.

Chapter
**23**

**9** | **17**

Nebuchadnezzar king of Babylon conquers Judah. Jehoiakim rebels. When Jehoichin becomes king after Jehoiakim dies, Nebuchadnezzar replaces him with Zedekiah.

Chapter
**24**

**9** | **17**

Zedekiah rebels, so Nebuchadnezzar attacks, kills his sons, blinds him, and takes him away. Nebuchadnezzar destroys Jerusalem and the Temple, exiling all but the poor to Babylon.

Chapter
**25**

# 1 Chronicles

## Overview

Chronicles lists genealogies and focuses on the details of how Saul was unfaithful to God and God chose David to take his place, followed by the details of how David's kingdom was established. 1 Chronicles is notable for the number of lists it contains.

Some of the differences between Chronicles and Samuel–Kings raise historical problems, most noticeably that Chronicles vastly inflates financial and military figures. This might be the ancient equivalent

## Chapter 1: **Commentary**

Why all the genealogies in the first nine chapters of Chronicles? For modern readers, such lists of names are incredibly boring. However, their prevalence in the Bible suggests that they served an important purpose.

First, the original authors and readers wanted to know who their ancestors were. Second, a theological point was being made: individuals are important. God was not concerned with just the community as a whole, or only with those who were kings and generals: God cared about individual human beings. Every single person is important and matters. The roots of western individualism grow from the soil of the Bible.

## Chapter 3: **Commentary**

Amon, David's firstborn and the heir to the throne, raped his half-sister Tamar. Absalom, David's third-born son then murders Amnon and subsequently leads a coup against his father David. The coup fails and he is killed. The fourth-born son, Adonijah, will attempt to take the throne shortly before his father David dies, but he fails and Solomon becomes king instead, despite the fact that he is far down the list of sons. The succession from one king to the next in ancient monarchies was rarely smooth or predictable: there was always much jostling for power, with many claimants to the throne. The question of succession was very often solved through murder and exile, as it was in Solomon's time.

*Jabez was more honorable than his brothers. His mother had named him Jabez, saying, "I gave birth to him in pain." Jabez cried out to the God of Israel, "Oh, that you would bless me and enlarge my territory! Let your hand be with me, and keep me from harm so that I will be free from pain." And God granted his request.*

**1 Chronicles 4:9–10**

| 16 | 17 |
|---|---|

**Chapter 1**

The genealogies of Noah's sons, Japheth, Ham, and Shem, including the descendants of Abraham, Ishmael, Esau's sons, and the kings of Edom.

| 16 | 17 |
|---|---|

**Chapter 2**

Israel, also known as Jacob, has 12 sons. The genealogy of Israel's son Judah.

| 16 | 17 |
|---|---|

**Chapter 3**

The genealogy of David, listing those who become kings down to the Babylonian exile, and his descendants after the Babylonian exile.

| 16 | 17 |
|---|---|

**Chapter 4**

The genealogies of the other clans of Judah and the genealogy of Simeon.

| 16 | 17 |
|---|---|

**Chapter 5**

The genealogies of Reuben, Gad, and the half-tribe of Manasseh.

of adjusting for inflation, though more likely the differences in numbers are simply the result of textual corruption.

Though 1 Chronicles covers much the same ground as 1–2 Samuel, the emphasis, point of view, and purpose of the book are radically different. Where Samuel presents an unvarnished view of David, 1 Chronicles in contrast limits the story of David to his positive behavior.

> *All Israel was listed in the genealogies recorded in the book of the kings of Israel and Judah. They were taken captive to Babylon because of their unfaithfulness. Now the first to resettle on their own property in their own towns were some Israelites, priests, Levites and temple servants.*
>
> **1 Chronicles 9:1–2**

> *Saul died because he was unfaithful to the Lord; he did not keep the word of the Lord and even consulted a medium for guidance, and did not inquire of the Lord. So the Lord put him to death and turned the kingdom over to David son of Jesse.*
>
> **1 Chronicles 10:13–14**

### Capturing Jerusalem
*David led his army in the conquest of Jerusalem, against the original Canaanite inhabitants of Palestine.*

**17** | **17**

The genealogies of Levi and its various clans, along with the towns that are allotted to them from the other tribes.

Chapter **6**

**16** | **17**

The genealogies of Issachar, Benjamin, Naphtali, Manasseh, Ephraim, and Asher.

Chapter **7**

**16** | **17**

The genealogies of Benjamin, focusing on the line of King Saul.

Chapter **8**

**16** | **17**

The list of several of those who are first to return to Jerusalem following the Babylonian exile, followed by a genealogy of King Saul.

Chapter **9**

**17**

The Philistines attack Israel. King Saul and his sons fight them and die in battle. Saul dies because he was "unfaithful" to Yahweh.

Chapter **10**

**16** | **17**

David becomes king in place of Saul and conquers the Jebusite city of Jerusalem and makes it his own. A list of David's best soldiers, along with some of their exploits.

Chapter **11**

**16** | **17**

A list of those who join David while he is hiding from Saul at Ziklag. A listing of how many people join David in Hebron when they make him king over all Israel.

Chapter **12**

**17**

David begins to move the Ark of the Covenant from Kiriath Jearim to Jerusalem, but when Uzzah is killed during the process, he leaves it in the house of Obed-Edom the Gittite.

Chapter **13**

| | |
|---|---|
| **16** **17** | |
| Chapter **14** | Hiram, king of Tyre, supplies David with what's needed for building a palace in Jerusalem. David marries women and has many children. He repeatedly defeats the Philistines. |
| **16** **17** | |
| Chapter **15** | David brings the Ark of the Covenant to Jerusalem, carried by the Levites. David dances before the Ark, but his wife, Michal, despises him for it. |
| **5** **11** | |
| Chapter **16** | At the Tabernacle, there are sacrifices and music. Asaph and his associates praise Yahweh. The priests continue daily sacrifices at the high place in Gibeon. |
| **7** **12** | |
| Chapter **17** | God will not let David build a permanent Temple. God promises him an everlasting kingdom and throne. His son will build the Temple, instead. David offers thanks to God. |
| **16** **17** | |
| Chapter **18** | A list of David's military victories over the Philistines, Moabites, Arameans, Edomites, Ammonites, and Amalekites. A list of important government officials. |
| **17** | |
| Chapter **19** | Hanun, the new king of Ammon, insults David's messengers, leading David to attack and conquer him. David also subjugates the Arameans who had allied with the Ammonites. |
| **17** | |
| Chapter **20** | David captures Rabbah, the capital of Ammon, and fights against the Philistines at Gezer and Gath. |
| **10** **15** **17** | |
| Chapter **21** | David takes a census of Israel despite Joab's opposition. God sends a plague against Israel that stops when David purchases the threshing floor of Araunah and offers a sacrifice. |

## Chapter 16: Commentary

Asaph was a Levite and a musician. David placed him in charge of the worship music in the Tabernacle (1 Chronicles 16:4–7). According to 2 Chronicles 5:12, after Solomon built the Temple in Jerusalem, Asaph was among those playing music at the dedication ceremony. According to 1 Chronicles 16:5 he played the cymbals; other instruments included harps and lyres.

According to tradition, Asaph was the author of several of the Psalms (Psalm 50 and Psalms 73–83). It is thought that these and the other Psalms were usually accompanied by music and regularly performed as part of the religious ceremonies in the Temple. Some of Asaph's descendants later served as gatekeepers in the Temple (1 Chronicles 26:1).

*And I will provide a place for my people Israel and will plant them so that they can have a home of their own and no longer be disturbed. Wicked people will not oppress them anymore, as they did at the beginning and have done ever since the time I appointed leaders over my people Israel. I will also subdue all your enemies.*

*"I declare to you that the Lord will build a house for you..."*

**1 Chronicles 17:9–10**

*In still another battle, which took place at Gath, there was a huge man with six fingers on each hand and six toes on each foot—twenty-four in all. He also was descended from Rapha. When he taunted Israel, Jonathan son of Shimea, David's brother, killed him.*

**1 Chronicles 20:6–7**

*Araunah said to David, "Take it! Let my Lord the king do whatever pleases him. Look, I will give the oxen for the burnt offerings, the threshing sledges for the wood, and the wheat for the grain offering. I will give all this."*

*But King David replied to Araunah, "No, I insist on paying the full price. I will not take for the Lord what is yours, or sacrifice a burnt offering that costs me nothing."*

**1 Chronicles 21:23–24**

**The Ark of the Covenant**
*Until David conquered Jerusalem and made it his capital, the Tabernacle and the Ark of the Covenant had wandered from place to place in Israel.*

*The duty of the Levites was to help Aaron's descendants in the service of the temple of the Lord: to be in charge of the courtyards, the side rooms, the purification of all sacred things and the performance of other duties at the house of God. They were in charge of the bread set out on the table, the special flour for the grain offerings, the thin loaves made without yeast, the baking and the mixing, and all measurements of quantity and size. They were also to stand every morning to thank and praise the Lord. They were to do the same in the evening.*

**1 Chronicles 23:28–30**

*David did not take the number of the men twenty years old or less, because the Lord had promised to make Israel as numerous as the stars in the sky. Joab son of Zeruiah began to count the men but did not finish. God's wrath came on Israel on account of this numbering, and the number was not entered in the book of the annals of King David.*

**1 Chronicles 27:23–24**

## Chapter 28: **Commentary**

The books of Samuel–Kings and Chronicles cover much of the same ground. In both 2 Samuel and I Chronicles, David wants to build a Temple to God in Jerusalem. In both accounts of the story, the prophet tells him that God won't let him do it. Only in the account given in 1 Chronicles 28:3 are we finally told God's reason for turning David down: it is because David was a warrior and had blood on his hands. Even so, although Solomon—who built the Temple—was not noted as a warrior, he was not innocent of blood, either (I Kings 2:13–46).

---

16 · 17

David declares that the future Temple will be built on that threshing floor. Then he makes extensive preparations for building it, giving Solomon and the leaders of Israel instructions.

Chapter **22**

---

16 · 17

David makes Solomon king before he dies. He counts the Levites, organizes them, and puts them in charge of helping Aaron's descendants minister at the future Temple.

Chapter **23**

---

16 · 17

David organizes Aaron's descendants. The various Aaronic families will have to take turns at the Temple. The Levitical families will also have to take turns at the Temple.

Chapter **24**

---

16 · 17

David organizes the musical service at the Temple, determining who will perform and when—and over what each family will be placed in charge.

Chapter **25**

---

16 · 17

A list of the families and individuals who are to serve as gatekeepers. A list of the treasurers and other government officials.

Chapter **26**

---

16 · 17

A list of the heads of families. A list of the commanders of the army and its divisions that serve on a rotating basis. A list of the tribal leaders and other government officials.

Chapter **27**

---

16 · 17

David reiterates his desire to build a Temple and then he gives a detailed overview of his design for the Temple.

Chapter **28**

---

5 · 12 · 17

David and other wealthy people in Israel make large donations for the future Temple. David praises God. Solomon is acknowledged as the next king. Then David dies.

Chapter **29**

# 2 Chronicles

## Overview

The Hebrew title for the books of 1 and 2 Chronicles (which were originally one book) is *dibere ha-yamim*, "The Words of the Days." In the Septuagint, it receives the title *Paraleipomenon*, "Of things that have been left untold." Some copies of the Septuagint add "concerning the kings of Judah." Jerome accepted the Greek title, but suggested that the Hebrew title would be better represented by a derivative from the Greek word *chronos*. He thought such a designation would better fit the character of the book, which he saw as a chronicle of the whole of sacred history. Jerome's suggestion is followed in the title give to the book in English.

2 Chronicles picks up with Solomon as king and tells his story and that of the subsequent kings of Judah until it is conquered by the Babylonian Empire and its people are taken into exile. The Book of 2 Chronicles largely ignores the history of the

| Chapter 1 | After Solomon becomes king, God grants him wisdom, so he can better govern the people of Israel. God also gives him wealth and honor. |
| Chapter 2 | Solomon orders the building of the Temple. Hiram king of Tyre supplies the wood and skilled labor. Solomon conscripts non-Israelites to do much of the hard, unskilled labor. |
| Chapter 3 | Solomon then builds the Temple. A list of the materials used in its construction. |
| Chapter 4 | A detailed list of the Temple's furnishings and the materials used in making them. |

*God said to Solomon, "Since this is your heart's desire and you have not asked for wealth, possessions or honor, nor for the death of your enemies, and since you have not asked for a long life but for wisdom and knowledge to govern my people over whom I have made you king, therefore wisdom and knowledge will be given you. And I will also give you wealth, possessions and honor, such as no king who was before you ever had and none after you will have."*

**2 Chronicles 1:11–12**

*Then Solomon began to build the temple of the Lord in Jerusalem on Mount Moriah, where the Lord had appeared to his father David. It was on the threshing floor of Araunah the Jebusite, the place provided by David. He began building on the second day of the second month in the fourth year of his reign.*

**2 Chronicles 3:1–2**

northern kingdom of Israel, except as it impinges on the history of the southern kingdom of Judah. The purpose of 2 Chronicles is to demonstrate the decline in the religious life and the faithfulness to Yahweh of both the kings and people of Judah. Although there were moments of obedience and repentance, the overall thrust of the nation was one of decline, with idolatry and disobedience run rampant, despite the work of God's prophets who attempted to warn the nation of its wicked ways. Therefore, God's judgment upon the nation was both just and inevitable. Even the best of the kings after Solomon are shown to have significant flaws, so that they suffer in comparison with both David and Solomon. Where Solomon built the Temple and consecrated it, devoting himself to Yahweh, the kings that followed were but pale shadows of that former greatness both in terms of worship as well as in terms of wealth and power.

**The Temple**
*With a capital city for the nation, Solomon finally replaces the wandering Tabernacle when he builds a permanent Temple in Jerusalem.*

*"When I shut up the heavens so that there is no rain, or command locusts to devour the land or send a plague among my people, if my people, who are called by my name, will humble themselves and pray and seek my face and turn from their wicked ways, then I will hear from heaven, and I will forgive their sin and will heal their land. Now my eyes will be open and my ears attentive to the prayers offered in this place."*

**2 Chronicles 7:13–15**

## Chapter 8: **Commentary**

In the Ancient world, it was common for kings in a region to marry their children off to neighboring kingdoms in order to ensure good relations. The most famous of Solomon's wives was one of Pharaoh's daughters, though according to 1 Kings 11:3 Solomon ended up being married to hundreds of women. For rulers to have harems was not unusual and, like Solomon, the Pharaohs of Egypt ordinarily had multiple wives. Considering the enormous number of children the Pharaoh would have, it is not odd that he would give Solomon, the ruler of a strategically located kingdom, one of his daughters.

| 11 | | 17 |
|---|---|---|

Once built, the Ark of the Covenant is brought to the Temple and set in the Most Holy Place. There are sacrifices and celebrations. God's glory fills the Temple.

Chapter **5**

| 1 | 12 | 11 |
|---|---|---|

Solomon pronounces a blessing on the assembled people, praises God, and offers a prayer of dedication.

Chapter **6**

| 1 | 14 | 17 |
|---|---|---|

Fire consumes the sacrifices and the glory of God fills the Temple. The celebration lasts for weeks. God promises to bless Solomon if he follows Yahweh, and curse him if he doesn't.

Chapter **7**

| 17 |
|---|

Solomon enslaves the non-Israelites within Israel's borders, builds a palace for his wife, Pharaoh's daughter, performs sacrifices to Yahweh, builds a trading fleet, and grows wealthy.

Chapter **8**

**Hezekiah's sign from God**
*God gave Hezekiah a sign that he would be healed from his illness: the shadow on the stairs moved backward ten steps.*

---

**⑰**

Chapter
**9**

The Queen of Sheba visits Solomon because of his wisdom. She praises him and the prosperity of his kingdom. Solomon dies after reigning 40 years.

---

**⑨ ⑰**

Chapter
**10**

The ten tribes north of Judah rebel against Solomon's son Rehoboam because he refuses to lighten their tax burden. So they set up a rival kingdom under Joroboam.

---

**⑰**

Chapter
**11**

God prevents Rehoboam from attacking Israel. Most of the Levites and priests leave Israel and move to Judah. Rehoboam has many wives and children.

---

**⑦ ⑨ ⑰**

Chapter
**12**

The Egyptian Pharoah Shishak attacks Jerusalem. The prophet Shemiah proclaims it is God's judgment. A state of war exists between Rehoboam and Jeroboam until Rehoboam dies.

---

**⑰**

Chapter
**13**

Abijah, Rehoboam's son, becomes king of Judah. He criticizes the northern tribes for following Jeroboam, then defeats Jeroboam in battle. He has many wives and children.

---

**⑰**

Chapter
**14**

After Abijah dies, his son Asa becomes king, enjoys ten years of peace, eliminates high places, builds up Judah's defenses, and successfully defends Judah against the Cushites.

---

*She said to the king, "The report I heard in my own country about your achievements and your wisdom is true. But I did not believe what they said until I came and saw with my own eyes. Indeed, not even half the greatness of your wisdom was told me; you have far exceeded the report I heard. How happy your people must be! How happy your officials, who continually stand before you and hear your wisdom! Praise be to the Lord your God, who has delighted in you and placed you on his throne as king to rule for the Lord your God. Because of the love of your God for Israel and his desire to uphold them forever, he has made you king over them, to maintain justice and righteousness."*

**2 Chronicles 9:5–8**

## Chapter 9: **Commentary**

During Solomon's reign, the Queen of Sheba came to visit. She is otherwise unknown in the Old Testament and she appears for the purpose of demonstrating Solomon's power and fame. The people of Sheba, the Sabeans, apparently occupied a portion of southwest Arabia in what is today Yemen. At the time it was relatively well irrigated. They gained their wealth as a consequence of their location along a major trade route. Traffic in myrrh, frankincense, gold, and precious stones passed through their land on its way between Africa and India and other parts of Asia.

*The young men who had grown up with him replied, "The people have said to you, 'Your father put a heavy yoke on us, but make our yoke lighter.' Now tell them, 'My little finger is thicker than my father's waist. My father laid on you a heavy yoke; I will make it even heavier. My father scourged you with whips; I will scourge you with scorpions.'"*

**2 Chronicles 10:10–11**

*Then the prophet Shemaiah came to Rehoboam and to the leaders of Judah who had assembled in Jerusalem for fear of Shishak, and he said to them, "This is what the Lord says, 'You have abandoned me; therefore, I now abandon you to Shishak.'"*
*The leaders of Israel and the king humbled themselves and said, "The Lord is just."*

**2 Chronicles 12:5–6**

*The Spirit of God came on Azariah son of Oded. He went out to meet Asa and said to him, "Listen to me, Asa and all Judah and Benjamin. The Lord is with you when you are with him. If you seek him, he will be found by you, but if you forsake him, he will forsake you. For a long time Israel was without the true God, without a priest to teach and without the law. But in their distress they turned to the Lord, the God of Israel, and sought him, and he was found by them.*

**2 Chronicles 15:1–4**

## Chapter 17: **Commentary**

For most of Israel's history, religious instruction and the practice of the Jewish faith was largely a matter left to individual households. There were no regularly scheduled religious services beyond the various annual festivals and occasional sacrifices, certainly no corporate worship services on a weekly basis. The basic pattern for religious instruction appears in Deuteronomy 6. However, during the reign of Jehoshaphat the beginnings of a more formal method of religious instruction began, setting the stage for what would come after the Babylonian captivity (about 597–520 BC) when the synagogue system was developed for weekly religious instruction.

## Chapter 18: **Commentary**

Ramoth Gilead was one of the cities of refuge east of the Jordan. It had once been a part of the territorial allotment granted to the tribe of Gad (Deuteronomy 4:43, Joshua 20:8; 21:38) before being conquered by the Arameans. Ahab, the king of Israel, decided to recover it.

Kings kept prophets on their staff and paid them to serve as advisors. Micaiah was one such prophet, but Ahab hated him because, as Ahab told Jehoshaphat, "he never prophesies anything good about me, but always bad." (2 Chronicles 18:7). True to form, Micaiah predicted that the military operation against Ramoth Gilead would fail, and that Ahab would die in the attempt. Since other prophets predicted success, and since Ahab didn't like Micaiah, he went with the majority and died as predicted. This same story is repeated in 1 Kings 22.

*When Jehoshaphat king of Judah returned safely to his palace in Jerusalem, Jehu the seer, the son of Hanani, went out to meet him and said to the king, "Should you help the wicked and love those who hate the Lord? Because of this, the wrath of the Lord is on you. There is, however, some good in you, for you have rid the land of the Asherah poles and have set your heart on seeking God."*

**2 Chronicles 19:1–3**

---

*17*

Asa removes idols, swears allegiance to Yahweh, and deposes his grandmother Maakah as queen mother because she set up an Asherah pole.

Chapter
15

*7*    *9*    *17*

Asa allies with Ben-Hadad, king of Aram, against Israel. When the prophet Hanani criticizes Asa for relying on Aram, Asa imprisons him. Asa suffers a severe foot disease.

Chapter
16

*16*    *17*

Jehoshaphat removes the high places and Asherah poles. He sends Levites to teach the people from the Book of the Law. He keeps a large standing army and fortifies the country.

Chapter
17

*7*    *9*    *17*

Ahab asks Jehoshaphat to fight against Ramoth Gilead. The prophet Micaiah prophesies disaster: Ahab will die. Neither Jehoshaphat nor Ahab listen and Ahab dies.

Chapter
18

*7*    *17*

The prophet Jehu prophesies against Jehoshaphat. Jehoshaphat appoints judges from the Levites, priests, and heads of Israelite families to settle disputes and administer justice.

Chapter
19

**The prophet Huldah**
*When the priests discovered a copy of the Law of Moses, King Josiah sent them to the prophet Huldah to find out about it.*

| ⑦ | ⑫ | ⑰ |
| --- | --- | --- |

Chapter
**20**

The Moabites and Ammonites attack Jehoshaphat. He prays and Jehaziel prophesies victory. He builds trading ships with Ahaziah, king of Israel. Eliezer predicts their destruction.

| ⑦ | ⑰ |
| --- | --- |

Chapter
**21**

Jehoram becomes king. He kills his brothers, marries one of Ahab's daughters, and worships other gods. Edom and Libnah revolt and the prophet Elijah prophesies his death.

**Jehoshaphat leading Judah**
After prayer, Jehoshaphat leads Judah to victory over the Moabites and the Ammonites who had attacked him.

| ⑰ |
| --- |

Chapter
**22**

Ahaziah king of Judah is killed with Joram king of Israel when Jehu rebels against Joram. Ahaziah's mother, Athaliah, kills all but Joash and sets herself up as queen of Judah.

| ⑰ |
| --- |

Chapter
**23**

Seven years later, when Joash is eight, Jehoida leads a coup against Athaliah, kills her, and Joash becomes king. Jehoida eliminates idolatry throughout Judah.

| ⑦ | ⑨ | ⑰ |
| --- | --- | --- |

Chapter
**24**

Joash renovates the Temple, but worships idols. Zechariah prophesies against him and Joash has him stoned to death. Severely wounded in an Aramean attack, Joash is assassinated in his bed.

*Our God, will you not judge them? For we have no power to face this vast army that is attacking us. We do not know what to do, but our eyes are on you."*

**2 Chronicles 20:12**

## Chapter 20: **Commentary**

Dietrich Bonhoeffer was a Lutheran pastor who was part of what was called the Confessing Church during the Nazi years in Germany. Arrested in 1943, he was convicted on April 8, 1945 and hanged the next day.

One of his favorite passages in the Bible was the second half of 2 Chronicles 20:12: "We do not know what to do, but our eyes are on you." That sentence occurs at the end of a prayer that Jehoshaphat, the king of Judah, offered to God in the face of a vast army coming against Judah from Edom and Moab. It is a common occurrence in life to face problems; an army or something smaller. It is also common to have no clue what to do about them.

No matter the outcome, we can still look to God and know that he will be with us as we experience whatever he has chosen for us, knowing that he will see us through, even if we don't like what happens.

*When Jehoram established himself firmly over his father's kingdom, he put all his brothers to the sword along with some of the officials of Israel. Jehoram was thirty-two years old when he became king, and he reigned in Jerusalem eight years. He followed the ways of the kings of Israel, as the house of Ahab had done, for he married a daughter of Ahab. He did evil in the eyes of the Lord.*

**2 Chronicles 21:4–6**

## Chapters 22–23: **Commentary**

Ahaziah became the king of Judah at the age of 22. After only a year on the throne, he was killed when he went to visit the king of Israel, Joram, who had been wounded in battle. When Jehu, one of Joram's generals rebelled and murdered him, he also killed Ahaziah.

Ahaziah's mother was a woman named Athaliah. She was the granddaughter of Omri, the king of Israel. Omri was the father of Ahab. Athaliah decided to become queen herself when Ahaziah died, so she killed all of Ahaziah's sons and other males of royal descent. However, one escaped her notice: Joash. Ahaziah's sister, the wife of one of the priests, rescued him and kept him hidden. Six years later, when he was only seven years old, the priests conducted a coup against Athaliah, killed her, and set up Joash as king in her place. The only woman to ever be the supreme ruler of Judah had reigned for only six years.

*When Amaziah returned from slaughtering the Edomites, he brought back the gods of the people of Seir. He set them up as his own gods, bowed down to them and burned sacrifices to them. The anger of the Lord burned against Amaziah, and he sent a prophet to him, who said, "Why do you consult this people's gods, which could not save their own people from your hand?"*

*While he was still speaking, the king said to him, "Have we appointed you an adviser to the king? Stop! Why be struck down?"*

*So the prophet stopped but said, "I know that God has determined to destroy you, because you have done this and have not listened to my counsel."*

**2 Chronicles 25:14–16**

## Chapter 26: **Commentary**

The word translated "leprosy" in the Old Testament afflicted human beings, fabrics, and houses. Modern scholars assume that it was some sort of mold, and many doubt that the leprosy of the Bible is the same as the modern Hansen's Disease, which is also known as leprosy.

Those afflicted with leprosy were outcasts. Any home that a leper visited was rendered unclean, as were any clothing or any other items touched by a leper. Recovering from the illness was possible, however. Regulations were in place on how to be ceremonially cleansed and returned to human society (Leviticus 14:2–32).

Uzziah's affliction with leprosy meant that he could no longer rule as king; his son took over and Uzziah was relegated to living separated from everyone else in his own place. Even kings were subject to the law.

*Jotham was twenty-five years old when he became king, and he reigned in Jerusalem sixteen years. His mother's name was Jerusha daughter of Zadok. He did what was right in the eyes of the Lord, just as his father Uzziah had done, but unlike him he did not enter the temple of the Lord. The people, however, continued their corrupt practices.*

**2 Chronicles 27:1–2**

*He followed the ways of the kings of Israel and also made idols for worshiping the Baals. He burned sacrifices in the Valley of Ben Hinnom and sacrificed his children in the fire, engaging in the detestable practices of the nations the Lord had driven out before the Israelites.*

**2 Chronicles 28:2–3**

**Uzziah contracts leprosy**
*King Uzziah tries to present incense in the Temple, only to contract leprosy in the process.*

**⑦** **⑨** **⑰**

Amaziah executes Joash's assassins, restores the worship of Yahweh in Judah, but later starts worshiping Edomite idols. He loses a war with Israel. Ultimately, he is assassinated.

Chapter **25**

**⑦** **⑨** **⑰**

Uzziah burns incense in the Temple. The priest Azariah challenges him, but Uzziah reacts with fury until he suddenly develops leprosy, which forces him to live out his days in isolation.

Chapter **26**

**⑰**

Uzziah's son Jotham rules for 16 years. Although he is faithful to Yahweh, the people of Judah are not. He conquers the Ammonites.

Chapter **27**

**⑦** **⑰**

Ahaz worships Baal and sacrifices his children. Israel takes many people captive from Judah, until the prophet Oded says they should be released. Ahaz buys help from Assyria.

Chapter **28**

**⑯** **⑰**

Hezekiah rules 29 years and is faithful to God. He restores Yahweh worship and purifies the Temple.

Chapter **29**

**11** **17**

Chapter
**30**

Hezekiah celebrates the Passover, inviting people from all over Judah and Israel to participate. They celebrate the holiday for two weeks.

**16** **17**

Chapter
**31**

Sacred stones and Asherah poles are destroyed throughout Israel and Judah. The Israelites bring huge numbers of animals in tithe and for sacrifice to the temple in Jerusalem.

**Jerusalem burns**
*Nebuchadnezzar's army destroys the city of Jerusalem, takes its people captive, and burns the Jewish Temple to the ground.*

**7** **8** **17**

Chapter
**32**

Sennacherib, king of Assyria, threatens Jerusalem, but a plague wipes out his army. Hezekiah recovers from illness, entertains visiting Babylonians, and builds a water channel for Jerusalem.

**2** **9** **17**

Chapter
**33**

Manasseh worships other gods and sacrifices his children. He repents after exile in Babylon and returns to his kingdom. His son Amnon worships false gods and is assassinated.

**7** **17**

Chapter
**34**

Josiah renovates the Temple and destroys the idols. Priests find the Book of the Law. The prophetess Huldah prophesies that God will judge Judah, though not during Josiah's life.

*The couriers went from town to town in Ephraim and Manasseh, as far as Zebulun, but people scorned and ridiculed them. Nevertheless, some from Asher, Manasseh and Zebulun humbled themselves and went to Jerusalem. Also in Judah the hand of God was on the people to give them unity of mind to carry out what the king and his officials had ordered, following the word of the Lord.*
**2 Chronicles 30:10–12**

## Chapter 30: **Commentary**

The celebration of Passover, a holiday devoted to remembering the Exodus from Egypt, was supposed to happen every year (Exodus 12, Leviticus 23:4–8, Numbers 28:16–25, and Deuteronomy 16:1–8). But just as the Israelites had failed to worship Yahweh properly, so they had failed to celebrate his holidays. Until the time of Hezekiah the Jewish people had never celebrated Passover. Even then, they did not follow the rules: they did it at the wrong time of year, and those taking part in the celebration were ceremonially "unclean." So badly was it celebrated in Hezekiah's time, a few years later when Josiah celebrated it again, the author of 2 Chronicles writes, "The Passover had not been observed like this in Israel since the days of the prophet Samuel; and none of the kings of Israel had ever celebrated such a Passover as did Josiah, with the priests, the Levites and all Judah and Israel who were there with the people of Jerusalem." (2 Chronicles 35:18; see also 2 Kings 23:22.)

## Chapter 32: **Commentary**

Sennacherib attacked Jerusalem and laid siege to it, but according to 2 Chronicles 32, and the parallel accounts in 2 Kings 18–19 and Isaiah 36–37, Sennacherib's army was devastated by a plague, forcing him to withdraw. Sennacherib's Prism contains a record of the same events, but from the perspective of the Assyrians. The prism is hexagonal in shape, made of red baked clay. It is about 15 in (38 cm) high and 5½ in (14 cm) wide, and is covered with six paragraphs of Akkadian cuneiform. It was discovered in Nineveh, the capital of the Assyrian Empire, in 1830 and is currently stored at the Oriental Institute in Chicago. The prism dates to about 690 BC and describes how Sennacherib destroyed 46 of Judah's cities and trapped Hezekiah in Jerusalem "like a caged bird." But the prism fails to state that Jerusalem was ever destroyed or captured—in contrast to the description of the fate of the other cities listed on the prism. It also—unsurprisingly—does not mention the plague that devastated Sennacherib's army. Two other similar prisms are known, produced in the same time period, and both with nearly identical inscriptions.

*After all this, when Josiah had set the temple in order, Necho king of Egypt went up to fight at Carchemish on the Euphrates, and Josiah marched out to meet him in battle. But Necho sent messengers to him, saying, "What quarrel is there, king of Judah, between you and me? It is not you I am attacking at this time, but the house with which I am at war. God has told me to hurry; so stop opposing God, who is with me, or he will destroy you."*

**2 Chronicles 35:20–21**

## Chapter 36: **Commentary**

Pharaoh Necho, allied with the Assyrians, fought the rising Babylonian Empire, led by Nebuchadnezzar. He lost to the Babylonians at the Battle of Carchemish about 605 BC. Judah soon came under the control of the Babylonians; after a series of puppet kings installed by Nebuchadnezzar, he finally attacked Jerusalem, destroying both it and the Temple around 586 BC. About 70 years would pass before the Jewish people returned and rebuilt Jerusalem and the temple, no longer an independent nation, but a vassal of Persia.

| 11 | 17 |
|---|---|
| Josiah celebrates the Passover with the people of Judah and the people of Israel who had not been deported to Assyria. Josiah fights against Pharaoh Necho and dies in battle | Chapter **35** |

| 7 | 9 | 17 |
|---|---|---|
| Necho dethrones Jehoahaz. Nebuchadnezzar replaces Jehoiakim, first with Jehoiachin and then Zedekiah. Then he destroys Jerusalem and sends the Israelites captive to Babylon. | | Chapter **36** |

**Evil king**
*Hezekiah's son, Manasseh, was an evil king who worshiped other gods, sacrificed his children as a burnt offerings, and murdered the prophet Isaiah.*

# Ezra

## Overview

The title of the Book of Ezra is taken from the name of one of the principle characters in the book. The name is Aramaic, and means "help." It is a shortened form of the name "Azariah," which means "Yahweh helps." The Greek form of his name is Esdras. The book contains the story of Ezra and his return, with many of the Jewish people, to the land of Israel following the Babylonian captivity.

Ezra is linked closely with the book that follows it in the canon, Nehemiah. In fact, the two books are counted as one in the Talmud, in Josephus, and in the traditional Hebrew Masoretic Text.

The author of the book of Ezra–Nehemiah is unknown, though Ezra chapters 7–9 were apparently written by Ezra, since they are written in the first person. The account in chapters 1–6 is compiled from records, including decrees (1:2–4;

---

**16** **17**

| Chapter | Cyrus announces that the people of Judah and Jerusalem can return home and gives the articles Nebuchadnezzar removed from the Temple to Sheshbazzar to take back with them. |
|---|---|
| **1** | |

*In the first year of Cyrus king of Persia, in order to fulfill the word of the Lord spoken by Jeremiah, the Lord moved the heart of Cyrus king of Persia to make a proclamation throughout his realm and also to put it in writing:*

*"This is what Cyrus king of Persia says:*

*"'The Lord, the God of heaven, has given me all the kingdoms of the earth and he has appointed me to build a temple for him at Jerusalem in Judah. Any of his people among you may go up to Jerusalem in Judah and build the temple of the Lord, the God of Israel, the God who is in Jerusalem, and may their God be with them."*

**Ezra 1:1–3**

**The exiles return**
*During his first year, the Persian King Cyrus issued a decree that allowed the exiled Jewish people to return to their homeland.*

6:3–12), genealogies and name lists (2), and letters (4:7–22; 5:6–17). There are two sections that have been preserved in Aramaic (4:8–6:18 and 7:12–26). Aramaic was the diplomatic language during this period.

When Ezra went to Jerusalem is the subject of great controversy. Two possibilities exist. The text tells us that Ezra went to Jerusalem during the reign of Artaxerxes. This should be enough, except that there were two Artaxerxes. Therefore, Ezra might have gone to Jerusalem about 458 BC, during the reign of Artaxerxes I, or he might have gone about 398 BC, during the reign of Artaxerxes II.

As to when the book was finally composed, it was obviously sometime after Ezra and Nehemiah. The evidence generally suggests a date sometime during the fourth century BC.

**Ezra returning to the Jewish homeland**
*Ezra, the priest and scribe, returned to the Jewish homeland and taught the Law of Moses to the returning Israelites.*

## Chapters 2–4: **Commentary**

The letters in verses 11–22 are not written in Hebrew. Rather they are written in Aramaic, a closely related Semitic language. Why does Ezra, which is otherwise written in Hebrew, include sections of Aramaic? Aramaic was the most widely understood language in the Ancient Near East, much as Arabic is the mostly widely understood language today in that part of the world. The Jewish people who returned from exile in Babylon during this period of time had become primarily Aramaic speakers rather than Hebrew speakers. Aramaic would remain the dominant language in Israel through the time of Jesus; it even affected the alphabet. The alphabet we now think of as "Hebrew" is actually the Aramaic alphabet that the Jewish people brought back from Babylon.

| 16 | | 17 | |
|---|---|---|---|
| The list of the people who returned to Judah. | | | Chapter 2 |

| 17 | |
|---|---|
| The returned exiles rebuild the altar to Yahweh, perform sacrifices, and then begin rebuilding the Temple. | Chapter 3 |

| 17 | |
|---|---|
| Zerubbabel refuses to allow any of the non-Israelites to help them rebuild the Temple. The non-Israelites send letters to Artaxerxes king of Persia to get him to halt the rebuilding. | Chapter 4 |

**⑰**

Chapter
5

The prophets Haggai and Zechariah encourage the people to start rebuilding again. They send a letter to King Darius explaining that Cyrus had commanded them to rebuild.

**⑰**

Chapter
6

Darius discovers that they are correct and orders that the Temple be rebuilt at once. So the Temple is rebuilt and the Israelites celebrate Passover.

**⑰**

Chapter
7

During the reign of Artaxerxes, Ezra came to Jerusalem along with priests, Levites, and other officials. He is to supervise the Israelites, train them, and appoint judges.

**⑯**   **⑰**

Chapter
8

A list of the people who went to Jerusalem with Ezra. Ezra and the people make a successful journey and offer sacrifices upon their arrival.

**⑫**   **⑰**

Chapter
9

Ezra is appalled by the intermarriage of Israelites and non-Israelites. He prays for God to forgive the Israelites of their many sins. He fears for the future of the people.

**⑨**   **⑯**   **⑰**

Chapter
10

Ezra orders the Israelites with non-Israelite wives to divorce them. He also forces them to expel their children. There is a list of those Israelites who had married non-Israelites.

*So the elders of the Jews continued to build and prosper under the preaching of Haggai the prophet and Zechariah, a descendant of Iddo. They finished building the temple according to the command of the God of Israel and the decrees of Cyrus, Darius and Artaxerxes, kings of Persia. The temple was completed on the third day of the month Adar, in the sixth year of the reign of King Darius.*

**Ezra 6:14–15**

## Chapters 7–9: **Commentary**

The time of Ezra and Nehemiah saw the introduction of two important innovations into Judaism. One was the synagogue system: the Jewish people began gathering once a week to be instructed in the Bible. The second was the beginnings of the Pharisee sect. The reason for these two innovations was simple: the people of Israel believed they had gone into exile in Babylon because they had failed to keep God's laws. They were therefore determined to do whatever it took to keep them in the future. They believed these two innovations would help them do just that.

*I am too ashamed and disgraced, my God, to lift up my face to you, because our sins are higher than our heads and our guilt has reached to the heavens. From the days of our ancestors until now, our guilt has been great. Because of our sins, we and our kings and our priests have been subjected to the sword and captivity, to pillage and humiliation at the hand of foreign kings, as it is today.*

*"But now, for a brief moment, the Lord our God has been gracious in leaving us a remnant and giving us a firm place in his sanctuary, and so our God gives light to our eyes and a little relief in our bondage."*

**Ezra 9:6–8**

**Ezra's tomb**
*According to one tradition, Ezra was buried near Basra, beside the Tigris River in Iraq.*

**Dedication of the replacement Temple**
*When the Israelites returned to Jerusalem after their 70 years of captivity, they rebuilt the Temple that Nebuchadnezzar had destroyed and dedicated it to Yahweh.*

# Nehemiah

## Overview

The name "Nehemiah" means "comforted by Yahweh." The Book of Nehemiah contains the story of Nehemiah's return to Israel and how he got the people to rebuild Jerusalem's city walls. The books of Ezra and Nehemiah, however, were originally one work. As an integral whole, the compiler/editor/author of Ezra–Nehemiah was concerned with showing how the Jewish community that came to live within the walls of rebuilt Jerusalem (Nehemiah 11:1–2) was united in its faithfulness to the Pentateuch (Nehemiah 8), begged forgiveness for their previous disobedience to the Pentateuch (Nehemiah 9), and resolved to maintain their fidelity to the smallest detail of the law (Nehemiah 10).

Sources for the section labeled "Nehemiah" include what appear to be memoirs of Nehemiah, written in the first person: Nehemiah 1:1–7:73a; 11:1–2; 12:31–43; and 13:4–31.

---

**12**          **17**

### Chapter 1

Nehemiah prays to God about the sorry state of Jerusalem and asks that God let him do something about it. He is the king's cupbearer.

*We have acted very wickedly toward you. We have not obeyed the commands, decrees and laws you gave your servant Moses.*
  *"Remember the instruction you gave your servant Moses, saying, 'If you are unfaithful, I will scatter you among the nations, but if you return to me and obey my commands, then even if your exiled people are at the farthest horizon, I will gather them from there and bring them to the place I have chosen as a dwelling for my Name.'"*
**Nehemiah 1:7–9**

---

**17**

### Chapter 2

Artaxerxes, the king of Persia, sends Nehemiah to Judah to rebuild Jerusalem along with the necessary money and materials. He also makes Nehemiah the new governor.

*But when Sanballat the Horonite, Tobiah the Ammonite official and Geshem the Arab heard about it, they mocked and ridiculed us. "What is this you are doing?" they asked. "Are you rebelling against the king?"*
  *I answered them by saying, "The God of heaven will give us success. We his servants will start rebuilding, but as for you, you have no share in Jerusalem or any claim or historic right to it."*
**Nehemiah 2:19–20**

---

**17**

### Chapter 3

The Israelites begin rebuilding the walls. Those who were involved in the rebuilding are listed as well as the sections of the walls that they worked upon.

The other main source of the book is a section of the Ezra narrative that is inserted within the story (Nehemiah 7–8). It is inserted here either because the activity of Ezra and Nehemiah overlapped or because the editor of this material, called the Chronicler by scholars, has arranged the material thematically.

Other sources for the Book of Nehemiah were lists of various kinds: (Nehemiah 3; 7:6–73a; 9:38–10:39; 11:3–19; 11:25–36; and 12:1–26).

There is little controversy regarding the dating of Nehemiah. Although the Book of Nehemiah does not specify Artaxerxes I or II, there is enough information in the text to make it clear that Nehemiah arrived in Jerusalem during the reign of Artaxerxes I. Thus, we can conclude that Nehemiah was appointed governor there in 445 BC.

As to when the Book of Nehemiah was actually put into its current form, that is uncertain.

**Rebuilding the city walls**
*When Nehemiah arrived in Jerusalem as the new governor, he quickly saw to rebuilding the city walls, completing them in only 52 days.*

*From that day on, half of my men did the work, while the other half were equipped with spears, shields, bows and armor. The officers posted themselves behind all the people of Judah who were building the wall. Those who carried materials did their work with one hand and held a weapon in the other, and each of the builders wore his sword at his side as he worked. But the man who sounded the trumpet stayed with me.*

**Nehemiah 4:16–18**

## Chapter 5: Commentary

Prior to the Babylonian captivity, the prophets had criticized the Israelites primarily for two issues: worshiping gods other than Yahweh, and mistreating the poor and weak. Nehemiah's fear—and his motivation for his harsh condemnation of the rich mistreating the poor—was that it was precisely because of such behavior that Jerusalem had been destroyed by the Babylonians. Nehemiah did not want to see that happen all over again, right after they had returned from captivity.

17

Sanballat, Tobiah, the Arabs, and the Ammonites at first ridicule the efforts to rebuild Jerusalem's walls. Soon, they threaten violence. Nehemiah arms the builders.

Chapter
4

3                                              17

Nehemiah criticizes the wealthy for charging interest and enslaving some of their fellow Israelites. He gets them to cancel the debts and free their slaves.

Chapter
5

**Ezra reads the law**
When Ezra read the Law of Moses to the assembled people
newly returned from exile, they celebrated for seven days.

*So the wall was completed on the twenty-fifth of Elul, in fifty-two days.*

**Nehemiah 6:15**

## Chapter 8: **Commentary**

The Israelites returned to their homeland following 70 years of captivity in Babylon. One day after they had rebuilt the city of Jerusalem and the Temple, they gathered outside one of the city gates. Then the priests read the Law of Moses, "making it clear" to them (Nehemiah 8:7–8). The phrase "making it clear" most likely refers to the need for the Law of Moses to be translated from the Hebrew in which it was written to Aramaic. During their 70 years of captivity in Babylon, they had gone from speaking Hebrew to speaking the language of the neo-Babylonian Empire. Aramaic remained the primary language of the Near East from that time on until it was superseded by Arabic.

It became common practice in the synagogues for the Bible to be read in Hebrew first, before being translated into the common Aramaic. Such a translation was called a *targum*—the Aramaic word for "translation." Originally these *targumim* were strictly oral. But eventually, they came to be written down, and were produced from the time of Ezra through the early Middle Ages.

## Chapter 13: **Commentary**

Nehemiah is concerned that all of God's laws be kept by all of God's people. Therefore, he forced compliance with the Sabbath regulations, based on what Moses said about the Sabbath (see Exodus 31:12–17) and on the actions he'd taken against a man who had gathered wood on the Sabbath (see Numbers 15:32–36). Although Nehemiah's actions may seem extreme, they are mild and merciful by comparison to Moses.

Who is Tobiah and why was Nehemiah so annoyed with him? Tobiah had been one of the active opponents of Nehemiah in 2:10, 19; 4:3, 7; and 6:1–19. Tobiah had fought against the restoration of Jerusalem.

*On that day the Book of Moses was read aloud in the hearing of the people and there it was found written that no Ammonite or Moabite should ever be admitted into the assembly of God, because they had not met the Israelites with food and water but had hired Balaam to call a curse down on them. (Our God, however, turned the curse into a blessing.) When the people heard this law, they excluded from Israel all who were of foreign descent.*

**Nehemiah 13:1–3**

**17**

Despite the threats against Nehemiah by those opposed to building the wall, the wall of Jerusalem is successfully rebuilt in only 52 days.

Chapter
6

**17**

The population of Jerusalem was small. The houses had not been rebuilt. Nehemiah got a list of the returned exiles and called them to an assembly in Jerusalem.

Chapter
7

**11**        **17**

Ezra reads and explains the Law of Moses to the people. They celebrate for seven days.

Chapter
8

**11**        **14**        **17**

They confess their sins, wear sackcloth and ashes, and fast while the Book of the Law of Moses is read. They make a binding agreement to serve God faithfully.

Chapter
9

**14**        **16**        **17**

A listing of all those who made the binding agreement. The other Israelites bound themselves with a curse and an oath to worship only Yahweh and to obey his commandments.

Chapter
10

**16**        **17**

One out of ten of the Israelites agree to take up residence in Jerusalem. Who will live in Jerusalem is determined by casting lots. There is a list of those who decide to live in Jerusalem.

Chapter
11

**16**        **17**

A list of the priests and Levites who returned with Zerubbabel and Joshua to Israel from Babylonian exile. The new wall of Jerusalem is dedicated with song and sacrifice.

Chapter
12

**9**        **17**

The Israelites exclude all those of foreign descent. Nehemiah throws Tobiah out of his home, prevents work on the Sabbath, and rebukes those who married non-Israelites.

Chapter
13

# Esther

## Overview

The Book of Esther tells the story of a young Jewish woman who becomes the queen of Persia and saves her people from destruction. The book is named after her. Although she had a Hebrew name, Haddassah, she is better known by her Persian name, Esther. "Esther" is the Hebraised form of "Ishtar," a pagan goddess of fertility. It is where the English word "star" originates.

The author of the Book of Esther is unknown. The story is set during the time of Xerxes, the king of Persia from 486 to 464 BC. Xerxes is also called Ahasuerus in some translations of the Bible.

After three years of preparation, Xerxes led his army into battle against Greece, intending to punish them for the way they had humiliated his father Darius I when the Athenians defeated him

---

**9**      **17**

Chapter **1**

King Xerxes has a party and asks his queen, Vashti, to dance for his guests. She refuses and so he deposes her.

**17**

Chapter **2**

King Xerxes has a contest to find a replacement for Vashti and selects Esther, the cousin of Mordecai. Mordecai uncovers an assassination plot against Xerxes.

**9**      **17**

Chapter **3**

Mordecai offends Haman, an official of Xerxes, by not bowing down to him. So Haman decides to kill Mordecai and all the Jews. Xerxes orders their extermination.

**17**

Chapter **4**

Mordecai begs Esther to do something about the situation.

---

*Then Memukan replied in the presence of the king and the nobles, "Queen Vashti has done wrong, not only against the king but also against all the nobles and the peoples of all the provinces of King Xerxes. For the queen's conduct will become known to all the women, and so they will despise their husbands and say, 'King Xerxes commanded Queen Vashti to be brought before him, but she would not come.' This very day the Persian and Median women of the nobility who have heard about the queen's conduct will respond to all the king's nobles in the same way. There will be no end of disrespect and discord."*

**Esther 1:16–18**

## Chapter 2: **Commentary**

Though often described as a beauty contest, the selection of the new queen was not made on a runway, but rather in the bedroom. All the women selected from the kingdom as the potential new queen were taken into the king's harem. He then slept with each of them in turn and only afterward decided that Esther would take the place of his old queen, Vashti. Those not selected to be queen remained a part of his harem.

at the battle of Marathon (490 BC). Xerxes accompanied his forces on their march through Thrace, Thessaly, and Locris. Although he was at first successful in the battle of Thermopylae, his hopes of reversing his father's defeat were dashed at Salamis (480) and Plataea (479). Defeated, he returned to Asia and stayed there for the rest of his life.

The Book of Esther begins in the third year of Xerxes' rule (Esther 1:3). Some have suggested that the banquet of chapter 1 may have taken place just before Xerxes led his army off to attack Greece, while Esther 2 through the end of the book may take place after Xerxes' defeats. He was ultimately murdered in 465 BC by Artabanus, one of his sons. Artaxerxes, another son, succeeded him to the throne.

*Afterward Mordecai returned to the king's gate. But Haman rushed home, with his head covered in grief, and told Zeresh his wife and all his friends everything that had happened to him.*

*His advisers and his wife Zeresh said to him, "Since Mordecai, before whom your downfall has started, is of Jewish origin, you cannot stand against him—you will surely come to ruin!" While they were still talking with him, the king's eunuchs arrived and hurried Haman away to the banquet Esther had prepared.*

**Esther 6:12–14**

## Chapter 9: **Commentary**

The Jewish holiday Purim grows out of the events described in the Book of Esther. According to the story, Haman, a member of Xerxes' royal government, decided to destroy all the Jews in the Persian Empire on a day that was chosen by casting lots. The Hebrew word for "lots" is *purim*. Today, Jewish people celebrate the holiday by reading the Book of Esther in the synagogue. Each time Haman's name is mentioned, the congregation makes loud noises to drown out the sound of his name. Afterward, a festive meal is enjoyed by all.

### Esther and Xerxes
*Queen Esther comes before King Xerxes and reveals the evil plot of Haman to slaughter all the Jews in the Persian Empire.*

**17**

Esther asks Xerxes and Haman come to a banquet. Meanwhile, Haman erects a pole to impale Mordecai on.

Chapter
**5**

**17**

Haman is humiliated when he is forced to help honor Mordecai for uncovering the assassination plot against the king. Then he leaves for Esther's banquet.

Chapter
**6**

**9**  **17**

Esther begs the king for the lives of herself and her people, blaming Haman for the problem. Haman is quickly impaled on the pole he built for Mordecai.

Chapter
**7**

**1**  **17**

Xerxes gives Mordecai Haman's job and gives Haman's property to Esther. Xerxes allows the Jews to fight their enemies. The Jews celebrate and many people convert to Judaism.

Chapter
**8**

**1**  **17**

The Jews defeat their enemies. Every year since then, the Jews celebrate Purim to remember their victory over those who would have destroyed them.

Chapter
**9**

**17**

Xerxes prospers and so does Mordecai, who is forever after held in high esteem by all the Jewish people.

Chapter
**10**

# Job
## Overview

The Book of Job is named after the principle character in the book. The title is the same in Hebrew as it is in English.

The author and era of the Book of Job are unknown. The name "Yahweh" appears in the story repeatedly, a name that was unknown prior to the time of Moses (see Exodus 6:2–3). A poetic name for Egypt is used twice (Job 9:12–13, 26:12–13) in a way that suggests the author knew of the Exodus from Egypt (cf. Isaiah 30:7, 51:9–10, Psalm 87:4, 89:9–10). Thus, the story is clearly set in a time following the Exodus from Egypt.

Though some commentaries will discuss Job in terms of the question of "why do the righteous suffer?" this is not the actual question being answered by the Book of Job. The real question comes in Job 1:9–11: "Why does Job serve God?"

## Chapter 1: **Commentary**

| | |
|---|---|
| **18** | |
| Chapter **1** | Job, a righteous man, loses his wealth and children when God gives Satan permission to attack him. Job accepts his loss and does not lose his trust in God. |
| **18** | |
| Chapter **2** | God gives Satan permission to take Job's health and still Job does not curse God, despite his wife telling him he should. His friends Eliphaz, Bildad, and Zophar arrive to offer comfort. |
| **5**  **18** | |
| Chapter **3** | Job finally speaks to his friends. He tells them that he wishes that he had never been born or at least had died at birth. He expresses his utter misery. |
| **5**  **18** | |
| Chapter **4** | Eliphaz tells him that the innocent are not destroyed; God only destroys the wicked. Of course, no humans are really good. |

Although many people have said that the question being discussed in the Book of Job is "why do the righteous suffer?" that's actually not the question being addressed at all. Satan believed that Job was righteous only because God had made him prosperous. Both Satan and Job's three friends believe the same thing: they believe that they must be good in order to be blessed by God, while being bad will bring punishment. In essence, they believe that people are good because God pays them to be good.

*"Does Job fear God for nothing?" Satan replied. "Have you not put a hedge around him and his household and everything he has? You have blessed the work of his hands, so that his flocks and herds are spread throughout the land. But now stretch out your hand and strike everything he has, and he will surely curse you to your face."*

**Job 1:9–11**

*His wife said to him, "Are you still maintaining your integrity? Curse God and die!"*

*He replied, "You are talking like a foolish woman. Shall we accept good from God, and not trouble?"*

*In all this, Job did not sin in what he said.*

**Job 2:9–10**

God and Satan argue over Job's reasons for obeying God. Job loses everything in order to demonstrate that faithfulness to God is not dependent upon health or prosperity—and that health and prosperity are not a consequence of obedience, either. Job's friends argue for Satan's point of view throughout the book. Job repeatedly denounces them.

Job wanted to know why he was suffering. God never tells him. Instead, God asks him questions that he can't answer. God's point is simply that there are many things in life Job doesn't know that he can't explain, and none of those puzzles make him question God's justice. Why should not being able to explain his suffering be any different?

| 5 | 18 | Chapter |
|---|---|---|
| Eliphaz tells Job that while fools and wicked people lose everything, if Job will just repent of his crimes, then God will restore him to prosperity. | | 5 |

| 5 | 18 | Chapter |
|---|---|---|
| Job wishes that God would just kill him and he tells his friends that they are not helpful at all. He hasn't done anything wrong. Can his friends show him what he has done wrong? | | 6 |

| 5 | 18 | Chapter |
|---|---|---|
| Job points out that his lifespan is brief. Even if he had misbehaved, why couldn't God just forgive him since he's going to be dead soon anyhow, no matter what. | | 7 |

| 5 | 18 | Chapter |
|---|---|---|
| Bildad responds: Job's words are worthless. Is God unjust? The blameless don't suffer, only the wicked suffer. | | 8 |

"What is mankind that you make so much of them,
that you give them so much attention,
that you examine them every morning
and test them every moment?
Will you never look away from me,
or let me alone even for an instant?
If I have sinned, what have I done to you,
you who sees everything we do?
Why have you made me your target?
Have I become a burden to you?
Why do you not pardon my offenses
and forgive my sins?
For I will soon lie down in the dust;
you will search for me, but I will be no more."

**Job 7:17–21**

**Job's suffering**
*Job loses his children, his wealth, and his health but refuses to turn against God, even though he cannot explain why he is suffering.*

| 5 | 18 |
|---|---|

**Chapter 9**

Job responds: how can I argue with God? But I am innocent and so yes, God does destroy both the innocent and the guilty. God is unjust. If only someone could arbitrate between us.

| 5 | 18 |
|---|---|

**Chapter 10**

Job continues: God, why have you done this to me? Why did you let me be born if it was going to end this way? Why can't you just leave me in peace, since I'll be dead soon?

| 5 | 18 |
|---|---|

**Chapter 11**

Zophar replies: Job, you're ignorant and arrogant. How dare you question God? Of course you're guilty. If you were righteous, you wouldn't be suffering. So repent. Then all will be well with you.

**The argument**
Job argues with his friends Eliphaz, Bildad, and Zophar over the cause of his suffering. They believe suffering only comes as a result of evil behavior, but Job disagrees.

## Chapter 9: Commentary

In Job 8, Bildad the Shuhite asked Job, "Does God pervert justice?" In chapter 9, Job responds to Bildad's question with a resounding "yes!" Job points out that bad things can easily happen to good people through no fault of their own, while wicked people can prosper. Job's friends then wonder what the point of being good is. They challenge him furiously, certain that he must be guilty of some horrible, hidden crime. Otherwise, Job's fate is terrifying: it means that they are not in control of how their lives turn out. What has happened to Job—his horrible tragedy and suffering—could just as easily happen to them and there is nothing they can do to prevent it.

*"Although I am blameless,*
*I have no concern for myself;*
*I despise my own life.*
*It is all the same; that is why I say,*
*'He destroys both the blameless and the wicked.'*
*When a scourge brings sudden death,*
*he mocks the despair of the innocent.*
*When a land falls into the hands of the wicked,*
*he blindfolds its judges.*
*If it is not he, then who is it?"*

**Job 21:34**

*Though he slay me, yet will I hope in him;*
*I will surely defend my ways to his face.*

**Job 13:15**

## Chapter 14: **Commentary**

Job's friends were convinced that bad things happened to bad people and good things to good people. Since Job had suffered a terrible tragedy, losing his wealth and children, they were certain that he must be guilty of a serious sin. Job disagreed and argued that the righteous could, in fact, suffer unjustly.

Job pointed out an obvious reality that his friends had missed: why should God bother to bring judgments against human beings, given how short their lifespans are? Isn't their inevitable and soon-coming death judgment enough? Job believed that suffering during one's life generally has nothing to do with one's behavior. In fact, good and bad happen pretty much randomly to human beings. God is satisfied with the ultimate judgment of death. The brevity of human lifespans in comparison to human history, let alone cosmic history, is the ultimate solution to the problem of evil. Even the worst human being eventually dies, bringing relief to his victims.

## Chapter 15: **Commentary**

Job's friend Eliphaz argues for what he believes: that though the wicked may prosper for a time, in the end God will judge them. And he believes that Job is that sort of wicked individual who is now, at long last, receiving his just penalty. His description of the suffering that befalls the wicked wealthy is not being argued in the abstract. Eliphaz believes it is a description of Job himself.

*But you even undermine piety*
*and hinder devotion to God.*

**Job 15:4**

*"I have heard many things like these;*
*you are miserable comforters, all of you!*
*Will your long-winded speeches never end?*
*What ails you that you keep on arguing?*
*I also could speak like you,*
*if you were in my place;*
*I could make fine speeches against you*
*and shake my head at you.*
*But my mouth would encourage you;*
*comfort from my lips would bring you relief."*

**Job 16:2–5**

| | | |
|---|---|---|
| **5** | **18** | |
| Job replies: Indeed, Zophar, you know everything. It's so easy to judge when you're not suffering. God can do whatever he wants and people cannot resist him. | | Chapter **12** |
| **5** | **18** | |
| Job continues: I know the same things you know. But I'm innocent. If I could stand before God, I would prove it. | | Chapter **13** |
| **5** | **18** | |
| Job continues. Life is short and full of trouble. What is the point of God doing this to me now when I'll be dead soon? | | Chapter **14** |
| **5** | **18** | |
| Eliphaz responds: Job, you're wrong. God destroys the wicked. They only briefly seem to prosper. If you're right and good people can suffer, then what's the point of being good? | | Chapter **15** |
| **5** | **18** | |
| Job responds: You're not comforting me at all; in fact, you're only making me feel worse. I'm innocent. I've lost everything. And you're just compounding my misery. | | Chapter **16** |
| **5** | **18** | |
| Job continues: I'm destroyed, my life is ruined, and only the grave awaits me. | | Chapter **17** |
| **5** | **18** | |
| Bildad responds: Job, you don't know what you're talking about. Only the wicked, those who don't know God, suffer horribly. | | Chapter **18** |

**5**   **18**

Chapter
**19**

Job responds: why do you keep on adding to my misery? Even if I have done something wrong, why is that your concern? But in fact, God has mistreated me for no good reason.

*I know that my redeemer lives,*
*and that in the end he will stand on the earth.*
*And after my skin has been destroyed,*
*yet in my flesh I will see God;*
*I myself will see him*
*with my own eyes—I, and not another.*
*How my heart yearns within me!*

**Job 19:25–27**

**5**   **18**

Chapter
**20**

Zophar responds: though the evil might prosper for a while, in the end, God will bring him down and punish him as he deserves, making him suffer horribly.

**5**   **18**

Chapter
**21**

Job responds: why don't you pay attention to what I say and what has happened to me? Bad things can happen to good people and good things to bad people. God does whatever wants.

## Chapter 21: **Commentary**

Job faces the reality of the world and he admits that it terrifies him (Job 21:6). His friends imagine that they are in control of their fates: that if they live good lives, make careful and wise choices, and do everything just as they are supposed to, then they will have good and satisfying lives free from serious turmoil. And Job now knows—and his friends are resisting—that it simply isn't that way at all. Job's description of the wicked living well and comfortably serves the point he is attempting to make: that prosperity lasts only as long as God doesn't choose to stop it. But as to when or whether God will intervene, there's no way to predict. Some people prosper and some people don't and there's no way to know why; it is part of the inscrutable mystery of God, who does as he pleases and doesn't bother to tell his creatures why or when.

**5**   **18**

Chapter
**22**

Eliphaz responds: do you really think God is punishing you for being good? God is righteous and you're not. So repent and then he'll forgive you and restore your fortunes.

**5**   **18**

Chapter
**23**

Job responds: he wishes that he could present his innocence. But he can't oppose God or do anything to stop God's actions against him.

**5**   **18**

Chapter
**24**

Job continues: he wishes that it was as his friends suggest; that the wicked were swiftly punished by God when they misbehaved. But in reality, justice doesn't always happen.

*"Can anyone teach knowledge to God,*
*since he judges even the highest?*
*One person dies in full vigor,*
*completely secure and at ease,*
*well nourished in body,*
*bones rich with marrow.*
*Another dies in bitterness of soul,*
*never having enjoyed anything good.*
*Side by side they lie in the dust,*
*and worms cover them both."*

**Job 21:22–26**

**5**   **18**

Chapter
**25**

Bildad responds: God is powerful and humans are weak and wicked.

**5**   **18**

Chapter
**26**

Job responds: you have done nothing to help me or make me feel better.

*"As surely as God lives, who has denied me justice,*
*the Almighty, who has made my life bitter,*
*as long as I have life within me,*
*the breath of God in my nostrils,*
*my lips will not say anything wicked,*
*and my tongue will not utter lies.*
*I will never admit you are in the right;*
*till I die, I will not deny my integrity.*
*I will maintain my innocence and never let go of it;*
*my conscience will not reproach me as long*
*as I live."*

**Job 27:2–6**

**Job's complaint**
*Job complains to both God and his friends about how badly they are treating him.*

## Chapter 28: **Commentary**

Job describes wisdom as valuable beyond compare, worth any price that one might pay to obtain it. But he also describes it as a hidden thing belonging to God alone. The "hymn to wisdom" is not a non sequitur that appears in the text without connection to what has gone before or what comes after. Rather, Job is stressing the inscrutability of God's plans. We imagine justice should be a sort of tit for tat, with punishment falling swiftly and surely on misbehavior just as much as reward should follow good behavior. Job is pointing out that apparently things are not as simple as they seem, or as simple as he would wish. Instead, only God really knows what wisdom is, just as he alone understands justice, which grows from it.

*But where can wisdom be found?*
*Where does understanding dwell?*
*No mortal comprehends its worth;*
*it cannot be found in the land of the living.*
**Job 28:12–13**

## Chapter 32: **Commentary**

Some scholars believe that Elihu and his words, which appear in Job chapters 32–37, were added by a later editor disturbed by the argument of the Book of Job, who wanted to present a more traditional notion of justice, reward, and punishment. Indeed, Elihu's arguments are little different from those of Job's other three friends, and Elihu is otherwise unmentioned anywhere else in the book. At the beginning only Eliphaz, Bildad, and Zophar are mentioned as those who came to visit him (Job 2:11). And at the end of the book God criticizes only those three friends (Job 42:9). Elihu is uncounted and unnamed, as if he and his words are so unimportant and inconsequential as to not even be worth God's time.

| 5 | 18 | |
|---|---|---|
| Job continues: God has mistreated me. Why do you keep repeating meaningless platitudes about how God makes the wicked suffer? | | Chapter **27** |
| Job continues: wisdom is rare and rarely seen among people; only God has it. | | Chapter **28** |
| Job continues: I wish my life could be the way it used to be, when I was happy and prosperous and people respected me. | | Chapter **29** |
| Job continues: instead, my life is miserable—and stupid, insignificant people are berating me. | | Chapter **30** |
| Job continues: I've been a good person and I didn't deserve to have these bad things happen to me. If I'd been bad, it would have made sense. | | Chapter **31** |
| Job's friends give up on him. Elihu, a young man who has been listening to the discussion between Job and his friends, decides that he has something to say. | | Chapter **32** |

**The suffering ends**
*Job thanks God for the return of his health, for a new family, and for renewed prosperity.*

| 5 | 18 |
|---|---|

**Chapter 33**
Elihu claims to be upright and wise. He says that Job is wrong to claim innocence, and wrong about suffering unjustly. God makes people suffer only to make them repent.

| 5 | 18 |
|---|---|

**Chapter 34**
Elihu continues: God repays people for what they do: he punishes the evil. So Job is a sinner and a rebel.

| 5 | 18 |
|---|---|

**Chapter 35**
Elihu continues: God is unaffected by human sin and has never responded to the just complaints of the oppressed, so why would you expect him to answer your worthless charges?

He does not answer when people cry out
because of the arrogance of the wicked.
Indeed, God does not listen to their empty plea;
the Almighty pays no attention to it.
How much less, then, will he listen
when you say that you do not see him,
that your case is before him
and you must wait for him,
and further, that his anger never punishes
and he does not take the least notice of wickedness.
**Job 35:12–15**

| 5 | 18 |
|---|---|

**Chapter 36**
Elihu continues: God helps the righteous and punishes the wicked in order to get them to turn back to God. God does whatever he wants, so we can't ever tell him he's wrong.

| 5 | 18 |
|---|---|

**Chapter 37**
Elihu continues: God is beyond our understanding, and he only does what is right. He is just in all his dealings.

"Can you bind the chains of the Pleiades?
Can you loosen Orion's belt?
Can you bring forth the constellations in
their seasons
or lead out the Bear with its cubs?
Do you know the laws of the heavens?
Can you set up God's dominion over the earth?"
**Job 38:31–33**

| 5 | 18 |
|---|---|

**Chapter 38**
God responds to Job from the storm: you don't know what's going on. So here are some questions: do you understand how I created the universe? Do you comprehend its laws?

## Chapters 39–40: **Commentary**

God's questions to Job are intended to be unanswerable. Job was beginning to doubt God's goodness and justice because he could not come up with an answer to the question of "why is this happening to me?" God then presents an overwhelming set of questions that Job is unable to answer. Yet, Job's inability to explain where rain comes from, the laws of physics, or, in this chapter, to understand or control Behemoth, never made Job distrust God's goodness or justice. In the end, all unanswered questions are alike. Why should his inability to explain why he is suffering trouble him more than his inability to explain the behavior of ostriches? Why is his inability to control the outcome of his life any more troubling to him than his inability to control Behemoth or Leviathan?

*"Would you discredit my justice?*
*Would you condemn me to justify yourself?*
*Do you have an arm like God's,*
*and can your voice thunder like his?*
*Then adorn yourself with glory and splendor,*
*and clothe yourself in honor and majesty.*
*Unleash the fury of your wrath,*
*look at all who are proud and bring them low,*
*look at all who are proud and humble them,*
*crush the wicked where they stand.*
*Bury them all in the dust together;*
*shroud their faces in the grave.*
*Then I myself will admit to you*
*that your own right hand can save you."*

**Job 40:8–14**

## Commentary: **Chapter 42**

God told Job's friends that what they had said about Job and about God were all wrong, while Job had actually been right all along. So God told them to perform a sacrifice, while Job prayed for them. God would overlook their folly, not because of their sacrifice, however, but because of Job's prayer.

*After the LORD had said these things to Job, he said to Eliphaz the Temanite, "I am angry with you and your two friends, because you have not spoken the truth about me, as my servant Job has. So now take seven bulls and seven rams and go to my servant Job and sacrifice a burnt offering for yourselves. My servant Job will pray for you, and I will accept his prayer and not deal with you according to your folly. You have not spoken the truth about me, as my servant Job has."*

**Job 42:7–8**

| 5 | 18 | |
|---|---|---|
| God continues: can you tell me all about goats? Donkeys? Wild oxen? Ostriches? Horses? Hawks? | | Chapter **39** |

| 5 | 18 | |
|---|---|---|
| God continues: Are you ready to correct me? Job has nothing to say. God continues: If you were powerful like me, you could save yourself. So how powerful are you? Can you control Behemoth? | | Chapter **40** |

**Sacrificing for his friends**
*Job performs sacrifices for his friends so God will forgive them. Their arguments about God's motives and practices had been wrong, while everything Job had said was right.*

| 6 | 19 | |
|---|---|---|
| God continues: can you control the beast called the Leviathan? | | Chapter **41** |

| 6 | 19 | |
|---|---|---|
| Job responds: I know that you can do anything and know everything, while I am powerless and incredibly ignorant. God blesses Job and warns his friends that they were wrong. | | Chapter **42** |

# Psalms
## Overview

The final editor of the Book of Psalms arranged the various Psalms into five sections, perhaps imitating the five divisions of the Law: Genesis, Exodus, Leviticus, Numbers, and Deuteronomy.

**I** Book 1—1–41—Genesis

**II** Book 2—42–72—Exodus

**III** Book 3—73–89—Leviticus

**IV** Book 4—90–106—Numbers

**V** Book 5—107–150—Deuteronomy

The book is called the Book of Psalms; the English word "psalm" is derived from the Greek word *Psalmos*, which is itself a translation of the Hebrew word *mizmor*, which refers either to instrumental music or a song. For practical purposes, the English title means "Book of Songs." The traditional Hebrew title is *sefer tehilim*, which means "Book of Praises." The Psalms are a collection of poems expressing praise, despair, thankfulness, and requests for God's deliverance.

The Book of Psalms is an amalgam of the work of several individuals; the one responsible for arranging the Psalms in their current framework is unknown. The authorship of the individual Psalms, as attributed by their titles, breaks down as follows (of the 150 Psalms, 116 are provided with a title):

**Song lyrics**
*The Psalms were the lyrics for the songs that the Ancient Jews sang during worship and prayer.*

## Book I (Psalms 1–41)

### Chapter 1: **Commentary**

The earliest examples of Hebrew poetry may be found in Exodus 15, the so-called Song of the Sea, and in Judges 5, the Song of Deborah.

Ordinarily, when a person who speaks English thinks of poetry, the word that comes to mind is "rhyme." A secondary characteristic is that it has rhythm. Today, the most common poetry that people hear is in music, which combines all aspects of English poetry in a pleasant format. Hebrew poetry lacks all these distinguishing characteristics. It rarely, if ever, has rhythm, and rhymes only by accident.

So how does Hebrew poetry differ from Hebrew prose? Through what is technically called "parallelism." This is responsible for the somewhat repetitive quality most readers of the Psalms (and other poetry in the Bible) have no doubt noticed. Perhaps the easiest way to describe parallelism would be to say that whereas in English, poems rhyme sounds, in Hebrew, poems rhyme ideas.

For instance, here in Psalm 1:1:
"Blessed is the man who does not walk in the counsel of the wicked,
or stand in the way of sinners
or sit in the seat of mockers."

Rather than three separate behaviors or individuals, the nature of Hebrew poetry reveals a single individual and a single idea. "Counsel of the wicked," "way of sinners," and "seat of mockers" are all parallel or synonymous concepts meaning simply: "those who behave wrongly."

**5**

Chapter
**1**

The righteous who obey God's law are blessed, in contrast to the wicked.

Moses—Psalm 90
Heman the Ezrahite—Psalm 88
Ethan the Ezrahite—Psalm 89
Solomon—Psalms 72, 127
David (73 times)—Psalms 3–9; 11–32; 34–41;
51–65; 68–70; 86; 103; 108–110; 122; 124; 131;
133; 138–145
Asaph (12 times)—Psalms 50; 73–83
Sons of Korah (9 times)—Psalm 42; 44–45;
47–49; 84–85; 87
Author unknown (49 times)
The Septuagint, the ancient Greek translation of
the Bible from the second century BC gives
additional authorship identifications as follows:
Jeremiah—Psalm 137
Haggai and Zechariah—Psalms 146–147
Ezra—Psalm 119
Hezekiah (15 times) Psalms 120–134

## Chapter 2: **Commentary**

Psalm 2:7 is quoted three times in the New Testament,
where it is applied to Jesus. The first quotation occurs in
Acts 13:33, when Paul was speaking in a synagogue. The
author of the New Testament Book of Hebrews uses it
twice, first in Hebrews 1:5, to demonstrate that Jesus is
superior to the angels and in 5:5 to indicate his superiority
to the High Priest at the Temple in Jerusalem.

*I will proclaim the Lord's decree:*
*He said to me, "You are my son;*
*today I have become your father."*

**Psalm 2:7**

## Chapter 3: **Commentary**

Psalm 3:2 displays the first use of the odd Hebrew word
*selah* in the Book of Psalms. Some modern translations,
such as NIV, don't bother to show the word at all, since it
has no effect on our understanding of the passage. The
word *selah* had something to do with the music that
accompanied the Psalm but its exact meaning is unknown.
It appears 74 times in the Bible. 71 times in Psalms (Psalms
3, 4, 7, 9, 20, 21, 24, 32, 39, 44, 46, 47, 48, 49, 50, 52, 54,
55, 57, 59, 60, 61, 62, 66, 67, 68, 75, 77, 81, 82, 83, 84,
85, 87, 88, 89, 140, and 143) and three times in Habakkuk
(all in Habakkuk 3).

**Illuminated manuscript**
*A handwritten page of the first Psalm, dating from
the fourteenth century, shows King David, the
traditional author of many Psalms, playing a harp.*

| 5 | 9 |
|---|---|

The nations may rise up against God and his
appointed king, but God will rebuke them. The
nations would be wise to submit to God and his
appointed king.

Chapter
2

| 5 | 12 |
|---|---|

I have many enemies; but I believe God will protect
me. Please God, destroy my enemies and protect me.

Chapter
3

**5**      **12**

Chapter

**4**

I am suffering. Please God, relieve my distress and bring me joy once again. I am not an idolater. I know only you can help me, God.

*In peace I will lie down and sleep,*
*for you alone, Lord,*
*make me dwell in safety.*

**Psalm 4:8**

**5**      **12**

Chapter

**5**

God, I need your help; save me from my enemies. I know you will judge the wicked and protect the righteous because you are righteous.

*Turn, Lord, and deliver me;*
*save me because of your unfailing love.*
*Among the dead no one proclaims your name.*
*Who praises you from the grave?*
*I am worn out from my groaning.*
*All night long I flood my bed with weeping*
*and drench my couch with tears.*
*My eyes grow weak with sorrow;*
*they fail because of all my foes.*

**Psalm 6:4–7**

**5**      **12**

Chapter

**6**

Please God, show me mercy. I'm in anguish. How long before you deliver me and rescue me from my enemies? I know you've heard my prayer and will answer it.

**5**      **12**

Chapter

**7**

I trust you God. If I'm guilty, then may I be punished. But if not, then punish my enemies, instead. I know you are just and will punish my enemies and so I praise you for it.

## Chapter 8: **Commentary**

The Psalmist wonders why God has paid any attention to human beings. The Psalmist's goal is to demonstrate both the glory of God and the value of human beings. The author comments in verse 5, as it is worded in most translations, that humans were made "a little lower than the heavenly beings" or "a little lower than the angels." However, the Hebrew word translated as "heavenly beings" or "angels" is actually the word normally translated as "God." Translating it as "angels" goes back to the ancient Greek translation known as the Septuagint; it is also found in the Aramaic Targums, the Syriac Peshita, and Jerome's Latin translation, known as the Vulgate. It arises from the discomfort felt by some translators in making any comparison between human beings and God. The Psalmist is playing off what God himself said about humanity when he created them: human beings were created in his image and were given dominion over God's creation (Genesis 1:26–28). They are second only to God.

**1**      **5**      **18**

Chapter

**8**

God, compared to you and the universe you've made, human beings are insignificant. And yet you care about us and made us rulers over that universe. You're wonderful!

**1**      **5**

Chapter

**9**

Praise God for all you've done and for your justice. Please continue to judge my enemies and all those who are opposed to you.

*When I consider your heavens,*
*the work of your fingers,*
*the moon and the stars,*
*which you have set in place,*
*what is mankind that you are mindful of them,*
*human beings that you care for them?*

**Psalm 8:3–4**

**5**      **12**

Chapter

**10**

Why have you been so slow to rescue us from our wicked enemies? Look how evil they are! Please do something about them. We know you care about those who suffer.

**5**      **12**

Chapter

**11**

Since I take refuge in Yahweh, why do you tell me to run away? Yahweh will take care of the righteous, but destroy the wicked, because he is just.

*How long, Lord? Will you forget me forever?*
*How long will you hide your face from me?*
*How long must I wrestle with my thoughts*
*and day after day have sorrow in my heart?*
*How long will my enemy triumph over me?*

**Psalm 13:1–2**

## Chapter 14: **Commentary**

Psalm 14:1–7 is nearly identical to Psalm 53:1–6. There are two differences. First is the use of God's name "Yahweh" in Psalm 14 in verses 2, 4, 6, and 7 (usually rendered "Lord") taking the place of the Hebrew word *elohim* (usually translated "God") in Psalm 53. Second, compare Psalm 53:5 with Psalm 14:5–6:

"But there they are, overwhelmed with dread,
where there was nothing to dread.
God scattered the bones of those who attacked you;
you put them to shame, for God despised them."
(Psalm 53:5)

"But there they are, overwhelmed with dread,
for God is present in the company of the righteous.
You evildoers frustrate the plans of the poor,
but the Lord is their refuge." (Psalm 14:5–6)

The presence of these nearly identical Psalms illustrates how texts were edited and adapted over time to fulfill different purposes in the Israelite community, until they were gathered together in the final form of the Book of Psalms.

| 5 | | 12 | |
|---|---|---|---|
| Yahweh, help us because we can't believe anyone else. The poor are suffering. But what God says is trustworthy. God will take care of us and protect us from the wicked. | | | Chapter **12** |

| 5 | | 12 | |
|---|---|---|---|
| How long do I have to be miserable, God? Please answer me and rescue me. I trust your unfailing love, rejoice in your salvation, and will sing praise to you. | | | Chapter **13** |

| 1 | | 5 | |
|---|---|---|---|
| Only fools don't believe in God. Everyone is wicked, but God will protect the righteous. We will rejoice when Yahweh rescues his people Israel. | | | Chapter **14** |

**The creator cares**
*The Psalmist wonders how the God who made the sun, moon, and stars could care for human beings, who seem so insignificant in the vastness of the universe.*

| 3 | | 5 | |
|---|---|---|---|

Chapter **15**

Who will live with God? Those who do the right thing, speak the truth, abhor wrongdoers, keep their promises, reject bribes, and give to the poor without charging interest.

| 1 | | 5 | | 12 |
|---|---|---|---|---|

Chapter **16**

Protect me, God. You have given me everything that is good in my life. Thank you for your instructions and for your care. You will protect me from death and make me happy.

| 5 | | 12 | |
|---|---|---|---|

Chapter **17**

Yahweh, please hear my prayer and vindicate me. I am not a liar and I have followed your ways. Protect me and destroy my enemies who are falsely accusing me.

| 1 | | 5 | |
|---|---|---|---|

Chapter **18**

I love you Yahweh, you are my rock. Thank you for rescuing me from my enemies. You always rescue the humble and righteous because of your perfect, flawless ways.

| 1 | | 3 | | 5 | |
|---|---|---|---|---|---|

Chapter **19**

The sky above displays God's glory and power to everyone. God's law is perfect and gives us life and protects us from going the wrong way.

| 5 | | 12 | |
|---|---|---|---|

Chapter **20**

May God grant all your requests and give victory to the king who trusts in God rather than in his own power.

| 1 | | 5 | |
|---|---|---|---|

Chapter **21**

The king rejoices because God has granted his requests and given him victory. The king trusts God. God will destroy the king's enemies.

| 4 | | 5 | | 12 |
|---|---|---|---|---|

Chapter **22**

God, I beg for help, but no help comes. Everyone is against me. I will praise you in front of everyone once you take care of me, which will encourage others when they face problems.

## Chapter 19: **Commentary**

When theologians speak of the "revelations" of God, they are not referring to the last book of the New Testament. Instead, they are describing God's "self-disclosure." That is, the idea that God opens himself to humanity, so humanity can get to know him. Theologians put God's revelations into two categories: "Special Revelation" and "General Revelation." Special Revelation refers to God's self-disclosure through the pages of the Bible, the voices of prophets, and all that Jesus said and did on Earth. General Revelation is what is described in Psalm 19: the universe that God created tells humanity about the God who created it.

*The heavens declare the glory of God;*
*the skies proclaim the work of his hands.*
*Day after day they pour forth speech;*
*night after night they reveal knowledge.*
*They have no speech, they use no words;*
*no sound is heard from them.*
*Yet their voice goes out into all the earth,*
*their words to the ends of the world.*
*In the heavens God has pitched a tent for the sun.*
**Psalm 19:1–4**

## Chapter 22: **Commentary**

Christians refer to Psalm 22 as a "messianic" Psalm because it makes reference to Jesus—especially his suffering on the cross. Jesus quoted the first line of the first verse, "My God, my God, why have you forsaken me?" shortly before he died (Matthew 27:46 and Mark 15:34). All four gospel writers quote or allude to verse 18, "They divide my clothes among them/and cast lots for my garment." (see Matthew 27:35, Mark 15:24, Luke 23:34, and John 19:24). Likewise, the words of verses 7–8 are alluded to by Matthew 27:41–43, Mark 15:31 and Luke 23:36.

*My God, my God, why have you forsaken me?*
*Why are you so far from saving me,*
*so far from my cries of anguish?*
*My God, I cry out by day, but you do not answer,*
*by night, but I find no rest.*
**Psalm 22:1–2**

## Chapter 23: **Commentary**

God will pursue us with goodness and mercy all our lives. The word translated as "follows" is most commonly used of predators in pursuit of their prey, or armies in pursuit of their enemies. It carries the sense of "hunting something down." The Psalmist has taken a word with negative connotations and twisted it to something positive in order to heighten the emotional impact of how strongly God will take care of his people and how much he wants to bless them.

*Surely your goodness and love will follow me all the days of my life, and I will dwell in the house of the Lord forever.*

**Psalm 23:6**

## Chapter 27: **Commentary**

Many of the Psalms have a superscription at the beginning, identifying the author and sometimes adding details about the time or context of the Psalm. Sometimes, the superscription includes instructions on how the Psalm was to be performed as a piece of music. In the Hebrew text, the superscription is verse 1, while in English, it is set apart without a verse number. The consensus among biblical scholars is that the superscriptions were added long after the individual Psalms were originally composed and are not part of the original text of the Bible. Even so, the superscriptions reflect tradition and a reasonable reading of the poems. Psalm 27 is attributed to David and certainly the words of verse 3 suggest that the author was indeed a king, since he comments, "though an army besiege me" and "though war break out against me." Armies rarely targeted ordinary farmers, priests, or city dwellers. But a king such as David could, and in fact did, face such problems regularly.

*One thing I ask from the Lord,*
*this only do I seek:*
*that I may dwell in the house of the Lord*
*all the days of my life,*
*to gaze on the beauty of the Lord*
*and to seek him in his temple.*
*For in the day of trouble*
*he will keep me safe in his dwelling;*
*he will hide me in the shelter of his sacred tent*
*and set me high upon a rock.*

**Psalm 27:4–5**

| 1 | | 5 | | |
|---|---|---|---|---|

Yahweh cares for his people and he supplies all their needs, just as a shepherd takes care of his sheep.

**Chapter 23**

| 1 | | 5 | | |
|---|---|---|---|---|

Everything belongs to God and he made it all. The righteous can come before God and receive God's blessing. God is strong and powerful, so be encouraged.

**Chapter 24**

| 3 | | 5 | | 12 |
|---|---|---|---|---|

I trust God. Teach me to live the right way. You, God, are good. You guide me, and you forgive me when I do the wrong thing. Please take care of me in my loneliness and affliction.

**Chapter 25**

| 5 | | 12 |
|---|---|---|

Vindicate me, God, because I am innocent and blameless, so don't destroy me like the bloodthirsty who plot evil.

**Chapter 26**

| 1 | | 5 | | 12 |
|---|---|---|---|---|

Yahweh is my light and salvation, so I have nothing and no one to fear. Please protect me and don't reject me. I know you'll take care of me and I'll see your goodness.

**Chapter 27**

| 1 | | 5 | | 12 |
|---|---|---|---|---|

Yahweh, don't ignore me; show me mercy. Repay the wicked for their evil. Thank you for helping me. I praise you with joy.

**Chapter 28**

| 5 | | 18 |
|---|---|---|

Ascribe glory and power to Yahweh, who shakes the world with thunder and storm, rules over all, and blesses his people with peace.

**Chapter 29**

| 1 | | 5 |
|---|---|---|

Thank you Yahweh for saving me from my enemies, when I was at my lowest ebb. I called for mercy and you showed me mercy, turning my sadness to dancing.

**Chapter 30**

| 1 | 5 | 12 |
|---|---|---|

### Chapter 31

Yahweh, I have taken refuge in you, I am in distress, consumed by anguish. Be merciful to me. I'm trusting in you. You are good, a shelter to all. We can all trust and praise you.

| 1 | 5 |
|---|---|

### Chapter 32

Those who are forgiven are blessed. I was miserable until I told you about my sins and you forgave me. You will protect me in my troubles and I can rejoice in you.

| 1 | 5 |
|---|---|

### Chapter 33

Sing joyfully to Yahweh! His word is faithful and true; he made the universe and no one can thwart his plans. Yahweh takes care of his own and only Yahweh can really help us.

| 1 | 5 |
|---|---|

### Chapter 34

When I sought Yahweh, he delivered me from all my fears. So taste and see that Yahweh is good and listens to the righteous. They may have troubles, but Yahweh will rescue them.

*Be merciful to me, Lord, for I am in distress;*
*my eyes grow weak with sorrow,*
*my soul and body with grief.*
*My life is consumed by anguish*
*and my years by groaning;*
*my strength fails because of my affliction,*
*and my bones grow weak.*
*Because of all my enemies,*
*I am the utter contempt of my neighbors*
*and an object of dread to my closest friends—*
*those who see me on the street flee from me.*
*I am forgotten as though I were dead;*
*I have become like broken pottery.*
*For I hear many whispering,*
*"Terror on every side!"*
*They conspire against me*
*and plot to take my life.*

**Psalm 31:9–13**

*Blessed is the one*
*whose transgressions are forgiven,*
*whose sins are covered.*
*Blessed is the one*
*whose sin the Lord does not count against them*
*and in whose spirit is no deceit.*

**Psalm 32:1–2**

## Chapters 33–34: **Commentary**

The individual Psalms, like any part of the Bible, grow out of specific circumstances. But they also, like any part of the Bible, deal with universal human experience and emotion. According to the superscription of Psalm 34, David composed this Psalm while he was on the run from his father-in-law, king Saul, who was determined to murder him (see 1 Samuel 21). He had thought to find a safe haven in the Philistine city of Gath, but discovered he was not welcome there and had to pretend to be insane in order to escape with his life. But the Psalm also speaks to anyone who is facing serious trouble.

**David asks for mercy**
*In Psalm 38 David begs God to relieve his suffering, which he recognizes as a punishment from God for his sins.*

## Chapters 35–40: **Commentary**

Verses 13–17 of Psalm 40 are modified slightly and appear as a separate Psalm, Psalm 70. Verses 6–8 are quoted in Hebrew 10:5–7 and applied to the sacrifice of Jesus. The ancient Hebrew text of verse 6 is worded "but my ears you have opened." As quoted by the author of the New Testament Book of Hebrews, however, that line is radically different: "but a body you have prepared for me." Why that difference? The author of Hebrews is not quoting from the Hebrew text. Instead, he is quoting from a translation into Greek made around 200 BC, known as the Septuagint. The difference between what appears in the Septuagint and the traditional Hebrew text is a consequence of textual variation that appears as a result of alterations of the sort anyone can make upon copying a text where they misread a word.

## Textual criticism

There are thousands of copies of the biblical texts. In fact, there are more copies of the books of the Bible than of any other ancient text. Unsurprisingly, since they were all written by hand, no two copies are exactly the same. The overwhelming majority of the differences between copies are spelling-related. On rare occasion, the differences are more substantive. Sometimes the differences will be the replacement of an uncommon word with a more common word of the same meaning. Other times, it will be the change of one word to another word spelled only slightly differently from the intended word, like using "lift" instead of "left." Occasionally a scribe will leave out a word or group of words as his eye slipped from one line to another; other times, he may add words, as for instance when he includes the words someone might have scribbled into the margin of his copy of a text as if they are part of the original text. Scholars have developed a methodology for comparing the multiplicity of texts and figuring out what the original readings of the texts actually were, before the introduction of the scribal variants.

*Blessed are those who have regard for the weak;*
*the Lord delivers them in times of trouble.*
*The Lord protects and preserves them—*
*they are counted among the blessed in the land—*
*he does not give them over to the desire of their foes.*
*The Lord sustains them on their sickbed*
*and restores them from their bed of illness.*
**Psalm 41:1–3**

**1** **5** Yahweh, fight against those who fight against me. How much longer will I have to suffer? I'm tired of your silence. I want to praise you and thank you for deliverance. **Chapter 35**

**1** **12** The wicked have no fear of God; all they do is plot evil. But your love is neverending and people can take refuge in you. Protect me from the wicked; I know they will be destroyed. **Chapter 36**

**1** **5** Don't envy the wicked. Their time is short. Instead, trust Yahweh. The righteous will prosper, while the wicked won't. Yahweh will deliver the righteous from their troubles. **Chapter 37**

**4** **5** **12** I am overwhelmed by my guilt. My body is falling apart. I'm in enormous pain. I confess my sin; please don't forsake me. Rescue me, please. **Chapter 38**

**4** **5** **12** I tried to keep silent, but I couldn't hold it in. Life is fleeting. Remove your scourge from me. Hear my cry for help. And let me enjoy my life once again. **Chapter 39**

**1** **5** **12** I waited patiently for Yahweh to hear me and rescue me from my problems. When he did, he restored my joy. I tell everyone about you. May my enemies be destroyed. **Chapter 40**

**4** **5** **12** Yahweh takes care of those who take care of the weak. Heal me, because I've sinned. My enemies plot against me. Even my closest friend rejects me. Restore me so I can repay them. **Chapter 41**

# Book II (Psalms 42–72)

| 4 | 5 | 12 |
|---|---|---|

**Chapter 42**

I long for God. I remember how happily I used to worship God. Why am I so sad now? Why has God forgotten me? I need to put my hope in God. Someday I will praise him again.

| 4 | 5 | 12 |
|---|---|---|

**Chapter 43**

God, vindicate me! Why do I have to mourn, oppressed by the enemy? Why am I so sad? When you rescue me, I will praise you. Why am I so sad? I should trust God.

| 5 | 12 |
|---|---|

**Chapter 44**

God, we remember how you brought our ancestors from Egypt to the Promised Land. But now, our enemies have been victorious. Why don't you do something? We don't deserve this.

| 1 | 5 |
|---|---|

**Chapter 45**

The king is the most excellent and exalted of men. Let him be enthralled by your beauty; you are his princess. Enjoy your new home. Your sons will be princes!

| 1 | 5 |
|---|---|

**Chapter 46**

God is our refuge when we face trouble. Look at what Yahweh has done for us: he has brought peace. So relax. Yahweh is with us. He is our fortress.

| 1 | 5 |
|---|---|

**Chapter 47**

Clap and shout praise to God with joy. God has subdued all the nations. The kings of the earth belong to God. God is king of the whole world.

| 1 | 5 |
|---|---|

**Chapter 48**

Jerusalem is beautiful, the place where God has his Temple. God keeps it secure and will guide us forever.

*As the deer pants for streams of water,*
*so my soul pants for you, my God.*
*My soul thirsts for God, for the living God.*
*When can I go and meet with God?*
*My tears have been my food*
*day and night,*
*while people say to me all day long,*
*"Where is your God?"*
*These things I remember*
*as I pour out my soul:*
*how I used to go to the house of God*
*under the protection of the Mighty One*
*with shouts of joy and praise*
*among the festive throng.*

*Why, my soul, are you downcast?*
*Why so disturbed within me?*
*Put your hope in God,*
*for I will yet praise him,*
*my Savior and my God.*

**Psalm 42:1–5**

## Chapters 43–45: **Commentary**

The superscription of Psalm 45 describes it as a "wedding song." It relates the marriage of a woman to the king, who is described as impressive and wonderful; in fact, as was common throughout the Ancient Near East, the king is apparently described as being divine (verse 6). The author of the New Testament Book of Hebrews quotes verses 6–7 and applied them to Jesus in Hebrews 1:8–9, using them to demonstrate that Jesus is greater than the angels because Jesus is God.

*Come and see what the Lord has done,*
*the desolations he has brought on the earth.*
*He makes wars cease*
*to the ends of the earth.*
*He breaks the bow and shatters the spear;*
*he burns the shields with fire.*
*He says, "Be still, and know that I am God;*
*I will be exalted among the nations,*
*I will be exalted in the earth."*

**Psalm 46:8–10**

*But God will redeem me from the
realm of the dead;
he will surely take me to himself.
Do not be overawed when others grow rich,
when the splendor of their houses increases;
for they will take nothing with them when they die,
their splendor will not descend with them.
Though while they live they count
themselves blessed—
and people praise you when you prosper—
they will join those who have gone before them,
who will never again see the light of life.*

    *People who have wealth but lack understanding
are like the beasts that perish.*

**Psalm 49:15–20**

---

**5**      **18**

Why be troubled by your problems? Why put your trust in money? Death comes to all. Trusting in yourself or your money is silly. Only God can redeem you from death.

Chapter
**49**

---

**3**      **5**

God says, "I already own all the cattle, so I don't need your sacrifices. Just thank me and I'll deliver you. But you wicked have no right to recite my laws, since you don't keep them."

Chapter
**50**

---

**4**      **5**      **12**

God, have mercy on me! I've sinned against you. Please clean me and make me pure once again. Deliver me from my guilt. My broken spirit is the only sacrifice you want.

Chapter
**51**

---

## Chapter 51: **Commentary**

According to the superscription on Psalm 51, this Psalm was composed by David in reaction to the exposure of his adulterous affair with Bathsheba. The affair culminated in David's murder of Bathsheba's husband Uriah, when his attempts to hide the affair failed (see 2 Samuel 11–12). Certainly the Psalm serves as a model prayer of repentance, expressing the sorrow of an individual as he confronts his sinful behavior.

*Have mercy on me, O God,
according to your unfailing love;
according to your great compassion
blot out my transgressions.
Wash away all my iniquity
and cleanse me from my sin.*

*For I know my transgressions,
and my sin is always before me.
Against you, you only, have I sinned
and done what is evil in your sight;
so you are right in your verdict
and justified when you judge.*

**Psalm 51:1–4**

**David admits his guilt**
*The prophet Nathan confronted David for his adultery with Bathsheba.
David confessed his sin and begged forgiveness in Psalm 51.*

**Chapter 52**
You are evil and deceitful and boastful. You're a disgrace and God will destroy you. You trusted in your wealth instead of in God. But I trust in God and so I will praise him forever.

**Chapter 53**
Only fools don't believe in God. Everyone is wicked, but God will protect the righteous. We will rejoice when Yahweh rescues his people Israel.

**Chapter 54**
God, please save me. Those who don't care about God are attacking me. I will sacrifice in thanks when you save me from my troubles and let me look triumphantly over my enemies.

**Chapter 55**
God, please answer my prayer. I'm in anguish. I want to hide and run away. Someone that was once my friend has become my enemy. Destroy my enemies. I trust you, God.

**Chapter 56**
My enemies are after me. They never let up. When I'm afraid, I look to God and my fear leaves me. What can people do to me when God stands by me? I thank God for saving me from death.

**Chapter 57**
Have mercy on me, God. I'm trusting you to vindicate me. My enemies are like lions. They plot against me. But I will praise you, God, because you are powerful and you love me.

**Chapter 58**
The rulers are unjust and oppressive; they've been wicked from birth. God, destroy them! Make them vanish! The righteous will rejoice when at long last they are avenged.

## Chapter 53: **Commentary**

The words of Psalm 53 are nearly identical to those of Psalm 14. But there are some differences. Where Psalm 53 consistently uses only the word "God," Psalm 14 sometimes replaces it with "Yahweh," God's name, rendered "Lord" in most translations. Also, the wording of the three lines following "But there they are, overwhelmed with dread" in Psalm 53 (verse 5) are entirely different in Psalm 14 (verses 5–6).

*The fool says in his heart,*
*"There is no God."*
*They are corrupt, and their ways are vile;*
*there is no one who does good.*
    *God looks down from heaven*
*on all mankind*
*to see if there are any who understand,*
*any who seek God.*
*Everyone has turned away, all have become corrupt;*
*there is no one who does good, not even one.*
**Psalm 53:1–3**

## Chapter 58: **Commentary**

Psalm 58 is an example of an "imprecatory" Psalm: that is, the author calls upon God to avenge his enemies, to judge the guilty, and to right injustice. Some modern critics dislike the whole idea of such Psalms, imagining them to be examples of a less enlightened theology. However, one must remember that the Psalms are poetry, and their purpose is to express emotion. As anyone who has experienced injustice and horrible tragedy can attest, anger is a common reaction. The victims of slavery, genocide, political oppression, and terror would all attest to the feelings that the Psalmist here expresses. To pretend such feelings and wishes don't arise in human beings is pious nonsense. To say that feeling them is wrong is itself an injustice against those who have suffered. Emotions simply are; how you behave is what is wrong or right. To ask that a loving and just God right our wrongs is preferable to taking it into our own hands, since we can trust God to judge rightly. His justice and vengeance are perfect in contrast to human efforts, which are often marred and can make things worse—or themselves be unjust.

*Break the teeth in their mouths, O God;*
*Lord, tear out the fangs of those lions!*
*Let them vanish like water that flows away;*
*when they draw the bow, let their arrows fall short.*
*May they be like a slug that melts away as it moves*
*along, like a stillborn child that never sees the sun.*
**Psalm 58:6–8**

## Chapters 59–60: **Commentary**

Psalm 60:5–12 and Psalm 108:6–13 are nearly identical. What differs between the two Psalms is their opening lines. Psalm 60 begins with a complaint, accusing God of having rejected the people of Israel. Psalm 108 begins with praise to God and describes his love and faithfulness. Psalm 60 has a superscription that describes the Psalm as a response to various battles against the Arameans and Edomites, as described in 2 Samuel 8–10. Psalm 108 does not describe any specific occasion for the Psalm.

The poetry and prayers of ancient Israel were reused and adapted to changing circumstances, much as traditional written prayers that are used today by Jews and Christians can be, and are, constantly modified and fitted to their current needs.

*Truly my soul finds rest in God;*
*my salvation comes from him.*
*Truly he is my rock and my salvation;*
*he is my fortress, I will never be shaken.*

**Psalm 62:1–2**

*Say to God, "How awesome are your deeds!*
*So great is your power*
*that your enemies cringe before you.*
*All the earth bows down to you;*
*they sing praise to you,*
*they sing the praises of your name."*
*Come and see what God has done,*
*his awesome deeds for mankind!*

**Psalm 66:3–5**

**God omnipotent**
*An image from a twelfth-century manuscript shows God standing on a snake and a lion to illustrate His power over his creation, as described in Psalm 65.*

God, deliver me from my enemies! I'm innocent. When you punish them, don't kill them. I want them to remember their crimes and know that God is in charge. I can rely on you.

Chapter **59**

You have rejected us, God. But now, please restore us, and save us from our enemies. Go out with our armies and fight. Give us victory against the enemies of Israel.

Chapter **60**

Hear my prayer. You're my refuge. Protect me. Protect the king. I will always praise you and I promise to fulfill all my vows to you.

Chapter **61**

I can rest secure in God, a rock that will never be shaken. My salvation and honor depend upon God and I know I can trust him. He is powerful and his love will never fail.

Chapter **62**

I earnestly seek God, like a thirsty person looking for water. I know I can rely on you and that you will overcome my enemies.

Chapter **63**

God, protect me from my enemies who plot injustice. I know you will destroy them and turn their evil plans against them. The righteous will rejoice and rest securely in you.

Chapter **64**

God, people will praise you in Zion, because you forgave us and answered our prayers. You provided us with what we need to live, giving us our water and food in abundance.

Chapter **65**

Israel should praise God for what he's done for them before. I will bring sacrifices to the Temple and fulfill my vows. Thank you for your forgiveness and for listening to my prayers.

Chapter **66**

| 1 | | 5 |
|---|---|---|

### Chapter 67

May God give us what we don't deserve and may the peoples of the world praise God. Give us what we need and bless us.

| 5 | | 9 | | 12 |
|---|---|---|---|---|

### Chapter 68

May God destroy his enemies. May the righteous rejoice. You care for the powerless. You will save us from all our troubles and bring us victory. Therefore, we praise you.

| 5 | | 12 |
|---|---|---|

### Chapter 69

Save me, God! My problems are overwhelming. You know I'm foolish and you know my guilt. Forgive and rescue me because you love me. My thanks are better than sacrifice.

| 5 | | 12 |
|---|---|---|

### Chapter 70

Hurry up and rescue me from those who are trying to harm me. May they suffer the harm instead. May all those who seek your help rejoice. Don't delay in rescuing me.

| 5 | | 12 |
|---|---|---|

### Chapter 71

I've depended upon you all my life. So don't abandon me now that I'm old. Save me from my enemies. I always have hope. I will tell everyone about your righteous acts.

| 5 | | 12 |
|---|---|---|

### Chapter 72

May the king be righteous and just. May he and his people prosper. May he deliver those who suffer and may he live a long time.

---

*You, God, know my folly;*
*my guilt is not hidden from you.*
*Lord, the Lord Almighty,*
*may those who hope in you*
*not be disgraced because of me;*
*God of Israel,*
*may those who seek you*
*not be put to shame because of me.*

**Psalm 69:5–6**

## Chapter 70: **Commentary**

Psalm 70 is almost identical to verses 13–17 of Psalm 40. The superscription describes this Psalm as a "petition" and both are identified as having been composed by David. Apparently a section of Psalm 40 was commonly used by the Jewish people as a prayer separate from the larger context of Psalm 40 since it was used in a different way from the longer Psalm.

---

*Do not cast me away when I am old;*
*do not forsake me when my strength is gone.*

**Psalm 71:9**

## Chapter 72: **Commentary**

The final verse of this Psalm records that "here concludes the prayers of David." But in fact, they don't. Psalm 143, for instance, is identified in the superscription as being by David; its first line begins, "Lord, hear my prayer..." This concluding line in Psalm 72, therefore, tells us something about the process of putting together the Book of Psalms as it currently appears in the Bible; this line was written before the rest of the Book of Psalms was included. Such construction marks in the Bible may make some people uncomfortable. But while believers affirm that the Bible is the word of God, they also affirm that the Bible was written by human beings. Thus, the word of God was put together by human beings, with all that goes into putting together any document: rewriting, editing, and copying. We should not be surprised by the evidence of people at work on the text. And it shouldn't make us think any less of the Bible, either.

**Sacrifice for sin**
*Regular sacrifices were performed for sin, but the author of Psalm 69 knows that his thanks are better than any sacrifice (Psalm 69:30–31).*

# Book III (Psalms 73–89)

**5** **18**

God is good to Israel, but it bothers me how the wicked prosper. It makes me wonder if there's any reason to be good. God, I trust you to give everyone what they deserve.

Chapter **73**

*O God, why have you rejected us forever?*
*Why does your anger smolder against the sheep of*
*your pasture?*
*Remember the nation you purchased long*
*ago, the people of your inheritance, whom you*
*redeemed—*
*Mount Zion, where you dwelt.*
*Turn your steps toward these everlasting ruins,*
*all this destruction the enemy has brought on*
*the sanctuary.*

**Psalm 74:1–3**

**4** **5** **12**

Why are you angry with us, God? We're suffering and there is no sign of you. How long will it be before you rescue us? You saved us in the past, so save us now.

Chapter **74**

**1** **5**

We praise you God, for all the wonderful things you've done; you judge the wicked in your own way, in your own time, in your own place, and exalt the righteous when you please.

Chapter **75**

## Chapters 75–77: **Commentary**

One of the reasons the Bible still speaks to people even after the passage of thousands of years is because, despite all the changes brought about by technology and culture, human beings remain mostly unchanged: the questions, the suffering, the nature of relationships, the problems we all face, and the questions we all ask ourselves are universal, no matter where we were born, where we grew up, or when. The author of this Psalm was suffering, he prayed, and nothing changed: neither his circumstances nor how he was feeling. If we are honest with ourselves, we must admit to facing similar circumstances during the course of our lives. How do we deal with prayer that doesn't seem to work? Some may lose their faith; others, like the author of this Psalm, instead chose to remember how God has worked in times past—both in the people of history and the Bible, as well as his or her experiences from earlier stages in his life.

**1** **5**

God is well known in Israel. His power is unassailable, his enemies are defeated, and the oppressed are rescued. Keep the promises you make to God. All should fear him.

Chapter **76**

**5** **12** **18**

When I asked God to solve my problems, nothing happened. No matter how much I prayed, I didn't feel any better. All I can do is remember how God rescued his people in times past.

Chapter **77**

*I cried out to God for help;*
*I cried out to God to hear me.*
*When I was in distress, I sought the Lord;*
*at night I stretched out untiring hands,*
*and I would not be comforted.*

**Psalm 77:1–2**

**When God is silent**
*The author of Psalm 77, illustrated by a young woman in prayer, asks for help from God. Even though nothing has changed and she feels no peace—she trusts God anyway.*

**Jerusalem destroyed**
*The destruction of Jerusalem traumatized the Ancient Israelites and forced them to become more faithful to Yahweh.*

| 3 | 5 | 9 |
|---|---|---|

Chapter
**78**

God gave his laws to prevent rebellion. Ephraim broke those laws so God judged them. But God chose Judah and picked David, who has led them with integrity.

| 5 | 12 |
|---|---|

Chapter
**79**

God, Jerusalem has been destroyed, your people slaughtered, and your Temple defiled. How long will you stay angry with us? Please rescue us and destroy our enemies.

*In spite of all this, they kept on sinning;*
*in spite of his wonders, they did not believe.*
*So he ended their days in futility*
*and their years in terror.*
*Whenever God slew them, they would seek him;*
*they eagerly turned to him again.*
*They remembered that God was their Rock,*
*that God Most High was their Redeemer.*

**Psalm 78:32–35**

| 5 | 12 |
|---|---|

Chapter
**80**

Restore us, God. How much longer will you be angry with us? Your land has been devastated. Rescue us and we will not turn from you.

| 1 | 5 |
|---|---|

Chapter
**81**

Sing praises to God. God rescued Israel from Egypt, warning them to worship him alone. But they didn't and so now he has judged them. If they repent, God will forgive.

*Sing for joy to God our strength;*
*shout aloud to the God of Jacob!*
*Begin the music, strike the timbrel,*
*play the melodious harp and lyre.*

**Psalm 81:1–2**

## Chapter 82: **Commentary**

In the New Testament Gospel of John (10:34), Jesus quotes from Psalm 82:6 as he defends himself against the charge of blasphemy for calling himself God. Jesus points out that this Psalm quotes God as calling the kings of the Ancient Near East "gods." If God could call kings divine, then what was blasphemous about Jesus calling himself God? Especially since he in fact was God?

When God calls the ancient kings "gods" he is being sarcastic. The Pharaoh of Egypt was supposed to be the incarnation of the sun-god Re. The king of Babylon was supposedly an incarnation of Marduk, while the later Roman Caesars were all worshiped as gods. But in Psalm 82, God points out that these kings are mere mortals and not gods at all (Psalm 82:6-7, Ezekiel 28:2, 9-10).

*"The 'gods' know nothing, they understand nothing.*
*They walk about in darkness;*
*all the foundations of the earth are shaken.*
*"I said, 'You are "gods";*
*you are all sons of the Most High.'*
*But you will die like mere mortals;*
*you will fall like every other ruler."*
**Psalm 82:5–7**

*Love and faithfulness meet together;*
*righteousness and peace kiss each other.*
**Psalm 85:10**

## Chapter 87: **Commentary**

The Psalmist argues that Yahweh is not the exclusive possession of the Israelites. He is also the God of Israel's enemies: the Philistines, the Babylonians and the Egyptians (Rahab is a poetic name for Egypt). And although Jerusalem—Zion—is the capital of the nation of Israel, it does not belong exclusively to Israel. It is the "city of God" (Psalm 87:3). Therefore, like God, it belongs to the world.

In the Ancient Near East, only the heretic king of Egypt, Akhenatan, and the Israelites are known to have believed in the universal dominion of God. Even for the Israelites, the recognition that God was the God of all humanity was not always recognized (Judges 11:21–24). It was a radical notion in a world that believed the gods were geographically limited (1 Kings 20:23, 28), with the wars between nations a reflection of the wars between the gods over territory. For instance, Sennacherib king of Assyria wrote to Hezekiah king of Israel, "Do you not know what I and my predecessors have done to all the peoples of the other lands? Were the gods of those nations ever able to deliver their land from my hand? Who of all the gods of these nations that my predecessors destroyed has been able to save his people from me? How then can your god deliver you from my hand?" (2 Chronicles 32:13–14).

**Chapter 82**

5 | 9

God presides over the kings of the world, kings who believe they are gods but are unjust. You're not really gods. You're just arrogant mortals who will die for your evil behavior.

**Chapter 83**

5 | 9 | 12

God, do something: your enemies are plotting to destroy Israel. Treat them like you've treated your enemies before. Let them know who you are: the only God over all the world.

**Chapter 84**

1 | 5

God, where you dwell is beautiful! How blessed are those who live there, and even those who only visit. A moment in Jerusalem is better than a lifetime anywhere else.

**Chapter 85**

5 | 10 | 12

You've forgiven your people before. Please forgive us once again. Don't be angry with us forever. Salvation is close to those who worship God. He will be good to the righteous.

**Chapter 86**

5 | 12

God, please answer me: my enemies are coming. But I am faithful to you, so give me joy and make me obedient. You are compassionate, merciful, and gracious. Destroy my enemies.

**Chapter 87**

1 | 5

The city of Zion belongs to God and God belongs to the whole world: to Egypt, Babylon, Philistia, Tyre, and Cush. They will all sing to God and be treated as if they were born in Zion.

**Chapter 88**

4 | 5 | 12

I am overwhelmed by my problems night and day. Why don't you do something, God? Can I praise you when I'm dead? Why have you rejected me? I'm all alone.

**Chapter 89**

5 | 10 | 12

God, your love is forever. You promised to always care for David and his descendants, but now you've punished him. How much longer before you rescue him and our nation?

# Book IV (Psalms 90–106)

**Moses on Mount Sinai**
*In Psalm 90, Moses asks God for compassion in the face of human frailty and sin, both his own and that of the people of Israel in the wilderness.*

| 5 | 18 |
|---|---|

## Chapter 90

You were God before the world existed but our lives are short and your punishment is heavy. Relent! How long before you forgive us? May your favor rest on us.

| 5 | 10 | 12 |
|---|---|---|

## Chapter 91

God will protect those that belong to him. If he is your refuge, then no harm can befall you. God will save us because we love him. He will answer our prayers.

| 1 | 5 | 18 |
|---|---|---|

## Chapter 92

It is good to praise Yahweh and make music to him. His acts are great: he blesses the righteous and judges the wicked. God's enemies perish, but the righteous flourish.

| 1 | 5 |
|---|---|

## Chapter 93

God reigns in power; he has existed forever. He is more powerful than the ocean waves. His laws are firmly established forever.

### Chapter 90: **Commentary**

The superscription attributes this Psalm to Moses, the only Psalm in fact that is attributed to him, though not the only poem in the Bible attributed to him. Exodus 15 includes a song that is attributed to Moses, a celebration of God rescuing Israel from Egypt and destroying Pharaoh's army in the Red Sea. Psalm 90 is a prayer to God. The phrase "a thousand years in your sight are like a day that has just gone by" is alluded to and paraphrased by the author of 2 Peter: "But do not forget this one thing, dear friends: With the Lord a day is like a thousand years, and a thousand years are like a day. The Lord is not slow in keeping his promise, as some understand slowness. Instead he is patient with you, not wanting anyone to perish, but everyone to come to repentance." (2 Peter 3:8–9).

*Before the mountains were born*
*or you brought forth the whole world,*
*from everlasting to everlasting you are God.*
*You turn people back to dust,*
*saying, "Return to dust, you mortals."*
*A thousand years in your sight*
*are like a day that has just gone by,*
*or like a watch in the night.*

**Psalm 90:2–4**

*You will not fear the terror of night,*
*nor the arrow that flies by day,*
*nor the pestilence that stalks in the darkness,*
*nor the plague that destroys at midday.*
*A thousand may fall at your side,*
*ten thousand at your right hand,*
*but it will not come near you.*

**Psalm 91:5–7**

*Blessed is the one you discipline, Lord,*
*the one you teach from your law;*
*you grant them relief from days of trouble,*
*till a pit is dug for the wicked.*

**Psalm 94:12–13**

## Chapter 95: **Commentary**

Psalm 95:7–8 is used by Hebrews 3:15 and 4:7:
"Today, if you hear his voice,
do not harden your hearts
as you did in the rebellion."
The author of Hebrews depends upon the ancient Greek translation of the Hebrew text. The Hebrew text has the word *Meribbah* which means "quarreling." The translator of the Greek text used the Greek word "rebellion." But most English translations of the Psalm do not translate the word since it is used as a place name. The incident that the Psalmist is referring to is described in Exodus 17:1–7.

*Shout for joy to the Lord, all the earth.*
*Worship the Lord with gladness;*
*come before him with joyful songs.*
*Know that the Lord is God.*
*It is he who made us, and we are his;*
*we are his people, the sheep of his pasture.*

**Psalm 100:1–3**

**The Ark of the Covenant**
*Yahweh was pictured as sitting enthroned between the cherubim on the Ark of the Covenant, which was kept in the Temple in the Most Holy Place (Psalm 99:1).*

| 5 | 10 | 12 |

Yahweh avenges. So how long will the wicked endure? God's discipline brings wisdom. God will judge the wicked and restore the righteous. I can take joy in God's unfailing love.

Chapter **94**

| 1 | 5 |

Come, let us sing for joy to Yahweh. He is greater than all gods; he made both land and sea. Worship him and obey him, unlike our ancestors who suffered for their disobedience.

Chapter **95**

| 1 | 5 |

Sing a new song to Yahweh. God is great and worthy of our praise. May the heavens, earth, and all creation rejoice before Yahweh who will judge the world in righteousness.

Chapter **96**

| 1 | 5 | 10 |

God is in control. His power is irresistible. May those who love Yahweh hate what is evil. God will protect the righteous, so rejoice in Yahweh and praise him.

Chapter **97**

| 1 | 5 | 10 |

Sing a new song to Yahweh. He has revealed himself to the world. He shows love and faithfulness to Israel. Shout for joy, all of creation. He will judge the world in righteousness.

Chapter **98**

| 1 | 5 | 10 |

Yahweh is in control. He is powerful, he loves justice. God spoke to his priests in the past and answered their prayers. God punishes and forgives. So worship God.

Chapter **99**

| 1 | 5 | 10 |

Shout for joy to Yahweh. He made us and we belong to him. He loves us forever and will always be good to us. There is much to be thankful for.

Chapter **100**

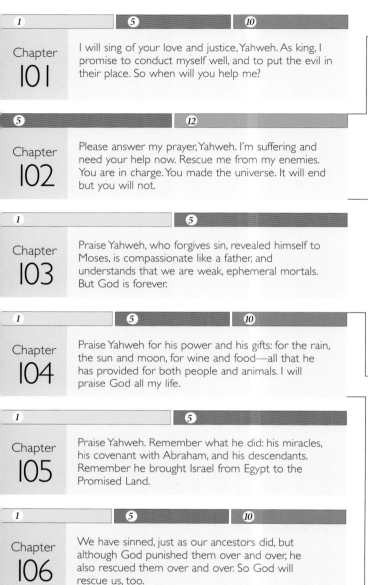

**Chapter 101**

I will sing of your love and justice, Yahweh. As king, I promise to conduct myself well, and to put the evil in their place. So when will you help me?

**Chapter 102**

Please answer my prayer, Yahweh. I'm suffering and need your help now. Rescue me from my enemies. You are in charge. You made the universe. It will end but you will not.

**Chapter 103**

Praise Yahweh, who forgives sin, revealed himself to Moses, is compassionate like a father, and understands that we are weak, ephemeral mortals. But God is forever.

**Chapter 104**

Praise Yahweh for his power and his gifts: for the rain, the sun and moon, for wine and food—all that he has provided for both people and animals. I will praise God all my life.

**Chapter 105**

Praise Yahweh. Remember what he did: his miracles, his covenant with Abraham, and his descendants. Remember he brought Israel from Egypt to the Promised Land.

**Chapter 106**

We have sinned, just as our ancestors did, but although God punished them over and over, he also rescued them over and over. So God will rescue us, too.

## Chapter 102: **Commentary**

The author of Hebrews quotes Psalm 102:25–27 in Hebrews 1:10–12 and ascribes it to Jesus, making Jesus the creator of the universe. The author of the Psalm indicates that while God will endure forever, the universe will not. The Psalmist views God as being separate from the universe he created, a concept inherent in the word used commonly in the Bible to describe God. He is said to be "holy." The Hebrew word's basic meaning is simply "separate," a description both of God's separateness as compared to the world, and the condition of those people and items that become dedicated to God's use.

*In the beginning you laid the foundations of the earth, and the heavens are the work of your hands.*
*They will perish, but you remain;*
*they will all wear out like a garment.*
*Like clothing you will change them*
*and they will be discarded.*
*But you remain the same,*
*and your years will never end.*

**Psalm 102:25–27**

## Chapter 104: **Commentary**

The concept that drinking alcohol is wrong has become common in many branches of Protestant Christianity, especially in the United States. This expressed itself in the temperance movement of the late nineteenth and early twentieth centuries and resulted in the short-lived Eighteenth Amendment to the U.S. Constitution that prohibited the sale and consumption of alcohol from 1920 to 1933. In contrast, the Bible does not view the consumption of alcohol as necessarily evil. Psalm 104 is a Psalm of thanksgiving for a variety of good things that God has given humanity, including, in verse 15, "wine that gladdens human hearts." The Hebrew word for wine, *yayin*, is actually one of the few Hebrew words cognate with an English word.

*He makes grass grow for the cattle,*
*and plants for people to cultivate—*
*bringing forth food from the earth:*
*wine that gladdens human hearts,*
*oil to make their faces shine,*
*and bread that sustains their hearts.*

**Psalm 104:14–15**

**Like a bird alone**
*This illustration from a page of an ancient, handwritten psaltar appears in Psalm 102, where the psalmist compares himself to birds that are alone and in distress.*

Renouabi

EN

anim

&om

intra

nom

Bene

mea

oblu

retr

Qui

oĩbʒ

qui ʃanac omſ infirmitateſ t̃

Qui redimit de interitu uitam

q coronat te inmiʃedia ɤ mĩ

**Mighty works of God**
*The Psalmist recounts all of God's mighty works on behalf of the Israelites, including rescuing them from Egypt.*

*Let them give thanks to the Lord for his unfailing love and his wonderful deeds for mankind, for he satisfies the thirsty and fills the hungry with good things.*
**Psalm 107:8–9**

| 1 | 5 | 18 |
|---|---|---|

### Chapter 107
Give thanks to Yahweh. Those God has rescued have many stories about how bad things were before he rescued them. God is good, merciful, and he forgives.

| 1 | 5 | 9 |
|---|---|---|

### Chapter 108
I will praise God with music. May God's glory cover the earth. May he save us from our enemy Edom and grant us victory.

| 5 | 9 | 12 |
|---|---|---|

### Chapter 109
God, please don't remain silent. Instead, curse my enemy. May he suffer horribly for all the bad things he ever did to me and for all his other evil deeds.

| 5 | 9 |
|---|---|

### Chapter 110
Yahweh told the king that he would make his enemies his footstool. He announced that the king is a priest like Melchizedek. God will use the king to judge the nations.

| 1 | 5 |
|---|---|

### Chapter 111
Praise Yahweh! His works are great. He is compassionate and takes care of his people. God's laws are permanently established. Fearing God is the beginning of wisdom.

| 1 | 5 |
|---|---|

### Chapter 112
Praise Yahweh! The children of those who worship God will become powerful and prosperous. The righteous will never be afraid of bad news. But the wicked will suffer.

## Chapter 108: **Commentary**

Psalm 108 is constructed from the parts of two other Psalms. 108:1–5 is nearly identical to Psalm 57:7–11 while Psalm 108:6–13 is nearly identical to Psalm 60:5–12. There are some differences, but it illustrates how earlier materials could be and were reworked and reused. As to which of the three Psalms came first—57, 60, or 108—there is no way of telling.

## Chapter 110: **Commentary**

Melchizedek, mentioned in verse 4 of Psalm 110, appears in only three books in the Bible. He is first mentioned in Genesis 14:18–20 when he meets Abram, who gives him a tenth of the spoils from a battle. Psalm 110 is the second occurrence. Melchizedek will appear again in the New Testament Book of Hebrews, when the author explains that Jesus is a priest like Melchizedek (Hebrews 6:16–7:28).

In context, Psalm 110 was probably composed for the purpose of celebrating the coronation of a king. Yahweh has chosen him and he promises that the king will be victorious against his enemies. The Psalm is attributed to David. Jesus suggests that Psalm 110 is talking about the Messiah in Matthew 22:42–45. The apostle Peter applies 110 to Jesus in Acts 2:34. Paul applies it to Jesus in 1 Corinthians 15:25, as does the unknown author of Hebrews in Hebrews 1:13. Paul probably is alluding to the Psalm in Ephesians 1:20–22 and Philippians 2:9–11, as is the author of Hebrews in Hebrews 10:12–13.

## Chapters 111–112: **Commentary**

Psalms 111 and 112 are examples of acrostic poems. Each line of these Psalms, following the opening word "hallelujah" (translated as "praise the Lord"), begins with a successive letter of the Hebrew alphabet. So, the line in Psalm 111:1 "I will extol the Lord with all my heart" begins with the first letter of the Hebrew alphabet, *aleph*, while the next line begins with the second letter, *beth*, and so on. There are no translations in English that preserve the acrostic format of the poems. Similar acrostics occur a few other times in the Bible, in Psalms 25, 34, 37, 119, 145, Proverbs 31:1–31, and Lamentations 1, 2, and 4.

*He raises the poor from the dust*
*and lifts the needy from the ash heap;*
*he seats them with princes,*
*with the princes of his people.*
*He settles the childless woman in her home*
*as a happy mother of children.*

**Psalm 113:7–9**

*But their idols are silver and gold,*
*made by human hands.*
*They have mouths, but cannot speak,*
*eyes, but cannot see.*
*They have ears, but cannot hear,*
*noses, but cannot smell.*
*They have hands, but cannot feel,*
*feet, but cannot walk,*
*nor can they utter a sound with their throats.*
*Those who make them will be like them,*
*and so will all who trust in them.*

**Psalm 115:4–8**

## Chapter 119: **Commentary**

Psalm 119 is the most extensive example of the use of an acrostic in the Bible. It is the longest Psalm in the Book of Psalms and it is also the longest chapter in the whole Bible. It is divided into 22 sections, each labeled with one of the 22 letters of the Hebrew language. Each line in that section begins with that letter of the Hebrew alphabet.

*I am your servant; give me discernment*
*that I may understand your statutes.*
*It is time for you to act, Lord;*
*your law is being broken.*
*Because I love your commands*
*more than gold, more than pure gold,*
*and because I consider all your precepts right,*
*I hate every wrong path.*

**Psalm 119:125–128**

## Chapter 120: **Commentary**

The 15 Psalms, 120–134, are called the "Psalms of ascent." According to tradition, they were recited by pilgrims as they went up to Jerusalem on pilgrimage to sacrifice to God. Travel to Jerusalem is always described as "going up" because Jerusalem is in the mountains and so no matter where a pilgrim originated, their journey to Jerusalem was always an uphill climb.

---

**1**     **5**

Praise Yahweh! May Yahweh be praised forever and everywhere. No one is like Yahweh. He cares for the powerless and rescues those who are suffering.

**Chapter 113**

**1**     **5**

When Israel came from Egypt, the waters of the Red Sea and the Jordan River fled. Why? Because God made them flee, just as he brought water from the rocks in the wilderness.

**Chapter 114**

**1**     **5**     **10**

Praise Yahweh for his love and faithfulness. The nations around Israel worship powerless idols. But Israel worships Yahweh, who is powerful and who will rescue us.

**Chapter 115**

**1**     **5**

I love Yahweh because he answered my prayer and rescued me from my problems. I will praise him forever, thank him, and fulfill my vows.

**Chapter 116**

**1**     **5**     **10**

All the people on Earth should praise Yahweh for his great love and everlasting faithfulness.

**Chapter 117**

**1**     **5**     **10**

Give thanks to Yahweh because he is good and his love lasts forever. When I was suffering and prayed to God, he answered my prayer and rescued me.

**Chapter 118**

**3**     **5**     **14**

Those who keep God's laws will be blessed; those who don't will suffer the consequences of their folly. God's laws are perfect and wonderful. They make our lives good.

**Chapter 119**

**5**     **12**

Yahweh, please rescue me from those who are deceitful. Rescue me from those who hate peace and prefer war.

**Chapter 120**

**Chapter 121**

**1** **5**

My help comes from Yahweh, who made the universe. He watches over Israel and he watches over you to protect you from all harm, forever.

**Chapter 122**

**1** **5** **12**

I was happy when I learned we were going to God's house. And now we're here! May there always be peace in Jerusalem. I will pray for its security and prosperity.

**Chapter 123**

**5** **12**

As slaves look to their master, so we look to God, waiting for him to show us mercy. We've endured contempt for long enough.

**Chapter 124**

**1** **5**

If Yahweh hadn't been on our side we'd have been destroyed. Praise Yahweh for rescuing us. He is the one who made the universe.

**Chapter 125**

**1** **5** **12**

Those who trust Yahweh are as secure as the mountain on which Jerusalem sits. May Yahweh do good to those who do good, and punish the evil as they deserve.

**Chapter 126**

**1** **5**

When Yahweh restored our fortunes, it was like we were dreaming. We were so happy! Those who go out sowing seed with tears will reap a harvest with joy.

**Chapter 127**

**1** **5**

Unless Yahweh is involved in the building of a house or watching over it, it's a waste of time. Having many children is a gift from Yahweh that blesses and protects a person.

**Chapter 128**

**1** **5**

Those who obey Yahweh are blessed by him: their work and families prosper. So may Jerusalem be blessed by Yahweh and may Israel know peace.

*I lift up my eyes to the mountains—*
*where does my help come from?*
*My help comes from the Lord,*
*the Maker of heaven and earth.*

**Psalm 121:1–2**

*When the Lord restored the fortunes of Zion,*
*we were like those who dreamed.*
*Our mouths were filled with laughter,*
*our tongues with songs of joy.*
*Then it was said among the nations,*
*"The Lord has done great things for them."*

**Psalm 126:1–2**

**Worshiping Yahweh**
*The Ancient Jewish people made regular pilgrimages to Jerusalem in order to sacrifice and worship Yahweh in his Temple.*

| 1 | 5 | 9 |
|---|---|---|

Israel has long suffered oppression, but Yahweh has granted her victory. May those who hate Israel suffer and never be blessed by Yahweh.

Chapter
129

*If you, Lord, kept a record of sins,*
*Lord, who could stand?*
*But with you there is forgiveness,*
*so that we can, with reverence, serve you.*
**Psalm 130:3–4**

| 5 | 10 | 12 |
|---|---|---|

Answer my prayer. God forgives. I'm waiting for you and put my hope in you. Israel can be confident because God's love never fails. Yahweh will rescue his people.

Chapter
130

| 5 | 18 |
|---|---|

I'm not arrogant, I don't concern myself with great matters. My ambition is small, like that of a child. Israel can forever hope in Yahweh.

Chapter
131

*I know that the Lord is great,*
*that our Lord is greater than all gods.*
*The Lord does whatever pleases him,*
*in the heavens and on the earth,*
*in the seas and all their depths.*
*He makes clouds rise from the ends of the earth;*
*he sends lightning with the rain*
*and brings out the wind from his storehouses.*
**Psalm 135:5–7**

| 5 | 12 |
|---|---|

Remember all that David suffered, all his promises, so that Yahweh's Temple could be built. For David's sake, therefore, do not reject Israel's king. Bless Israel and its king.

Chapter
132

| 1 | 5 |
|---|---|

It is wonderful if people can live together in harmony. That is when Yahweh has given his blessing.

Chapter
133

## Chapter 136: **Commentary**

Psalm 136 is a hymn of praise to Yahweh for creating the universe and for saving and protecting the Israelites. It was designed for public worship, probably during the celebration of one of the annual Jewish festivals. Many commentators suspect it was used during Passover and it is so used today. It is referred to as the "Great Hallel." *Hallel*, the beginning of the word "hallelujah," is a Hebrew word that means "praise." The second half of each verse, "his love endures forever," would have been spoken or sung by the congregation in response to the first half of the verse, probably spoken or sung by a priest or choir.

The word translated "love" in the second half of each verse is a word that is used within the context of a covenant or contractual relationship. It describes the obligations and duties of those bound by such a contract, such as the contract that bound Israel to God as his vassal.

| 1 | 5 |
|---|---|

May all those who work in the Temple during the night praise Yahweh. And may Yahweh, the creator of the universe, bless you.

Chapter
134

| 1 | 5 |
|---|---|

Yahweh rescued Israel from its enemies in Egypt, in the wilderness, and in the Promised Land. Yahweh is real and powerful, but idols are powerless, manmade trinkets.

Chapter
135

| 1 | 5 | 10 |
|---|---|---|

Give Yahweh thanks for his power, for his victories over Israel's enemies, from the Pharaoh in Egypt to Sihon and Og. Yahweh's love endures forever.

Chapter
136

## Chapter 137: **Commentary**

The Psalm is anonymous, but the setting is clear from the opening line. It is a lament expressing the sorrow of those taken into exile by the Babylonians around 586 BC. Besides expressing sorrow, however, the Psalm also asks God to avenge his people. The author of the Psalm is hoping that what the Babylonians did to the Israelites would be done to them, as expressed in the horrific request that infants be dashed against rocks (verse 9). In the ancient world, it was not uncommon for armies to slaughter the children, especially the male children, of their conquered enemies (see 2 Kings 8:12, Nehemiah 3:10, Isaiah 13:16, and Hosea 13:16). This was considered a practical way to reduce the numbers of future rebels and vengeance seekers.

**4** **5** **9**

### Chapter 137

During our exile in Babylon we wept while our conquerors tried to make us sing for them. Yahweh, remember what they did to us. Destroy them like they have destroyed us.

*If I forget you, Jerusalem,*
*may my right hand forget its skill.*
*May my tongue cling to the roof of my mouth*
*if I do not remember you,*
*if I do not consider Jerusalem*
*my highest joy.*

**Psalm 137:5–6**

**1** **5**

### Chapter 138

I will praise you, Yahweh. May all the kings of the earth praise you. Though you are high and mighty, you care about the lowly. Rescue me from my troubles and vindicate me.

**1** **5**

### Chapter 139

Yahweh, you are all powerful, all knowing, and there's nowhere I can hide from you. You created me and know everything about me. Destroy the wicked. Wash away my sin.

## Chapter 139: **Commentary**

The author describes the power and knowledge of God as being essentially unlimited. Theologians use the words of this Psalm to formulate their concepts of God as "all knowing" (Psalm 139:1–6) and "present everywhere" (Psalm 139:7–12). The concept of God controlling everything, of being "all powerful" also grows from the wording of this Psalm, specifically verse 16: "All the days ordained for me were written in your book before one of them came to be" which seem to argue that God has decided ahead of time what will happen in an individual's life.

However, the point of the Psalm is one of comfort, rather than to suggest that human beings lack free will or that the world is controlled by fate. The Psalmist's purpose is to demonstrate that God is in control even when everything seems out of control. The Psalmist concludes with a prayer that God will overthrow those responsible for the Psalmist's current suffering.

**1** **5** **12**

### Chapter 140

Rescue me from my enemies who are plotting against me. Protect me. I know you give the poor justice. Surely the righteous will praise you.

**5** **12**

### Chapter 141

Answer my prayer quickly. Keep me from sin. I know the wicked will perish, but I'm looking to you to rescue me from my enemies. May my enemies suffer instead of me.

**1** **5** **12**

### Chapter 142

Yahweh, I need mercy. I'm in desperate trouble. Please listen to me and rescue me from my enemies. Then the righteous will praise you because you've been good to me.

*Listen to my cry,*
*for I am in desperate need;*
*rescue me from those who pursue me,*
*for they are too strong for me.*
*Set me free from my prison,*
*that I may praise your name.*
*Then the righteous will gather about me*
*because of your goodness to me.*

**Psalm 142:6–7**

**5** **12**

### Chapter 143

I depend upon your righteousness and faithfulness to bring me relief. I'm suffering. Answer my prayer quickly. Rescue me from my enemies. Teach me to do your will.

*Great is the Lord and most worthy of praise;*
*his greatness no one can fathom.*
*One generation commends your works to another;*
*they tell of your mighty acts.*
*They speak of the glorious splendor of your*
*majesty—and I will meditate on your*
*wonderful works.*

**Psalm 145:3–5**

*Do not put your trust in princes,*
*in human beings, who cannot save.*
*When their spirit departs, they return to the*
*ground;*
*on that very day their plans come to nothing.*
*Blessed are those whose help is the God of Jacob,*
*whose hope is in the Lord their God.*

**Psalm 146:3–5**

*He has revealed his word to Jacob,*
*his laws and decrees to Israel.*
*He has done this for no other nation;*
*they do not know his laws.*

**Psalm 147:19–20**

*Let everything that has breath praise the Lord.*
*Praise the Lord.*

**Psalm 150:6**

| 1 | 5 | 18 |

Praise Yahweh who helps me train for war. You are loving and kind; why do you even care about ephemeral humans? Rescue me from my enemies. Then I will praise you.

Chapter
144

| 1 | 5 |

Yahweh, you should be praised for your power, love, and compassion. You exist forever and forever keep your promises. You take care of those who put their trust in you.

Chapter
145

| 1 | 5 |

Praise Yahweh and trust him, rather than humans who will soon die. Yahweh made the universe. He takes care of the oppressed and powerless. He feeds the hungry.

Chapter
146

| 1 | 5 | 18 |

Praise Yahweh who restored the fortunes of the Israelites after their exile. He brings the rain and provides food for all. Only to Israel has Yahweh revealed his law.

Chapter
147

| 1 | 5 |

May everyone and everything in heaven and everyone and everything on earth praise Yahweh. Yahweh has restored his people.

Chapter
148

| 1 | 5 | 9 |

Praise Yahweh with a new song. Let Israel praise him with music and dance. May their praise of Yahweh inflict vengeance on their enemies.

Chapter
149

| 1 | 5 |

Praise Yahweh for his power and his greatness with music and dancing. May everything that breathes praise Yahweh.

Chapter
150

**Free at last**
*In Psalm 142 David asks God to set him free from the prison of his problems, suffering, fear, and worry.*

# Proverbs

## Overview

The English title of the book is simply the translation of the Hebrew title, *Mishle Shlomo*—Proverbs of Solomon. The Book of Proverbs is a collection of wise sayings that give general guidance for a life well-lived.

The primary function of the Book of Proverbs is to instruct youth. The recurrent phrase "my son" (which is typical of all Ancient Near Eastern wisdom literature) points to this purpose. Youth is warned against the adulteress, to hold his tongue, to pay diligent attention to wisdom's teachings, to deal honestly with his fellow human beings, and to avoid association with the wicked.

There are approximately 375 proverbs written down in Proverbs 10:1–22:16. 1 Kings 4:32 indicates that Solomon spoke over 3,000 proverbs. Therefore, it is obvious that not all of his proverbs have been preserved. The current Book of Proverbs is obviously a composite work. Its current form is the result of the activities of later editors.

**King Solomon**
*King Solomon, noted for his wisdom, is the traditional author of the Book of Proverbs.*

## Chapter 1: **Commentary**

Proverbs 1:10–19 is a good illustration of a common structure that appears in Hebrew literature and storytelling. While we may be accustomed to telling stories in chronological order, chronology is not always so important for the biblical narrative. In Hebrew, thematic elements sometimes become more important. The opening line or two in a story will often be a summary of what is then explained in greater detail in the paragraphs that follow. Such is what happens here in Proverbs 1:10–19. Verse 10, line one says, "My son, if sinners entice" (1:10a). Verses 11–14 then expound on how sinners might entice. Verse 10, line two says "do not go" (1:10b). Verses 15–19 explain in detail why one should not go with sinners. This same structuring technique can be found throughout the Bible.

| 3 | 5 | 18 |
|---|---|---|

**Chapter**

**1**

The purpose of the Proverbs is to make people wise. Don't listen to those who entice you to do wrong. Instead, listen to wisdom, which offers you a long and happy life. Don't be a fool.

The date for when the book was put into its current form is unknown, though most scholars assume a date long after the time of Solomon, perhaps during or following the Babylonian exile.

Proverbs 1:1–24:22 is attributed to Solomon, who was king of Israel during the second third of the tenth century BC.

Proverbs 24:23–34 are attributed to "the Wise."

Proverbs 25:1–29:27 are Solomon's, but they were collected and recorded by "Hezekiah's men." Hezekiah was king of Judah from 727–698 BC.

Proverbs 30:1–33 are attributed to Agur, who is otherwise unknown in scripture.

Proverbs 31:1–31 are attributed to Lemuel, also unknown elsewhere in scripture.

Proverbs are poetic, so they follow the pattern of the Psalms, with the lines either repeating synonymous phrases, or as is more common for the Proverbs, stating the opposite of the previous line.

**The value of wisdom**

*Wisdom is presented in Book of Proverbs as the most valuable thing a person can obtain. The author personifies it as a woman who offers help and hope to the young.*

## Chapters 2–3: **Commentary**

The author of Proverbs describes wisdom as so valuable as to be worth whatever price one might have to pay for it. He stresses wisdom's origin in God. He explains that God used wisdom as a tool in creating the universe. The author of Proverbs does not suggest that wisdom prevents all problems or guarantees prosperity. The Proverbs are not promises. Instead, they are rules of thumb. Wisdom gives people their best chance for a good life, barring the unfortunate accidents that can come to anyone. He contrasts the advantage of being wise with the almost certain disastrous consequences of folly. While the wise person maximizes the chances of a good life, the fool is doomed to nearly certain misery. Good choices and bad choices are their own rewards.

*Trust in the Lord with all your heart*
*and lean not on your own understanding;*
*in all your ways submit to him,*
*and he will make your paths straight.*

**Proverbs 3:5–6**

| 3 | 5 | 18 |
|---|---|---|

If you follow the way of wisdom, you'll know to do what's right, instead of what's wrong. Choosing wisdom will protect you from many easily avoidable problems.

Chapter
2

| 3 | 5 | 18 |
|---|---|---|

The way of wisdom will prolong your life and grant you peace and prosperity. God used wisdom to make the universe, so don't lose sight of wisdom. Wisdom will protect you.

Chapter
3

| 3 | 5 | 18 |
|---|---|---|

Wisdom is valuable: it's worth whatever you have to pay to get. Be wise and be righteous. Don't be foolish and wicked. Wisdom is the road to life; folly is the road to death.

Chapter
4

| 3 | 5 | 18 |
|---|---|---|

Wisdom will protect you from adultery; adultery may seem like fun at first, but in the end, it only leads to embarrassment and loss. Adultery will destroy your life.

Chapter
5

| 3 | 5 | 18 |
|---|---|---|

### Chapter 6

Don't be foolish. Work hard, like the ant. Don't be lazy. People will forgive someone who steals bread because they're starving. An adulterer will forever be disgraced.

| 3 | 5 | 18 |
|---|---|---|

### Chapter 7

Be wise. Avoid the fate of the foolish young man I saw having an affair with a married woman. He wasn't the first one she seduced. And the affair destroyed him.

| 3 | 5 | 18 |
|---|---|---|

### Chapter 8

Wisdom is offering to help you. God created wisdom before he made anything else, and it was by wisdom that he created the universe. So listen to wisdom.

**Solomon's judgments**
*Solomon, the traditional author of Proverbs, was well-known for his wisdom and learning and for rendering enlightened judgments.*

| 3 | 5 | 18 |
|---|---|---|

### Chapter 9

Wisdom may be more difficult at first, but it offers genuine security and joy. Folly claims to offer a shortcut to security and joy, but the ways of folly really lead only to death.

| 5 | 18 |
|---|---|

### Chapter 10

Wise children are a joy to their parents, but foolish ones bring them grief. Wisdom brings wealth, but folly brings poverty. Trouble destroys the foolish, but the wise will survive.

*How long will you lie there, you sluggard?*
*When will you get up from your sleep?*
*A little sleep, a little slumber,*
*a little folding of the hands to rest—*
*and poverty will come on you like a thief*
*and scarcity like an armed man.*

**Proverbs 6:6–11**

## Chapter 8: **Commentary**

Hebrew assigns one of two genders to every noun, either masculine or feminine. There is no neuter in Hebrew. The Hebrew words for "wisdom" and "folly" both happen to be feminine. Therefore, it is quite natural for the author of Hebrews to personify them both as women. When they speak in the first person, they describe their accomplishments and call out to the crowds, competing as if they were merchants selling trinkets.

*I was there when he set the heavens in place,*
*when he marked out the horizon on the face of the*
*deep, when he established the clouds above*
*and fixed securely the fountains of the deep,*
*when he gave the sea its boundary*
*so the waters would not overstep his command,*
*and when he marked out the foundations of the*
*earth. Then I was constantly at his side.*
*I was filled with delight day after day,*
*rejoicing always in his presence,*
*rejoicing in his whole world*
*and delighting in mankind.*

**Proverbs 8:27–31**

## Chapters 9–10: **Commentary**

The first nine chapters of the Book of Proverbs serve as an introduction to the actual Proverbs that make up the bulk of the book, which do not seem to have been organized in any thematic way.

In studying the various Proverbs, their overall cultural and religious context must be considered. The author of Proverbs was writing in the context of the relationship the people of Israel had with God. Israel is God's vassal, according to their formal, ratified treaty. The nation is bound to certain objective requirements, with specific blessings or punishments the consequence of their performance. The blessings and cursings as described in the treaty document, the Book of Deuteronomy (see Deuteronomy 28, page 49) are guarantees to the nation as a whole, not to individuals. The Proverbs are not necessarily universal. Instead, they are specific to the people of Israel in their time and place.

*Whoever spares the rod hates their children,*
*but the one who loves their children is careful*
*to discipline them.*

**Proverbs 13:24**

*Each heart knows its own bitterness,*
*and no one else can share its joy.*

**Proverbs 14:10**

*The simple believe anything,*
*but the prudent give thought to their steps.*

**Proverbs 14:15**

*A gentle answer turns away wrath,*
*but a harsh word stirs up anger.*

**Proverbs 15:1**

## Chapter 16: Commentary

Do human beings have free will or are their lives predestined? In the Bible, God appears powerful and in complete control of all that happens. He is able to predict the future with certainty, turning events precisely as he desires. But human beings are held responsible for their actions and are frequently told to make choices. Proverbs 16:9 suggests that God's power is expressed through the free actions of human beings. God is powerful, but he has chosen for people to be free.

*In their hearts humans plan their course,*
*but the Lord establishes their steps.*

**Proverbs 16:9**

*Better to meet a bear robbed of her cubs*
*than a fool bent on folly.*

**Proverbs 17:12**

*A friend loves at all times,*
*and a brother is born for a time of adversity.*

**Proverbs 17:17**

**5** **18**

Pride leads to disgrace, but humility brings wisdom. The righteous survive problems. Gossip is destructive. Both nations and individuals depend upon wisdom for their survival.

Chapter 11

**5** **18**

Discipline may seem unpleasant, but in the end, discipline is what will make you successful. For the best life, watch your tongue, persevere, work hard, and be honest.

Chapter 12

**5** **18**

Spend time with the wise and you'll start to become wise; spend time with fools and you'll start to become foolish. Trouble is the lot of those who are wicked and stupid.

Chapter 13

**5** **18**

Simple-minded people believe everything they hear; those who are wise are a bit more discerning. Be careful. Consider the potential consequences of the choices you make.

Chapter 14

**5** **18**

Speak kindly, rather than harshly if you want to fix problems. Think about what's most likely to be effective long term, rather than what feels good in the moment.

Chapter 15

**5** **18**

God is the only one really in control. People may think their motives are pure, they may believe they're doing the right thing, but most of the time they're just fooling themselves.

Chapter 16

**5** **18**

It's better to be poor and at peace, than wealthy and facing strife. And it's better to face an angry mother bear than to spend time with a fool. A real friend will always love you.

Chapter 17

**5** — **18**

## Chapter 18

Fools don't really care about the facts, they just want to win the argument. Get all the facts before deciding what to do. Find and hold onto your real friends.

**5** — **18**

## Chapter 19

If you are careful, work hard, watch your tongue, and in general practice good self-control, you'll live longer and be more successful than those who don't.

**5** — **18**

## Chapter 20

Don't lose your temper, don't be lazy. Be respectful of those with power on their side. Let God avenge you, don't do it yourself. Plan for the future carefully.

**5** — **18**

## Chapter 21

You're better off doing the right thing to begin with than having to ask for forgiveness later. Justice brings joy to the righteous, even as it terrorizes the wicked.

**5** — **18**

## Chapter 22

Your reputation is a precious thing, worth more than any other possession. What people first learn to do is what they will tend to keep on doing ever after. Discipline is important.

**5** — **18**

## Chapter 23

Watch yourself around those with power. Don't make wealth your priority. Avoid fools. Discipline your children. Obey your parents. Don't get drunk all the time.

**5** — **18**

## Chapter 24

Don't envy the wicked and foolish. In the end, you'll be better off with wisdom. Don't let your problems get the best of you. Help those you see struggling. God is in control.

## Chapter 19: **Commentary**

That God is powerful and in control does not mean that it is his fault when you do something stupid. In fact, God has given human beings the ability, as the Book of Proverbs indicates clearly, to make either good or bad choices. When life goes badly because of the bad choices a person makes, it is not uncommon for him or her to blame God. Shifting the blame, rather than taking responsibility for their actions, is a common human failing. Proverbs 19:3 is a clear expression of that experience.

*Who can say, "I have kept my heart pure;*
*I am clean and without sin"?*
**Proverbs 20:9**

## Chapter 22: **Commentary**

It has been common among some Christians to read Proverbs 22:6 as a promise from God that means that while one's children may turn away from the right path and disappoint us, sooner or later, "when they are old" they will return to the path that we taught them.

But in point of fact, that is not at all what the verse is talking about. First, the Proverbs are not promises. Second, Proverbs 22:6 is merely stating the obvious: children tend to grow up to be the people they were taught to be by their caregivers.

*Start children off on the way they should go, and*
*even when they are old they will not turn from it.*
**Proverbs 22:6**

## Chapters 23–24: **Commentary**

Although it is human nature to be happy when an enemy falls, it is not God's nature. God is never happy when the wicked suffer or die. He'd much rather see them change for the better than see them suffer destruction. God is more interested in granting mercy and forgiveness than punishment. It is in the redemption of enemies that God rejoices, rather than in their destruction (see Ezekiel 18:23 and 33:11, for example). God does not rejoice in the destruction of the wicked; he doesn't want people to do it either.

*Do not gloat when your enemy falls; when they*
*stumble, do not let your heart rejoice, or the Lord*
*will see and disapprove and turn his wrath away*
*from them.*
**Proverbs 24:17–18**

## Chapter 26: **Commentary**

On the surface, verses 4 and 5 of Proverbs 26 may seem to contradict each other, since one verse tells the reader to answer fools according to their folly while the one right after instructs the reader not to. But in the course of reading the Book of Proverbs, it becomes clear that fools are best avoided, since they are nothing but trouble for those around them (Proverbs 17:12). Thus, the two verses together make a simple point: no matter how one responds to fools, it's not going to work out well for them or anyone else. Nothing good can come from any interaction with a fool.

*The righteous detest the dishonest;*
*the wicked detest the upright.*

**Proverbs 29:27**

## Chapter 30: **Commentary**

The attributed author of this chapter of Proverbs, Agur, is otherwise unknown, appearing only here in the Bible. The first verse of the passage is also problematic, with many proposed translations and no consensus as yet in the scholarly community. Some translate "I can prevail" as a name, Ucal. Others, take Ithiel not as a name, but as the phrase "with God." Others have suggested that "to Ithiel," with a few alterations in the vowels, can better be translated as "there is no God" with what follows then being a commentary on the flawed concept of atheism that the Bible elsewhere describes as foolish (see Psalm 53:1 and 14:1)

## Chapter 31: **Commentary**

King Lemuel is otherwise unknown but for his mention here. The "woman of virtue" or "noble character" is described as a rarity to be treasured, much as wisdom at the beginning of the Book of Proverbs is described as a treasure. The word that is translated as "virtuous" or "of noble character" in this passage is never elsewhere translated that way. Instead, it is usually translated as either "powerful" or as "army" (see Exodus 14:28 and Joshua 1:14 as examples). It is only when it is applied to women that the translators of the Bible, mostly men, have softened it to "virtuous."

In fact, the wife of Proverbs 31 is a powerful woman. She is wise, strong-willed, and able to accomplish great things on her own. In a society that tended to be patriarchal, where the status of women—though better than in the rest of the Ancient Near East—was still low by modern standards, this wife stands out as remarkable. She is praised and worth emulating.

---

**5** — **18**

The ways of kings and the powerful are hard to predict. Be circumspect, speak softly and respectfully, and don't visit them too frequently. Be kind to your enemies.

Chapter **25**

**5** — **18**

Fools are trouble, so stay away from them if you can. The lazy will find any excuse to avoid work. Gossip is destructive. Beware of flattery.

Chapter **26**

**5** — **18**

You don't know the future, so be careful about boasting about what hasn't happened yet. Let other people praise you, but don't let it go to your head. Be loyal. Be careful out there.

Chapter **27**

**5** — **18**

Being foolish and wicked is a punishment in itself. Wisdom and righteousness can be its own reward. Guilt is a neverending torment.

Chapter **28**

**5** — **18**

Wisdom will bring joy and prosperity, but folly will bring sorrow and destruction. Accept correction and become better for it. Hold your temper. Discipline your children.

Chapter **29**

**5** — **18**

It's best to be neither too poor nor too rich. Besides, you'll never be fully satisfied. You'll always want something more. Only God fully satisfies.

Chapter **30**

**5** — **18**

Kings shouldn't get drunk. A powerful woman is a rarity that will make the man who finds her happier than any other man. She'll create prosperity for herself and for her family.

Chapter **31**

# Ecclesiastes

## Overview

The title of the Book of Ecclesiastes comes from the Septuagint, the Greek translation of the Hebrew Old Testament. The word "Ecclesiastes" is an attempt to translate the Hebrew title, Qohelet, on the analogy of the rendering of *qahal*, "congregation," by the Greek word *ekklesia*, meaning "assembly" or "church." The *ekklesiastes* is then understood as the leader or speaker of an assembly. Because of this, some translations render the first line in the book as "the words of the preacher" or "the words of the teacher." Traditionally the book was thought to be written by Solomon, but most modern scholars now believe it was written centuries later by an anonymous author.

The Book of Ecclesiastes discusses the meaning of life. Its argument can be summarized this way:

| 5 | 18 |
|---|---|

**Chapter 1**

Life seems to lack meaning because everything repeats. So I'm going to see if I can figure out the meaning of life. It's not wisdom: the more you know, the sadder you'll be.

| 5 | 18 |
|---|---|

**Chapter 2**

So I tried to find the meaning of life in endless pleasures, but life was still meaningless because no matter what, I'm going to die, whether I'm wise or foolish.

| 5 | 18 |
|---|---|

**Chapter 3**

There is a time for everything that happens: things come and go. And so we gain nothing from our work. We're no better than the animals: we live, we breathe, and then we die.

| 5 | 18 |
|---|---|

**Chapter 4**

The world is filled with suffering and all accomplishment is due to envy. It's better not to be alone, but no matter what you accomplish, people will soon forget you. Life is meaningless.

## Chapters 2–3: **Commentary**

The author of Ecclesiastes argues that life is unpredictable. The will and workings of God are obscured and unfathomable. Nothing that a human being can build or accomplish will last any length of time. Therefore, both human beings and their accomplishments are ultimately worthless.

*What do workers gain from their toil? I have seen the burden God has laid on the human race. He has made everything beautiful in its time. He has also set eternity in the human heart; yet no one can fathom what God has done from beginning to end. I know that there is nothing better for people than to be happy and to do good while they live. That each of them may eat and drink, and find satisfaction in all their toil—this is the gift of God. I know that everything God does will endure forever; nothing can be added to it and nothing taken from it. God does it so that people will fear him.*

**Ecclesiastes 3:9–14**

"Life is meaningless. God's actions appear to be capricious, with good and bad happening randomly, having nothing to do with behavior. Since we will soon die no matter how we conduct our lives, we must try to enjoy life as long as we have it."

Theologians argue that God has revealed himself to the human race by two separate paths: Special Revelation and General Revelation. Special Revelation refers to the Bible, while General Revelation refers to the natural realm of life, history, and the universe at large.

The author of Ecclesiastes has chosen to ignore what can be read about the purpose of life and the plan of God from Moses and the prophets. Instead, he set out to determine what life is all about on the basis of what he could witness happening around him.

*Do not pay attention to every word people say,*
*or you may hear your servant cursing you—*
*for you know in your heart*
*that many times you yourself have cursed others.*
**Ecclesiastes 7:21–22**

## Chapters 11–12: **Commentary**

The author's conclusion, as he summarizes the essence of his argument throughout his book, is one of utter despair. Many theologians believe when the word "fear" is applied to God, it carries the sense of reverential awe or "worship" rather than terror. But the author of Ecclesiastes believes otherwise. He believes that human beings should, in fact, be terrified of God. Why? Because when all is said and done, no matter how individuals conduct their affairs, God is going to judge them for it: without exception, everyone dies and is quickly forgotten.

*Now all has been heard; here is the conclusion of*
*the matter: Fear God and keep his commandments,*
*for this is the duty of all mankind. For God will*
*bring every deed into judgment, including every*
*hidden thing, whether it is good or evil.*
**Ecclesiastes 12:13–14**

| 5 | 18 | |
|---|---|---|
| If you make a promise to God, keep it. Wealth is meaningless, too. The more you have, the more you want. You'll never be satisfied and in the end, you die and can't take it with you. | | Chapter **5** |
| Maybe you can enjoy yourself for a while, but you'll never be satisfied, no matter how much you get. And no one can reveal the meaning of life or the future. | | Chapter **6** |
| There's no such a thing as "the good old days." Good comes to the bad and bad to the good. So don't be so bad that you suffer, but don't be so good that you don't have any fun. | | Chapter **7** |
| Obey the powerful; you'll have an easier life. And try to enjoy yourself; you'll never figure out what it all means. Anyone who claims he has it all figured out is wrong. | | Chapter **8** |
| No matter what you do, no matter how you live, in the end you're going to die. Time and chance happen to everyone. Life has no guarantees. You can do everything right and still lose. | | Chapter **9** |
| People get promoted who don't deserve it. Good things happen to fools. Of course, if you do everything wrong, if you are a fool, you increase your chances of things going badly. | | Chapter **10** |
| So be wise in your ventures, but there is still no guarantee that you'll succeed. | | Chapter **11** |
| Enjoy your life while you're young. When you're old, it won't be as much fun. But it's all meaningless, because in the end, whether you're good or bad, God will judge you. | | Chapter **12** |

# Song of Songs

## Overview

The book is called "Song of Songs" in Hebrew and in most modern English translations. In the King James version, it received the title "Song of Solomon." The Latin Vulgate called it "Canticles." The phrase "Song of Songs" is a Hebraism that means "The Best Song."

Its Solomonic authorship is widely credited, though the occurrence of some apparent Persian and Greek terms has led some scholars to postulate a post-exilic date.

The Song of Songs, more than any other book of the Bible, has been kept in the dark ages in the thoughts of many interpreters, who continue to insist on the medieval approach of allegorical interpretation—even though they would never approach any other book of the Bible allegorically. The allegorical approach to the Song of Songs

**Chapter 1** — 5 · 10 · 18

A Shulamite woman is in love with a prince and wants him to kiss her. He agrees that she is beautiful, comparing her eyes to doves. She describes her desire for him.

**Chapter 2** — 5 · 10 · 18

The woman describes the prince, his embrace, his strength, and how handsome he is. She wants him to go away with her. The prince longs for her and the sound of her voice.

**Chapter 3** — 5 · 10 · 18

The woman spends all night wishing that the prince were making love to her. Then she describes how he finally does make love to her and how aroused he was.

**Chapter 4** — 5 · 10 · 18

The prince describes her beauty, comparing her body parts to animals. She has stolen his heart. He says that she is his private garden. She tells him to come into his garden.

*Let him kiss me with the kisses of his mouth—*
*for your love is more delightful than wine.*
*Pleasing is the fragrance of your perfumes;*
*your name is like perfume poured out.*
*No wonder the young women love you!*
*Take me away with you—let us hurry!*
*Let the king bring me into his chambers.*
**Song of Songs 1:2–4**

## Chapter 4: Commentary

In chapter 4, the author of the Song of Songs describes his beloved as a garden (verse 12). Her response is to ask that he come into his garden and taste its fruits. The man and the woman compare one another and parts of their bodies to gardens, fruits, animals, and other objects. For the reader that pays attention to the descriptions and imagery, the erotic nature of the poem is obvious.

*You have stolen my heart, my sister, my bride;*
*you have stolen my heart*
*with one glance of your eyes,*
*with one jewel of your necklace.*
*How delightful is your love, my sister, my bride!*
*How much more pleasing is your love than wine,*
*and the fragrance of your perfume more than any spice!*
**Song of Songs 4:9–10**

results in teaching that the story is figurative, representing Yahweh's love for Israel, and by extension, Christ's love for the church. Those who cling to this approach argue that if a wholly literalistic approach is taken to the poem, it is impossible to understand why the Song of Songs would have been included as part of Scripture.

However, only if one takes the position that romantic love and sexual desire are evil would one find such a book inexplicable. As important as male–female relationships and romantic love are to human beings, it would be very odd if at least one book in the Bible were not devoted to the topic.

Therefore, it is best to take the Song of Songs at face value—as an erotic love poem. Like the Book of Esther, the Song of Songs never once mentions God. These are the only two books of the Bible that fail to mention him.

> *How beautiful you are and how pleasing,*
> *my love, with your delights!*
> *Your stature is like that of the palm,*
> *and your breasts like clusters of fruit.*
> *I said, "I will climb the palm tree;*
> *I will take hold of its fruit."*
> *May your breasts be like clusters of grapes on*
> *the vine,*
> *the fragrance of your breath like apples,*
> *and your mouth like the best wine.*
>
> **Song of Songs 7:6–9**

## Chapter 8: **Commentary**

According to the author of the Song of Songs, love is more than eroticism and momentary passion. Love is an insatiable hunger that can be but temporarily sated. Love lasts as long as life endures and can be satisfied only by the one who is loved. True love can never end and never be undone. Passion comes and goes, but love abides forever.

| 5 | 10 | 18 |
|---|----|----|

The prince says he has come into the garden and eaten its honey and drunk its wine. She describes how she engaged in intercourse with him and how handsome he is.

**Chapter 5**

| 5 | 10 | 18 |
|---|----|----|

The woman speaks of how much the prince has enjoyed his garden. The prince describes how beautiful she is and how much he desires her.

**Chapter 6**

**The Shulamite**
*The beloved woman of the Song of Songs is identified as a "Shulamite" in 6:13, perhaps identifying her hometown, or perhaps identifying her as belonging to Solomon.*

| 5 | 10 | 18 |
|---|----|----|

She stands tall like a palm tree; her breasts are clusters of fruit; her mouth like wine. He climbs the palm tree and grabs hold of the fruit. He drinks deeply from the wine.

**Chapter 7**

| 5 | 10 | 18 |
|---|----|----|

The woman delights in the prince's embrace. Love, she says, is as strong as death, a flame that can never be extinguished, and she wouldn't trade her love for anything.

**Chapter 8**

# Isaiah

## Overview

The title of the book is derived from the name of its author. Isaiah's name means "Yahweh saves" or the "Salvation of Yahweh." According to Jewish tradition, King Manasseh executed Isaiah by sawing him in half (cf. Hebrews 11:37).

At the same time Isaiah was prophesying in Judah, Amos and Hosea were busy in the northern kingdom of Israel, while Micah was writing in the south. The Book of Isaiah appears to be a compilation of a series of prophecies Isaiah received and committed to writing over the years 740 to 690 BC. The prophecies describe God's pending judgment against Israel and Judah and the surrounding nations, along with predictions of future hope and restoration (see 2 Kings 15:8–21:18). Destruction and exile were the consequence of breaking God's contract. The Israelites were worshiping other gods in addition

## Chapter 1: **Commentary**

God rejects the religious ceremonies and festivals of the people of Israel, despite the fact that the Laws of Moses require everything that He is rejecting. Has God changed his mind about how the Israelites were to worship him?

The Israelites had fallen into the easy trap of imagining that worship was only the performance of rituals. In fact, the rituals were intended to be symbolic of what the people were: lovers of God and lovers of their neighbors. Instead, they thought a kiss could take the place of love, and warm words could take the place of warm actions (see James 1:27 and 2:15–16).

The criticism that God is leveling against his people by the words of his prophet come down to two issues: the mistreatment of the poor and powerless, and the worship of other gods in addition to Yahweh. The Israelites were in violation of the two commandments that summarize the Bible: love people and love God (see Matthew 22: 34–40).

| 5 | 7 |
|---|---|

Chapter **1**

Israel worships other gods and so Yahweh has judged them. Don't bother with sacrifices: God wants obedience, justice, and the poor and orphans protected.

| 5 | 7 |
|---|---|

Chapter **2**

In the future, Yahweh's Temple will be exalted and people from around the world will visit. But since God's people have turned to idolatry, for now they will suffer God's judgment.

*He will judge between the nations*
*and will settle disputes for many peoples.*
*They will beat their swords into plowshares*
*and their spears into pruning hooks.*
*Nation will not take up sword against nation,*
*nor will they train for war anymore.*

**Isaiah 2:4**

to Yahweh, while the rich and powerful mistreated the poor and weak.

Assyria was gaining momentum and strength as a major world power. In Isaiah's lifetime, the northern kingdom of Israel, as a separate political entity, came to an end. Tiglath-Pileser III invaded Gilead and the northern kingdom in 734 BC; its capital, Samaria, finally fell between 724–722 BC. Sennacherib invaded Judah, the southern kingdom, in 701 BC.

The majority of scholars believe that the Book of Isaiah had two authors: chapters 1–39 were written by Isaiah son of Amoz in the eighth century BC, while 40–66 were composed by a so-called "Second Isaiah," an anonymous writer who lived during or shortly after the time of the Babylonian exile. Traditional scholars disagree and believe that the entire book was written by just one author in the eighth century BC.

**Isaiah bears witness**
*The prophet Isaiah lived and worked in Jerusalem, surrounded by those who followed the other gods and goddesses of the Ancient world.*

*The Lord takes his place in court;*
*he rises to judge the people.*
*The Lord enters into judgment*
*against the elders and leaders of his people:*
*"It is you who have ruined my vineyard;*
*the plunder from the poor is in your houses.*
*What do you mean by crushing my people*
*and grinding the faces of the poor?" declares the*
*Lord, the Lord Almighty.*

**Isaiah 3:13–15**

| 5 | 7 | |
|---|---|---|
| Jerusalem and Judah are going to face God's judgment. The righteous will survive, but the wicked will suffer. The proud will all be brought low. | | Chapter 3 |

| 5 | 7 | |
|---|---|---|
| Times will be desperate, especially for the women. But in the end, the city of Jerusalem will be cleansed and God will restore it. The survivors will prosper and be holy. | | Chapter 4 |

*Woe to those who call evil good and good evil,*
*who put darkness for light and light for darkness,*
*who put bitter for sweet and sweet for bitter.*

**Isaiah 5:20**

| 5 | 7 | |
|---|---|---|
| Because of their injustice and their worship of gods other than Yahweh, Israel and Judah are an unfruitful vineyard destined for invasion and destruction. | | Chapter 5 |

**5**    **7**    **15**

### Chapter 6

In the year that the king of Judah, Uzziah, died, Yahweh called Isaiah to be his prophet and showed him a vision of the heavenly throne room.

**5**    **7**    **17**

### Chapter 7

When Israel and Aram attacked Judah, Isaiah told Judah's king Ahaz to ask for a sign from God of victory. He refused, but God gave him a sign anyway: a child called Immanuel.

**The Tree of Jesse**
*Isaiah predicts a future descendant of Jesse, the father of King David, will someday come to the throne as a worthy and righteous successor.*

**5**    **7**

### Chapter 8

Isaiah's son Maher-Shalal-Hash-Baz fulfills the prophecy: before he knows how to speak, Assyria destroys Aram and Israel. Isaiah warns about consulting psychics.

**5**    **7**

### Chapter 9

Isaiah prophesies that the gloom facing Israel will eventually pass and that the Israelites will be restored to joy. But for now, they must suffer for their idolatry and wickedness.

## Chapter 6: **Commentary**

Isaiah 6 is the only place in the Bible that mentions the seraphim (or seraphs). The only other class of angel named in the Bible is the cherubim (or cherubs), first mentioned in Genesis 3 as the guardians blocking the way to the Tree of Life. Cherubs are later described in Ezekiel 1 (see also Ezekiel 10). Only two angels in the Bible are ever given personal names: Gabriel (Daniel 8:16, 9:21, Luke 1:19, 26) and the archangel Michael (Daniel 12:1, Jude 9, and Revelation 12:7).

*In the year that King Uzziah died, I saw the Lord, high and exalted, seated on a throne; and the train of his robe filled the temple. Above him were seraphim, each with six wings: With two wings they covered their faces, with two they covered their feet, and with two they were flying. And they were calling to one another:*
*"Holy, holy, holy is the Lord Almighty;*
*the whole earth is full of his glory."*
**Isaiah 6:1–3**

## Chapter 7: **Commentary**

Ahaz, the king of Judah, was facing an invasion from the north mounted by Aram and Israel. Isaiah told him that God would eliminate the threat. When he told Ahaz to ask for a sign from God to verify the truth of Isaiah's words, Ahaz refused to ask for a sign. Isaiah told him he'd get one anyway: a "virgin" would have a son and before he was old enough to tell the difference between right and wrong, his enemies from the north would be gone (7:14–17). The sign was fulfilled in chapter 8 when Isaiah's wife gave birth to Maher-Shalal-Hash-Baz (8:1–4). The Hebrew word that is often translated "virgin" in verse 14 can also be translated simply as "young woman."

In the New Testament, Matthew takes Isaiah's words for Ahaz and applies them to Jesus' virgin birth (Matthew 7:22).

## Chapter 9: **Commentary**

The composer George Frideric Handel used Isaiah 9:6–7 for his composition entitled "The Messiah" in 1741. Most Christians interpret the passage as a messianic prophecy and apply it to Jesus. Interestingly enough, however, the New Testament never quotes it.

The passage predicts that a descendant of David would one day again become king. The entire chapter is designed to reassure the people of Israel then facing exile that someday the nation, along with the Davidic monarchy, would be restored.

**Prophecy of Christ**
*Isaiah 53 was taken as a prophecy of the suffering, death, burial, and resurrection of Jesus by the authors of the New Testament.*

| 5 | 7 | Chapter 10 |
|---|---|---|
| God pronounces disaster on those who oppress the poor and powerless. God promises judgment against the Assyrians. Afterward, Israel's survivors will turn back to Yahweh. | | |

| 5 | 7 | Chapter 11 |
|---|---|---|
| The monarchy of David will be restored and the land of Israel will become prosperous, with all Israelites worshiping Yahweh. They will return from their places of exile. | | |

| 5 | 7 | Chapter 12 |
|---|---|---|
| When the people of Israel return to their Promised Land, they will praise and thank Yahweh, acknowledging their past infidelity, his restoration, and his forgiveness. | | |

| 5 | 7 | Chapter 13 |
|---|---|---|
| Isaiah prophesies against Babylon, predicting its conquest and destruction. Isaiah predicts that Babylon will never again be powerful or a threat to Israel. | | |

## Chapter 14: Commentary

The old King James version of the Bible translated the Hebrew word "morning star" as "Lucifer." But "Lucifer" was in fact simply the Latin word for "morning star" that Jerome had used in his translation of the Bible known as the Latin Vulgate. Puzzled English readers who missed the context of verses 12–15, had trouble figuring out what "Lucifer" meant. Eventually, someone decided that "Lucifer" must be another name for the Devil.

In reality, Isaiah was not discussing the Devil at all. The "morning star" was the king of Babylon. That Isaiah was not thinking of the infernal being is clear since he refers to him as "a man" (14:16) and speaks of his soon-coming death (14:9–11, 19). The fulfillment of Isaiah's prophecy occurred when the Persians conquered Babylon around 539 BC and killed the reigning Babylonian monarch, an event described by the Book of Daniel (see Daniel 5:18–31).

| 5 | 7 | Chapter 14 |
|---|---|---|
| God will restore Israel to its land and make it dominant over its neighbors. The Israelites will make fun of the king of Babylon's destruction. The Philistines will be defeated. | | |

| 5 | 7 | Chapter 15 |
|---|---|---|
| Isaiah prophesies against Moab, predicting its defeat and destruction, listing the fate of various regions within the nation. | | |

| 5 | 7 | Chapter 16 |
|---|---|---|
| Isaiah continues to describe Moab's defeat and destruction, the wailing and mourning of its people. He predicts that his prophecy will be fulfilled within three years. | | |

| 5 | 7 | Chapter 17 |
|---|---|---|
| Isaiah prophesies against the city of Damascus, predicting that it will become a heap of ruins. He also predicts a similar fate for Israel because of its idolatry. | | |

*In that day people will look to their Maker and turn their eyes to the Holy One of Israel. They will not look to the altars, the work of their hands, and they will have no regard for the Asherah poles and the incense altars their fingers have made.*
**Isaiah 17:7–8**

<table>
<tr><td>5</td><td>7</td></tr>
</table>

Chapter **18**

Isaiah prophesies against Cush, predicting its downfall. But then he promises that in the future, the people of Cush will worship Yahweh and bring gifts to Jerusalem.

Chapter **19**

Isaiah predicts civil war, conquest, and famine in Egypt. But some day Egypt and Assyria will worship Yahweh, becoming God's people as much as the Israelites.

Chapter **20**

By walking around naked for three years, Isaiah illustrates his prophecy that the Egyptians and the people of Cush will be taken away naked as captives to Assyria.

Chapter **21**

Isaiah prophesies about the fall of Babylon, predicting the siege by the Medes. He also predicts the downfall of Edom and Arabia.

Chapter **22**

Isaiah predicts that Jerusalem will suffer in the Valley of Vision. He prophesies that the palace steward Shebna will be deposed and die, while Eliakim will take his place.

Chapter **23**

Isaiah predicts Tyre's destruction and the subsequent mourning among its trading partners. Though Tyre will rise again in 70 years, all its profits will go to Yahweh.

## Chapter 19: **Commentary**

Although the creation account in Genesis 1 made clear that the God of Israel was not an exclusively Israelite God, the Israelites were slow to grasp Yahweh's universal dominion. In the Ancient Near East, gods belonged to a specific nation. So, Re was the god of the Egyptians, and Marduk was the god of the Babylonians. Each city had its own patron deity. The Israelite prophets battled against these prevailing cultural beliefs. In Isaiah 19, Isaiah clearly proclaims the radical notion that Yahweh isn't Israel's alone. The Egyptians and Assyrians also belonged to Yahweh (Isaiah 19:16–24).

*So the Lord will make himself known to the Egyptians, and in that day they will acknowledge the Lord. They will worship with sacrifices and grain offerings; they will make vows to the Lord and keep them. The Lord will strike Egypt with a plague; he will strike them and heal them. They will turn to the Lord, and he will respond to their pleas and heal them.*

*In that day there will be a highway from Egypt to Assyria. The Assyrians will go to Egypt and the Egyptians to Assyria. The Egyptians and Assyrians will worship together. In that day Israel will be the third, along with Egypt and Assyria, a blessing on the earth. The Lord Almighty will bless them, saying, "Blessed be Egypt my people, Assyria my handiwork, and Israel my inheritance."*

**Isaiah 19:21–25**

## Chapter 20: **Commentary**

The prophets sometimes acted out their messages. Just as Jesus would use parables to teach about God and his kingdom, so the prophets would use objects, their behavior, even events in their lives to illustrate God's message to his people. On occasion, such illustrations could be very embarrassing, as when Isaiah was required to run about without any clothes on for three long years, simply to illustrate that the people of Egypt and Cush would be dragged naked into Babylonian captivity.

*At that time Tyre will be forgotten for seventy years, the span of a king's life. But at the end of these seventy years, it will happen to Tyre as in the song of the prostitute:*
*"Take up a harp, walk through the city,*
*you forgotten prostitute;*
*play the harp well, sing many a song,*
*so that you will be remembered."*

**Isaiah 23:15–16**

## Chapter 24: **Commentary**

The Hebrew word translated "earth" in chapter 24 is more commonly translated as "land." It would be more accurate to translate it "land," here. Isaiah was not predicting an alien invasion of planet Earth, nor was he predicting that its inhabitants would be scattered around the galaxy. Instead, Isaiah predicted what will happen to God's land—specifically, the land of Israel: that Israel and Jerusalem would be laid waste and their inhabitants would be taken and scattered. Exile occurred for the northern kingdom of Israel around 722 BC and for the southern kingdom of Judah about 586 BC.

*See, the Lord is going to lay waste the earth*
*and devastate it;*
*he will ruin its face*
*and scatter its inhabitants—*

**Isaiah 24:1**

*On this mountain the Lord Almighty will prepare*
*a feast of rich food for all peoples,*
*a banquet of aged wine—*
*the best of meats and the finest of wines.*
*On this mountain he will destroy*
*the shroud that enfolds all peoples,*
*the sheet that covers all nations;*
*he will swallow up death forever.*
*The Sovereign Lord will wipe away the tears*
*from all faces;*
*he will remove his people's disgrace*
*from all the earth. The Lord has spoken.*

**Isaiah 25:6–8**

## Chapter 27: **Commentary**

According to Isaiah, God will punish Leviathan. Who or what is Leviathan? In Ugaritic mythology, Leviathan battles Baal as an ally of Mot, the god of the underworld. Baal ultimately defeated Leviathan. That mythological language and imagery is then taken by the authors of the Bible and transformed. Yahweh takes on the role of the victor over Leviathan. The mythological imagery is used poetically to show the power of God over his foes. In this case, God's enemies are also the enemies of Israel: the Assyrians who will conquer and exile the Israelites. So God reassures his people that one judging them—the Assyrians—will ultimately be judged by God.

**5** | **7**

Yahweh is going to lay waste to the "earth"—that is, to the land of Judah. All its inhabitants from highest to lowest will suffer equally.

Chapter
**24**

**5** | **7**

When God forgives and restores the people of Israel, they will praise and thank him. They will rejoice over the destruction of their enemies. God is just, faithful, and dependable.

Chapter
**25**

**The concept of resurrection**
One of the earliest references to the concept of resurrection appears in Isaiah 26, where the restoration of prosperity to the nation is compared to the resurrection of the dead.

**5** | **7**

They will praise God for forgiving Judah and destroying Judah's enemies. They will trust Yahweh, obey him, and worship him exclusively. He will grant them peace and prosperity.

Chapter
**26**

**5** | **7**

God will punish the nations that attacked and oppressed his people. God will bring Israel back to its land and restore its prosperity. Israel will bless the rest of the world.

Chapter
**27**

| **5** | **7** |
|---|---|
| Chapter **28** | The love of drinking will be replaced by the love of God. God will make sure that his people in Ephraim and Judah obey him. |

| **5** | **7** |
|---|---|
| Chapter **29** | Ariel—the city of Jerusalem—will be destroyed. Then, instead of just performing empty rituals, the Israelites, purged of their wickedness, will genuinely worship him. |

| **5** | **7** |
|---|---|
| Chapter **30** | Israel has turned to everything and everyone but God. Their hope of Egyptian help will prove futile. Only when they turn to God will they be rescued. Then they will praise God. |

| **5** | **7** |
|---|---|
| Chapter **31** | The Egyptians are merely mortals; they cannot be relied upon like God. The Israelites need to turn back to God and reject their idolatry. Some day they will repent. |

| **5** | **7** |
|---|---|
| Chapter **32** | A righteous king will come. Those who couldn't see the truth will suddenly see it. Before then, the women of Jerusalem will mourn until God's spirit comes and restores prosperity. |

**The great scroll of Isaiah**
*Among the Dead Sea Scrolls discovered in 1948 is a copy of the Book of Isaiah, the earliest complete copy of Isaiah's work in existence, dating from about 100 BC.*

*The Lord says:*
*"These people come near to me with their mouth*
*and honor me with their lips,*
*but their hearts are far from me.*
*Their worship of me is based on merely human*
*rules they have been taught.*
*Therefore once more I will astound these people*
*with wonder upon wonder;*
*the wisdom of the wise will perish,*
*the intelligence of the intelligent will vanish."*
*Woe to those who go to great depths*
*to hide their plans from the Lord,*
*who do their work in darkness and think,*
*"Who sees us? Who will know?"*
*You turn things upside down,*
*as if the potter were thought to be like the clay!*
*Shall what is formed say to the one who formed it,*
*"You did not make me"?*
*Can the pot say to the potter,*
*"You know nothing"?*

**Isaiah 29:13–16**

## Chapter 30: **Commentary**

Isaiah warned the Israelites that Egypt could not help them: "Egypt's shade will bring you disgrace" (Isaiah 30:3) and Egypt is a "splintered reed of a staff, which pierces the hand of anyone who leans on it." (Isaiah 36:6). The Third Intermediate Period in Egypt (1070–664 BC) saw its decline as a world power. The kingdom was split, with rival kings. The Assyrian Empire was ascendant and Egypt's allies were defecting to it. By Isaiah's day it was only a matter of time before war would erupt. Despite its wealth, Egypt lacked timber. This was important, because charcoal, produced from timber, was necessary for smelting iron for making weapons. In 664 BC the Assyrians sacked Thebes and Memphis. Thereafter, the kings of Egypt were clients of the Assyrian Empire. The Babylonians ultimately defeated the Egyptians and their Assyrian masters at the battle of Carchemish in 605 BC. Egypt would not become an independent nation again until the modern era.

*See, a king will reign in righteousness*
*and rulers will rule with justice.*
*Each one will be like a shelter from the wind*
*and a refuge from the storm,*
*like streams of water in the desert*
*and the shadow of a great rock in a thirsty land.*
*Then the eyes of those who see will no longer be*
*closed, and the ears of those who hear will listen.*
*The fearful heart will know and understand,*
*and the stammering tongue will be fluent and clear.*
*No longer will the fool be called noble*
*nor the scoundrel be highly respected.*

**Isaiah 32:1–5**

*Then will the eyes of the blind be opened*
*and the ears of the deaf unstopped.*
*Then will the lame leap like a deer,*
*and the mute tongue shout for joy.*
*Water will gush forth in the wilderness*
*and streams in the desert.*
*The burning sand will become a pool,*
*the thirsty ground bubbling springs.*
*In the haunts where jackals once lay,*
*grass and reeds and papyrus will grow.*

**Isaiah 35:5–7**

*Hezekiah received the letter from the messengers*
*and read it. Then he went up to the temple of the*
*Lord and spread it out before the Lord. And*
*Hezekiah prayed to the Lord: "Lord Almighty, the*
*God of Israel, enthroned between the cherubim, you*
*alone are God over all the kingdoms of the earth.*
*You have made heaven and earth. Give ear, Lord,*
*and hear; open your eyes, Lord, and see; listen to*
*all the words Sennacherib has sent to ridicule the*
*living God.*
  *"It is true, Lord, that the Assyrian kings have*
*laid waste all these peoples and their lands."*

**Isaiah 37:14–18**

## Chapter 40: **Commentary**

In chapter 40, Isaiah offers comfort to the Israelites. Though God is punishing them for idolatry and the mistreatment of the poor, in the future God will forgive them. He will restore them to their land and to their prosperity. Isaiah 40:3 is quoted in each of the four New Testament gospel accounts: in Matthew 3:3, Mark 1:3, Luke 3:4 and in John 1:23. His words are applied to John the Baptist, Jesus' cousin, who announced him as the long promised Jewish Messiah.

*A voice of one calling:*
*"In the wilderness prepare*
*the way for the Lord;*
*make straight in the desert*
*a highway for our God.*
*Every valley shall be raised up,*
*every mountain and hill made low;*
*the rough ground shall become level,*
*the rugged places a plain.*
*And the glory of the Lord will be revealed,*
*and all people will see it together. For the mouth of*
*the Lord has spoken."*

**Isaiah 40:3–5**

**⑤** **⑦**

God is gracious and powerful. The wicked will be punished. Jerusalem will be restored and people will faithfully worship Yahweh. Then Jerusalem will be secure and prosperous.

Chapter
**33**

**⑤** **⑦**

The nations surrounding Israel will be judged by God for their sins and for how they mistreated the Israelites. They will be destroyed.

Chapter
**34**

**⑤** **⑦**

The redeemed will rejoice. They will inhabit a peaceful and prosperous land without fear. The blind will see, the deaf will hear, the lame will walk, the mute will speak.

Chapter
**35**

**⑦** **⑰**

During the fourteenth year of Hezekiah, king of Judah, the Assyrian King Sennacherib attacks Jerusalem and tells the people to turn against Hezekiah. He promises to treat them well.

Chapter
**36**

**⑤** **⑦** **⑰**

Isaiah tells Hezekiah that God will rescue Jerusalem. Then Sennacherib's army suddenly dies, forcing Sennacherib to leave. Back in Nineveh, two of his sons assassinate him.

Chapter
**37**

**⑤** **⑦** **⑰**

Hezekiah becomes ill. Isaiah tells him he will not recover, but he prays and God grants him 15 more years of life. Hezekiah thanks God for his recovery.

Chapter
**38**

**⑦** **⑰**

Babylonians visit Jerusalem and Hezekiah reveals all his wealth to them. Isaiah predicts that the Babylonians will soon come back and strip Jerusalem of all that wealth.

Chapter
**39**

**⑤** **⑦**

God promises comfort, restoration, and good news for the people of Israel. God is in charge, he made the universe, he is incomparable, and he will restore hope and prosperity.

Chapter
**40**

## Chapter 41

**5** · **7**

God subdues the nations, but Israel is God's chosen servant, who has nothing to fear. Idols are powerless, unable to tell the future. Only Yahweh tells the future.

## Chapter 42

**5** · **7**

God's servant will be cared for and protected. God delights in his servant and has called him to righteousness. Israel was blind and deaf. They suffered because they had sinned.

## Chapter 43

**5** · **7**

Yahweh is Israel's only savior. He will restore them: the blind will see and the deaf will hear. Despite Israel's unfaithfulness, God will rescue them from Babylon.

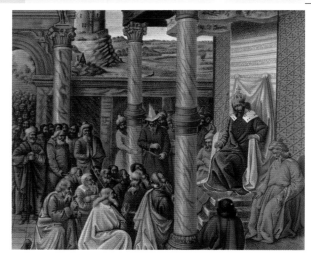

**Cyrus the Great**
*Cyrus the Great, following his conquest of the Babylonian Empire, did just as the prophet Isaiah predicted and let the Jewish people return to their homeland.*

## Chapter 44

**5** · **7**

Israel is God's servant. He chose them for himself. Idols are nothing, simply powerless and useless statues, unlike Yahweh the true God. Jerusalem will be re-inhabited.

## Chapter 45

**5** · **7**

Cyrus is God's anointed and he will send the Israelites home. God is invisible but he is powerful. The visible idols are powerless. God knows the future. Idols don't. Trust God.

## Chapters 41–43: **Commentary**

The Israelites were slow to accept the concept of monotheism. Although the creation account of Genesis clearly assumes a monotheistic perspective, as does the entire Pentateuch (see, for instance Deuteronomy 6:4) the belief in multiple deities remained constant among the ancient Jewish people. So the prophets tried to teach them that there were no other gods than Yahweh.

*Lead out those who have eyes but are blind,*
*who have ears but are deaf.*
    *All the nations gather together*
*and the peoples assemble.*
*Which of their gods foretold this*
*and proclaimed to us the former things?*
*Let them bring in their witnesses to prove they were*
*right, so that others may hear and say, "It is true."*
    *"You are my witnesses," declares the Lord,*
*"and my servant whom I have chosen,*
*so that you may know and believe me*
*and understand that I am he.*
*Before me no god was formed,*
*nor will there be one after me.*
    *I, even I, am the Lord,*
*and apart from me there is no savior."*

**Isaiah 43:8–11**

*"This is what the Lord says—*
*Israel's King and Redeemer, the Lord Almighty:*
*I am the first and I am the last;*
*apart from me there is no God.*
    *Who then is like me? Let him proclaim it.*
*Let him declare and lay out before me*
*what has happened since I established my ancient*
*people, and what is yet to come—yes, let them*
*foretell what will come.*
    *Do not tremble, do not be afraid.*
*Did I not proclaim this and foretell it long ago?*
*You are my witnesses. Is there any God besides me?*
*No, there is no other Rock; I know not one."*

**Isaiah 44:6–8**

## Chapter 45: **Commentary**

Isaiah calls Cyrus, the future ruler of Persia and the conqueror of Babylon, God's "anointed." The Hebrew word translated "anointed" is the word *Messiah*. The Greek form of the word is *Christ*. At the time Isaiah wrote, the term *Messiah* had not yet acquired the narrow theological meaning it later developed.

## Chapters 46–51: **Commentary**

Isaiah 46:

"Bel bows down, Nebo stoops low" says Isaiah (Isaiah 46:1). He explains that such idols are lifeless and powerless—so powerless that people have to carry them around since they can't even walk. When Isaiah makes fun of Bel and Nebo he is belittling the two most powerful and important gods of the most powerful nation in the world. Bel is a title meaning "lord" or "master" and it was used by the Babylonians of the neo-Babylonian period for their chief god, Marduk. It is thought that the Babylonian creation epic, *Enuma Elish*, was written to explain how Marduk seized power over the older gods. The story relates how Marduk was born. It describes the civil war between the gods that resulted, ultimately, in the creation of the world and how human beings were designed to be the gods' slaves. The Babylonians believed that Marduk was the chief god, master of all.

Nebo, also called Nabu, was the Babylonian god of writing and wisdom. He was Marduk's son. The Babylonians believed he engraved upon sacred tablets the destiny of each human, a destiny that the gods themselves had determined. Nebo, the Babylonians believed, could shorten or lengthen a person's life at will.

*This is what the Lord says—*
*your Redeemer, the Holy One of Israel:*
*"I am the Lord your God,*
*who teaches you what is best for you,*
*who directs you in the way you should go.*
*If only you had paid attention to my commands,*
*your peace would have been like a river,*
*your well-being like the waves of the sea.*

**Isaiah 48:17–18**

*"I, even I, am he who comforts you.*
*Who are you that you fear mere mortals,*
*human beings who are but grass,*
*that you forget the Lord your Maker,*
*who stretches out the heavens*
*and who lays the foundations of the earth,*
*that you live in constant terror every day*
*because of the wrath of the oppressor,*
*who is bent on destruction?*
*For where is the wrath of the oppressor?*
*The cowering prisoners will soon be set free;*
*they will not die in their dungeon,*
*nor will they lack bread."*

**Isaiah 51:12–14**

**5** **7**

The Babylonian idols have to be carried by people who themselves will be carried into captivity. Remember what God has done in the past. He is still the same powerful God.

Chapter **46**

**5** **7**

Babylon will fall and God will rescue his captive people. God was angry with his people, but he forgives them. Babylon will suffer for its idolatry, its pride, and its trust in its wealth.

Chapter **47**

**5** **7**

God warns Israel of the consequences of its idolatry. What happened to them was no surprise. But now, God will rescue them from Babylon and forgive them.

Chapter **48**

**5** **7**

Before he was even born, God calls his servant to bring Israel back to Yahweh and to make him a light to the Gentiles. Israel will once again be restored to its land.

Chapter **49**

**5** **7**

Yes, Israel sinned and went into captivity; but God was not rejecting his people. God has the power to forgive and restore.

Chapter **50**

**5** **7**

There is no reason to fear mortals. God is in charge, God is powerful, and God will save. Jerusalem suffered, but soon the suffering will end. Those in bondage will be set free.

Chapter **51**

**Chapter 52**

Jerusalem will be freed from its shackles. God is in control. He will give the Israelites reasons to sing. God will bring his people home. God's servant is wise, though disfigured.

**Chapter 53**

God's servant will suffer for the sins of his people; he will be pierced and crushed for the iniquities of his people. He will go like a lamb to the slaughter, becoming an offering for sin.

**Chapter 54**

Jerusalem is like a barren woman. God is like her husband, who rescues her and calls her back to himself after his anger has passed. God will never punish Jerusalem again.

**Chapter 55**

God invites all those who are thirsty and hungry to come to him so he can satisfy their needs. He asks people to turn from their ways and to choose God's way instead.

**Chapter 56**

God wants to see justice. No one should feel excluded. A relationship with God is available to everyone. But Israel's rulers are only want to satisfy their own appetites.

**Chapter 57**

The righteous suffer and die. Those who worship idols think their idols will save them. They won't. Only God can help. God will forgive and restore the wicked.

**Chapter 58**

Religious ritual doesn't matter. What matters is rescuing the oppressed, feeding the hungry, and helping the poor. Concern yourself with God's concerns if you want joy.

## Chapters 52–53: Commentary

The New Testament authors understood Isaiah 52:13–53:12 as a prophecy of Jesus' death as a sacrifice for the sins of the world (see Matthew 8:17, John 12:38, Acts 8:32–33, Romans 10:16, 15:21, and 1 Peter 2:24–25). In contrast, Jewish scholars believe that the passage refers to the suffering of the nation of Israel.

*Surely he took up our pain*
*and bore our suffering,*
*yet we considered him punished by God,*
*stricken by him, and afflicted.*
*But he was pierced for our transgressions,*
*he was crushed for our iniquities;*
*the punishment that brought us peace was on him,*
*and by his wounds we are healed.*
*We all, like sheep, have gone astray,*
*each of us has turned to our own way;*
*and the Lord has laid on him*
*the iniquity of us all.*

**Isaiah 53:4–6**

## Chapter 55: Commentary

The words of the biblical authors arise from particular times and places. Knowing that context is always important for accurate interpretation. When reading a passage from the Bible, its setting must always be kept in mind, along with the place of the words in the sentences and paragraphs around it.

For instance, when God says in verse 8 that "my thoughts are not your thoughts, neither are your ways my ways" and then continues in verse 9 that they are "higher than your ways" he is not suggesting that his thoughts are incomprehensible. Instead, the context makes it clear that God was merely criticizing the unrighteous behavior of the Israelites of that time, and contrasting their wickedness to his goodness: in verse 7 God tells the Israelites, "Let the wicked forsake their ways and the unrighteous their thoughts."

*Seek the Lord while he may be found;*
*call on him while he is near.*
*Let the wicked forsake their ways*
*and the unrighteous their thoughts.*
*Let them turn to the Lord, and he will have mercy*
*on them, and to our God, for he will freely pardon.*
*"For my thoughts are not your thoughts,*
*neither are your ways my ways," declares the Lord.*
*"As the heavens are higher than the earth,*
*so are my ways higher than your ways*
*and my thoughts than your thoughts."*

**Isaiah 55:6–9**

**The suffering servant**
*According to Isaiah, the suffering servant was pierced for our transgressions and crushed for our iniquities (Isaiah 53:5).*

*"Before they call I will answer;*
*while they are still speaking I will hear.*
*The wolf and the lamb will feed together,*
*and the lion will eat straw like the ox,*
*and dust will be the serpent's food.*
*They will neither harm nor destroy*
*on all my holy mountain," says the Lord.*
                                    **Isaiah 65:24–25**

## Chapter 66: Commentary

The imagery that concludes the Book of Isaiah, in which Isaiah predicts the future restoration and glory of the nation of Israel and the utter defeat of her foes, was taken up and quoted by Jesus in the New Testament. In Mark 9:48, the phrase "where 'their worm does not die, and the fire is not quenched'" is used to express the importance of avoiding sin, because its consequences are dire.

*"As the new heavens and the new earth that I make will endure before me," declares the Lord, "so will your name and descendants endure. From one New Moon to another and from one Sabbath to another, all mankind will come and bow down before me," says the Lord. "And they will go out and look on the dead bodies of those who rebelled against me; the worms that eat them will not die, the fire that burns them will not be quenched, and they will be loathsome to all mankind."*
                                    **Isaiah 66:22–24**

God has the power to rescue, but your sins get in the way. So turn back to God and he'll turn back to you. God understands that you can't rescue yourself; so he'll do the job for you.
**Chapter 59**

The world will be attracted to Yahweh. The nations will bring wealth and help rebuild Jerusalem. Those who do not serve Jerusalem will perish. God will be the light of Jerusalem.
**Chapter 60**

Freedom for the captives has come; the city of Jerusalem will be rebuilt. God loves justice and he will save his people. God will make righteousness spring up before the world.
**Chapter 61**

God will protect and watch over Jerusalem and its people. Israel's savior is coming, bringing his reward. The Israelites will be a holy people, redeemed by God.
**Chapter 62**

Israel suffered for a little while, but no more. God has saved his people and brought vengeance against their enemies. God is their savior. When Israel suffered, he suffered.
**Chapter 63**

Oh that God would come down and rescue his people! Even our best deeds are nothing but filthy rags. Please forgive us; Israel is a wasteland; the Temple has been destroyed.
**Chapter 64**

God showed himself to people who didn't want him. Those who abandon God, God will abandon. But God will forgive them. Once again, the land will prosper and be at peace.
**Chapter 65**

Sacrifices don't really matter. What matters is humility and contrition. Jerusalem can rejoice. The righteous will proclaim God's glory to the nations of the world.
**Chapter 66**

# Jeremiah

## Overview

**I** Early prophecies—under Josiah and Jehoiakim 1–20

- **a** The commission of Jeremiah 1
- **b** Judah, Yahweh's unfaithful wife 2–6
- **c** Judah, the hypocrite 7–10
- **d** Judah, breaker of the covenant 11–12
- **e** Five parables of judgment 13–20

**II** Later prophecies—under Jehoiakim and Zedekiah 21–39

- **a** Captivity in Babylon predicted 21–29
- **b** Restoration predicted 30–33
- **c** Captivity anticipated 34–39

**III** Prophecies after the fall of Jerusalem 40–45

- **a** Gedaliah as governor 40–41
- **b** Johanan's rebellion 41–43
- **c** Jeremiah's prophecies in Egypt 43–44
- **d** Jeremiah's prophecy for Baruch 45

**IV** Prophecies concerning foreign nations 46–51

- **a** Southwest 46–47
- **b** Southeast 48–49:22
- **c** North 49:23–33
- **e** East 49:34–51:64

**V** The fall of Jerusalem 52

The Book of Jeremiah is called by the name of its author, which means "Yahweh establishes." Jeremiah was a priest, the son of Hilkiah, and lived in the priestly town of Anathoth, about 3 miles (5.4 km) north of Jerusalem (1 Chronicles 6:60). There is little disagreement over Jeremiah being the author of the book that bears his name, though its arrangement is probably due to Baruch, his secretary. The Book of Jeremiah is a collection of prophecies regarding God's judgment against Judah, along with promises of hope for the future. Interspersed among the prophecies are descriptions of the prophet's experiences as he lived through the destruction of his homeland.

Jeremiah lived from about about 627 to 580 BC, a crucial period in the history of Judah. Except for a brief period of independence under Josiah, Judah existed as a vassal under Assyria, Egypt, and Babylon. Jeremiah began writing during the thirteenth year of Josiah's reign (Jeremiah 1:2, 25:3) and continued until after the fall of Jerusalem around 586 BC. Jeremiah was not the only prophet at this time: preaching with him, were Zephaniah, Habakkuk, and Huldah. Meanwhile,

(5) (7) (17)

**Chapter 1**

God calls Jeremiah to be his prophet shortly before Judah goes into Babylonian captivity. No one will overcome Jeremiah, because God will be with him and will rescue him.

(5) (7)

**Chapter 2**

God compares Israel to a wife having an affair, even though her husband is good and kind. Other nations are faithful to their gods, but Israel is not.

*"Get yourself ready! Stand up and say to them whatever I command you. Do not be terrified by them, or I will terrify you before them. Today I have made you a fortified city, an iron pillar and a bronze wall to stand against the whole land—against the kings of Judah, its officials, its priests and the people of the land. They will fight against you but will not overcome you, for I am with you and will rescue you," declares the Lord.*

**Jeremiah 1:17–19**

Daniel and Ezekiel were busy prophesying from Babylonian captivity.

On the world scene, empires were jockeying for world domination. The Assyrian Empire began to disintegrate after the death of Ashurbanipal in 626 BC, with its capital, Nineveh, falling to Nebuchadnezzar in 612 BC. In 609 BC Josiah was killed in battle at Megiddo when he foolishly went out to fight Pharaoh Necho. Judah was a vassal to Egypt until 605 BC when Nebuchadnezzar defeated Egypt at Carchemish, thus gaining control of all of western Asia, including Judah. In 586 BC, Nebuchadnezzar besieged Jerusalem, sacked the city, and burned it to the ground (2 Kings 21–25 and 2 Chronicles 33–36).

**God speaks to Jeremiah**
*God told Jeremiah that he had decided to make him a prophet even before he was born.*

## Chapter 3: **Commentary**

Although Jeremiah predicted the destruction of Jerusalem and the Temple, he also offered hope. Near the beginning of his book, he predicts that the people will return and prosper. Despite recent popular fictional representations and other speculation, Jeremiah indicates in 3:16 that the Ark of the Covenant will be neither recovered nor recreated.

*"In those days, when your numbers have increased greatly in the land," declares the Lord, "people will no longer say, 'The ark of the covenant of the Lord.' It will never enter their minds or be remembered; it will not be missed, nor will another one be made."*
**Jeremiah 3:16**

| 5 | 7 | |
|---|---|---|
| If a divorced woman remarries, will her first husband take her back? Judah is like a prostitute. She knows what happened to her sister Israel, but she isn't changing. | | Chapter **3** |

| 5 | 7 | |
|---|---|---|
| Even so, God asks for Israel and Judah to return to him. But if they won't, then a nation from the north is going to come and invade Judah and destroy Jerusalem. | | Chapter **4** |

| 5 | 7 | |
|---|---|---|
| Since everyone worships other gods, why should Yahweh forgive them? They chase other gods like a man chasing someone else's wife. But they wonder why God judged them. | | Chapter **5** |

| 5 | 7 | |
|---|---|---|
| Jerusalem will be besieged and destroyed, even though everyone seems convinced that it will never happen. The other prophets predict peace and prosperity that will never be. | | Chapter **6** |

**7**

Chapter
**7**

The Israelites worship idols and oppress the weak. God tells Jeremiah that no one will listen, so he should cut off his hair, throw it away, and lament for the coming wrath.

**5**  **7**

Chapter
**8**

The graves will be dug up and the corpses will be exposed before the sun, moon, and stars that the Israelites worship. The living will go into captivity.

**4**  **5**  **7**

Chapter
**9**

God mourns for the coming destruction of his people, brokenhearted over their rejection, their mistreatment of one another, and dismayed at the pain they will endure.

**5**  **7**

Chapter
**10**

Don't be like the idolatrous nations. Idols are powerless, but God, the creator, has the power to punish. Jeremiah wants God to judge the nations who destroyed Israel.

**5**  **7**

Chapter
**11**

God made a contract with Israel when he rescued them from Egypt. They broke it, so God is obligated to punish them. Some want Jeremiah to stop prophesying and plot to kill him.

**5**  **7**

Chapter
**12**

Jeremiah complains to God, asking why the wicked prosper. He wants God to judge them. God tells him that even his own family will reject him, and Judah will be destroyed.

**5**  **7**

Chapter
**13**

Jeremiah buries a belt. When he later digs it up, it is ruined. God says Israel is as worthless to God now as that belt. Israel will go into captivity because of its idolatry.

*"The harvest is past, the summer*
*has ended, and we are not saved."*
*Since my people are crushed, I am crushed;*
*I mourn, and horror grips me.*
*Is there no balm in Gilead?*
*Is there no physician there?*
*Why then is there no healing*
*for the wound of my people?*
*Oh, that my head were a spring of water*
*and my eyes a fountain of tears!*
*I would weep day and night*
*for the slain of my people.*
**Jeremiah 8:20–9:1**

*This is what the Lord says:*
*"Let not the wise boast of their wisdom*
*or the strong boast of their strength*
*or the rich boast of their riches,*
*but let the one who boasts boast about this:*
*that they have the understanding to know me,*
*that I am the Lord, who exercises kindness,*
*justice and righteousness on earth,*
*for in these I delight," declares the Lord.*
**Jeremiah 9:23–24**

## Chapter 12: Commentary

Jeremiah became frustrated with the course of his life. He was obeying God, serving as his prophet. But not only did no one believe him, he was actively opposed and even threatened physically. He wonders why it is that the wicked seemed to be prospering while he is suffering. Why didn't God do something to punish the wicked? Where was God's justice? God's response was to tell him to stop whining and to just be patient.

*"If you have raced with men on foot*
*and they have worn you out,*
*how can you compete with horses?*
*If you stumble in safe country,*
*how will you manage in the thickets by the Jordan?"*
**Jeremiah 12:5**

***An unhappy Jeremiah***
*Jeremiah complains to God about how the wicked are prospering while he, God's servant, is suffering unjustly.*

*The heart is deceitful above all things*
*and beyond cure.*
    *Who can understand it?*
    *"I the Lord search the heart and examine the*
*mind, to reward each person according to their*
*conduct, according to what their deeds deserve."*
                                                    **Jeremiah 17:9–10**

*If at any time I announce that a nation or*
*kingdom is to be uprooted, torn down and*
*destroyed, and if that nation I warned repents*
*of its evil, then I will relent and not inflict on it*
*the disaster I had planned. And if at another time*
*I announce that a nation or kingdom is to be built*
*up and planted, and if it does evil in my sight and*
*does not obey me, then I will reconsider the good*
*I had intended to do for it.*
                                                    **Jeremiah 18:7–10**

## Chapter 20: **Commentary**

Jeremiah believes that God has misled him, because rather than having success as God's prophet, he is suffering constant criticism from everyone around him—and worse, God is not doing anything to fix it. In fact, Jeremiah feels as if God has turned against him, as if God has become his enemy. Jeremiah wishes that he had never been born, so low have his fortunes sunk.

   Even though Jeremiah heard from God on a regular basis, knew precisely what God wanted him to do, and knew the future—Jeremiah still suffered from feelings of discouragement. Despite those feelings, God continued working with him—and Jeremiah continued doing what God asked him to do.

*Cursed be the day I was born!*
*May the day my mother bore me not be blessed!*
*Cursed be the man who brought my father the*
*news, who made him very glad, saying,*
*"A child is born to you—a son!"*
*May that man be like the towns*
*the Lord overthrew without pity.*
*May he hear wailing in the morning,*
*a battle cry at noon.*
*For he did not kill me in the womb,*
*with my mother as my grave,*
*her womb enlarged forever.*
*Why did I ever come out of the womb*
*to see trouble and sorrow*
*and to end my days in shame?*
                                                    **Jeremiah 20:14–18**

| 5 | 7 | |
|---|---|---|
| God tells Jeremiah again not to pray for the wellbeing of the people: they are going into exile for their idolatry. Jeremiah prays that God has not rejected his people forever. | | Chapter **14** |

| 5 | 7 | |
|---|---|---|
| God tells Jeremiah that even if Moses and Samuel asked for the people to be forgiven, he wouldn't forgive them now. They must be punished. But God promises to protect Jeremiah. | | Chapter **15** |

| 5 | 7 | |
|---|---|---|
| God tells Jeremiah not to get married or to have any children. He tells him not to mourn for the dead or celebrate with the living. Someday Judah will be forgiven. But not now. | | Chapter **16** |

| 5 | 7 | |
|---|---|---|
| God describes Judah's idolatry. They have not kept the Sabbath. Those who trust in Yahweh will be blessed; those who trust in themselves will be cursed. | | Chapter **17** |

| 5 | 7 | |
|---|---|---|
| Just as a potter does what he wants with clay, so God does what he wants with Israel: unless they repent, judgment will fall. People plot against Jeremiah. He asks God to protect him. | | Chapter **18** |

| 7 | |
|---|---|
| Yahweh tells Jeremiah to take some of the elders and priests to the Valley of Ben Hinnom. There, he smashes a clay jar and announces that God intends to smash Jerusalem. | Chapter **19** |

| 5 | 7 | 17 | |
|---|---|---|---|
| The priest Pashhur has Jeremiah arrested, beaten, and locked in stocks. Jeremiah says that he and his family will die in Babylon. Jeremiah wishes that he wasn't a prophet or even born. | | | Chapter **20** |

| ⑤ | ⑦ | ⑰ |

**Chapter 21**

Zedekiah, king of Judah, asks Jeremiah if maybe God would rescue them from Nebuchadnezzar. Jeremiah tells him no, only those who surrender to the Babylonians will live.

| ⑤ | ⑦ |

**Chapter 22**

The king, Jehoahaz, will never return. King Jehoiakim will have the burial of a donkey. His son, Jehoiachin will go into exile; none of his children will ever sit on David's throne.

| ⑤ | ⑦ |

**Chapter 23**

A righteous branch will come back from David's line to rule Judah and Israel and the captives will come home. The other prophets and priests offer false hope.

| ⑦ |

**Chapter 24**

After Jehoiachin and others had gone into exile, God showed Jeremiah two baskets of figs: one good, one bad. The exiles are the good figs, those still in Jerusalem, the bad ones.

| ⑤ | ⑦ |

**Chapter 25**

Jeremiah announces that the Jewish captivity in Babylon will last 70 years, but afterward, God will destroy the Babylonian Empire. God will judge Egypt, Judah, and others.

| ⑤ | ⑦ | ⑰ |

**Chapter 26**

After Jeremiah prophesied in the Temple courtyard, the religious establishment plans to kill him, until they remember a prophet named Micah who was never executed for similar words.

| ⑦ | ⑰ |

**Chapter 27**

Jeremiah wears a yoke to symbolize that Judah, Edom, Moab, Ammon, Tyre, and Sidon will be conquered and oppressed by the Babylonians. Those who resist will be killed.

| ⑦ | ⑰ |

**Chapter 28**

The prophet Hananiah removes and breaks Jeremiah's yoke, predicting that within two years the power of Babylon would be broken. Jeremiah tells Hananiah he is wrong and will die.

## Chapter 23: **Commentary**

Jeremiah predicts the coming of a future king who will reign over Israel as a "righteous Branch." (23:5). Christian expositors view this as a messianic prophecy of Jesus who is described as a descendant of David, the Messiah, and the rightful king of Israel (Matthew 2:2, 1:1).

*"The days are coming," declares the Lord,*
*"when I will raise up for David a righteous Branch,*
*a King who will reign wisely*
*and do what is just and right in the land.*
*In his days Judah will be saved*
*and Israel will live in safety.*
*This is the name by which he will be called:*
*The Lord Our Righteous Savior.*

**Jeremiah 23:5–6**

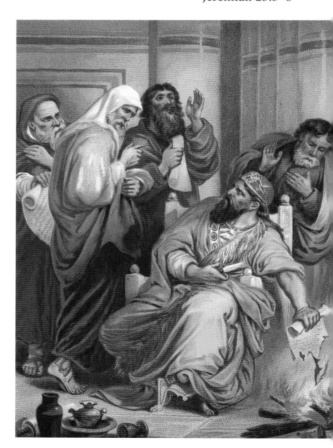

***King Jehoiakim rejects Jeremiah***
*King Jehoiakim rejects Jeremiah and his prophecies and tries to destroy both Jeremiah and the words that he has written.*

## Chapter 31: **Commentary**

Jeremiah predicted that God would make a New Covenant with the people of Israel, that would differ from the earlier one made by Moses. Instead of being written on tablets of stone, the New Covenant would be written on the hearts of His people. The author of Hebrews (Hebrews 8) quotes Jeremiah's words and argues that Jesus' death and resurrection, followed by the arrival of the Holy Spirit, is the fulfillment of Jeremiah's prophecy.

It is on the basis of Jeremiah's prophecy that the books written by the early Christians are called "the New Testament." "Testament" is just an older word meaning "covenant." Thus, the "Old Testament" refers to the "Old Covenant" of Moses while the "New Testament" is the "New Covenant" predicted by Jeremiah and fulfilled by Jesus' resurrection and the coming of the Holy Spirit.

## Chapter 33: **Commentary**

Jeremiah argues that God's contractual relationship with Israel, with David and his descendants, and with the Levitical priests is as firm and unbreakable as the laws of physics. As a result, most modern theologians do not define "miracle" as a violation of natural law. Instead, they define "miracle" as the intervention of God in the affairs of the world. Such spectacular interventions as the parting of the Red Sea or the resurrection of the dead do not require the breaking of natural laws, which God says he will not break. Instead, it simply requires power and knowledge, both of which God has in abundance. As Sir Arthur C. Clark is quoted as saying: "any sufficiently advanced technology is indistinguishable from magic." Miracles simply demonstrate that God is far more advanced, and far more powerful, than human beings.

*"Therefore this is what the Lord says: You have not obeyed me; you have not proclaimed freedom to your own people. So I now proclaim 'freedom' for you, declares the Lord—'freedom' to fall by the sword, plague and famine. I will make you abhorrent to all the kingdoms of the earth. Those who have violated my covenant and have not fulfilled the terms of the covenant they made before me, I will treat like the calf they cut in two and then walked between its pieces. The leaders of Judah and Jerusalem, the court officials, the priests and all the people of the land who walked between the pieces of the calf, I will deliver into the hands of their enemies who want to kill them. Their dead bodies will become food for the birds and the wild animals."*

**Jeremiah 34:17–20**

---

**7** **17**

Jeremiah writes to the Babylonian exiles, encouraging them to settle down and make a new life for themselves. Shemaiah opposes Jeremiah, but will be punished as a false prophet.

Chapter **29**

---

**7** **7**

God promises to bring his people Israel and Judah back from captivity in Assyria and Babylonia. They do not need to fear. God's wrath is not forever.

Chapter **30**

---

**5** **7**

The Israelites' tears will turn to joy. God will make a New Covenant with them, inscribing it on their hearts instead of on stone tablets. God can never reject his people Israel.

Chapter **31**

---

**7** **17**

As a sign that God will restore the people to their land, Jeremiah buys a field from his cousin Hanamel while the city of Jerusalem is besieged by the Babylonian army.

Chapter **32**

---

**5** **7**

In the future, God will bring the Israelites back to rebuild Jerusalem. God can no more break his covenant with David and the priests than the laws of physics can be broken.

Chapter **33**

---

**7** **17**

Jeremiah tells King Zedekiah that Jerusalem will be destroyed and he will be carried captive to Babylon. The rich are condemned for failing to free their slaves as promised.

Chapter **34**

---

**7** **17**

God contrasts the Rekabites' faithfulness to their ancestor's strange rules with the Israelites' failure to keep the reasonable rules of God. God blesses the Rekabites.

Chapter **35**

---

**7** **17**

Jehoiakim, the king, burns the words of Jeremiah's prophecies as they are read to him. But then God has Jeremiah write it all down again on another scroll.

Chapter **36**

**Jeremiah weeps**
*Jeremiah, known as the weeping prophet, mourned the coming destruction of his nation, its capital, and God's Temple.*

| 7 | 17 |
|---|---|
| Chapter **37** | After being falsely accused of deserting to the Babylonians, Jeremiah is arrested. Jeremiah prophesies the destruction of Jerusalem and Zedekiah's exile. |

| 7 | 17 |
|---|---|
| Chapter **38** | King Zedekiah allows Jeremiah to be put into a cistern for a while because Jeremiah is encouraging people to surrender to the Babylonians during the siege. |

| 9 | 17 |
|---|---|
| Chapter **39** | The Babylonians destroy Jerusalem while Jeremiah is still imprisoned. Zedekiah sees his children executed. He is blinded, then taken to Babylon. The Temple is burned. |

| 17 | |
|---|---|
| Chapter **40** | Released from prison, Jeremiah goes to Gedaliah, the governor appointed by Nebuchadnezzar. Gedaliah does not take seriously reports that Ishmael planned to assassinate him. |

| 17 | |
|---|---|
| Chapter **41** | Ishmael assasinates Gedaliah and his associates. Johanan, many soldiers, women, children and court officials want to flee to Egypt, afraid of Nebuchadnezzar's reaction. |

| 7 | 17 |
|---|---|
| Chapter **42** | Johanan and the others then ask Jeremiah to inquire of God about what they should do. They promise to obey God. Jeremiah tells them that God wants them to stay in Israel. |

| 7 | 17 |
|---|---|
| Chapter **43** | Johanan and the rest tell Jeremiah he's lying. So they go to Egypt and take Jeremiah and his secretary Baruch with them. Jeremiah prophesies that Nebuchadnezzar will attack Egypt. |

| 7 | 17 |
|---|---|
| Chapter **44** | Jeremiah tells them to abandon their idols. They reject Jeremiah's message, convinced that the reason they are suffering is because they have not been faithful enough to the gods. |

*When Jeremiah had finished telling the people all the words of the Lord their God—everything the Lord had sent him to tell them—Azariah son of Hoshaiah and Johanan son of Kareah and all the arrogant men said to Jeremiah, "You are lying! The Lord our God has not sent you to say, 'You must not go to Egypt to settle there.' But Baruch son of Neriah is inciting you against us to hand us over to the Babylonians, so they may kill us or carry us into exile to Babylon."*

**Jeremiah 43:1–3**

## Chapter 43: **Commentary**

Following the fall of Jerusalem, the Babylonian king made Gedaliah governor of Judah, now a new district in the Babylonian Empire. Gedaliah was soon assassinated however, and in the confusion following that event, several of the leading citizens approached Jeremiah and asked him where they should go and what they should do. They were terrified at the prospect of Babylonian retribution for Gedaliah's assassination and wanted to flee south to Egypt as a refuge from the Babylonians. At the time, Egypt was considered a world power equal in strength to Babylon and opposed to Babylonian expansionism.

Jeremiah's response to their request for guidance went contrary to their desires and what seemed the only logical course of action. Therefore, they rejected Jeremiah's words, even though he claimed to have divine sanction, and they did what they had planned to do from the beginning. The request for advice was in fact a request for divine sanction for their decision and desire. They already knew what they wanted to do and they really didn't care what God wanted when it conflicted with their plans.

*"Do not be afraid, Jacob my servant;*
*do not be dismayed, Israel.*
*I will surely save you out of a distant place,*
*your descendants from the land of their exile.*
*Jacob will again have peace and security,*
*and no one will make him afraid.*
*Do not be afraid, Jacob my servant,*
*for I am with you," declares the Lord.*
*"Though I completely destroy all the nations*
*among which I scatter you,*
*I will not completely destroy you.*
*I will discipline you but only in due measure;*
*I will not let you go entirely unpunished."*

**Jeremiah 46:27–28**

*"Flee from Babylon!*
*Run for your lives!*
*Do not be destroyed because of her sins.*
*It is time for the Lord's vengeance;*
*he will repay her what she deserves.*
*Babylon was a gold cup in the Lord's hand;*
*she made the whole earth drunk.*
*The nations drank her wine;*
*therefore they have now gone mad."*

**Jeremiah 51:6–7**

## Chapter 52: **Commentary**

Most scholars believe that Jeremiah 52 is a later addition to the work. Jerusalem was burned and the Temple destroyed during the summer of 586 or 587 BC. Traditionally, the date for the Temple's destruction is the ninth of Av (which falls in July or August).

On that day, Jewish people now annually commemorate the destruction of the Temple by the Babylonians in 586 BC, and then again by the Romans in AD 70. It is a day of fasting and mourning. Traditionally the Book of Lamentations is read in synagogues, occasionally along with the Book of Job and sections of Jeremiah. Jewish people are prohibited from eating or drinking, bathing, applying creams or oils, wearing leather shoes, or engaging in sex.

| | | |
|---|---|---|
| **7** **17** | Jeremiah prophesies to Baruch, his secretary, that he should not expect great things for himself. However, he reassures him that God will protect him and spare his life. | **Chapter 45** |
| **5** **7** | Jeremiah's prophecy to Egypt: Nebuchadnezzar will defeat Egypt, but in the future, Egypt will prosper. He prophesies that Israel will be punished but not destroyed. | **Chapter 46** |
| **5** **7** | Jeremiah's prophecy to the Philistines: God says that they will be attacked and destroyed all along the coast, with their cities of Gaza and Ashkelon being wiped out. | **Chapter 47** |
| **5** **7** | Jeremiah's prophecy to Moab: their cities will be destroyed and the people and their gods will be taken away to exile. But someday their fortunes will be restored. | **Chapter 48** |
| **5** **7** | Israel will attack Amon, but someday their fortunes will be restored. Edom will become uninhabited. Damascus, Kedar, Hazor, and Elam will be destroyed. | **Chapter 49** |
| **5** **7** | Babylon will be attacked from the north and overthrown because of what they did to the Israelites. The Israelites will be forgiven and will return to their homeland. | **Chapter 50** |
| **5** **7** | Jeremiah warns that when Babylon is destroyed, the people of Israel should flee. God, who made the universe, is determined to repay Babylon for its crimes against the Jewish people. | **Chapter 51** |
| **16** **17** | An account of the destruction of Jerusalem: the wealth stolen, and the people taken away into exile. Jehoiachin king of Judah is granted a measure of freedom in Babylon. | **Chapter 52** |

# Lamentations

## Overview

Lamentations is a series of acrostic poems mourning the destruction of Jerusalem by the Babylonians. In Hebrew, the title of the book is *ekah*, which means "how." It is the first word in the book. In the Babylonian Talmud and other early Jewish writings, the book is referred to as *qinot*, which is equivalent to the English word "lamentations." The title in the Greek Septuagint, *threnoi*, and the Latin Vulgate, *threni*, are translations of the Hebrew name *qinot*. It is not uncommon for manuscripts and printed editions to add the phrase "of Jeremiah" or "of Jeremiah the prophet."

## Chapters 1–2: **Commentary**

In the Book of Lamentations, Zion is personified as a distraught woman mourning the loss of her children. The meaning of the Hebrew word *Zion* is most likely "citadel" or "fortress." It is used in the Bible primarily as a symbol for the city of Jerusalem through metonymy—a figure of speech where one part of something can be used to represent the whole. The word "Zion" was originally applied only to the ridge upon which the Temple was constructed. In 2 Samuel 5:6–10, Zion is equated with both Jerusalem and "the city of David" which consisted at the time of just that fortified ridge. Ultimately, the term was then used for the entire city and became a synonym for Jerusalem.

**Chapter 1**

The great city of Jerusalem is deserted. She is weeping for all her children who have been taken away to Babylon. Jerusalem is guilty and so she now suffers for her crimes.

**Chapter 2**

God pours out his wrath on the city of Jerusalem. He has become Jerusalem's enemy and utterly destroyed it. God has never done anything like this before. Jerusalem mourns.

*The Lord is like an enemy;*
*he has swallowed up Israel.*
*He has swallowed up all her palaces*
*and destroyed her strongholds.*
*He has multiplied mourning and lamentation*
*for Daughter Judah.*

**Lamentations 2:5**

**Chapter 3**

God has unleashed his anger on Jerusalem, taking away everything that brought joy. We have sinned. All we can do is cry until God grants relief. Judge Babylon for what it did to us.

**Chapter 4**

God has done this to us because of our sins. He scattered the people among the nations. But someday the punishment will end. The exile in Babylon will not last long.

*You, Lord, reign forever;*
*your throne endures from generation to generation.*
*Why do you always forget us?*
*Why do you forsake us so long?*
*Restore us to yourself, Lord, that we may return;*
*renew our days as of old*
*unless you have utterly rejected us*
*and are angry with us beyond measure.*

**Lamentations 5:19–22**

**Chapter 5**

God, don't forget our pain. We sinned. Please forgive us. Do not forget about us. Restore us—unless you really have rejected us for all time.

# Ezekiel

## Overview

The title of the Book of Ezekiel is the same in Hebrew as it is in English. The name Ezekiel means "God is strong."

The Book of Ezekiel is a long series of oracles received by the priest Ezekiel, son of Buzi, who began to prophesy in Babylonia in the fifth year of Jehoiachin's exile, around 593 BC. He was therefore probably born around 622 BC, and had been taken captive to Babylon with Jehoiachin in 597 BC (cf. 2 Kings 24).

The entire book is dated according to the reign of Jehoiachin, and covers the years from about 593 through 570 BC. The first deportation of captives to Babylon from Judah had occurred about 605 BC, leaving Jehoiachin as king in Jerusalem. This is when the prophet Daniel was taken captive. The second deportation occurred about 597 BC.

---

## Chapter 1: Commentary

The Book of Ezekiel opens with Ezekiel's vision of God's throne room. The strange creatures are cherubs (see Ezekiel 10:20–22), commonly portrayed as winged lions. The cherubs also appeared as decorations in the Temple of Yahweh in Jerusalem, and overshadowed the Ark of the Covenant (see Exodus 25:10–22). Wheels were often attached to the bottoms of the thrones of Ancient Near Eastern kings. The overall shape of Ezekiel's vision matches an earlier description of God's throne from the time of Moses in Exodus 24:9–11, when Moses, Aaron, Aaron's sons, and 70 of the elders of Israel ascended Mount Sinai, saw Israel's God, and had a meal with him.

*"Son of man, I have made you a watchman for the people of Israel; so hear the word I speak and give them warning from me. When I say to a wicked person, 'You will surely die,' and you do not warn them or speak out to dissuade them from their evil ways in order to save their life, that wicked person will die for their sin, and I will hold you accountable for their blood. But if you do warn the wicked person and they do not turn from their wickedness or from their evil ways, they will die for their sin; but you will have saved yourself."*

**Ezekiel 3:17–19**

**11**  **15**  **17**

Ezekiel sees four living creatures with four faces: human, lion, ox, and eagle. Each has four wings. They stand beside wheels supporting a blue dome where Yahweh sits on his throne.

Chapter **1**

**7**

Yahweh tells him to be a prophet to the Israelites, to never fear them, and to never be rebellious like them. Then God has Ezekiel eat a scroll.

Chapter **2**

**7**

The scroll tastes like honey. God tells Ezekiel to be a watchman for Israel. Ezekiel will be unable to speak except on those occasions when God speaks through him.

Chapter **3**

**7**  **9**

Ezekiel draws the city of Jerusalem on a brick and lays siege to it, then must lie on his side next to it for over a year, eating bread he bakes over cow dung.

Chapter **4**

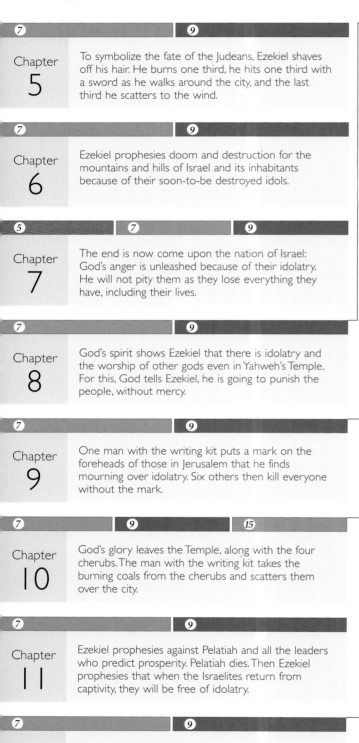

**Chapter 5**

To symbolize the fate of the Judeans, Ezekiel shaves off his hair. He burns one third, he hits one third with a sword as he walks around the city, and the last third he scatters to the wind.

**Chapter 6**

Ezekiel prophesies doom and destruction for the mountains and hills of Israel and its inhabitants because of their soon-to-be destroyed idols.

**Chapter 7**

The end is now come upon the nation of Israel: God's anger is unleashed because of their idolatry. He will not pity them as they lose everything they have, including their lives.

**Chapter 8**

God's spirit shows Ezekiel that there is idolatry and the worship of other gods even in Yahweh's Temple. For this, God tells Ezekiel, he is going to punish the people, without mercy.

**Chapter 9**

One man with the writing kit puts a mark on the foreheads of those in Jerusalem that he finds mourning over idolatry. Six others then kill everyone without the mark.

**Chapter 10**

God's glory leaves the Temple, along with the four cherubs. The man with the writing kit takes the burning coals from the cherubs and scatters them over the city.

**Chapter 11**

Ezekiel prophesies against Pelatiah and all the leaders who predict prosperity. Pelatiah dies. Then Ezekiel prophesies that when the Israelites return from captivity, they will be free of idolatry.

**Chapter 12**

Ezekiel packs as if going into exile, then digs a hole through the wall of his house at dusk. This illustrates how the prince and people of Israel would soon be exiled.

---

*I looked, and I saw a figure like that of a man. From what appeared to be his waist down he was like fire, and from there up his appearance was as bright as glowing metal. He stretched out what looked like a hand and took me by the hair of my head. The Spirit lifted me up between earth and heaven and in visions of God he took me to Jerusalem, to the entrance of the north gate of the inner court, where the idol that provokes to jealousy stood. And there before me was the glory of the God of Israel, as in the vision I had seen in the plain.*

**Ezekiel 8:2–4**

## Chapter 9: **Commentary**

In Ezekiel 9:4–6, God's angel marks the foreheads of the faithful in order to protect them from judgment. Such "marking" is widespread in the Bible. In Genesis 4:14 God placed a mark on Cain to protect him from suffering vengeance for the murder of his brother Abel. In Exodus 13:9, God tells the Israelites that their annual celebration of Passover will "be for you like a sign on your hand and a reminder on your forehead that this law of the Lord is to be on your lips." (Exodus 13:9). In Deuteronomy 6, the Israelites were told to bind the law as symbols "on your hands and bind them on your foreheads. Write them on your houses and on your gates." (Deuteronomy 6:8–9). In the New Testament Book of Revelation, 144,000 will receive a seal on their foreheads to protect them from the coming judgment (Revelation 7:3–4), while in contrast, those who receive the "mark of the Beast" on their foreheads will be judged by God (Revelation 13:16–17, 14:9–11). Finally, those who are part of God's kingdom will receive his name on their foreheads (Revelation 22:4).

---

*These were the living creatures I had seen beneath the God of Israel by the Kebar River, and I realized that they were cherubim. Each had four faces and four wings, and under their wings was what looked like human hands. Their faces had the same appearance as those I had seen by the Kebar River. Each one went straight ahead.*

**Ezekiel 10:20–22**

---

*The word of the Lord came to me: "Son of man, the Israelites are saying, 'The vision he sees is for many years from now, and he prophesies about the distant future.'*

*"Therefore say to them, 'This is what the Sovereign Lord says: None of my words will be delayed any longer; whatever I say will be fulfilled, declares the Sovereign Lord.'"*

**Ezekiel 12:26–28**

## Chapter 16: **Commentary**

As with the other prophets, Ezekiel used the imagery of adultery and prostitution to picture Israel's idolatry. Like an adulterous spouse engaged in relationships with other people, the Israelites worshiped other gods while still worshiping Yahweh. Ezekiel takes that picture to an extreme with his description of Jerusalem as an adulterous wife. Ezekiel's language is explicit, even vulgar. No translations would dare to use such language. Ezekiel's point was not to be prurient. Instead, he wanted to shock his audience into understanding just how badly they had offended God by their idolatry. He uses similar graphic language and imagery in Ezekiel 23.

*You slaughtered my children and sacrificed them to the idols. In all your detestable practices and your prostitution you did not remember the days of your youth, when you were naked and bare, kicking about in your blood.*

*"Woe! Woe to you, declares the Sovereign Lord. In addition to all your other wickedness, you built a mound for yourself and made a lofty shrine in every public square. At every street corner you built your lofty shrines and degraded your beauty, spreading your legs with increasing promiscuity to anyone who passed by. You engaged in prostitution with the Egyptians, your neighbors with large genitals, and aroused my anger with your increasing promiscuity."*

**Ezekiel 16:21–26**

## Chapter 18: **Commentary**

Ezekiel's emphasis that only the guilty would suffer for their wrongdoing was not new to Judaism. Ezekiel, like all the prophets, was not innovative. Instead, he tried to remind his audience of what God had already taught. Deuteronomy 24:16 is clear: "Parents are not to be put to death for their children, nor children put to death for their parents; each of you will die for your own sin." Ezekiel merely restates and expands upon the preexisting command.

*"What do you people mean by quoting this proverb about the land of Israel:*

*"'The parents eat sour grapes, and the children's teeth are set on edge'?*

*"As surely as I live, declares the Sovereign Lord, you will no longer quote this proverb in Israel. For everyone belongs to me, the parent as well as the child—both alike belong to me. The one who sins is the one who will die."*

**Ezekiel 18:2–4**

---

**7** **9**

The prophets predicting peace are just making it up out of their own imaginations. There will be no peace. The false prophets will be destroyed with the destruction of Jerusalem.

Chapter **13**

**7** **9**

Those with idols in their hearts will hear only one message from God: repent! Jerusalem will be devastated by sword, famine, wild beasts, and plague. Few will survive.

Chapter **14**

**7** **9**

The wood of a vine is useless for building anything, so it is burned. Jerusalem is such a worthless vine: it will burn because of its unfaithfulness.

Chapter **15**

**6** **7** **9**

God loves Jerusalem, marries her, and gives her everything she could want. But she repays God's kindness by becoming a prostitute. So God will destroy her like her sister Samaria.

Chapter **16**

**6** **7**

An eagle plants a cedar of Lebanon that prospers. But then it turns to another eagle. Babylon replaces the exiled king, but the replacement turns to Egypt. Destruction comes.

Chapter **17**

**3** **5** **7**

People will suffer the consequences of only their own sins. God takes no pleasure in the death of the wicked. He'd rather they repent and gain forgiveness.

Chapter **18**

**4** **5** **6**

Ezekiel laments over what happened to the princes of Israel because of their rebellion and idolatry. He compares them to a lion and a vine.

Chapter **19**

**2** **7**

God explains that he was very slow to punish the Israelites for their evil ways, but now they are suffering the exile they deserve. When they repent, God will bring them back home.

Chapter **20**

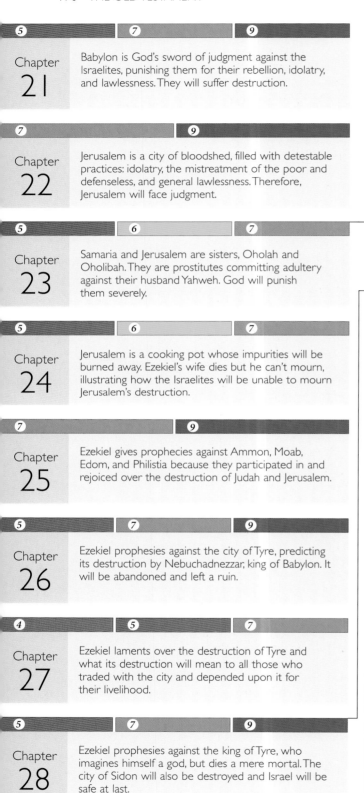

**Chapter 21**

Babylon is God's sword of judgment against the Israelites, punishing them for their rebellion, idolatry, and lawlessness. They will suffer destruction.

**Chapter 22**

Jerusalem is a city of bloodshed, filled with detestable practices: idolatry, the mistreatment of the poor and defenseless, and general lawlessness. Therefore, Jerusalem will face judgment.

**Chapter 23**

Samaria and Jerusalem are sisters, Oholah and Oholibah. They are prostitutes committing adultery against their husband Yahweh. God will punish them severely.

**Chapter 24**

Jerusalem is a cooking pot whose impurities will be burned away. Ezekiel's wife dies but he can't mourn, illustrating how the Israelites will be unable to mourn Jerusalem's destruction.

**Chapter 25**

Ezekiel gives prophecies against Ammon, Moab, Edom, and Philistia because they participated in and rejoiced over the destruction of Judah and Jerusalem.

**Chapter 26**

Ezekiel prophesies against the city of Tyre, predicting its destruction by Nebuchadnezzar, king of Babylon. It will be abandoned and left a ruin.

**Chapter 27**

Ezekiel laments over the destruction of Tyre and what its destruction will mean to all those who traded with the city and depended upon it for their livelihood.

**Chapter 28**

Ezekiel prophesies against the king of Tyre, who imagines himself a god, but dies a mere mortal. The city of Sidon will also be destroyed and Israel will be safe at last.

*Then the Babylonians came to her, to the bed of love, and in their lust they defiled her. After she had been defiled by them, she turned away from them in disgust. When she carried on her prostitution openly and exposed her naked body, I turned away from her in disgust, just as I had turned away from her sister. Yet she became more and more promiscuous as she recalled the days of her youth, when she was a prostitute in Egypt. There she lusted after her lovers, whose genitals were like those of donkeys and whose emission was like that of horses. So you longed for the lewdness of your youth, when in Egypt your bosom was caressed and your young breasts fondled.*

**Ezekiel 23:17–21**

## Chapter 28: **Commentary**

Many of the kings of the Ancient Near East believed themselves to be gods. The Egyptian Pharaoh was supposed to be an incarnation of the sun-god Re. When Hatshepsut, a woman, became Pharaoh she created new mythology in order to explain her ascension to the throne. Alexander the Great was proclaimed divine after he conquered Egypt, while the later rulers of Rome, the Caesars, also claimed to be gods.

In Ezekiel 28 the prophet mocks the supposed divinity of the king of Tyre. Yahweh points out that the king would be forced to recognize his own humanity when those who conquered his city killed him.

Although some commentators have tried to see Satan's downfall in the destruction of the king of Tyre, the Devil is not discussed in the passage. The imagery describing the king of Tyre is instead similar to that used of the Pharaoh of Egypt in Ezekiel 31.

Eden is a trading partner of Tyre (see Ezekiel 27:23), not the garden home of Adam and Eve. In fact, Eden was commonly used metaphorically for any beautiful and lush region (see Isaiah 51:3, Ezekiel 36:35 and Joel 2:3).

*"I am going to bring foreigners against you,*
*the most ruthless of nations;*
*they will draw their swords against your beauty and*
*wisdom and pierce your shining splendor.*
*They will bring you down to the pit,*
*and you will die a violent death*
*in the heart of the seas.*
*Will you then say, "I am a god,"*
*in the presence of those who kill you?*
*You will be but a mortal, not a god,*
*in the hands of those who slay you.*
*You will die the death of the uncircumcised*
*at the hands of foreigners.*
*I have spoken, declares the Sovereign Lord."*

**Ezekiel 28:7–10**

## Chapter 29: **Commentary**

Ezekiel gives more attention to judgments against Egypt than to any other nation besides his own. The Pharaoh of Egypt at the time of his prophesies was Hophra, who reigned from 588 to 569 BC. His grandfather, Pharaoh Neco, had killed the Jewish king Josiah at Megiddo in 609 BC. Pharaoh, unsurprisingly, is described as a monster; the hooks in the jaw describe the tools that were used in capturing crocodiles in the Nile. Thus, the imagery that Ezekiel uses for Nebuchadnezzar's conquest of Egypt is in keeping with an Egyptian setting. A fragmentary British museum tablet describes Nebuchadnezzar's invasion of Egypt during his 37th year on the throne (he ruled from 605 to 562 BC).

## Chapter 33: **Commentary**

An important concept is made explicit in Ezekiel 33:11, but is seen throughout the biblical record: God is the God of second chances. God takes no pleasure in the death of the wicked, or in any kind of punishment, but would rather see people repent and turn from their sin. The Israelites had been guilty of worshiping other gods for generations. They were idolaters during the time of Jacob, when they left Egypt, when they conquered Canaan, and even during the time of David. God was very slow to bring punishment against them, waiting many generations before the Assyrians (around 722 BC) and the Babylonians (between 605 and 586 BC) finally conquered and exiled them.

**⑤ ⑦**

Ezekiel prophesied against the Pharaoh of Egypt, predicting that Nebuchadnezzar would conquer him. Because Nebuchadnezzar's battle against Tyre netted him no reward, God gives him Egypt in payment.

Chapter **29**

**④ ⑤ ⑦**

Ezekiel laments over the destruction of Egypt and its dependent peoples by Nebuchadnezzar, king of Babylon.

Chapter **30**

**⑤ ⑥ ⑦**

Assyria was once a mighty cedar, but it was cut down by Babylon. Egypt's Pharaoh is a mighty cedar and he too will be cut down by Babylon.

Chapter **31**

**④ ⑦**

Ezekiel laments over Pharaoh, the king of Egypt, comparing him to a lion captured in a net. Babylon will destroy Pharaoh who will die and be buried with the uncircumcised.

Chapter **32**

**⑦**

God calls Ezekiel to serve as a watchman to warn the people of Israel. In the twelfth year of his exile, Ezekiel hears that Jerusalem has been destroyed for its idolatry and lawlessness.

Chapter **33**

*"Son of man, say to the Israelites, 'This is what you are saying: "Our offenses and sins weigh us down, and we are wasting away because of them. How then can we live?"' Say to them, 'As surely as I live, declares the Sovereign Lord, I take no pleasure in the death of the wicked, but rather that they turn from their ways and live. Turn! Turn from your evil ways! Why will you die, people of Israel?"'*
**Ezekiel 33:10–11**

**Cherubim**
*The cherubim that appear in Ezekiel 1, 10, and elsewhere throughout the Bible were well known in the ancient world, for instance as the winged lions on Assyrian monuments.*

| 7 | |
|---|---|
| Chapter **34** | Ezekiel prophesies that God will become Israel's shepherd: he will seek the lost, heal the sick, strengthen the weak, make a covenant of peace with them, and eliminate their enemies. |

| 7 | 9 |
|---|---|
| Chapter **35** | Ezekiel prophesies against Edom: it will be destroyed and become a desolate waste because of how it treated the Israelites and rejoiced over their destruction. |

| 2 | 7 |
|---|---|
| Chapter **36** | The mountains and hills will flourish, and the Israelites will be cleansed and restored to their homeland. Their heart of stone will be replaced with a heart of flesh. |

| 6 | 7 |
|---|---|
| Chapter **37** | A valley of dry bones reassembles and comes back to life, symbolizing the restoration of the nation. Judah and Israel will reunite and be ruled by one king, a descendant of David. |

| 7 | 13 |
|---|---|
| Chapter **38** | When Israel is peaceful and prosperous, Gog will invade from the north, advancing like a cloud. |

| 7 | 13 |
|---|---|
| Chapter **39** | God will destroy Gog and his army, feeding their flesh to the birds and animals. The Israelites will be restored to their land, where they will prosper and live securely. |

| 7 | 16 |
|---|---|
| Chapter **40** | God gives Ezekiel a vision of a new Jerusalem and its Temple, where a man like bronze shows him its gates, inner court, and inner rooms, measuring them all with a measuring rod. |

## Chapter 37: **Commentary**

The concept of the afterlife was slow to make an appearance in the Bible. Although the Egyptians, by whom the Israelites were enslaved before Moses led them to the Promised Land, spent much of their lives planning for the afterlife, the Israelites barely mention it through most of the Old Testament. Ezekiel's vision of the dry bones that come to life is one of the first pictures of resurrection in the Bible. Israel had been destroyed, first by the Assyrians and then by the Babylonians. The country was in ruins. It seemed improbable that the Israelites would continue as a people. But the prophet Ezekiel described a vision from God of a valley filled with dry bones that come back to life: though their nation had been destroyed, God would restore it. By the time of the New Testament, a belief in personal immortality—personal resurrection—was firmly a part of first-century Judaism.

## Chapters 38–39: **Commentary**

Who are Gog, Magog, Meshek, and Tubal? Gog and Magog are only mentioned in Ezekiel 38–39 and in Revelation 20:8. Most scholars believe that Gog is a reference to the seventh-century BC king of Lydia, Gyges. Lydia is in Asia Minor. Magog is probably derived from an Akkadian phrase that means "land of Gog." Meshek has been identified as the region of Lydia and Tubal is also located in Asia Minor. Most scholars believe that Gog should not be identified with any specific individual, but instead should be pictured as simply the leader of any who attempt to exterminate the people of God. The fate of those who go against God's people is the same as those who would attempt to oppose God, because God treats his people as if they were himself.

## Chapter 40: **Commentary**

Why does Ezekiel's description of a new Temple in Jerusalem not match either Solomon's Temple nor the Temple that the Jewish people built when they returned from exile? As with the story of Gog and Magog, most scholars assume that the description of a new Jerusalem and Temple, in a restored Jewish state, is an idealized one. It simply means that God's people will forever be with him.

In the New Testament Book of Revelation, the same imagery appears. In Revelation 20:7–8 Satan assembles the nations of the world, described as Gog and Magog, against God's people, only to be entirely defeated and destroyed. What follows in Revelation parallels what follows Gog and Magog in Ezekiel: the eternal kingdom of God, a new heaven and earth, with the bride of the Lamb, the New Jerusalem, descending from heaven (see Revelation 21). The bride of the Lamb, however—the "New Jerusalem" of Revelation 21—is not a physical city. Instead, it is the people of God themselves (see Revelation 19:7, 22:17, Ephesians 5:21–33).

*Then the man brought me to the gate facing east, and I saw the glory of the God of Israel coming from the east. His voice was like the roar of rushing waters, and the land was radiant with his glory. The vision I saw was like the vision I had seen when he came to destroy the city and like the visions I had seen by the Kebar River, and I fell facedown. The glory of the Lord entered the temple through the gate facing east.*

**Ezekiel 43:1–4**

*This land will be his possession in Israel. And my princes will no longer oppress my people but will allow the people of Israel to possess the land according to their tribes.*

*"'This is what the Sovereign Lord says: You have gone far enough, princes of Israel! Give up your violence and oppression and do what is just and right. Stop dispossessing my people, declares the Sovereign Lord. You are to use accurate scales, an accurate ephah and an accurate bath."*

**Ezekiel 45:8–10**

*Then he led me back to the bank of the river. When I arrived there, I saw a great number of trees on each side of the river. He said to me, "This water flows toward the eastern region and goes down into the Arabah, where it enters the Dead Sea. When it empties into the sea, the salty water there becomes fresh. Swarms of living creatures will live wherever the river flows. There will be large numbers of fish, because this water flows there and makes the salt water fresh; so where the river flows everything will live. Fishermen will stand along the shore; from En Gedi to En Eglaim there will be places for spreading nets. The fish will be of many kinds—like the fish of the Mediterranean Sea. But the swamps and marshes will not become fresh; they will be left for salt. Fruit trees of all kinds will grow on both banks of the river. Their leaves will not wither, nor will their fruit fail. Every month they will bear fruit, because the water from the sanctuary flows to them. Their fruit will serve for food and their leaves for healing."*

**Ezekiel 47:6–12**

The man measures the rest of the new Temple, inside and out: the inner sanctuaries, entrances, and main hall.

Chapter
41

The man shows Ezekiel the rooms for the priests, then measures all four sides of the area around the Temple.

Chapter
42

God's glory then returns to the Temple. The great altar is measured and God gives detailed instructions for performing the sacrifices.

Chapter
43

God gives detailed regulations for the Levites and priests. God warns that the Israelites must not disobey him again.

Chapter
44

A large section of the land of Israel around the Temple is designated a sacred district for the Levites. God gives additional regulations for sacrifices and Passover celebrations.

Chapter
45

God gives instructions for proper behavior on the Sabbath and other appointed festivals. He also explains the proper sacrifices.

Chapter
46

A river, lined with fruit trees, flows from the Temple to the Dead Sea. The fruit is for food and the leaves are for healing. God describes the boundaries for the new land of Israel.

Chapter
47

Each of the 12 tribes receives a section of the new land of Israel. The new city of Jerusalem has three gates on each of its four sides, each named for a tribe of Israel.

Chapter
48

# Daniel

## Overview

The Book of Daniel is named after the prophet Daniel. The name means "God is Judge." Daniel's friends in captivity are remembered by their Babylonian names rather than their Hebrew names. Esther is likewise remembered for her Persian name rather than her Hebrew name. But Daniel, though given the Babylonian name Belteshazzar, is not well remembered by it.

The Book of Daniel is the story of a young man taken to Babylon following the conquest of his nation by the Babylonian Empire, his rise to a position of responsibility, and his visions of God's plans for Babylon and Israel. The prophet was taken captive by Nebuchadnezzar in 605 BC, during the first deportation recorded in 2 Kings 24:8–17. Daniel continued to minister through the reign of King Cyrus, under whom the Israelites began to return to Israel (Ezra 1:1–4 and 2 Chronicles 36:22–23).

**Chapter 1**

Daniel and his friends Shadrach, Meshach, and Abednego are taken to Babylon, receive training in the language and literature of their captors, and are assigned jobs in the bureaucracy.

**Chapter 2**

Daniel explains Nebuchadnezzar's dream of a statue representing current and future kingdoms in the Middle East. Nebuchadnezzar praises Daniel's God and rewards Daniel.

**Chapter 3**

Nebuchadnezzar builds a statue, then orders all to worship it. Shadrach, Meshach, and Abednego refuse and are cast into a fiery furnace. They survive and Nebuchadnezzar rewards them.

**Chapter 4**

Nebuchadnezzar dreams of a tree being felled. Daniel explains that it means Nebuchadnezzar will go crazy. When he later returns to his senses, Nebuchadnezzar praises God for his deliverance.

## Chapter 1: **Commentary**

Nebuchadnezzar II ruled from 605 to 562 BC. He was the most powerful and longest reigning king of the neo-Babylonian Empire, an empire that lasted from 625 BC until it was conquered by the Persians in 539 BC. Nebuchadnezzar's name means "O Nabu, preserve the boundary stone." Properly defined boundaries were important in the Ancient world. Curses were written on boundary stones against any who dared move them. The Bible records multiple warnings against moving such markers (Deuteronomy 19:14, 27:17; Proverbs 22:28, 23:10). Nabu was the Babylonian god of writing and wisdom, and the son of Marduk, the chief god of Babylon.

## Chapter 2: **Commentary**

Daniel explains that Nebuchadnezzar's dream reveals future events, specifically, the coming and going of four kingdoms. Scholars are not in agreement about the kingdoms. The first kingdom is identified with the neo-Babylonian Empire. Most believe the second kingdom is the Persian Empire. Many think the third kingdom is a reference to the Greek empire of Alexander the Great. When he dies, it breaks apart, becoming the fourth empire. Other scholars wish to identify the fourth empire with Rome. Many Christian scholars believe that the final "kingdom" replacing the world's kingdoms is the Christian Church.

*Then the men went as a group to King Darius and said to him, "Remember, Your Majesty, that according to the law of the Medes and Persians no decree or edict that the king issues can be changed."*

*So the king gave the order, and they brought Daniel and threw him into the lions' den. The king said to Daniel, "May your God, whom you serve continually, rescue you!"*

**Daniel 6:15–16**

## Chapter 9: **Commentary**

Daniel 9 builds upon Jeremiah's prediction that the Babylonian captivity would last 70 years (see Jeremiah 29:10 and 2 Chronicles 36:21). Following Daniel's prayer, the angel Gabriel appears and explains that there are an additional 70 "sevens" decreed for the people of Israel. Many Christian interpreters believe that the "anointed one" that is cut off is a prophecy of Jesus and his crucifixion, while the reference to seven years, with sacrifice ending halfway through, is a reference to the Jewish revolt against Rome. Others have taken these verses about a coming desolation as indicating the end of the world and the time of the antichrist. Still others believe Daniel's vision has something to do with the Antiochus IV Ephiphanes, who ended proper sacrifice in the Temple by his sacrifice of a pig—an unclean animal—on its altar.

## Chapters 10–11: **Commentary**

When Alexander the Great died, his newly conquered empire was divided among his generals, with Ptolemy receiving Egypt and Seleucus gaining control of Asia. Antiochus IV Epiphanes was one of Seleucus' descendants. He took the Seleucid throne in 175 BC and reigned until 163 BC. In 168 BC he nearly conquered Egypt but was prevented from success by the newly ascendant Romans who threatened him with war if he did not withdraw. While he was in Egypt, the rumor spread in Israel, then a part of the Seleucid Empire, that he had been killed. The high priest that Antiochus had put in charge, Menelaus, was forced to flee from Jerusalem when the previous high priest gathered a force of 1,000 soldiers and attacked the city. After Antiochus left Egypt, he headed north, restored order in Jerusalem, and put Menelaus back in power. Then he executed many of the rebels and outlawed Jewish religious rites and traditions. He ordered the Jewish people to worship Zeus instead and headed home.
This united the population against both Antiochus and Menelaus—the opposite of what he had hoped for. The rebel armies were soon defeating the armies that Antiochus sent against them. But with the death of Antiochus IV in 163 BC, his army commander agreed to permit the restoration of the Jewish religious rites and practices. The revolt was officially over. The holiday of Hanukkah has its origin in the events following the cleansing of the Temple in Jerusalem.

| 7 | 9 | 17 |
|---|---|---|

King Belshazzar sees a hand write three words on the wall. Daniel explains that the Persians are going to conquer Babylon. That night, the Persians kill Belshazzar.

**Chapter 5**

| 17 | | |
|---|---|---|

King Darius decrees that no one may pray to anyone but him for a month. Daniel refuses and is cast into a den of lions. He survives and Darius praises Daniel's God.

**Chapter 6**

| 7 | 13 | |
|---|---|---|

During the reign of Belshazzar, Daniel dreams of four powerful beasts. The angel Gabriel interprets them as four future kingdoms.

**Chapter 7**

| 7 | 13 | |
|---|---|---|

Daniel has a vision of a goat destroying a ram. Gabriel explains that the ram is Persia and the goat is Greece. A small horn on the goat is a future evil king.

**Chapter 8**

| 7 | 12 | 13 |
|---|---|---|

During the reign of Xerxes, Daniel confesses the sins of Israel in prayer. Gabriel explains that 70 "sevens" will end with desolation and an abomination in the Temple.

**Chapter 9**

| 7 | 13 | 15 |
|---|---|---|

During the reign of Cyrus, Daniel has a vision of a great war and mourns for three weeks. The angel Michael tells him not to be afraid and promises him an explanation.

**Chapter 10**

| 7 | 13 | 15 |
|---|---|---|

Michael explains that there will be war between Persia and Greece. A future mighty king will devastate the people of Israel and God's Temple before he is finally overthrown.

**Chapter 11**

| 7 | 13 | 15 |
|---|---|---|

There will be a great period of distress and trouble, but then the righteous will be resurrected. It will all happen in the distant future.

**Chapter 12**

# Hosea

## Overview

The book title is the same both in Hebrew and in the Greek and English translations. Hosea is a variant form of the name "Joshua." "Jesus" is the Anglicized Greek form of the same name, which means "salvation."

Very little is known about Hosea, since he is never mentioned outside this book. His prophecies cover the period from about 753 BC to 715 BC, from the end of the reign of Jeroboam II of Israel to the beginning of the reign of King Hezekiah of

**Chapter 1**

To illustrate how Israel was treating God, God has Hosea marry a prostitute named Gomer. The names of his children signify the future judgment on Israel and Judah.

**Chapter 2**

God rebukes and punishes Israel for idolatry, comparing her to an adulteress. Nevertheless, God will someday be reconciled to the Israelites as his people.

**Chapter 3**

Hosea's wife had left him and been sold into slavery. He buys her back and reconciles with her, illustrating God's intentions for the Israelites.

**Chapter 4**

God brings his charges against the Israelites, accusing them of unfaithfulness, idolatry, and law breaking. He tells them that they will be punished.

**Chapter 5**

God says that Ephraim will be destroyed and taken captive. The Israelites will feel the wrath of God: God will attack them like a lion attacks its prey.

**Chapter 6**

Israel is unrepentant. The Israelites outwardly practice their religion, but their hearts are not in it. Therefore, they will be judged.

## Chapter 1: Commentary

In 2 Kings 9–10 Jehu, the commander of Israel's army, leads a rebellion against Joram, the king of Israel, the son of Ahab and Jezebel. In Jezreel, Jehu kills Joram, his mother Jezebel, and all the remaining members of the royal household. Then Jehu gathers all the priests and leaders of Baal-worship together and slaughters them.

Though the author of 2 Kings seems to praise Jehu for exterminating an evil king and the worshipers of Baal (see 2 Kings 10:30), the prophet Hosea pronounces God's judgment against the slaughter. Though God himself is now judging his people for their worship of Baal and other false gods, he is not in favor of murdering them. Instead, by this criticism, the prophet seems to suggest that God does not wish to see the wicked killed, but rather wishes to see them repent and change their behavior (cf. Ezekiel 33:11). When God speaks of the destruction of his enemies, he often means it metaphorically: to destroy them by changing them into his friends.

## Chapters 5–6: Commentary

God is not a vending machine that dispenses goodies as a result of paying the right amount of money and performing the right rituals. The prophet believes that there is a difference between superstition and real faith. For him, superstition is an attempt to control God. Real faith is being open to letting God control you. The used car dealer will promise you tickets to the game and cookies from his mother—but as soon as you sign and pay for the car, he disappears. He merely simulated friendship, manipulating you until he got what he wanted. God is not interested in a used-car relationship with his people. He wants them to be his real friends, just as he intends to be their real friends.

Judah. Jeroboam II died about 753 BC, while Hezekiah began his reign around 715 BC.

The golden age of prosperity for Israel was ending with Jeroboam II. There was political, moral, and religious chaos. The people of Israel worshiped Yahweh, but also worshiped other gods as well.

Hosea's prophecies were directed to the people of the northern kingdom of Israel. Prophets contemporary with Hosea were Amos and perhaps Jonah, in Israel. In Judah, Micah and Isaiah were prophesying.

*"They sow the wind*
*and reap the whirlwind.*
*The stalk has no head;*
*it will produce no flour.*
*Were it to yield grain,*
*foreigners would swallow it up.*
*Israel is swallowed up;*
*now she is among the nations*
*like something no one wants."*

**Hosea 8:7–8**

## Chapter 11: **Commentary**

God expresses his displeasure at having to bring judgment upon the Israelites. The phrase translated in 11:8 as "my heart is changed within me" would better be rendered as, "my insides are churning." God is upset about what he is being forced to do by his contract with the people of Israel. That contract—the Book of Deuteronomy— requires God to discipline them for their idolatry and mistreatment of one another. Nevertheless, despite how painful it will be for both God and his people, God will do it because he knows it is necessary and for the best, like a parent disciplining his child. When the Israelites return from captivity in Babylon and Assyria, they will return worshiping only Yahweh, never again tempted by idolatry.

*Who is wise? Let them realize these things.*
*Who is discerning? Let them understand.*
*The ways of the Lord are right;*
*the righteous walk in them,*
*but the rebellious stumble in them.*

**Hosea 14:9**

| 5 | 7 | 9 |

Whenever God thought about restoring Israel, they just sinned even more. The Israelites are foolish. God wants to restore them, but they have rejected him.

**Chapter 7**

| 5 | 7 | 9 |

Israel has rejected what is good. The Israelites follow idols and ignore all of God's commandments. As a result, God does not appreciate or accept their sacrifices.

**Chapter 8**

| 5 | 7 | 9 |

Israel has worshiped other gods besides Yahweh, so the time of punishment is at hand for all their many sins. They will become wanderers among the nations.

**Chapter 9**

| 5 | 7 | 9 |

Israel has been deceitful and idolatrous. Instead of righteousness, they have sown wickedness. Therefore, they will harvest judgment.

**Chapter 10**

| 5 | 7 | 10 |

God loves Israel. He rescued them from Egypt. He made them prosperous. He would rather not punish them, but he must, since he is bound by the contract he made with them.

**Chapter 11**

| 5 | 7 | 9 |

The Israelites seek for help from everyone but God; they practice idolatry and break God's commandments, despite the warning of God's prophets.

**Chapter 12**

| 5 | 7 | 9 |

The Israelites have worshiped idols, even though God warned them since they left Egypt to worship only him. So God will judge them and destroy them.

**Chapter 13**

| 2 | 5 | 7 |

When the Israelites repent and turn back to God, then God will forgive them, heal them, and bring them back home.

**Chapter 14**

# Joel
## Overview

The name of the Book of Joel is the same both in Hebrew and English. It means "Yahweh is God." Joel prophesied to Judah and Jerusalem and is mentioned nowhere else in the Bible. The date for Joel's prophecy is uncertain. Those who suggest a date before the Babylonian exile point out that Joel 3:10 matches Isaiah 2:4 and Micah 4:3, while Joel 3:16 is identical to Amos 1:2 and 4:8. However, Joel could just as easily be quoting the other prophets as they could be quoting him. Judah is referred to as Israel in 3:1–2 and 2:27, improbable as long as the northern kingdom still existed. There is no mention of a locust plague of the sort described by Joel in either Kings or Chronicles. More significantly, however, there is no mention of the sin of idolatry, the central issue for pre-exilic prophets, which allows us to distinguish pre-exilic from post-exilic prophets. Therefore, the majority of scholars assume that Joel was prophesying after the Babylonian captivity, making the date for Joel's prophecies sometime after 520 BC.

It should be noted that the use of the phrase "Day of the Lord" which appears in the Book of Joel is not necessarily to be understood as a reference to the end of the world. Rather, it was

**Devastation**
*In an agricultural society, a plague of locusts could lead to widespread famine and loss of life.*

| 4 | 5 | 7 |
|---|---|---|

Chapter

1

Joel prophesies about a plague of locusts that will come and devastate Israel like an army, stripping the land of all its crops. Israel will mourn.

| 2 | 5 | 7 |
|---|---|---|

Chapter

2

The army of locusts devours the land like a fire. God asks for repentance and promises to replace what has been lost. He will pour his spirit upon the people of Israel and deliver them.

## Chapter 1: **Commentary**

The language of the Old Testament is primarily Hebrew. Although the Jewish community survived exile in Babylon, the Hebrew language did not. For nearly 2,000 years until its revival as part of the Zionist movement at the end of the nineteenth century it was a dead language, like Latin. Thus our understanding of that ancient tongue is dependent upon how it is used in the Bible, almost the only example of Ancient Hebrew still in existence. Scholars don't necessarily understand all the words clearly. An example of that lack of understanding occurs in chapter 1 of Joel, in verse 4, which lists four kinds of locusts. English translations attempt to distinguish between them, but translating them as "swarm," "great," "young," and "other" is simply guesswork.

Similar problems exist for some of the more unusual gems, plants, and animals that occur elsewhere in the Bible. As a consequence, different translations will sometimes vary wildly, one calling an animal a baboon and another calling it a peacock (cf. 1 Kings 10:22 in NIV and in KJV).

used to describe any period when God was acting in bringing judgment against a people. Below is a listing of all the occurrences of the phrase in the Bible. A perusal should give the reader a good overview of the range of meanings for the phrase.

**Old Testament**
Isaiah 2:6–12; 13:6, 9; 22:5; 34:8; 61:2
Lamentations 2:22
Ezekiel 7:7–19; 13:5; 30:3
Joel 1:15; 2:1; 2:11; 2:31; 3:14
Amos 5:18, 20
Obadiah 15
Zephaniah 1:7–18; 2:2–3
Zechariah 14:1
Malachi 4:5

**New Testament**
Romans 2:5
1 Corinthians 1:8; 1:14
2 Corinthians 1:14
Philippians 1:6–10; 2:16
1 Thessalonians 5:2
2 Thessalonians 2:2
2 Peter 3:10–12
Revelation 16:14

## Chapter 3: **Commentary**

The normal war cry, which appears in Joel 3:10, calls for the nation's inhabitants to take their farming implements and convert them into weapons. That call to arms was transformed into a call for peace by the prophets Isaiah and Micah (see Isaiah 2:4 and Micah 4:3).

*Proclaim this among the nations:*
*Prepare for war!*
*Rouse the warriors!*
*Let all the fighting men draw near and attack.*
*Beat your plowshares into swords*
*and your pruning hooks into spears.*
*Let the weakling say,*
*"I am strong!"*
*Come quickly, all you nations from every side,*
*and assemble there.*
*   Bring down your warriors, Lord!*

**Joel 3:9–11**

**The prophet Joel**
*The prophet Joel son of Pethuel is known only through the prophecy that bears his name. When he wrote, where he lived, and what became of him remain a mystery.*

5   7   9

God calls upon the Israelites to prepare for war against their enemies, whom they will successfully defeat. Israel's enemies will be destroyed on the day of the Lord.

Chapter
3

# Amos

## Overview

The title for the Book of Amos is the same in Hebrew as it is in English. The name means "burden" or "burdensome." The prophecies Amos announced predicted God's judgment against Israel and the nations around it. Prophets who were working at the same time as Amos include Hosea and Jonah.

Amos is not mentioned anywhere else in the Bible. He was from Tekoa, a village about 6 miles (10 km) south of Bethlehem, in Judah. Amos was placed after Joel in the canon because it seemed to be an expansion of Joel 3:16: "The Lord will roar from Zion." In the same way, Obadiah seemed to be an expansion of Amos 9:12: "that they may possess the remnant of Edom." Rather than

**The prophet Amos**
*The prophet Amos was a shepherd and keeper of sycamore-fig trees who came from the small village of Tekoa, about 6 miles (10 km) south of Bethlehem.*

He said:
  "The Lord roars from Zion
and thunders from Jerusalem;
the pastures of the shepherds dry up,
and the top of Carmel withers."

**Amos 1:2**

## Chapter 2: **Commentary**

God announces, "I will send fire" in Amos 1:4, 7, 10, 12, 14, 2:2, and 2:5 against the various nations around Israel. At chapter 2:6, Amos turns his attention at last to Israel, announcing God's displeasure and pending judgment, but he does not announce that he will send fire against Israel. Instead, he speaks in some detail about their pending destruction and captivity at the hands of Assyria. Why does God not announce that he will send fire against Israel? Because "fire" is in fact shorthand for whatever unspecified judgment would befall the neighboring nations. Throughout the Bible, "fire" will be used as a metaphor meaning God's discipline, judgment, or punishment. The prophet's condemnation of Israel's enemies was kept short—mere summaries that were designed to get his listeners' attention and to get them on his side as he condemned Israel's neighbors, who were often Israel's enemies. But when he turns to Israel, he goes into specifics, rather than a summary of what will happen to the nation, because the whole focus of God's message through Amos is for Israel, rather than her neighbors.

| 5 | 7 | 9 |
|---|---|---|

Chapter 1

Amos describes God's coming judgment against Israel's neighbors. Damascus, Gaza, Tyre, Edom, and Amon are judged for four sins: fire will consume them.

| 5 | 7 | 9 |
|---|---|---|

Chapter 2

Amos describes God's coming judgment against Israel's neighbors. Moab and Judah will be judged for four sins. Then Amos announces that Israel, too, will be judged for four sins.

preaching to the people of Judah, Amos prophesied to the northern kingdom of Israel.

The book is dated between 767 and 753 BC. Both the northern kingdom under Jeroboam II and the southern kingdom, under Uzziah, were at the height of their prosperity. They had subjugated most of the nations around them, freeing them from worry about external powers. Given their prosperity and comfortable circumstances, neither Israel nor Judah had any obvious reason to anticipate God's coming judgment, although both kings were suffering a time of moral corruption, idolatry, luxury, and vice. And corruption existed not only in politics, but also in religion: most of the prophets and priests of both Judah and Israel were serving God only for profit and prestige.

*You levy a straw tax on the poor*
*and impose a tax on their grain.*
*Therefore, though you have built stone mansions,*
*you will not live in them;*
*though you have planted lush vineyards,*
*you will not drink their wine.*
*For I know how many are your offenses*
*and how great your sins.*

**Amos 5:11–12**

## Chapter 7: **Commentary**

Being a prophet was a recognized profession in both Israel and Judah. Most kings kept a group of court prophets as official advisors. For instance, we have the story of Ahab calling for his prophets to come before him and let him know if he and Jehoshaphat should go to war against Aram (1 Kings 22:1–6). Likewise, the king of Babylon, Nebuchadnezzar, had his official seers: court astrologers and magicians (see Daniel 2:1–3).

Thus Amaziah, the priest of Bethel, told Amos to go back to where he came from in Judah and to "earn his bread" by prophesying there. Amaziah assumed Amos was a prophet from the Judean court, come north to create dissension and trouble for Israel. Amos responds to his critic by announcing that he is not a professional prophet working for the Judean government. Instead, he claims to have been called by God out of his normal job as a shepherd and keeper of sycamore-fig trees to bring a specific message to Israel. He is merely following God's orders.

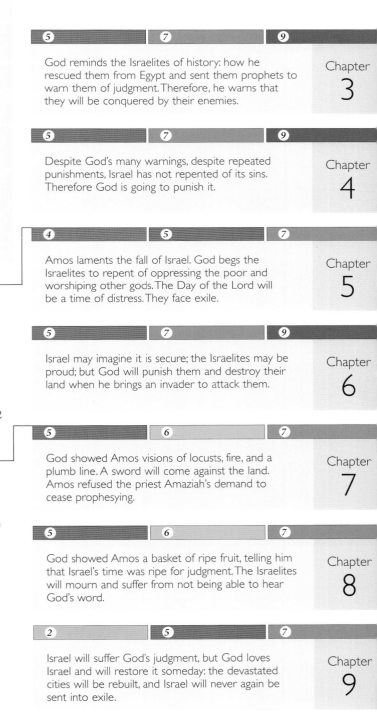

**5 7 9**

God reminds the Israelites of history: how he rescued them from Egypt and sent them prophets to warn them of judgment. Therefore, he warns that they will be conquered by their enemies.

Chapter **3**

**5 7 9**

Despite God's many warnings, despite repeated punishments, Israel has not repented of its sins. Therefore God is going to punish it.

Chapter **4**

**4 5 7**

Amos laments the fall of Israel. God begs the Israelites to repent of oppressing the poor and worshiping other gods. The Day of the Lord will be a time of distress. They face exile.

Chapter **5**

**5 7 9**

Israel may imagine it is secure; the Israelites may be proud; but God will punish them and destroy their land when he brings an invader to attack them.

Chapter **6**

**5 6 7**

God showed Amos visions of locusts, fire, and a plumb line. A sword will come against the land. Amos refused the priest Amaziah's demand to cease prophesying.

Chapter **7**

**5 6 7**

God showed Amos a basket of ripe fruit, telling him that Israel's time was ripe for judgment. The Israelites will mourn and suffer from not being able to hear God's word.

Chapter **8**

**2 5 7**

Israel will suffer God's judgment, but God loves Israel and will restore it someday: the devastated cities will be rebuilt, and Israel will never again be sent into exile.

Chapter **9**

# Obadiah

## Overview

I  Edom will be destroyed 1–9

II  Edom will be punished because of its sin against Israel 10–21

The title of the Book of Obadiah is the same in Hebrew as it is in English. The name Obadiah means "servant of Yahweh." It was a relatively common Old Testament name. Obadiah proclaims God's judgment against Israel's neighbor, Edom, for its mistreatment of God's people.

Virtually nothing is known about the prophet Obadiah. Even the time when he was alive and made his prophecy is obscure, though two time periods dominate the scholarly discussion.

Some postulate that Obadiah wrote the book between 847 and 841 BC. Just before King Jehoram died, the Philistines and Arabs invaded Jerusalem, while Edom watched from the sidelines. Those who hold to such an early date point out that there are many identical phrases in Obadiah 1–9 and Jeremiah 49:7–22, suggesting some literary relationship between the two.

Most scholars believe that the calamity Obadiah describes in verses 11–14 is the Babylonian conquest of Jerusalem in 586 BC. Several phrases that Obadiah uses are also found in the book of Joel:

• Obadiah 10 is the same as Joel 3:19
• 11 is the same as 3:3
• 15 is the same as 1:15, 2:1, 3:4, 3:7, and 3:14
• 18 is the same as 3:8.

It is possible that in Joel 2:32, when the prophet uses the words "as the Lord has said," Joel is, in fact, quoting from Obadiah 18. If so, it seems likely that Obadiah came before Joel, and influenced him. Therefore, the majority view is that the Book of Obadiah was written following the Babylonian conquest, during the post-exilic period.

**The prophet Obadiah**
*Obadiah's name was a popular one, used by at least 11 people in the Bible. But nothing definite is known of the prophet beyond his name.*

 5    7    9

| Chapter 1 | Edom will be destroyed on account of its poor treatment of Israel. They will suffer as Israel suffered and their kingdom will become God's kingdom. |

## Chapter 1: **Commentary**

Esau, the hairy brother of Jacob (Genesis 25:25) was also called Edom (Genesis 36:1, 8). According to Genesis, his descendants became a nation too, just as the descendants of Jacob became the Israelites. The nation of Edom was located to the east and south of the Dead Sea in part of what is today the nation of Jordan. Edom was often dominated and controlled by the Israelites and the relations between the two nations were never good. Later, an Edomite named Herod would become King of Judah—the Herod who slaughtered the babies of Bethlehem in his attempt to kill Jesus after he was born.

# Jonah
## Overview

**Jonah and the whale**
*When Jonah tried to run away from God, God sent a whale to swallow Jonah and bring him back.*

*The sea was getting rougher and rougher. So they asked him, "What should we do to you to make the sea calm down for us?"*

*"Pick me up and throw me into the sea," he replied, "and it will become calm. I know that it is my fault that this great storm has come upon you."*
**Jonah 1:11–12**

## Chapters 2–4: Commentary

The lesson of Jonah is a simple one commonly forgotten: God is not just our God. Rather he is everyone's God and he cares not just about us, but about all people, everywhere. God also wants Jonah to understand that God's preferred method for destroying the evil is not brimstone, but repentance. The evil person can be transformed into a righteous person.

Jonah's hatred of Nineveh leads him to disobey God's command to warn them of their impending doom. After spending time in a whale, Jonah finally obeys and is dismayed when the people of Nineveh repent and God forgives them.

The book is an anonymous composition; it is a story about Jonah, not by Jonah. Jonah was the son of Amittai, and according to 2 Kings 14:25, he prophesied during the reign of Jeroboam II. Jonah was raised in Galilee, in the city of Gath-hepher, which is located just a few miles north of Nazareth. The book therefore dates to somewhere between 775 and 750 BC, and it describes how his special message to Nineveh was finally delivered.

Much argument ensues over whether to call the creature that swallowed Jonah a whale or a fish. The Hebrew word used is ambiguous.

**7** — **17**

When God asks Jonah to go to Nineveh, he refuses and boards a ship going the other way. When a storm arises, Jonah tells the sailors to toss him overboard. A whale swallows him.

Chapter **1**

**5** — **12**

After three days in the whale, Jonah prays for deliverance. God responds by having the whale vomit Jonah back up on the shore near where God first asked him to go to Nineveh.

Chapter **2**

**7** — **17**

God once again asks Jonah to go to Nineveh. This time Jonah obeys. To his dismay, the people of Nineveh repent, so God forgives them.

Chapter **3**

**3** — **10** — **17**

A disappointed Jonah sits down outside the city hoping that God will change his mind about Nineveh. God uses a vine that dies to teach Jonah that God loves everyone.

Chapter **4**

# Micah

## Overview

**I**   Judgment against Samaria and Jerusalem 1:1–2:13

**II**   Rebuke and promise 3:1–5:15

**III**   The case against Israel 6:1–7:20

The title of the Book of Micah is the same in Hebrew as it is in English. The name Micah means "who is like Yahweh?"

Micah was from Moresheth, about 20 miles (32 km) southwest of Jerusalem on the Philistine border, in Judah. Although he prophesied against both Jerusalem and Samaria, his primary focus and ministry was for the southern kingdom of Judah. Micah prophesies against both Jerusalem and Samaria, warning their rulers of God's impending judgment for their idolatry, injustice, and oppression.

| 5 | 7 | 9 |
|---|---|---|

**Chapter 1**

Micah predicts that God is going to judge Samaria and Jerusalem for their sins; the result will be much suffering and weeping.

| 2 | 5 | 7 |
|---|---|---|

**Chapter 2**

The Israelites don't want to listen to Micah's warnings of judgment; they'd rather hear happy predictions of prosperity. But they will be forgiven and restored only after punishment.

| 5 | 7 | 9 |
|---|---|---|

**Chapter 3**

God condemns Israel's leaders for their injustice and oppression and condemns the prophets who prophesied lies instead of the truth. Disaster is coming.

| 5 | 7 |
|---|---|

**Chapter 4**

In the last days many nations will come to worship in Jerusalem. The exiles will all come home and live in peace and prosperity, worshiping Yahweh faithfully.

| 5 | 7 |
|---|---|

**Chapter 5**

A ruler for Israel will arise from Bethlehem. But Israel will go into exile for a while, to cleanse them of their idolatry. Then God will restore them and destroy Israel's enemies.

| 3 | 5 | 7 |
|---|---|---|

**Chapter 6**

God calls on the mountains and foundations of the earth to bear witness to Israel's guilt. God wants to see repentance, justice, and mercy, not animal sacrifices.

| 2 | 5 | 7 |
|---|---|---|

**Chapter 7**

Israel is in misery; wickedness is rampant. But its sin will be forgiven and it will be restored to the land where it will once again find peace and prosperity.

## Chapters 2–4: **Commentary**

In the Ancient Near East, the gods were limited by geography. Each nation, each city, sometimes even each family, had its own deity. The gods could act only within the borders of his or her nation or city, facing severe limitations if they strayed beyond their home. Wars between nations were believed to be not just battles between armies, but also battles between the gods those armies worshiped. But the Israelite prophets believed that the God of Israel was not just their God. Instead, they believed Yahweh was the only deity. Based on this conviction, the prophet Micah argues that a time will come when the other nations will finally recognize Yahweh as the only God and will come to Jerusalem to worship him (Micah 4:1–2).

## Chapter 5: **Commentary**

The author of the New Testament Gospel of Matthew quotes Micah 5:1, which predicts that a man from Bethlehem will arise to rule over the nation of Israel. The author of the Gospel of Matthew believes that Jesus' birth in Bethlehem fulfilled that prediction (Matthew 2:6). In the New Testament, only the Gospels of Matthew and Luke describe Jesus' birth and locate it in Bethlehem.

# Nahum

## Overview

I   Yahweh will avenge his people 1:1–15

I   The battle for Nineveh 2:1–13

III   The fate of Nineveh 3:1–19

**The prophet Nahum**
*Nahum predicted the conquest and destruction of the Assyrian capital, Nineveh.*

The title of the book is the same in Hebrew as it is in English. The name Nahum means "consoler," "consolation," or "comforter." Nahum prophesies the destruction of Nineveh, the capital of the Assyrian Empire.

Very little is known about Nahum's life. He is mentioned only in the first verse of the book that bears his name and in Luke 3:25. The only thing we know about Nahum is his hometown, Elkosh. But like the prophet, the town of Elkosh remains something of a mystery. Although there is an

Elkosh in Assyria, just north of Nineveh, this seems an improbable location for a Hebrew prophet's hometown. A more likely possibility places his hometown in Galilee, in a spot that is today known as Capernaum, which in Hebrew means "Village of Nahum."

Two different dates are generally accepted as possibilities for Nahum's ministry: between 661 and 612 BC, and between 722 and 701 BC (after the capture of Israel, but before the siege of Jerusalem by Sennacherib).

---

*The Lord has given a command concerning you, Nineveh:*
*"You will have no descendants to bear your name.*
*I will destroy the images and idols*
*that are in the temple of your gods.*
*I will prepare your grave,*
*for you are vile."*
*Look, there on the mountains,*
*the feet of one who brings good news,*
*who proclaims peace!*
*Celebrate your festivals, Judah,*
*and fulfill your vows.*
*No more will the wicked invade you;*
*they will be completely destroyed.*

**Nahum 1:14–15**

## Chapter 1: Commentary

The Assyrian Empire was one of the major empires of the Ancient Near East. The people of Assyria spoke a Semitic language known today as Akkadian, which was written with cuneiform, a writing system made up of symbols.

The Assyrians were a brutal and imperialistic people who repeatedly attacked the Jewish people, both the northern kingdom of Israel and the southern kingdom of Judah. The Assyrians finally conquered the northern kingdom around 722 BC. Nineveh fell to the Babylonian Empire in 612 BC. Nebuchadnezzar led the Babylonians to victory against the Assyrians in 605 BC at Carchemish.

| 5 | 7 | 9 |

Yahweh is angry with Nineveh, the capital of the Assyrian Empire, for what the Assyrians did in destroying Israel. Therefore God will avenge his beloved people.

**Chapter 1**

| 5 | 7 | 9 |

God is against Nineveh. An invader dressed in red, riding chariots, will attack and defeat Nineveh. Nineveh will be plundered and destroyed.

**Chapter 2**

| 5 | 7 | 9 |

God is against Nineveh for its cruelty. It will suffer the fate of Cush, Egypt, Put, and Libya: they were devastated; their infants were dashed to pieces. Nineveh will burn.

**Chapter 3**

# Habakkuk

## Overview

**Trust in God**
*Habakkuk could not make sense of what God was planning to do, but trusted God would make it work out for the best.*

The title of the book is the same in Hebrew as it is in English. The name Habakkuk may mean "embrace" or it may be related to the Assyrian plant name *hambakuku*. Habakkuk complains to God about the sin he sees among the Jewish people. He wants to know when and whether God will do something about it. Habakkuk is troubled to learn that God plans on judging the Israelites by sending the Babylonians against them.

Almost nothing is known about Habakkuk; his name appears only in his own book. Some have speculated that Habakkuk was the son of the Shunammite woman of 2 Kings 4:16, or the watchman of Isaiah 21:6. In Bel and the Dragon, Habakkuk is shown making a journey to Babylon in order to feed Daniel while he is in the lion's den.

## Chapter 1: **Commentary**

The prophet Habakkuk, troubled by Israel's sin, becomes even more troubled when he learns that God plans to judge his people with a Babylonian attack. Habakkuk thought he understood God, but with this new information he realizes that he doesn't understand him at all; the Babylonians are far worse sinners than the Israelites. As Habakkuk writes, "Why are you silent while the wicked swallow up those more righteous than themselves?" (Habakkuk 1:13.)

| 5 | | 7 | | 9 | |
|---|---|---|---|---|---|

| Chapter 1 | Habakkuk wants God to judge Israel's wickedness. God tells him that the Babylonians will destroy Israel. Habakkuk wonders how God can use the wicked to judge the more righteous. |
|---|---|

| 5 | | 7 | | 9 | |
|---|---|---|---|---|---|

| Chapter 2 | Habakkuk waits patiently for God's response. God tells him that although Israel will be judged for its idolatry and mistreatment of the poor, the Babylonians will also be judged. |
|---|---|

| 1 | | 5 | | 7 | |
|---|---|---|---|---|---|

| Chapter 3 | Habakkuk recognizes God's power, acknowledges that he does not understand, and affirms that he will rejoice in God even when everything is going wrong and makes no sense. |
|---|---|

*I heard and my heart pounded,*
*my lips quivered at the sound;*
*decay crept into my bones,*
*and my legs trembled.*
*Yet I will wait patiently for the day of calamity*
*to come on the nation invading us.*
*Though the fig tree does not bud*
*and there are no grapes on the vines,*
*though the olive crop fails*
*and the fields produce no food,*
*though there are no sheep in the pen*
*and no cattle in the stalls,*
*yet I will rejoice in the Lord,*
*I will be joyful in God my Savior.*
*    The Sovereign Lord is my strength;*
*he makes my feet like the feet of a deer,*
*he enables me to tread on the heights...*
**Habakkuk 3:16–19**

# Zephaniah
## Overview

The title is the same in Hebrew as it is in English. The name Zephaniah could mean "Yahweh hides" and may thus reflect the terror in the days of Manasseh, at the time of Zephaniah's birth. Other scholars have suggested that his name might be derived from a combination of Zaphon and Ya (an abbreviation for Yahweh). Zaphon was an important Canaanite deity. The combination of Zaphon and Ya could then be translated as "Zaphon is Yahweh."

Very little is known of the prophet Zephaniah, since he is only mentioned in this book. He prophesied during the reign of King Josiah (640–609 BC) against the worship of Baal and he warns of God's impending judgment against his people.

## Chapter 1: **Commentary**

The word commonly translated "earth" in the Bible rarely means the whole world. In fact, it never means a blue globe spinning in space, an image that no writer of the Bible could have conceived. Instead, "earth" refers to the ground that stretches to the horizon in all directions. Therefore, it would be better to translate the word as "land" in most cases, and certainly the context of the opening lines of Zephaniah's first chapter makes it abundantly clear that the prophet is announcing judgment against the land of Judah, not against the whole world. God's judgment against the land of Judah would fall within two decades of Zephaniah's prophecy. The Babylonians devastated the nation beginning in 605 BC and finally destroyed Jerusalem and its Temple in 586 BC.

*"I will stretch out my hand against Judah
and against all who live in Jerusalem.
I will destroy every remnant of Baal worship in
this place,
the very names of the idolatrous priests—
those who bow down on the roofs
to worship the starry host,
those who bow down and swear by the Lord
and who also swear by Molek,
those who turn back from following the Lord
and neither seek the Lord nor inquire of him."*
**Zephaniah 1:4–8**

| 5 | 7 | 9 |
|---|---|---|

God says that he will sweep away everything from the land of Judah and Jerusalem, both people and animals, birds and fish—and the idols. He will punish the rulers of Judah.

Chapter
1

| 5 | 7 | 9 |
|---|---|---|

God wants Judah to repent. Philistia, Moab, and Ammon will be destroyed and turned over to the people of Judah. Cush and Assyria will be judged and destroyed.

Chapter
2

| 2 | 5 | 9 |
|---|---|---|

Jerusalem's rulers, prophets, and priests are unrighteous. Therefore, God will send them into exile. When they repent, he will restore them to their land.

Chapter
3

# Haggai
## Overview

The Book of Haggai has the same title in Hebrew as it has in English. The name Haggai (pronounced ha-GUY, with the stress on the second syllable) seems to be an adjective derived from the Hebrew word for "feast"; therefore his name means "festive." He is referred to as a "prophet" in Haggai 1:1 and "the Lord's messenger" in 1:13, a phrase that elsewhere in the Bible is translated as "the Angel of the Lord."

There are two references to Haggai in the Bible outside of his own book: Ezra 5:1 and 6:14. Haggai's name is often linked with Zechariah (there may even be an allusion to him in Zechariah 8:9), since Zechariah was prophesying about the same time in Judah and Jerusalem. Haggai prophesied encouragement to the people to finally begin rebuilding the Temple in Jerusalem.

**The prophet Haggai**
*Haggai was a prophet who encouraged the people to rebuild the Temple in Jerusalem.*

## Chapter 1: **Commentary**

The Jewish Temple for worshiping Yahweh replaced the earlier tent, referred to as a Tabernacle, which was created during the time of Moses and the Israelite wanderings in the wilderness (Exodus 39:32–40:38). Solomon is credited with building this first Temple, around 906 BC (1 Kings 6). It was destroyed by the Babylonians under Nebuchadnezzar around 586 BC and then rebuilt, beginning around 520 BC. Haggai and Zechariah were two of the prophets that encouraged the people in this rebuilding process.

*'This is what I covenanted with you when you came out of Egypt. And my Spirit remains among you. Do not fear.'*
*"This is what the Lord Almighty says: 'In a little while I will once more shake the heavens and the earth, the sea and the dry land. I will shake all nations, and what is desired by all nations will come, and I will fill this house with glory,' says the Lord Almighty. 'The silver is mine and the gold is mine,' declares the Lord Almighty. 'The glory of this present house will be greater than the glory of the former house,' says the Lord Almighty. 'And in this place I will grant peace...'"*

**Haggai 2:5–9**

| 7 | |
|---|---|
| Chapter **1** | Haggai prophesies that the people who have returned from exile should rebuild God's Temple in Jerusalem. |

| 7 | |
|---|---|
| Chapter **2** | God promises to restore Israel's glory and he reassures Zerubbabel that he is doing what God wants to have done. In fact, he is like a signet ring on God's finger. |

# Zechariah

## Overview

I   The eight visions of Zechariah 1:1–6:15

II   Justice and mercy instead of fasting 7:1–14

III   Blessing will return to Jerusalem 8:1–23

IV   An oracle by Jeremiah 9:1–11:17

V   An oracle by an unknown prophet 12:1–21

The title of the Book of Zechariah is the same in Hebrew as it is in English. The name Zechariah probably means "Yahweh remembers." Zechariah the prophet was the son of Berechiah, the son of Iddo, who began prophesying in Judah about 520 BC. He is referred to as "the son of Berechia, the son of Iddo" in Zechariah 1:1 and 7 and simply as "the son of Iddo" in Ezra 5:1 and 6:14.

### Chapter 3: **Commentary**

Satan is mentioned in only three books of the Old Testament: 1 Chronicles (1 Chronicles 21:1, Job 1:6–12, 2:1–7), and Zechariah (Zechariah 3:1–2). The word Satan means "adversary" or "accuser" and is related to the verb that appears in 3:1 and is translated "accused." So minor a character is Satan in the Bible that he is never actually given a name; instead, he is merely given a designation. In essence, his role in Zechariah, as it is elsewhere, is to act as a tattler. He hopes to bring the high priest Joshua into disrepute and to get God to punish him. God, in contrast, is not interested in punishing him: instead, God wants to rehabilitate him, to forgive him, and to encourage him to do his priestly duty. Satan is never portrayed as a powerful figure in the Bible. He is always constrained by God's command.

### Chapter 5: **Commentary**

The only place in the Bible where female angels appear is in Zechariah 5:9–11, where two women that had "wings like those of a stork" carry a basket with a woman in it to Babylon. Elsewhere in the Bible the angels always appear as male. The only two angels who are named in the Bible are both male as well, Gabriel (Daniel 8:16, 21; Luke 1:19, 26) and Michael (Daniel 10:13, 21, 12:1; Jude 1:9; Revelation 12:7).

**6**  **7**

The men and horses among the myrtle trees signify God's concern for Jerusalem and the rebuilding of the Temple. The four horns represent the destruction of Israel's enemies.

Chapter 1

**7**  **15**

A man with a measuring line measures Jerusalem, which will become a city without walls. Babylon will be destroyed. God will bless his people.

Chapter 2

**7**  **15**

Satan makes accusations against the filthy, poorly clothed high priest Joshua. The angel of Yahweh rebukes Satan, cleans up Joshua, and grants him authority over the Temple. Judah is forgiven.

Chapter 3

**6**  **7**  **15**

A gold lampstand with two olive trees next to it symbolizes those anointed to serve the Lord of all the earth. Zerubbabel will complete the rebuilding of the Temple.

Chapter 4

**6**  **7**  **15**

A flying scroll represents the curse against thieves and liars. A woman in a basket represents wickedness, which two winged women carry to Babylon.

Chapter 5

**7**  **15**

Four chariots represent the four spirits of heaven going from God's presence out to the whole world. Zechariah had a crown made and placed it on the head of the high priest, Joshua.

Chapter 6

**3**  **7**

God is not interested in fasting. He wants the people to administer justice, cease oppressing the poor and weak, and stop planning evil against each other.

Chapter 7

**5**

God will bless Jerusalem and bring the scattered exiles home from all the nations to which they have been scattered. The days of fasting will become days of celebration.

Chapter 8

| 5 | 7 | 9 |
|---|---|---|

**Chapter 9**

Judgment is coming against Damascus, Tyre, Sidon, and the Philistines. God will protect Jerusalem and the Temple. Israel's king will arrive on a donkey and Yahweh himself will appear.

| 5 | 7 |
|---|---|

**Chapter 10**

God will take care of Israel. He will bring the Israelites back home from Egypt and Assyria. He will make them prosper once again.

| 5 | 6 | 7 |
|---|---|---|

**Chapter 11**

The shepherd used staffs called Favor and Union. When he quit, he broke the staff of Favor, accepted his final payment of 30 pieces of silver, and broke the staff of Union.

| 4 | 7 | 9 |
|---|---|---|

**Chapter 12**

Ultimately, all who attack Israel and Jerusalem will be destroyed. Then the house of David and the inhabitants of Jerusalem will look on the one they pierced and will mourn for him.

| 5 | 7 | 13 |
|---|---|---|

**Chapter 13**

The house of David and the inhabitants of Jerusalem will be cleansed: the idols and false prophets will disappear. The shepherd will be struck and the sheep will be scattered.

| 7 | 13 |
|---|---|

**Chapter 14**

Yahweh will assemble the nations against Jerusalem, so he can destroy them. Then God will rule the world. Every year the people of the world will worship Yahweh in Jerusalem.

*This is what the Lord Almighty says: "Many peoples and the inhabitants of many cities will yet come, and the inhabitants of one city will go to another and say, 'Let us go at once to entreat the Lord and seek the Lord Almighty. I myself am going.' And many peoples and powerful nations will come to Jerusalem to seek the Lord Almighty and to entreat him."*

*This is what the Lord Almighty says: "In those days ten people from all languages and nations will take firm hold of one Jew by the hem of his robe and say, 'Let us go with you, because we have heard that God is with you.'"*

**Zechariah 8:20–23**

## Chapter 11: Commentary

Matthew quotes Zechariah 11:12–13 in Matthew 27:9–10 and attributes it to Jeremiah. Most commentators believe that Matthew made a simple mistake. Others have suggested that Matthew is, in fact, correct in attributing this passage to Jeremiah, and our understanding of the composition of the Book of Zechariah needs some modification. A seventeenth-century Cambridge theologian, Joseph Mede, suggested that while Zechariah 1–8 was written by Zechariah, chapters 9–11 were written by Jeremiah and chapters 12–14 by an otherwise anonymous author.

Why would these sections by Jeremiah be added to the end of a book by Zechariah? Because Zechariah was the last book of the prophets. Zechariah 9–11, Zechariah 12–14, and Malachi are each given the heading *masa*, "a burden" or "a prophesy." Mede and some later scholars have suggested therefore that these were three floating and anonymous oracles arbitrarily assigned to their present position in the canon.

*I will gather all the nations to Jerusalem to fight against it; the city will be captured, the houses ransacked, and the women raped. Half of the city will go into exile, but the rest of the people will not be taken from the city. Then the Lord will go out and fight against those nations, as he fights on a day of battle. On that day his feet will stand on the Mount of Olives, east of Jerusalem, and the Mount of Olives will be split in two from east to west, forming a great valley, with half of the mountain moving north and half moving south. You will flee by my mountain valley, for it will extend to Azel. You will flee as you fled from the earthquake in the days of Uzziah king of Judah. Then the Lord my God will come, and all the holy ones with him.*

**Zechariah 14:2–5**

# Malachi

## Overview

I  Yahweh's complaints 1:1–2:17

II  Yahweh's arrival 3:1–4:6

**Malachi**
The Book of Malachi may just be a fragment of some other prophet's writing, perhaps Isaiah.

The title of the Book of Malachi is the same in Hebrew as it is in English. Malachi is not likely the name of the author of the book; it means simply "my messenger" and occurs in Malachi 1:1 and 3:1. Some scholars have suggested that the Book of Malachi was actually written by the prophet Isaiah.

Malachi never appears as a name anywhere else in the Bible and nothing else is known of him. He is said to have been born in Sopha, a place that is otherwise unknown. But there is no evidence to support this legend. Some scholars believe that whoever the author was, he wrote sometime in the fifth century BC, prophesying after Haggai and Zechariah and therefore after the Temple had been rebuilt. He delivers a series of God's complaints against his people, whose worship lacks faith and commitment.

## Chapter 3: **Commentary**

In the New Testament, the gospels of Matthew (Matthew 11:10), Mark (Mark 1:2), and Luke (Luke 7:27) quote Malachi 3:1 and apply the words to the ministry and message of John the Baptist. He preached a baptism of repentance, announced the imminent arrival of the Kingdom of God, and identified Jesus as the promised Messiah.

## Chapter 4: **Commentary**

During the celebration of Passover, a cup called Elijah's cup sits on the table. Filled with wine, no one drinks it throughout the celebration. Toward the end of the Seder service, the youngest child is sent to the door. He opens it and peers outside, to see if Elijah might be waiting there. The tradition, growing from Malachi 4:5, was that Elijah would come at Passover time and announce the arrival of the Messiah. In the New Testament, Jesus explains that John the Baptist fulfilled Elijah's role, becoming the "Elijah" who had announced his coming (see Matthew 11:11–15, 17:10–13, Mark 9:11–13, and Luke 1:17).

| 3 | 7 | Chapter |
|---|---|---------|
| Israel questions whether God really loves them. He tells them they've shown him contempt by bringing him diseased and disfigured animals for sacrifice. They need to stop. | | **1** |

| 3 | 7 | Chapter |
|---|---|---------|
| The prophet warns the priests to honor God and to listen to him. He wants them to teach what is good and true. He wants them to keep their promises. God hates divorce and injustice. | | **2** |

| 3 | 7 | Chapter |
|---|---|---------|
| God will send his messenger to prepare his way. Though many Israelites have been unfaithful, there is a remnant that is obedient and who worship God. | | **3** |

| 3 | 7 | 9 | Chapter |
|---|---|---|---------|
| A day of judgment is coming when God will destroy the wicked. But he will send the prophet Elijah before that dreadful day of the Lord comes, so many people will repent. | | | **4** |

# The New Testament

The New Testament includes four parallel accounts of the time Jesus spent with his disciples. All four Gospel stories, as they are called, end with Jesus' crucifixion and resurrection. The purpose of these Gospels is not to give a biography of Jesus in the modern sense, but rather, as the author of the Gospel of John states so clearly, "these are written that you may believe that Jesus is the Messiah, the Son of God, and that by believing you may have life in his name." (John 20:31). They have as their purpose the goal of convincing readers that Jesus is the Messiah, so that they will become Christians.

There is one book, the Book of Acts, that relates the actions of Jesus' followers in the three decades following his resurrection. It describes their persecutions and focuses on the actions of Peter and Paul in bringing the news of Jesus to the people of the Roman world and how they established churches across the empire.

There follow several letters written by Paul, Peter, James, John, and Jude to the early churches around the Roman Empire. In these letters, they discuss personal matters, as well as offering encouragement in the midst of persecution. They offer warnings about misbehavior or false teachings. They explain what it is that Christians believe and how they should live their lives both as individuals and in communities and families. They encourage the early churches to remain faithful to what the apostles have taught and they remind them of the hope that Jesus will return.

The final book in the New Testament, Revelation, is designed to encourage its first readers with the promise that God would triumph over evil, that the oppression and persecution would end, and that the kingdoms of Earth will someday become transformed into the kingdom of God. Specifically, most scholars believe it predicts the overthrow of the Roman Empire and its replacement with God's rule. Historically, Christians suffering under oppression have found comfort in reading it.

# Introduction to the Gospels (Matthew–John)

**Jesus as savior**
*The Gospels were written to explain that Jesus was the Messiah, the Son of God, who died for the sins of the world and rose again.*

The reader of the New Testament may wonder at the fact that there are four books, written by different authors, each of which describes the life of Christ. When one considers the nature and importance of parallelism in the Hebrew mind, perhaps the repetition is not so surprising. Where a Western writer would be concerned to present a single, unified account, the Jewish mind wished for a stereoscopic view; instead of relying on a single window into the life of Christ, the modern reader is able to view his life from more than one point of view, thereby getting a much clearer picture.

The careful reader of the Gospels will notice that the similarities between Matthew, Mark, and Luke are much greater than simply three authors telling the same story. In fact, these three Gospels often have nearly identical wording, which raises at least three questions:

• Who wrote these Gospels?
• Were the writers dependent upon each other, and if so, who depended on whom?
• What other sources did the authors of the Gospels make use of, that they might have had in common?

It seems clear that Matthew incorporated almost the entire Gospel of Mark into his narrative, although he condensed the accounts of the miracles, probably for thematic reasons. In addition to Mark, the author of Matthew inserted numerous sayings of Jesus, apparently taken from a source that both he and Luke had in common. This source is designated as "Q" by scholars. Q is an abbreviation for *Quelle*, the German word for "source." The order of the Gospels is as follows:

1. Mark
2. Matthew, making use of Mark and Q
3. Luke, making use of Mark, Q, and other sources
4. John, which apparently did not make reference to the earlier written Gospels, and is not, therefore, part of the synoptic problem.

# Matthew

## Overview

**Adoration of the Magi**
*The magi traveled from Persia to Bethlehem
to find the newly born king of the Jews, Jesus.*

The title of the book comes from its assumed author. Matthew appears in all the lists of the 12 apostles (Matthew 10:3, Mark 3:18, Luke 6:15, and Acts 1:13). In Matthew 10:3 he is described as "the tax-collector." Matthew 9:9 describes Matthew's call to be a disciple. In the parallel passages in Mark and Luke he is referred to as Levi; Mark says he was "the son of Alphaeus."

Papias, the early second-century bishop of Hierapolis—Phrygia (in Turkey)—wrote that Matthew "compiled the oracles" in Hebrew. This statement was taken by the early church as evidence that Matthew was the author of the Gospel, which had been handed down as being "according to Matthew."

Most modern scholars think that Papias was not referring to Matthew's Gospel at all, but rather to a compilation of sayings of Jesus, or of Messianic

| 15 | | 16 |
|----|----|----|

**Chapter 1**

The genealogy of Jesus from Abraham through Joseph is followed by the story of an angel telling Joseph that his fiancé is miraculously pregnant with the Messiah.

| 17 | | |
|----|----|----|

**Chapter 2**

When Zoroastrian priests arrive from Persia seeking the newborn king of Israel, Herod the Great seeks to kill him in Bethlehem.

| 7 | | 17 |
|----|----|----|

**Chapter 3**

John the Baptist, Jesus' cousin, proclaims that the Messiah is coming, then baptizes Jesus as a rite of initiation into his public ministry as a rabbi.

## Chapter 2: **Commentary**

The Magi are most likely Zoroastrian priests from Persia. The word *Magi*, sometimes rendered "wise men," is related to the English word "magic." Zoroastrianism was a dualistic religion that believed in two gods, one good and one bad, who were in conflict with one another, with the world as their battlefield. The Magi were astrologers. The star, many scholars believe, while meaningful to Persian astrologers, would not have necessarily been noticeable to anyone else. Its significance was a consequence of where it appeared among the constellations. For them, it signified the birth of a king in Judea—which is why they went to the palace of Herod, who was startled by their news since his wife had not recently given him a child.

## Chapter 3: **Commentary**

Jesus was Jewish. So were all his disciples and most of the other characters throughout the New Testament. Therefore, baptism here needs to be considered in the context of Judaism. In Judaism, baptism was always by immersion: it was a ritual washing undertaken for multiple purposes. It could indicate that a person had converted to Judaism. Baptism could also be a sign of repentance, as was the case for those John baptized. Or, baptism could indicate that a person was beginning a new role in life, for instance becoming a priest or a rabbi. In Jesus' case, it meant he was no longer going to be just a carpenter.

proof texts from the Old Testament, which might have served the author of Matthew (and the other Gospel writers) as source materials.

Matthew has two principle interests in his Gospel: 1) the fulfillment of God's purposes in and through Jesus; and 2) how this fulfillment will find expression in the Church that Jesus founded.

It has been argued that the Gospel of Matthew was likely written before AD 70, since Jesus predicts the destruction of Jerusalem in 24:2–23 and it would be odd that no mention of its fulfillment would appear in the book had it been written after this date. However, if the Gospel had been written after the destruction of Jerusalem, that destruction would have been so well known, it would have been unnecessary to point out that Jesus' words had been fulfilled.

Matthew 27:8 and 28:15 would seem to indicate that some time had passed since the crucifixion, since both have the phrase "to this day."

## Chapter 5: Commentary

The beatitudes in Matthew 5:3–11 are structured according to the rules of Hebrew poetry, with the two opening lines "Blessed are the poor in spirit," and "for theirs is the kingdom of heaven" serving as a summary of what will be explained by the words that follow. The next lines define who the "poor in spirit" are: they are "those who mourn," "the meek," "those who hunger and thirst for righteousness," "the merciful," "the pure in heart," "the peacemakers," and those "persecuted because of righteousness."

And what is the Kingdom of Heaven? It is defined as consisting of those who are "comforted," "inherit the earth," are "filled," are "shown mercy," "see God," and those who are "called the children of God."

*"Which of you, if your son asks for bread, will give him a stone? Or if he asks for a fish, will give him a snake? If you, then, though you are evil, know how to give good gifts to your children, how much more will your Father in heaven give good gifts to those who ask him! So in everything, do to others what you would have them do to you, for this sums up the Law and the Prophets."*

**Matthew 7:9–12**

---

**8**     **15**

Jesus is tempted by Satan after 40 days of fasting in the wilderness, then gathers his first disciples.

Chapter
**4**

---

**3**     **5**

Jesus gives his Sermon on the Mount, including the beatitudes and moral teachings about loving enemies.

Chapter
**5**

---

**3**

Jesus continues his Sermon on the Mount with instructions on giving to the needy, prayer, fasting, not worrying, and the importance of gathering treasures in Heaven rather than treasures on Earth.

Chapter
**6**

---

**3**

Jesus concludes his Sermon on the Mount with instructions about not judging, God's willingness to answer prayer, and wisdom versus folly.

Chapter
**7**

---

**8**     **15**

Jesus heals a leper, the servant of a Roman centurion, Peter's mother-in-law, and other sick people; warns about the difficulty of becoming a disciple, calms a storm, and sends demons into a herd of pigs.

Chapter
**8**

---

**8**

Jesus forgives and heals a paralyzed man, calls Matthew as his disciple, teaches about fasting, raises a dead girl back to life, heals a sick woman, and restores sight to the blind.

Chapter
**9**

---

**3**     **16**

Lists the 12 disciples of Jesus and then gives his instructions to them for ministry in the community.

Chapter
**10**

| **1** | **9** | **12** |
|---|---|---|

**Chapter 11**

Jesus praises John the Baptist, condemns the cities of Chorazin, Bethsaida, and Capernaum for their unwillingness to repent despite the miracles he performed, and then offers a prayer to God.

*"Come to me, all you who are weary and burdened, and I will give you rest. Take my yoke upon you and learn from me, for I am gentle and humble in heart, and you will find rest for your souls. For my yoke is easy and my burden is light."*
**Matthew 11:28–30**

| **3** | **7** | **15** |
|---|---|---|

**Chapter 12**

Jesus offers instructions about the Sabbath, heals a demon-possessed man who was blind and mute, and then uses the story of Jonah to illustrate his coming execution and resurrection.

*Coming to his hometown, he began teaching the people in their synagogue, and they were amazed.*
*"Where did this man get this wisdom and these miraculous powers?" they asked. "Isn't this the carpenter's son? Isn't his mother's name Mary, and aren't his brothers James, Joseph, Simon and Judas? Aren't all his sisters with us? Where then did this man get all these things?" And they took offense at him.*
*But Jesus said to them, "A prophet is not without honor except in his own town and in his own home."*
**Matthew 13:54–57**

| **6** |
|---|

**Chapter 13**

Jesus explains why he teaches in parables, then gives seven about what the Kingdom of Heaven is like, concluding that a prophet is without honor in his own home.

| **8** | **17** |
|---|---|

**Chapter 14**

When King Herod beheads John the Baptist, Jesus wants to be alone, but a crowd of 5,000 follows. He feeds them. He catches up to his disciples by walking across the water.

## Chapter 16: **Commentary**

Jesus announced to Peter that "On this rock I will build my church." Paul expresses a similar sense of things when he explains that the church is one body, made of all Christians everywhere "built on the foundation of the apostles and prophets, with Christ Jesus himself as the chief cornerstone." (Ephesians 2:20). The difference of opinion that commentators have regarding the interpretation of Jesus' words relates to precisely who or what Jesus identified as the rock on which the church would be built. For most of its history, the church believed the rock was to be identified with Peter, whose name actually means "rock." In contrast, Protestant scholars after the Reformation suggested that the rock actually meant Peter's affirmation of Jesus as the Messiah. Still others have argued that the rock was Jesus himself.

| **3** | **8** |
|---|---|

**Chapter 15**

Before healing the daughter of a Canaanite woman and feeding 4,000, Jesus tells the Pharisees that people are defiled by what comes out of their mouths, not what goes into them.

| **3** | **7** |
|---|---|

**Chapter 16**

The Pharisees ask for a sign. Jesus refuses. He tells his disciples to reject what the Pharisees teach. Peter declares that Jesus is the Messiah. Jesus predicts his crucifixion and resurrection.

| **8** |
|---|

**Chapter 17**

On a mountain, Jesus transforms and converses with Moses and Elijah. He heals a demon-possessed man. He predicts his death. Peter takes a coin from a fish's mouth to pay the Temple tax.

*Jesus replied, "Blessed are you, Simon son of Jonah, for this was not revealed to you by flesh and blood, but by my Father in heaven. And I tell you that you are Peter, and on this rock I will build my church, and the gates of Hades will not overcome it. I will give you the keys of the kingdom of heaven; whatever you bind on earth will be bound in heaven, and whatever you loose on earth will be loosed in heaven."*
**Matthew 16:17–19**

*At that time the disciples came to Jesus and asked, "Who, then, is the greatest in the kingdom of heaven?"*

*He called a little child to him, and placed the child among them. And he said: "Truly I tell you, unless you change and become like little children, you will never enter the kingdom of heaven. Therefore, whoever takes the lowly position of this child is the greatest in the kingdom of heaven.*
**Matthew 18:1–4**

## Chapter 20: **Commentary**

Rather than leaders being "the boss," Jesus portrays them as being the servants of those they lead. Jesus, the rabbi and leader of his disciples, takes on the role of a house slave when he washes their feet (see John 13:1–17). Elsewhere, Paul argues, "Follow God's example, therefore, as dearly loved children and walk in the way of love, just as Christ loved us and gave himself up for us as a fragrant offering and sacrifice to God." (Ephesians 5:1; cf. Ephesians 5:21, 25–30). And in Philippians Paul argues:

"In your relationships with one another, have the same attitude of mind Christ Jesus had:
Who, being in very nature God,
did not consider equality with God something to be used to his own advantage;
rather, he made himself nothing
by taking the very nature of a servant,
being made in human likeness.
And being found in appearance as a human being,
he humbled himself
by becoming obedient to death—
even death on a cross!" (Philippians 2:5–8)

Jesus, the servant God, calls upon his people to lead by being servants to one another, rather than seeking authority, power, and prestige.

*Jesus called them together and said, "You know that the rulers of the Gentiles lord it over them, and their high officials exercise authority over them. Not so with you. Instead, whoever wants to become great among you must be your servant, and whoever wants to be first must be your slave—just as the Son of Man did not come to be served, but to serve, and to give his life as a ransom for many."*
**Matthew 20:25–28**

**③ ⑥** The greatest in the kingdom of heaven are those who seem least significant. Forgive no matter how many times someone hurts you. Jesus tells a parable to illustrate the importance of forgiveness.
**Chapter 18**

**③** God would prefer that divorce never happen. The kingdom of heaven is made up of children. It is hard for the rich to enter the kingdom, but with God, all is possible.
**Chapter 19**

**③ ⑥ ⑧** The parable of the workers in the vineyard. Jesus predicts his death. A mother asks that her sons be leaders in the kingdom. True leadership comes from being the servant of all. Jesus heals two blind men.
**Chapter 20**

**Feeding of the 4,000**
*Jesus miraculously provided food for 4,000 men starting with just a few fish and seven loaves of bread.*

| 6 | 8 | 17 |

**Chapter 21**

Jesus enters Jerusalem triumphantly on a donkey's colt. He throws the moneychangers out of the Temple. He curses a fig tree. He tells the parable of the two sons and the parable of the tenants.

| 3 | 6 | 10 |

**Chapter 22**

Parable of the wedding banquet. The Pharisees wonder about paying taxes to Rome. Sadducees doubt the resurrection. The greatest commands are loving God and people. Whose son is the Messiah?

| 3 | 9 |

**Chapter 23**

Jesus gives a warning about the hypocrisy of the Pharisees and the teachers of the law. Then he pronounces a series of seven woes against them.

| 7 |

**Chapter 24**

Jesus predicts the destruction of Jerusalem and the Jewish Temple. He predicts the coming of his kingdom in the future. Only the Father knows when it will happen.

| 6 |

**Chapter 25**

Jesus gives the parable of the ten virgins, the parable of three servants given bags of gold to invest for their master while he is gone, and the parable of the sheep and goats.

| 7 | 17 |

**Chapter 26**

Judas agrees to betray Jesus for 30 pieces of silver. Jesus is anointed in Bethany, celebrates the Last Supper, is arrested in the Garden of Gethsemane, and Peter denies Jesus three times.

| 17 |

**Chapter 27**

Judas hangs himself. Jesus is condemned by Pilate, is crucified, and dies. He is buried in the tomb of a rich man named Joseph of Arimathea. Pilate agrees to post guards at the tomb.

| 8 | 17 |

**Chapter 28**

On Sunday morning, Jesus rises from the dead. He appears to women who visit his tomb, then later to his disciples. Jesus tells them spread the good news to the entire world.

## Chapter 22: **Commentary**

The phrase translated "Law and Prophets" was simply the first-century and modern Jewish term for the Old Testament. Jesus explains that the entire Old Testament can be summed up with just two commands: to love God and to love people. Paul also expounds on Jesus' teaching when he writes "The commandments, 'You shall not commit adultery,' 'You shall not murder,' 'You shall not steal,' 'You shall not covet,' and whatever other command there may be, are summed up in this one command: 'Love your neighbor as yourself.' Love does no harm to its neighbor. Therefore love is the fulfillment of the law." (Romans 13:9–10; cf. Galatians 5:14 and James 2:8.)

*One of them, an expert in the law, tested him with this question: "Teacher, which is the greatest commandment in the Law?"*

*Jesus replied: "'Love the Lord your God with all your heart and with all your soul and with all your mind.' This is the first and greatest commandment. And the second is like it: 'Love your neighbor as yourself.' All the Law and the Prophets hang on these two commandments."*

**Matthew 22:35–40**

*The chief priests picked up the coins and said, "It is against the law to put this into the treasury, since it is blood money." So they decided to use the money to buy the potter's field as a burial place for foreigners. That is why it has been called the Field of Blood to this day. Then what was spoken by Jeremiah the prophet was fulfilled: "They took the thirty pieces of silver, the price set on him by the people of Israel, and they used them to buy the potter's field, as the Lord commanded me."*

**Matthew 27:6–10**

## Chapter 28: **Commentary**

Women held a high status in the early Christian community. A woman was the first to know Jesus was the Messiah (Luke 1:26–38). All four Gospel accounts in the New Testament indicate that women were the first to know Jesus was resurrected (Matthew 28:1–8, Mark 16:1–8, Luke 24:1–12, and John 20:1–18). The writers acknowledge women as the first to see the risen Christ despite the fact that in Jewish society and most of the Roman world of the first century, women were not considered reliable eyewitnesses.

# Mark

## Overview

The title of the Gospel of Mark comes from the name of the traditional author of the book.

Tradition points to John Mark as the author of this Gospel, the same John Mark who was companion to Paul and Barnabas; it was Mark's behavior in leaving and Barnabas' desire to bring Mark with them that lead to Barnabas and Paul splitting up (see Acts 13:13, 15:36–40). Later, Paul was to accept Mark again (see Colossians 4:10; 2 Timothy 4:11). Tradition also asserts that Mark was in some way associated with Peter, and that Peter furnished the materials and information that make up this book. In fact, some ancient writers called this book Peter's Gospel.

In reality, the Gospel of Mark is an anonymous composition that does not identify an author. None of the other New Testament books identify the author of Mark's Gospel, either.

## Chapter 1: **Commentary**

The Kingdom of God—what is it? John the Baptist announced that it was coming. Jesus proclaimed that the Kingdom of God was "near" (Matthew 3:2, 10:7), and later that it had even arrived (Luke 17:20–21). In Matthew's Gospel, it is usually called the Kingdom of Heaven, rather than the Kingdom of God. "Heaven" was a circumlocution used by some Jewish people to avoid mentioning God or his name out of reverence and out of a desire to avoid the possibility of taking God's name in vain.

Jesus told several parables to explain what the kingdom of God is. He said it is like a man who sowed seed in his field (Matthew 13:24), it is like a mustard seed (Matthew 13:31), it is like yeast (Matthew 13:44), and it is like a merchant looking for fine pearls (Matthew 13:45), among other things. But Jesus never compared the Kingdom of God to an earthly government.

The Jewish people of Jesus' day, his disciples included, expected the Messiah to lead an army against Rome, overthrow it, and restore the monarchy of King David. They believed the Messiah would create a physical, earthly kingdom that would rule the earth, with Jerusalem replacing Rome as the center of an empire. In contrast, Jesus wanted his disciples to understand that the Kingdom of God is spiritual, not physical: it is the presence of God in the lives of his people, who act in love, showing grace and mercy.

**Baptism of Jesus**
*Jesus was baptized in the River Jordan by his cousin, John the Baptist.*

| 8 | 15 | 17 | Chapter 1 |
John the Baptist baptizes Jesus. Jesus is tempted by Satan, calls his first disciples, frees a man from a demon, heals Peter's mother-in-law, and heals a leper.

| 3 | 8 | 17 | Chapter 2 |
Jesus heals a paralyzed man, calls Matthew Levi as a disciple, has dinner with tax collectors, and faces questioning by the Pharisees over supposed violations of the Sabbath.

## Chapter 3

| 8 | 15 | 17 |

Jesus heals a man on the Sabbath and appoints the 12 apostles. The religious establishment accuses Jesus of casting out demons by using Satan. Even Jesus' own family oppose him.

## Chapter 4

| 6 | 8 | 17 |

Jesus tells the parables of the sower, the lamp, the growing seed, and the mustard seed. When Jesus and his disciples cross the Sea of Galilee, Jesus calms a storm.

## Chapter 5

| 8 | 15 | 17 |

In the region of the Gerasenes, Jesus sends demons from a possessed man into a herd of pigs. A woman is cured by touching Jesus' clothing. Jesus raises a dead girl back to life.

## Chapter 6

| 3 | 8 | 17 |

Jesus sends his 12 apostles out to preach the good news and to heal people. King Herod beheads John the Baptist. Jesus feeds the 5,000 and walks on water.

## Chapter 7

| 3 | 8 | 17 |

Jesus criticizes religious leaders for their legalism. Evil comes from within, not from without. Jesus heals a Canaanite woman's daughter in Tyre; then he heals a deaf and mute man.

## Chapter 8

| 3 | 8 | 17 |

Jesus feeds the 4,000, and warns against the teachings of the Pharisees and Herod. Jesus heals a blind man. Peter declares that Jesus is the Messiah. Jesus predicts his own death.

**Transfiguration of Christ**
*Jesus took Peter, James, and John up a mountain where they met Moses and Elijah and Jesus appeared glorified.*

*Then Jesus entered a house, and again a crowd gathered, so that he and his disciples were not even able to eat. When his family heard about this, they went to take charge of him, for they said, "He is out of his mind."*

*And the teachers of the law who came down from Jerusalem said, "He is possessed by Beelzebul! By the prince of demons he is driving out demons."*
**Mark 3:20–22**

## Chapter 5: **Commentary**

Demon possession is described in the Bible only in the New Testament and then only in the four Gospels and the early part of the Book of Acts. Although a distinction is made in the accounts between mental illness, physical illness, and demon possession, demon possession was sometimes accompanied by insanity or illness.

It is clear that Jesus and his followers were not alone in casting out demons (see Luke 9:49, 11:19). It is also clear that the expulsion of demons seems to have been a relatively quick and easy process for Jesus and his disciples, so much so that it surprised their contemporaries who apparently were accustomed to more of a struggle—or even failure (see Luke 10:17).

## Chapter 7: **Commentary**

Judaism of the first century was not a monolithic faith. As with any religion, differences of opinion had led to a variety of sects. Those mentioned in the New Testament include the Pharisees, Sadducees, Herodians, and Zealots. Who were these groups and what motivated them?

The Zealots were a nationalistic organization. They used violence against both the Roman government and those they saw as collaborating with it. Among Jesus' followers was at least one Zealot (Luke 6:15). The Herodians, in contrast, tended to support both Rome and the puppet ruler, Herod Antipas. The Sadducees were mostly wealthy, mostly priests, and were mostly members of the Jewish ruling council, the Sanhedrin. They were conservative in their religious beliefs, accepting only the Torah—the first five books of the Bible—as authoritative scripture. Consequently, they did not believe in angels, demons, or life after death. The Pharisees were the innovators, who accepted the Prophets and the Writings—the rest of the Old Testament. They believed in angels, demons, and the resurrection. Most rabbis and teachers were Pharisees, and came from a variety of socioeconomic backgrounds. They were generally much more popular and influential than the other groups.

On reaching Jerusalem, Jesus entered the temple courts and began driving out those who were buying and selling there. He overturned the tables of the money changers and the benches of those selling doves, and would not allow anyone to carry merchandise through the temple courts. And as he taught them, he said, "Is it not written: 'My house will be called a house of prayer for all nations'? But you have made it 'a den of robbers.'"

**Mark 11:15–17**

Later they sent some of the Pharisees and Herodians to Jesus to catch him in his words. They came to him and said, "Teacher, we know that you are a man of integrity. You aren't swayed by others, because you pay no attention to who they are; but you teach the way of God in accordance with the truth. Is it right to pay the imperial tax to Caesar or not? Should we pay or shouldn't we?"

But Jesus knew their hypocrisy. "Why are you trying to trap me?" he asked. "Bring me a denarius and let me look at it." They brought the coin, and he asked them, "Whose image is this? And whose inscription?"

"Caesar's," they replied.

Then Jesus said to them, "Give back to Caesar what is Caesar's and to God what is God's."

And they were amazed at him.

**Mark 12:13–17**

Peter declared, "Even if all fall away, I will not."

"Truly I tell you," Jesus answered, "today—yes, tonight—before the rooster crows twice you yourself will disown me three times."

But Peter insisted emphatically, "Even if I have to die with you, I will never disown you." And all the others said the same.

**Mark 14:29–31**

## Chapter 16: **Commentary**

The Book of Mark ends abruptly at verse 8. Because of how the Gospel ended, later scribes copying the text added some verses to "fill in" information gleaned from the other Gospel accounts. There are a variety of endings that appear in later manuscripts. The 1611 KJV had an ending that now appears in most modern translations, though most modern translations also indicate that this ending is not part of the original story.

| ③ | ⑧ | ⑮ |
|---|---|---|

Jesus is transfigured on a mountain. Jesus heals a possessed boy. Jesus predicts his own death and resurrection. Those not against us are for us. Don't be the cause of stumbling.

Chapter **9**

| ③ | ⑧ | ⑰ |
|---|---|---|

Jesus warns against divorce and blesses children. A rich man wonders how to enter God's kingdom. Jesus predicts his death and resurrection. James and John seek power. Jesus heals a blind man.

Chapter **10**

| ③ | ⑧ | ⑰ |
|---|---|---|

Jesus triumphantly enters Jerusalem riding a colt. Jesus curses a fig tree and drives the moneychangers from the Temple. The religious establishment questions Jesus' authority.

Chapter **11**

| ③ | ⑥ | ⑰ |
|---|---|---|

Jesus tells the parable of the tenants, answers a question about taxes, teaches about love, and warns against the teachers of the law. Jesus praises the offering given by a poor widow.

Chapter **12**

| ⑦ |
|---|

Jesus predicts that the Temple and Jerusalem will be destroyed. He tells his disciples that he is going to go away and that no one knows when he'll come back.

Chapter **13**

| ⑰ |
|---|

In Bethany, a woman anoints Jesus with expensive perfume. Jesus and his disciples eat the Last Supper. Judas betrays Jesus. Jesus stands before the Sanhedrin and Peter disowns Jesus.

Chapter **14**

| ⑰ |
|---|

The Roman governor Pilate condemns Jesus to crucifixion. Jesus dies on the cross and is buried in a new tomb belonging to Joseph of Arimathea.

Chapter **15**

| ⑧ | ⑰ |
|---|---|

Jesus rises from the dead. The first to know this are his female followers: Mary Magdalene, Mary, mother of James, and Salome.

Chapter **16**

# Luke

## Overview

With the opening lines of Luke's Gospel, it is clear that the author was not an eyewitness to Jesus' life. Rather, the author indicates that he gained his information about Jesus from other sources after extensive research (1:1–3). The book is called the Gospel of Luke because tradition has suggested him as the author. Nowhere does the Gospel account mention the author by name. However, the close similarity between the Book of Acts and Luke's Gospel has led some scholars to conclude that Luke actually did write the book:

• Both books are dedicated to Theophilus.
• Acts refers to a previous document, which is generally assumed to be the Gospel of Luke.
• The language and style of both books are similar.
• The first person plural replaces the normal third person in several sections of Acts, suggesting that

| 5 | 8 | 15 |
|---|---|---|
| **Chapter 1** | The parents of John the Baptist learn that he will be born. Gabriel tells Mary that she will give birth to the Messiah, even though she is a virgin. John the Baptist is born. | |

| 15 | 17 | |
|---|---|---|
| **Chapter 2** | Jesus is born in Bethlehem. Angels announce his birth to shepherds. Simeon blesses Jesus on the day of his circumcision. At the age of 12, Jesus stays behind at the Temple. | |

| 16 | 17 | |
|---|---|---|
| **Chapter 3** | John the Baptist baptizes people and tells them that the Messiah is coming. John baptizes Jesus. God announces that Jesus is his Son. The genealogy of Jesus from Joseph to Adam. | |

## Chapter 3: **Commentary**

An old problem for expositors has been the contradictory genealogies of Christ given in Matthew and Luke. Many scholars believe that the genealogies are merely a pious fiction designed to legitimize Jesus' claim to be the son of David and the Messiah.

Others scholars disagree. Since first proposed by Annius of Viterbo (c. AD 1490), it has been common to assume that Matthew's genealogy traces the lineage of Jesus through Joseph, while the one in Luke traces it through Mary. However, this explanation fails if one bothers to actually read the genealogies, since both genealogies are clearly Joseph's (cf. Matthew 1:15–16 and Luke 3:23).

It has been suggested instead that Matthew traces the lineage back through Joseph's father, and that Luke traces back through Joseph's mother. That Matthew should skip Joseph's mother in the genealogical listing is not peculiar since Matthew skips a number of other people in his genealogy (cf. Matthew 1:8 with 1 Chronicles 3:10–12). Matthew left out names so that he could get three sets of 14 names (Matthew 1:17), since the name David is written with three Hebrew letters whose numerical value is 14. Therefore, it is possible that Matthew left out the name of Joseph's mother so he could achieve the structural format he desired.

the author was accompanying Paul during those events (Acts 16:10–17, 20:5–15, 21:1–18, 27:1–28:16).
• In addition to the internal evidence suggesting Luke, the church fathers Irenaeus, Clement of Alexandria, Origen, and Tertullion all believed Luke was the author.

Regarding Luke himself, it seems clear that he was a gentile, rather than Jewish. (cf. Colossians 4:10–14 where he is contrasted with those "of the circumcision.") This may account for the statement in Luke 1:3 where he indicates that he intends to give an "orderly account" of Jesus' life. This would be in contrast to the tendency by Matthew and Mark and John to allow thematic elements to dominate the chronology of the story. Being a Greek, Luke would have found chronology of greater importance than it was to Jewish authors.

**The Annunciation**
*The angels' Annunciation to the shepherds.*

*Jesus, full of the Holy Spirit, left the Jordan and was led by the Spirit into the wilderness, where for forty days he was tempted by the devil. He ate nothing during those days, and at the end of them he was hungry.*
*The devil said to him, "If you are the Son of God, tell this stone to become bread."*
*Jesus answered, "It is written: 'Man shall not live on bread alone.'*

**Luke 4:1–4**

## Chapter 8: Commentary

Women were important in the early Christian movement. Luke 8:1–3 (see also Mark 15:41) answers the question of how Jesus and his disciples managed to supply their needs for food and shelter over the years of their wandering about Israel preaching and performing miracles. According to Luke, their financial support was taken care of by several wealthy women. The word translated "helping to support" is the verb form of the word for deacon, a noun that applied not just to men who served the church in an official capacity, but also to women who functioned in the same capacity (see Romans 16:1–2).

| ⑧ | ⑮ | ⑰ |
|---|---|---|

Jesus is tempted by the Devil for 40 days. When Jesus returns to Galilee, he teaches in the synagogues, heals a demon-possessed man, and heals the mother-in-law of Peter.

Chapter 4

| ③ | ⑧ | ⑰ |
|---|---|---|

Jesus calls his first disciples. He heals a leper and a paralyzed man. He calls Matthew as his disciple and has dinner with tax collectors. Jesus is questioned about why his disciples don't fast.

Chapter 5

| ③ | ⑤ | ⑥ |
|---|---|---|

Jesus heals a man on the Sabbath, appoints his 12 apostles, and gives the beatitudes. He tells parables about the blind, sawdust in the eye, fruit, and wise and foolish builders.

Chapter 6

| ⑧ | ⑰ |
|---|---|

Jesus heals a Roman centurion's servant and raises a widow's son back to life. In prison, John wonders if Jesus is really the Messiah. A sinful woman wipes Jesus' feet with her hair.

Chapter 7

| ⑥ | ⑧ | ⑮ |
|---|---|---|

Jesus tells the parables of the sower and the lamp. He calms the storm, and drives demons from a man and into a herd of pigs. Jesus heals a woman and raises a dead girl back to life.

Chapter 8

**Chapter 9**
7 | 8 | 15

Jesus sends out the 12 apostles and feeds the 5,000. Peter declares Jesus the Messiah. Jesus predicts his death and resurrection, is transfigured, and heals a demon-possessed boy.

**Chapter 10**
6 | 8 | 15

Jesus sends out the 72. They heal the sick, preach, and cast out demons. Jesus tells the parable of the Good Samaritan. Jesus visits the home of Martha and Mary.

**Chapter 11**
6 | 12 | 15

Jesus gives the Lord's Prayer, tells a parable of persistence in prayer, is accused of using Satan's power, gives the sign of Jonah, and pronounces woes upon the religious leadership.

**Chapter 12**
3

Jesus warns about Pharisaical hypocrisy. He says not to fear persecution and tells the parable about a rich fool. Don't worry, be alert, and there will be division rather than peace.

**Chapter 13**
3 | 6 | 8

Suffering is not from sin, but people should repent. Jesus heals a woman and tells the parables of the mustard seed and the yeast. He mourns the coming destruction of Jerusalem.

**Chapter 14**
3 | 6

Jesus is criticized for healing on the Sabbath, warns against taking the best seat, gives the parable of the great banquet, and explains the high cost of being one of his disciples.

**Chapter 15**
6

Jesus gives the parables of the lost sheep, the lost coin, and the lost son—also called the parable of the prodigal son.

**Chapter 16**
6

Jesus tells the parable about the shrewd manager and the story of the rich man and Lazarus: the rich man dies and faces torment, while Lazarus dies and finds paradise.

## Chapter 11: Commentary

Jesus' prayer in Luke 11:2–4 is called "the Lord's Prayer." It is also found in Matthew 6:9–13. The wording in Matthew and Luke is very similar, but not identical. The wording of the prayer also varies in the multiple ancient copies of Matthew and Luke that have survived. As texts were copied and recopied, it was inevitable that some variations would be created. Most differences between copies of the biblical texts involve spelling, though on occasion, the differences are more substantive. Thankfully, scholars have developed ways of comparing the thousands of copies of the New Testament that exist so as to recover, in most cases, the original reading. Modern translations of the Lord's Prayer are based on these corrected texts.

*He said to them, "When you pray, say:*
*'Father,*
*hallowed be your name,*
*your kingdom come.*
*Give us each day our daily bread.*
*Forgive us our sins,*
*for we also forgive everyone who sins against us.*
*And lead us not into temptation.'"*

**Luke 11:2–4**

*Someone in the crowd said to him, "Teacher, tell my brother to divide the inheritance with me."*
*Jesus replied, "Man, who appointed me a judge or an arbiter between you?" Then he said to them, "Watch out! Be on your guard against all kinds of greed; life does not consist in an abundance of possessions."*

**Luke 12:13–15**

## Chapter 13: Commentary

People would like to believe that good things will happen to good people and bad things to bad people. Suffering would be easy to explain then, and preventing bad things from happening in our lives would be as simple a process as always doing the right thing and always making good choices. But reality is not so simple. As the author of Ecclesiastes put it:

"The race is not to the swift or the battle to the strong, nor does food come to the wise or wealth to the brilliant or favor to the learned; but time and chance happen to them all." (Ecclesiastes 9:11)

Jesus simply reaffirms what Ecclesiastes—and experience with life—should teach: suffering does not come because the sufferer is a greater sinner than his or her neighbors. Sometimes bad things simply happen.

The apostles said to the Lord, "Increase our faith!" He replied, "If you have faith as small as a mustard seed, you can say to this mulberry tree, 'Be uprooted and planted in the sea,' and it will obey you."
**Luke 17:5–6**

To some who were confident of their own righteousness and looked down on everyone else, Jesus told this parable: "Two men went up to the temple to pray, one a Pharisee and the other a tax collector. The Pharisee stood by himself and prayed: 'God, I thank you that I am not like other people— robbers, evildoers, adulterers—or even like this tax collector. I fast twice a week and give a tenth of all I get.'

"But the tax collector stood at a distance. He would not even look up to heaven, but beat his breast and said, 'God, have mercy on me, a sinner.'

"I tell you that this man, rather than the other, went home justified before God. For all those who exalt themselves will be humbled, and those who humble themselves will be exalted."
**Luke 18:9–14**

## Chapter 21: **Commentary**

Jesus predicts the coming destruction of Jerusalem and its Temple by the Romans. Many Christians today believe that Jesus' words in Luke 21 (paralleling Matthew 24) predict a future battle just before Jesus returns to establish the Kingdom of God on Earth. But most modern scholars believe that his words instead describe the Jewish revolt against Rome that began in 66 AD and ended when Jerusalem fell and the Jewish Temple was burned by the Romans on July 29 or 30, 70 AD.

As Jesus looked up, he saw the rich putting their gifts into the temple treasury. He also saw a poor widow put in two very small copper coins. "Truly I tell you," he said, "this poor widow has put in more than all the others. All these people gave their gifts out of their wealth; but she out of her poverty put in all she had to live on."
**Luke 21:1–4**

When they came to the place called the Skull, they crucified him there, along with the criminals— one on his right, the other on his left. Jesus said, "Father, forgive them, for they do not know what they are doing." And they divided up his clothes by casting lots.
**Luke 23:33–34**

# John
## Overview

The title of the book is taken from the name of the traditional author, the apostle John.

The most important witness in the early Church to the authorship of the Gospel is Irenaeus, bishop of Lyons in the last quarter of the second century. That Irenaeus would affirm John's authorship is significant because he was acquainted with Polycarp, who had been a companion of John. Other early church fathers who affirmed John's authorship include Eusebius, Polycrates, and Clement of Alexandria.

Westcott's presentation of the internal evidence relating to the authorship of the Gospel is famous and follows five steps: 1) the author was Jewish; 2) he lived in Palestine; 3) he was an eyewitness; 4) he was an apostle; and finally, 5) he was the apostle John.

John 21:24 makes the statement "This is the

**The wedding in Cana**
*The first miracle Jesus performed was at a party in Cana celebrating a wedding. When they ran out of wine, Jesus made more.*

## Chapter 1: **Commentary**

The opening words of John's Gospel parallel the beginning of the Book of Genesis. John wanted his readers to understand that Jesus—"the Word"—is more than just a human being: he is the God of the Old Testament who created the universe and all that it contains. He then came to Earth, became a human being, and died for the sins of humanity. Paul echoes this same sentiment in Colossians 1:15–20 when he announces that "in him all things were created: things in heaven and on earth, visible and invisible, whether thrones or powers or rulers or authorities; all things have been created through him and for him." The authors of the New Testament believed that Jesus was the God of the Old Testament: Yahweh.

*In the beginning was the Word, and the Word was with God, and the Word was God. He was with God in the beginning. Through him all things were made; without him nothing was made that has been made. In him was life, and that life was the light of all mankind. The light shines in the darkness, and the darkness has not overcome it.*
**John 1:1–5**

**17**

Chapter
**1**

God becomes a human being named Jesus. John the Baptist announces Jesus is the Messiah. Andrew and John become Jesus' first disciples, followed by Peter, Philip, and Nathanael.

disciple who testifies to these things and who wrote them down. We know that his testimony is true." Westcott took this verse to be an addition by the elders of the church in Ephesus, bearing witness to the authorship and authenticity of this Gospel.

The majority opinion among traditional scholars, and even among a large number of critical scholars, is that John, the son of Zebedee, is the author of the Gospel that bears his name.

As for the date of the book, it is generally suggested that he wrote it sometime between AD 85 and 90, although dates as early as 45 and as late as 110 have sometimes been proposed. Tradition, based upon the statements of Irenaeus and Eusebius, has it that the book was written at Ephesus, in Asia Minor.

Although John's Gospel has much in common with the other three Gospel accounts, there are striking differences, especially in the order of events.

**Nicodemus**
*Nicodemus was a member of the Sanhedrin who visited Jesus at night to learn more about him. He became a disciple of Jesus.*

## Chapter 3: **Commentary**

When Jesus told Nicodemus that in order to see the Kingdom of God he must be "born again" Nicodemus was puzzled. He wondered how such a thing could happen. Jesus explained that those who enter the Kingdom must be born of the Spirit. Jesus was alluding to Joel 2:28–32, and Jeremiah 31:31–34. This Spirit, this New Kingdom, would be brought by the Messiah.

| **8** | **17** | |
|---|---|---|
| At the reception following a wedding, they run out of wine. At the urging of his mother, Jesus turns water into wine. Jesus drives the moneylenders out of the Temple in Jerusalem. | | Chapter **2** |

| **3** | **17** | |
|---|---|---|
| Nicodemus approaches Jesus at night to learn more about him. Jesus explains that he came to save humanity from its sins. John the Baptist testifies that Jesus is the Messiah. | | Chapter **3** |

| **3** | **8** | **17** |
|---|---|---|
| Jesus talks to a Samaritan woman by a well. Many Samaritans believe that he is the Messiah. Jesus heals the son of a royal official. | | Chapter **4** |

*Just as Moses lifted up the snake in the wilderness, so the Son of Man must be lifted up, that everyone who believes may have eternal life in him."*

*For God so loved the world that he gave his one and only Son, that whoever believes in him shall not perish but have eternal life. For God did not send his Son into the world to condemn the world, but to save the world through him.*

**John 3:14–17**

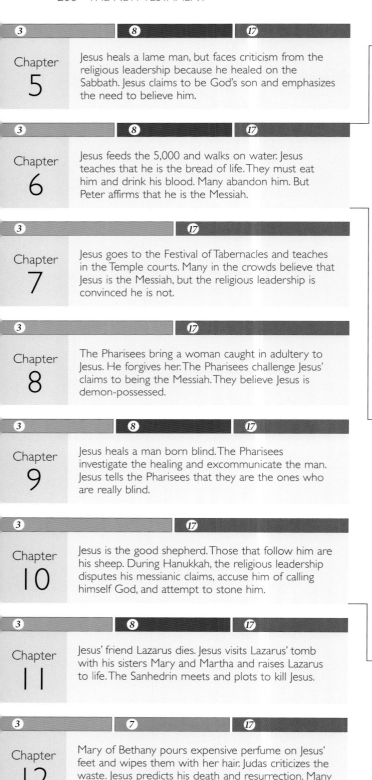

**Chapter 5**
Jesus heals a lame man, but faces criticism from the religious leadership because he healed on the Sabbath. Jesus claims to be God's son and emphasizes the need to believe him.

**Chapter 6**
Jesus feeds the 5,000 and walks on water. Jesus teaches that he is the bread of life. They must eat him and drink his blood. Many abandon him. But Peter affirms that he is the Messiah.

**Chapter 7**
Jesus goes to the Festival of Tabernacles and teaches in the Temple courts. Many in the crowds believe that Jesus is the Messiah, but the religious leadership is convinced he is not.

**Chapter 8**
The Pharisees bring a woman caught in adultery to Jesus. He forgives her. The Pharisees challenge Jesus' claims to being the Messiah. They believe Jesus is demon-possessed.

**Chapter 9**
Jesus heals a man born blind. The Pharisees investigate the healing and excommunicate the man. Jesus tells the Pharisees that they are the ones who are really blind.

**Chapter 10**
Jesus is the good shepherd. Those that follow him are his sheep. During Hanukkah, the religious leadership disputes his messianic claims, accuse him of calling himself God, and attempt to stone him.

**Chapter 11**
Jesus' friend Lazarus dies. Jesus visits Lazarus' tomb with his sisters Mary and Martha and raises Lazarus to life. The Sanhedrin meets and plots to kill Jesus.

**Chapter 12**
Mary of Bethany pours expensive perfume on Jesus' feet and wipes them with her hair. Judas criticizes the waste. Jesus predicts his death and resurrection. Many do not believe Jesus is the Messiah.

## Chapter 6: Commentary

In John 6:46 (cf. John 1:18) Jesus announces that no one has seen the Father. Some commentators find a problem with Jesus' words, given that in the Old Testament several people saw God, ranging from Abraham, who not only saw God, but gave him a meal (Genesis 18:1–22), to Moses, Aaron, Aaron's sons, and 70 elders who saw God and had a meal with him (Exodus 24:9–11). Samson's parents saw God (Judges 13:12–23), as did the prophets Isaiah (Isaiah 6:1–5) and Ezekiel (Ezekiel 1:25–28). So how could Jesus say that no one had seen his Father? Because the one people saw in the Old Testament was not Jesus' Father. Instead, they saw the Son: Jesus in his pre-incarnate state. The God of the Old Testament is not God the Father, but rather the Son of God. That is why the New Testament authors regularly refer to Jesus as "Lord." The Greek word translated "lord" was used by Greek-speaking Jewish people as a circumlocution for God's name, Yahweh. The standard Greek translation of the Old Testament, the Septuagint, used the word translated "lord" in place of God's name wherever it occurred. Jewish people—and later Christians—refused to say, as required by Roman law, that Caesar was "Lord." The word was used exclusively for God among the Jewish people and yet it was this word that they—the first Christians who were all Jewish—applied to Jesus.

*"No one has seen the Father except the one who is from God; only he has seen the Father. Very truly I tell you, the one who believes has eternal life. I am the bread of life. Your ancestors ate the manna in the wilderness, yet they died. But here is the bread that comes down from heaven, which anyone may eat and not die. I am the living bread that came down from heaven. Whoever eats this bread will live forever. This bread is my flesh, which I will give for the life of the world."*

**John 6:46–51**

*But Jesus said to them, "I have shown you many good works from the Father. For which of these do you stone me?"*

*"We are not stoning you for any good work," they replied, "but for blasphemy, because you, a mere man, claim to be God."*

**John 10:32–33**

*"You call me 'Teacher' and 'Lord,' and rightly so, for that is what I am. Now that I, your Lord and Teacher, have washed your feet, you also should wash one another's feet. I have set you an example that you should do as I have done for you. Very truly I tell you, no servant is greater than his master, nor is a messenger greater than the one who sent him. Now that you know these things, you will be blessed if you do them."*

*John 13:13–17*

## Chapters 14–16: **Commentary**

Beginning in chapter 14, the author of John's Gospel explains that Jesus will be sending the Holy Spirit to his followers. The expectation of God's Spirit coming to dwell among God's people grows out of the prophecies of Joel and Jeremiah. Peter will quote the words of Joel 2:28–32 on the day of Pentecost to explain what had happened when the Spirit arrived on the disciples (see Acts 1–2). So Jesus tells his disciples that the Holy Spirit will comfort them in his absence, empower them, and would have the task of convincing the world about the Gospel message, as well as what is right and wrong (John 16:8–10).

*Jesus said, "My kingdom is not of this world. If it were, my servants would fight to prevent my arrest by the Jewish leaders. But now my kingdom is from another place."*

*"You are a king, then!" said Pilate.*

*Jesus answered, "You say that I am a king. In fact, the reason I was born and came into the world is to testify to the truth. Everyone on the side of truth listens to me."*

*"What is truth?" retorted Pilate. With this he went out again to the Jews gathered there and said, "I find no basis for a charge against him."*

*John 18:36–38*

| 3 | 7 | 17 | |
|---|---|---|---|
| During the Last Supper, Jesus washes his disciples' feet, predicts Judas' betrayal, and warns Peter that he will deny he knows Jesus. | | | Chapter 13 |

| 3 | 7 | 17 | |
|---|---|---|---|
| Jesus comforts his disciples, tells them that he is the way, the truth, and the life. He promises that when he returns to his Father, that the Holy Spirit will come to them. | | | Chapter 14 |

| 3 | 17 | |
|---|---|---|
| Jesus tells his disciples that he is the vine and that they are the branches. He tells them that just as the world has hated Jesus, so the world will hate them. | | Chapter 15 |

| 3 | 7 | 17 | |
|---|---|---|---|
| The Holy Spirit will teach the disciples and convict the world of sin. The disciples' grief will soon turn to joy. Jesus offers them peace during the trouble they will experience. | | | Chapter 16 |

| 3 | 12 | 17 | |
|---|---|---|---|
| Jesus prays that he will be glorified. He prays for all who will ever follow him: that God will love them, protect them, make them holy, and guide them. | | | Chapter 17 |

| 3 | 17 | |
|---|---|---|
| Jesus is arrested and taken to the Sanhedrin. Peter denies Jesus three times. Jesus faces the Roman Governor Pilate. Jesus tells Pilate that his kingdom is not of this world. | | Chapter 18 |

**Woman caught in adultery**
*Jesus forgives a woman who committed adultery and shames those men who accused her.*

**17**

Chapter

**19**

Pilate sentences Jesus to death. Jesus is crucified, dies, and is buried in the tomb of Joseph of Arimathea.

*Later, knowing that everything had now been finished, and so that Scripture would be fulfilled, Jesus said, "I am thirsty." A jar of wine vinegar was there, so they soaked a sponge in it, put the sponge on a stalk of the hyssop plant, and lifted it to Jesus' lips. When he had received the drink, Jesus said, "It is finished." With that, he bowed his head and gave up his spirit.*

**John 19:28–30**

## Chapter 19: **Commentary**

Although the religious leadership of Israel conspired to get Jesus arrested and made the accusations to the Roman authorities that he was guilty of fomenting rebellion, it was the Roman government, in the person of the governor, Pontius Pilate, who had ultimate responsibility for executing Jesus. Crucifixion was an exclusively Roman method of punishment that they reserved for non-citizens. It was a harsh punishment, designed to send a message to subject peoples. Death from crucifixion sometimes took as long as a week, the consequence of exposure, hunger, thirst, and sometimes asphyxiation. In the case of Jesus and the two criminals executed with him, their deaths came much quicker. Because of the approaching Sabbath, the Romans feared insurrection if their dead or dying bodies were left hanging after sunset.

**Mary Magdalene**
*Mary Magdalene was the first person Jesus visited after his resurrection.*

*Jesus performed many other signs in the presence of his disciples, which are not recorded in this book. But these are written that you may believe that Jesus is the Messiah, the Son of God, and that by believing you may have life in his name.*

**John 20:30–31**

**3**     **8**     **17**

Chapter

**20**

Mary Magdalene and the other women find the tomb empty and tell Jesus' disciples. John and Peter visit the empty tomb. Jesus appears to Mary, other disciples, and last of all, to Thomas.

## Chapter 21: **Commentary**

Jesus tells Peter that he will suffer a martyr's death. Based on the wording describing Peter's death, the legend that Peter was executed by crucifixion during the Roman persecutions under Nero is reasonable. The author of John's Gospel also attempts to quash the rumors that John would not die until Jesus returned. This has sometimes been linked with the legend of the "wandering Jew," about a Jewish man condemned to walk the earth until the Second Coming of Christ.

**3**     **8**     **17**

Chapter

**21**

Jesus appears to his disciples in Galilee, where they catch an unusually large number of fish. Jesus forgives Peter. Peter affirms his love for Jesus.

# Acts

## Overview

The Book of Acts records the activities of some of the early followers of Jesus after his resurrection, focusing mostly on what Peter and Paul were doing.

The author of the Book of Acts has traditionally been assumed to be the same as the author of the Gospel of Luke: a gentile, a physician, and a companion of Paul. This assumption is based on the similar opening paragraph of the two works, both of which are addressed to the same person: Theophilus (see Acts 1:1–3 and Luke 1:1–4).

It is important to point out that without the Book of Acts, there would be no record of the early history of Christianity. All that is known about the beginnings of the early Church, except for what little can be gleaned from Paul's letters and the letters of a few others, comes from this work by Luke. It records the period from about AD 33 until about AD 63.

## Chapter 1: **Commentary**

From the beginning, Jesus instructed his disciples to tell others about who he was and what he had done, and its significance. (cf. Matthew 28:18–20, Luke 24:46–49, John 20:21.) He was underlining the importance of missionary activity to Christianity.

***The Day of Pentecost***
*On the Day of Pentecost, the Holy Spirit came upon the followers of Jesus, who had assembled together in a room.*

*Then they gathered around him and asked him, "Lord, are you at this time going to restore the kingdom to Israel?"*

*He said to them: "It is not for you to know the times or dates the Father has set by his own authority. But you will receive power when the Holy Spirit comes on you; and you will be my witnesses in Jerusalem, and in all Judea and Samaria, and to the ends of the earth."*

**Acts 1:6–8**

 (15)     (17)

Jesus gives his disciples final instructions to take the good news to the world and then ascends into heaven. The remaining 11 apostles select Matthias to replace Judas.

Chapter
1

 (3)     (5)     (12)

On the day of Pentecost, the Holy Spirit came upon the disciples gathered in an upper room in Jerusalem. Peter preached to a crowd that gathered; 3,000 became Christians.

Chapter
2

| | | |
|---|---|---|
| ③ | ⑧ | ⑰ |

**Chapter 3**

Peter and John went to the Temple. Peter healed a lame beggar, then spoke to the crowd about Jesus.

| | | |
|---|---|---|
| ③ | ⑫ | ⑰ |

**Chapter 4**

Peter and John were brought before the Sanhedrin because they were preaching about Jesus. They were warned to stop it. The believers shared their possessions with each other.

| | | |
|---|---|---|
| ⑧ | ⑮ | ⑰ |

**Chapter 5**

Ananias and his wife Sapphira died after lying to the church. An angel freed the apostles who were arrested and the Sanhedrin discussed what to do about followers of Jesus.

## Chapters 4–5: Commentary

The Jewish people of the first century were expecting the Messiah to arrive. They believed that the Messiah would lead a rebellion against the Romans, expel them from their land, and re-establish the monarchy under a descendant of King David. Several individuals arose during the first century AD claiming to be the Messiah. Gamaliel of the Sanhedrin listed two such individuals in his argument against doing anything to the followers of Jesus. One of those Gamaliel refers to, Judas of Galilee, may be mentioned by Josephus in his *Antiquities of the Jews* (13.1.1). In Luke 13:1–3 Jesus is asked about the Galileans killed by Pilate, which also may be a reference to Judas' rebellion. From Gamaliel's perspective, therefore, the Jesus movement seemed no different than the others. Like them, he expected it to fade away with the death of its leader. From the perspective of the Sanhedrin, these various pretenders to messiahship were dangerous. The Jewish leaders well understood the power of Rome and feared Roman invasion and retribution should an armed rebellion ever occur. They knew that the Romans would not only kill many people and devastate the land, they feared losing their comfortable positions of power.

**Stephen's martyrdom**
*Stephen, one of the first deacons, became the first Christian to die for his faith.*

*Then he addressed the Sanhedrin: "Men of Israel, consider carefully what you intend to do to these men. Some time ago Theudas appeared, claiming to be somebody, and about four hundred men rallied to him. He was killed, all his followers were dispersed, and it all came to nothing. After him, Judas the Galilean appeared in the days of the census and led a band of people in revolt. He too was killed, and all his followers were scattered. Therefore, in the present case I advise you: Leave these men alone! Let them go! For if their purpose or activity is of human origin, it will fail. But if it is from God, you will not be able to stop these men; you will only find yourselves fighting against God."*
**Acts 5:35–39**

## Chapter 6: Commentary

As the Christian community grew, so did the need for organization. Since the early believers had sold their property and held everything in common, it was necessary to dole out the food and supplies to the members of the community. There were problems with equitable and proper distribution, so the 12 apostles devised the solution of choosing seven men to be in charge of it. The names of these seven deacons betray them as members of the Hellenized Jewish community, rather than the Hebraic Jewish community.

| | |
|---|---|
| ③ | ⑰ |

**Chapter 6**

Because of disagreements between Hebraic and Hellenized Jews, the apostles selected seven Hellenized Jews as deacons. One, Stephen, is arrested by the Sanhedrin for blasphemy.

*At this they covered their ears and, yelling at the top of their voices, they all rushed at him, dragged him out of the city and began to stone him. Meanwhile, the witnesses laid their coats at the feet of a young man named Saul.*

*While they were stoning him, Stephen prayed, "Lord Jesus, receive my spirit." Then he fell on his knees and cried out, "Lord, do not hold this sin against them." When he had said this, he fell asleep.*

**Acts 7:57–60**

*Meanwhile, Saul was still breathing out murderous threats against the Lord's disciples. He went to the high priest and asked him for letters to the synagogues in Damascus, so that if he found any there who belonged to the Way, whether men or women, he might take them as prisoners to Jerusalem. As he neared Damascus on his journey, suddenly a light from heaven flashed around him. He fell to the ground and heard a voice say to him, "Saul, Saul, why do you persecute me?"*

*"Who are you, Lord?" Saul asked.*

*"I am Jesus, whom you are persecuting," he replied. "Now get up and go into the city, and you will be told what you must do."*

**Acts 9:1–6**

## Chapter 11: **Commentary**

In the beginning, the Christian movement was strictly Jewish: Jesus was Jewish, as were his disciples. Originally, their concept of the Messiah had been that he would lead the Jewish nation to freedom from Rome and the re-establishment of the Jewish monarchy under a descendant of king David. Up until the Jewish revolt that brought the destruction of the Jerusalem Temple in 70 AD, Christians were treated as a sect of Judaism, akin to the Pharisees or Sadducees. Initially, there was resistance and disagreement over whether and how non-Jews could become Christians. Peter's experience with Cornelius (Acts 10) began the expansion of Christianity into the non-Jewish Roman world. It expanded rapidly with the work of Paul and his companions who began targeting non-Jewish people for conversion. Ultimately, the majority of Christians ended up not being Jewish at all.

---

**3**   **17**

In his defense, Stephen summarizes Jewish history and affirms that Jesus is the Messiah. The Sanhedrin condemns him, so a mob stones him to death, while Paul watches with approval.

Chapter **7**

**8**   **15**   **17**

The Christians of Jerusalem are persecuted and flee, except for the apostles. Philip preaches in Samaria. Simon the Sorcerer converts. Philip baptizes an Ethiopian eunuch.

Chapter **8**

**8**   **17**

Saul persecutes Christians until he meets Jesus on his way to Damascus. Healed of blindness, he begins preaching the Gospel. Peter heals a paralyzed man and raises a dead woman.

Chapter **9**

**8**   **12**   **17**

The centurion Cornelius of Caesarea hears the Gospel from Peter after Peter's vision of being commanded to eat unclean animals. He and his family believe and receive the Holy Spirit and baptism.

Chapter **10**

**8**   **12**   **17**

Peter argues that the conversion of Cornelius demonstrates that Gentiles may also become Christians. The church in Antioch sends Barnabas and Paul to Judea with aid.

Chapter **11**

**8**   **12**   **15**

King Herod kills James, the brother of John, then arrests Peter. An angel comes and frees Peter while the church prays for his release. Herod soon dies from worms.

Chapter **12**

**3**   **8**   **17**

The church in Antioch sends Barnabas and Saul to preach about Jesus around the Roman world. In Paphos they blind a sorcerer. In Pisidian Antioch they preach to gentiles.

Chapter **13**

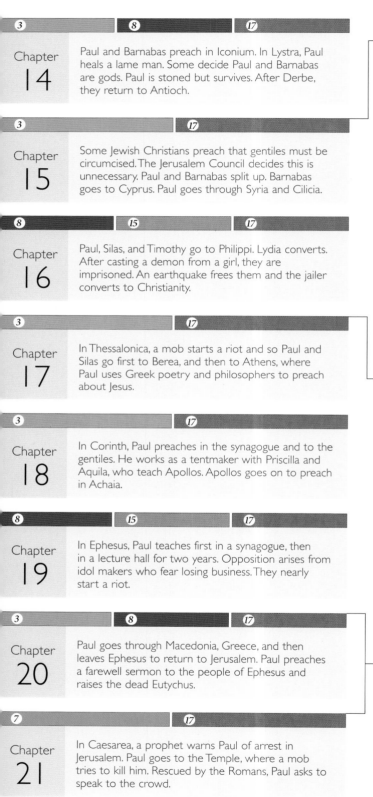

**Chapter**

**14**

Paul and Barnabas preach in Iconium. In Lystra, Paul heals a lame man. Some decide Paul and Barnabas are gods. Paul is stoned but survives. After Derbe, they return to Antioch.

**Chapter**

**15**

Some Jewish Christians preach that gentiles must be circumcised. The Jerusalem Council decides this is unnecessary. Paul and Barnabas split up. Barnabas goes to Cyprus. Paul goes through Syria and Cilicia.

**Chapter**

**16**

Paul, Silas, and Timothy go to Philippi. Lydia converts. After casting a demon from a girl, they are imprisoned. An earthquake frees them and the jailer converts to Christianity.

**Chapter**

**17**

In Thessalonica, a mob starts a riot and so Paul and Silas go first to Berea, and then to Athens, where Paul uses Greek poetry and philosophers to preach about Jesus.

**Chapter**

**18**

In Corinth, Paul preaches in the synagogue and to the gentiles. He works as a tentmaker with Priscilla and Aquila, who teach Apollos. Apollos goes on to preach in Achaia.

**Chapter**

**19**

In Ephesus, Paul teaches first in a synagogue, then in a lecture hall for two years. Opposition arises from idol makers who fear losing business. They nearly start a riot.

**Chapter**

**20**

Paul goes through Macedonia, Greece, and then leaves Ephesus to return to Jerusalem. Paul preaches a farewell sermon to the people of Ephesus and raises the dead Eutychus.

**Chapter**

**21**

In Caesarea, a prophet warns Paul of arrest in Jerusalem. Paul goes to the Temple, where a mob tries to kill him. Rescued by the Romans, Paul asks to speak to the crowd.

## Chapter 15: **Commentary**

The Jerusalem Council was the first time that the Church establishment came together to decide an issue of doctrine: in this case, they decided what was required in order for someone to be considered a Christian. There were those who believed that it was necessary for gentiles to convert to Judaism first, as signified by being circumcised. Peter's experience with Cornelius suggested no prerequisites were necessary and so Paul's beliefs prevailed. It was decided that a belief in Jesus was sufficient. The letter produced by the council stated that, although gentiles did not have to keep kosher, they should still pay attention to certain minimal requirements regarding their diet and their sexual behavior.

Paul later argued—in contrast to this letter—that abstaining from food sacrificed to idols was unnecessary (1 Corinthians 8:1–13). The fact that Paul felt comfortable disagreeing with this point, even though it had been produced by a Church council, and the fact that those who believed circumcision was necessary for becoming a Christian continued to preach that message (see Galatians 2:11–16, Titus 1:10, for example), argues that at this stage in Church history, the decisions of Church councils were not necessarily considered binding.

## Chapter 17: **Commentary**

The Areopagus was the hill of Ares in Athens. Ares was the god of war, equivalent to the Roman god Mars. Therefore, some translations render it as "Mars Hill." It was a court that traditionally met on that hill and it is possible that this was more than simply Paul lecturing. Socrates was accused of "introducing other new gods" and Paul is likewise described as "introducing strange ideas" which are described as "foreign gods" in verse 18. One of Paul's converts from this episode was Dionysius, a member of the Aeropagus (verse 34) which also suggests that this was a formal hearing, not just a lecture.

Epicureans were materialists who believed that everything came from particles of matter and they did not believe in any life beyond this one. Stoics believed in divine providence and tended toward pantheism, believing that the divine principle existed in everything. By calling Paul a "babbler" they meant that he was a dilettante who picked up ideas and passed them on with no understanding. Paul adapted his message to his audience.

## Chapters 20–21: **Commentary**

When Paul returned to Jerusalem, the church leaders there encouraged him to participate in some Jewish religious rites. Most likely, the rite was associated with the end of a Nazirite vow, something Paul himself had participated in recently (see Acts 18:18). The Nazirite vow (see Numbers 6) was a vow of dedication to God; during the time set for the vow, participants avoided wine and anything else associated with grapes. They also did not cut their hair. At the end of the vow, Nazirites brought offerings for sacrifice and shaved off their hair.

*The crowd listened to Paul until he said this. Then they raised their voices and shouted, "Rid the earth of him! He's not fit to live!"*

*As they were shouting and throwing off their cloaks and flinging dust into the air, the commander ordered that Paul be taken into the barracks. He directed that he be flogged and interrogated in order to find out why the people were shouting at him like this. As they stretched him out to flog him, Paul said to the centurion standing there, "Is it legal for you to flog a Roman citizen who hasn't even been found guilty?"*

**Acts 22:22–25**

**Paul on trial**
*Paul was arrested when he visited Jerusalem and defended himself before the Roman governor, Felix.*

*The soldiers planned to kill the prisoners to prevent any of them from swimming away and escaping. But the centurion wanted to spare Paul's life and kept them from carrying out their plan. He ordered those who could swim to jump overboard first and get to land. The rest were to get there on planks or on other pieces of the ship. In this way everyone reached land safely.*

**Acts 27:42–44**

## Chapter 28: **Commentary**

According to legend, Paul died during the persecutions against Christians that occurred during Emperor Nero's reign. The Book of Acts ends with Paul's situation unresolved. Some speculate that the author of Acts wrote the book during this imprisonment in Rome, and may have intended a sequel. According to 2 Timothy 4:16–17 Paul was released following this imprisonment. I Clement 5:7 says that Paul made more missionary journeys before being arrested again. Later, 2 Timothy 4:6–8 indicates that he was in prison awaiting execution, perhaps around 62 AD.

---

**3** · **17**

Paul explains how he came to be a Christian. When he tells them that God asked him to preach to the gentiles, they become enraged. The Romans arrest Paul, then send him to the Sanhedrin.

Chapter
**22**

**3** · **17**

Paul addresses the Sanhedrin, which splits and argues. After a death threat, the Romans move Paul to Caesarea. He meets the Roman Governor Felix, then is placed under guard in Herod's palace.

Chapter
**23**

**3** · **17**

The high priest Ananias and other elders go to Caesarea to level charges against Paul. Paul makes his defense. Two years later, when Festus replaces Felix, Paul is still imprisoned.

Chapter
**24**

**3** · **17**

Paul makes a defense before Festus, who asks Paul to stand trial in Jerusalem. Paul refuses and appeals to Caesar. King Agrippa and his wife arrive and decide to meet with Paul.

Chapter
**25**

**3** · **17**

Paul tells Agrippa about how he came to be a Christian. Agrippa agrees with Festus that Paul is guilty of nothing and that had he not appealed to Caesar he could have been released.

Chapter
**26**

**3** · **7** · **17**

Paul sails for Rome and reaches Crete. It is late in the season, but it is not a good place to winter so they sail on. A storm sinks the ship, but Paul and the crew reach dry land.

Chapter
**27**

**3** · **8** · **17**

They discover they have landed on Malta. Paul survives a snakebite. After three months, they finally reach Rome. Paul stays in a rented house for two years and preaches.

Chapter
**28**

**3**

Chapter

**1**

Paul writes to Christians in Rome, expressing his desire to visit them. The good news is for all humanity. Righteousness comes from faith. God's judgment is the consequence of sin.

**3**

Chapter

**2**

God's judgment is righteous. Those living by the law will be judged by it, while those without it will be judged by their consciences. Righteousness is from the Spirit, not from laws.

**3**  **5**

Chapter

**3**

Jewish people have the words of God, which gives them an advantage. But in the end, no human being is really righteous. Righteousness comes from faith, rather than from good works.

**3**

Chapter

**4**

Abraham was not justified by God on the basis of his actions, but on the basis of his faith: he believed God and by that belief, became the father of many nations.

**2**  **3**

Chapter

**5**

We are justified by faith, not by works. The death of Jesus made peace with God. Sin came to the world by one man, Adam. Salvation comes by one man, the new Adam, Jesus Christ.

**2**  **3**

Chapter

**6**

We were crucified with Jesus and died with him; likewise, we rose from the dead with him. Therefore, where before we were slaves to sin, now we are slaves to righteousness.

**2**  **3**

Chapter

**7**

After people die, they are freed from the law's authority. Therefore, since we died with Jesus, we are freed from the law. The law wasn't a bad thing. It taught us the need for a savior.

**2**  **3**  **10**

Chapter

**8**

We have been set free from the law of sin and death and have been given a new life through the Spirit in Christ. God is with us and loves us and so we can be victorious in the end.

# Romans

## Overview

**I**   Introduction 1:1–17

**II**  The world 1:18–3:20

**III** Justification 3:21–5:21

**IV** Sanctification 6:1–8:39

**V**  Israel 9:1–11:36

**VI** The practice of righteousness 12:1–15:13

**VII** Conclusion 15:14–16:27

It is believed that Paul wrote this epistle to the Christians in Rome to introduce his teachings to them. In it, Paul presents his belief that salvation is offered through the Gospel of Jesus Christ. It is given by God freely to human beings as a consequence of Jesus' sacrificial death on a cross.

## Chapter 1: **Commentary**

The message that Paul and the other early Christians proclaimed—the essence of the Gospel message—can be summarized in six statements:
• Jesus came from God.
• Jesus was crucified.
• Jesus was raised from the dead.
• God gave the Holy Spirit.
• Jesus is coming again.
• Repent and be baptized.
This same message can be summarized from sermons in the Book of Acts, as well as the various letters of the New Testament attributed to Paul, Peter, James, Jude, and the author of Hebrews.

## Chapter 5: **Commentary**

Paul stresses in his letter to the Romans that a human being's relationship with God is a consequence of Jesus' death on a cross, not the result of keeping the law. Good behavior and bad behavior have nothing to do with salvation; instead, salvation is a gift God offers through Jesus, freely given and freely available to any who want it. The sixteenth-century Protestant reformer, Martin Luther, argued from Paul, in the *Smalcald Articles*, that we do not gain righteousness by doing righteous things.

## Chapters 9–11: **Commentary**

In his discussion about the Jewish people, Paul argues that God's gifts and calling cannot be revoked. God's relationship and promises to the nation of Israel are permanent. Through much of Christian history it has been taught that Israel has been replaced by the Church, and that therefore the Jewish people have been cast aside by God. However, Paul's argument in Romans 11 strongly suggests otherwise. The idea that the Church has replaced Israel is called "replacement theology" or "supersessionism" and has been used too often as a justification for the hatred, persecution, and mistreatment of the Jews; it has gone hand in hand with the anti-Semitic notion that the Jews killed Christ.

## Chapter 14: **Commentary**

Paul affirms in Romans 14 that the concept of sin is sometimes a matter of individual conscience rather than a universal principle. While a given behavior may be widely considered good, if an individual feels guilty about it, then that makes it a sin for that person. It is similar to what the prophet Jeremiah found in his dealings with the descendants of Rekab, as recorded in Jeremiah 35. Jeremiah offered them wine and they refused to drink it, because their ancestor had forbidden it to them. God then praised them for their fidelity to their ancestor's commands, even though drinking the wine would otherwise have been unobjectionable. Paul likewise points out that while eating certain foods may offend some and not others, our choices in our behavior should not be made selfishly, but rather with due consideration for the feelings of those around us. Paul wants people to respect the conscientious choices of one another, not criticizing them for how they chose to restrict themselves, nor causing them problems for it.

## Chapter 16: **Commentary**

Among those that Paul greets are several important women, demonstrating that women had positions of authority and leadership in the early Church. Phoebe is described as a deacon in the church at Cenchreae. Priscilla, with her husband Aquila, is mentioned early on. Priscilla, who is normally listed ahead of her husband, helped to train the evangelist Apollos (Acts 18:26). In Romans 16:7 Paul mentions a woman named Junia who spent time in prison with him. He describes her as being "outstanding among the apostles." She is the only woman explicitly called an apostle in the New Testament, though there were many other women who followed Jesus as his disciples (see for instance Luke 8:2–3, Matthew 27:56, Luke 24:10, John 19:25) and fit the requirements for an apostle (Acts 1:21–22). Many women were involved in the formative days of the Christian community (Acts 1:12–14, Acts 12:12).

**3**

Paul loves the Jewish people and wants them to accept Jesus as the Messiah. God is just. For now, the gentiles are believing in Jesus more than the Jewish people.

Chapter **9**

**2** **3** **12**

But Paul's great desire and prayer to God is that his own people, the Jewish people, would accept that Jesus is the Messiah. All who call on his name will be saved.

Chapter **10**

**3** **10**

God has not rejected his people Israel. In fact, someday all of the Jewish people will be saved. The Jewish people are God's people forever and nothing can change that.

Chapter **11**

**3** **10**

All Christians should devote themselves fully to God. Each individual is important and has a role to play. We should love each other and everyone else, whether friend or foe.

Chapter **12**

**3** **10**

Obey the government and be good citizens. All the laws in the Bible can be summarized by the command to love others. So don't focus just on yourself. Focus on helping others.

Chapter **13**

**3**

Don't quarrel over disputable matters. Something you think is fine may be sinful for someone else and vice versa. So don't judge and don't do things that cause problems for others.

Chapter **14**

**3**

Encourage one another and help each other. Accept each other just as Jesus accepted you. Paul expresses his desire to visit and minister to the people in Rome.

Chapter **15**

**3**

Paul ends with personal greetings to people in Rome that he knows. He urges them to work together and to stay away from divisive people.

Chapter **16**

# I Corinthians

## Overview

he title of the book comes from the name of the city of Corinth, in Greece, where the church Paul wrote to was located. It is the first of two surviving letters that Paul wrote to the church in Corinth. He discusses the divisions and other serious problems facing that congregation.

According to 1 Corinthians 16:8–9, 20, it is clear that Paul wrote the letter while he was in Ephesus. Based on the long time he spent there, and the fact that it followed his time in Corinth, it is assumed that it was written during his stay in Ephesus as recorded in Acts 19–20, probably between 53 and 57 AD.

**Mosaic from Corinth**
*Bacchus, whose head appears in the center of this mosaic taken from a villa in Corinth, was the god of wine and ecstasy.*

*Brothers and sisters, think of what you were when you were called. Not many of you were wise by human standards; not many were influential; not many were of noble birth. But God chose the foolish things of the world to shame the wise; God chose the weak things of the world to shame the strong. God chose the lowly things of this world and the despised things—and the things that are not—to nullify the things that are, so that no one may boast before him. It is because of him that you are in Christ Jesus, who has become for us wisdom from God—that is, our righteousness, holiness and redemption. Therefore, as it is written: "Let the one who boasts boast in the Lord."*

**1 Corinthians 1:26–31**

---

**③**

| Chapter 1 | Paul warned the Christian community in Corinth against following people. Jesus' death on the cross is God's power and true wisdom and Christians have nothing to boast about except the Lord. |
|---|---|

**③**

| Chapter 2 | Paul claims no great wisdom or charisma; he imply preaches about Jesus dying on the cross. The message of the good news came from God, not from human reasoning. |
|---|---|

## Chapter 2: **Commentary**

Paul quotes a few lines from Isaiah, that "no human mind has conceived… these things God has prepared for those who love him." (Isaiah 64:4). His point was not, however, that these wonderful things were unknowable. Rather, he points out immediately that "God has revealed them to us by his Spirit." (1 Corinthians 2:10.) Paul then gives an explanation, in 1 Corinthians 2: 11–16 of God's work in the lives of Christians, expanding and building upon what Jesus had taught his disciples about the Spirit in the Gospel of John (see John 14:26–27, 15:26, 16:7–15).

*For no one can lay any foundation other than the one already laid, which is Jesus Christ. If anyone builds on this foundation using gold, silver, costly stones, wood, hay or straw, their work will be shown for what it is, because the Day will bring it to light. It will be revealed with fire, and the fire will test the quality of each person's work. If what has been built survives, the builder will receive a reward. If it is burned up, the builder will suffer loss but yet will be saved—even though only as one escaping through the flames.*

**1 Corinthians 3:11–15**

**Roman courtroom**
*Paul believed that Christians should not bring lawsuits against one another. Instead, disagreements between Christians were to be settled by the Church.*

## Chapter 7: Commentary

Paul spends chapter 7 discussing matters of status in society and among believers. Jesus had told his disciples that they were not to relate to one another as people in their world commonly did: no one was the boss, no one exercised authority over others. In the first century, women were an underclass, and slavery was widespread. In religion, Jewish people commonly looked down upon non-Jews and segregated themselves, viewing gentiles as corrupting and unclean. Paul encourages believers to accept their place in society and to not be consumed with attempts to alter status, as if that were all that mattered in life. The radical nature of what Paul was telling the recipients of his letter is clear when he writes that husbands and wives were the property of one another and therefore equally bound to the will of their life partner.

*The wife does not have authority over her own body but yields it to her husband. In the same way, the husband does not have authority over his own body but yields it to his wife.*

**1 Corinthians 7:4**

---

**3**

God is the one who is building the ministry and work of the church, not special people. God uses the inconsequential people to confound the self-important.

Chapter
**3**

---

**3**

True apostles are servants of Jesus, not masters. Paul speaks of his suffering and persecution and sarcastically speaks of how great the Corinthians must be in contrast.

Chapter
**4**

---

**3**        **9**

Paul criticizes the assembly in Corinth for tolerating a member of their fellowship who has taken his father's wife as his own. He tells them they should expel him.

Chapter
**5**

---

**3**        **9**

Paul criticizes the assembly in Corinth for suing one another. They instead should settle their differences among themselves. Although we are free in Christ, we shouldn't use our freedom to behave badly.

Chapter
**6**

---

**3**

Given the problems facing Christians from the Roman Empire, staying single might be wise. Nevertheless, marriage is good and divorce should be avoided if possible.

Chapter
**7**

---

**3**

Idols are nothing, so eating food sacrificed to them shouldn't bother you. But if it does, or if it would harm another's conscience, then refrain. Don't lead people to sin against their own consciences.

Chapter
**8**

**3**

Chapter

**9**

Although Paul, as an apostle, has certain rights, he has chosen not to exercise them. He's more concerned with the needs of others than with his own needs. Be self-disciplined.

**3**

Chapter

**10**

God can give us victory over temptations. As a believer, you have the right to do anything you want, but not everything is beneficial. Whatever you do, do it to God's glory.

**3**     **11**

Chapter

**11**

It is traditional for women to cover their heads in worship when they pray or prophesy. Take communion in a reverential manner. Remember it's not about satisfying your hunger.

**3**     **11**

Chapter

**12**

Every Christian has been given a spiritual gift from God for the purpose of helping the church. Therefore, all Christians are important and should exercise their gifts to benefit all.

**Women's conduct**
*Paul encouraged all women to cover their heads when praying or prophesying in church.*

*Who serves as a soldier at his own expense? Who plants a vineyard and does not eat its grapes? Who tends a flock and does not drink the milk? Do I say this merely on human authority? Doesn't the Law say the same thing? For it is written in the Law of Moses: "Do not muzzle an ox while it is treading out the grain." Is it about oxen that God is concerned? Surely he says this for us, doesn't he? Yes, this was written for us, because whoever plows and threshes should be able to do so in the hope of sharing in the harvest. If we have sown spiritual seed among you, is it too much if we reap a material harvest from you? If others have this right of support from you, shouldn't we have it all the more?*

*But we did not use this right. On the contrary, we put up with anything rather than hinder the gospel of Christ.*

**1 Corinthians 9:7–12**

*If I take part in the meal with thankfulness, why am I denounced because of something I thank God for?*

*So whether you eat or drink or whatever you do, do it all for the glory of God. Do not cause anyone to stumble, whether Jews, Greeks or the church of God—even as I try to please everyone in every way. For I am not seeking my own good but the good of many, so that they may be saved.*

**1 Corinthians 10:30–33**

## Chapter 11: **Commentary**

In the Roman world, high-born women who were properly married were allowed to wear head coverings. Those women who were slaves and those who had been prostitutes could not. Paul tells the people of Corinth that all women should be wearing head coverings, thereby making all of them equal to the proper, high-born married women. A visitor to a Christian congregation would not be able to tell, by looking at the way the participants were dressed, what any individual's social status might be. Paul wanted Christians to understand that in Christ, all were equal and loved by God. James will later discuss the same sort of problem in his letter (see James 2:1–13).

*Just as a body, though one, has many parts, but all its many parts form one body, so it is with Christ. For we were all baptized by one Spirit so as to form one body—whether Jews or Gentiles, slave or free— and we were all given the one Spirit to drink. Even so the body is not made up of one part but of many.*

**1 Corinthians 12:12–14**

**3**  **10**  **11**

Love is more important than anything else: it is patient, trusting, and never fails. It is concerned only with others. Everything else will fade, but love will endure forever.

Chapter
13

**3**  **11**

God is an orderly God, not a God of confusion. Therefore, if everything is confused, God isn't the cause. Conduct your worship services in an orderly and intelligible way.

Chapter
14

**3**  **8**

The good news is that Jesus died for our sins and rose again. If Jesus did not rise from the dead, then Christianity is a lie. Just as Jesus rose from the dead, so shall we.

Chapter
15

**3**

Paul explains that he is taking up a collection for the needy in Jerusalem. He gives other personal requests. He tells them to do everything in love and to greet one another with a kiss.

Chapter
16

*Love is patient, love is kind. It does not envy, it does not boast, it is not proud. It does not dishonor others, it is not self-seeking, it is not easily angered, it keeps no record of wrongs. Love does not delight in evil but rejoices with the truth. It always protects, always trusts, always hopes, always perseveres.*

**1 Corinthians 13:4–8**

## Chapter 15: **Commentary**

Paul points out that the resurrection of Jesus is central to Christianity. If Jesus did not rise from the dead, then Christianity is untrue and Christians are false teachers.

Christianity is a historically based religion. Unlike more philosophically oriented religions, Christianity is built upon an event in history. As a consequence, by affirming a historical event, Christianity more than most religions sets itself up for criticism and attack. Apologetics—that branch of theology that deals with answering criticism and giving evidence for what Christians profess—has therefore been an important aspect of Christianity since its inception.

*And if Christ has not been raised, our preaching is useless and so is your faith. More than that, we are then found to be false witnesses about God, for we have testified about God that he raised Christ from the dead. But he did not raise him if in fact the dead are not raised. For if the dead are not raised, then Christ has not been raised either. And if Christ has not been raised, your faith is futile; you are still in your sins. Then those also who have fallen asleep in Christ are lost. If only for this life we have hope in Christ, we are of all people most to be pitied.*

**1 Corinthians 15:14–19**

**The Resurrection**
*Paul points out that if Jesus did not come back to life after his crucifixion, then Christianity is meaningless, worthless, and wrong.*

# 2 Corinthians

## Overview

The book receives its title from the name of the church to which it is addressed. It is the second surviving letter that Paul wrote to the church in Corinth, most likely composed between 53 and 57 AD when Paul was in Ephesus.

Most scholars believe that Paul is responsible for the contents of 2 Corinthians, but some have speculated that the letter as it exists today is actually a combination of two letters, the "warning letter" and the "letter of tears." Other scholars disagree and believe that 2 Corinthians is one letter and that neither the "warning letter" nor the "letter of tears" has survived to the present day.

| | |
|---|---|
| **Chapter 1** | Paul explains that as much as he had hoped to return to Corinth again, his situation was such as to prevent him from making it yet, but that was all for the best. |
| **Chapter 2** | Paul tells the Corinthian congregation that they should forgive the man they expelled now that he has repented. Paul explains his opportunities for ministry in Troas and Macedonia. |
| **Chapter 3** | We don't sell God's word for profit. The Old Covenant of Moses was glorious, but the New Covenant of the Spirit is even better. The Old Covenant brought death. The new one brings life. |
| **Chapter 4** | Despite the current persecution, suffering, and rejection of the message of good news, still, we don't give up. God renews our spirit, because we keep an eternal perspective. |
| **Chapter 5** | We look forward to the resurrection and our new bodies which will never decay. In the meantime, we attempt to persuade people to believe the message of the good news. |

*Praise be to the God and Father of our Lord Jesus Christ, the Father of compassion and the God of all comfort, who comforts us in all our troubles, so that we can comfort those in any trouble with the comfort we ourselves receive from God. For just as we share abundantly in the sufferings of Christ, so also our comfort abounds through Christ. If we are distressed, it is for your comfort and salvation; if we are comforted, it is for your comfort, which produces in you patient endurance of the same sufferings we suffer. And our hope for you is firm, because we know that just as you share in our sufferings, so also you share in our comfort.*

**2 Corinthians 1:3–7**

## Chapter 3: **Commentary**

The Old Covenant was contained in the Law of Moses in Genesis–Deuteronomy. The New Covenant came with what Jesus achieved through his death and resurrection. Paul makes his argument for the superiority of what Jesus had done by alluding to the words of the prophet Jeremiah, when he compares "tablets of stone" and "tablets of human hearts" (2 Corinthians 3:3). Jeremiah had written that God would make a New Covenant with his people of Israel (Jeremiah 31:31) and that "I will put my law in their minds and write it on their hearts." Paul is not unique in making this argument. It is, in fact, the central theme of the entire Book of Hebrews (notice Hebrews 1 and 8, for instance). Paul also alludes to the incident in Exodus when Moses returned from Mount Sinai, after having received the Ten Commandments, and had to wear a veil over his glowing face (see Exodus 34:29–35).

**Paul arrested**
*While in Corinth, Paul was arrested and brought to the Bema to stand trial, but the charges were dismissed by Gallio, proconsul of Achaia.*

*Godly sorrow brings repentance that leads to salvation and leaves no regret, but worldly sorrow brings death.*

**2 Corinthians 7:10**

*For though we live in the world, we do not wage war as the world does. The weapons we fight with are not the weapons of the world. On the contrary, they have divine power to demolish strongholds. We demolish arguments and every pretension that sets itself up against the knowledge of God, and we take captive every thought to make it obedient to Christ.*

**2 Corinthians 10:3–5**

## Chapter 12: **Commentary**

Commentators have long speculated over what Paul's "thorn" in his flesh might be (2 Corinthians 12:7–10). Some have speculated that it was a physical ailment, perhaps something with his eyes, based upon his reference in a letter to the Christians in Galatia about an illness he suffered. He commented that they cared so much for him that they would "have torn out" their eyes and given them to him (Galatians 4:14–15). On the other hand, Paul often used the word "flesh" to mean "sinful nature" as in Galatians 5:19 where he lists the evil acts of the "sinful nature": the same Greek word that describes the location of the thorn that afflicts him in 2 Corinthians 12:7. Therefore, some have suggested that Paul wished to be freed from some temptation to wrongdoing.

**3** | **5**

Paul describes his sufferings. Thanks to God's help, he has managed to keep going despite it all. He warns the Christians in Corinth against idolatry.

Chapter **6**

**3** | **4**

Paul is happy that his previous letter led the church to repent. Though that letter hurt them, it was for their own good. He tells them how much Titus enjoyed his stay with them.

Chapter **7**

**3**

Paul talks about how generous the Macedonian church was in their collection for the needy in Jerusalem. He encourages them to also be generous. Titus will pick up their generous donation.

Chapter **8**

**3**

Paul knows how eager they are to help. Those who sow sparingly will reap sparingly. Those who sow abundantly will reap abundantly. But giving must be done voluntarily.

Chapter **9**

**3**

Paul defends his ministry with them. He's no different in person than he is in his letters. Don't take his outer "timidity" as an indication that inside he's anything other than bold.

Chapter **10**

**3**

Paul reluctantly lists his accomplishments, since they are so concerned with status. What they should really be impressed with is simply the message of God, regardless of the messenger.

Chapter **11**

**3** | **15**

Paul admits he is less than perfect. He is concerned about how easily the Corinthians let people take advantage of them. They should avoid gossip, arrogance, disorder, and other sins.

Chapter **12**

**3**

Paul issues final warnings. He encourages the Corinthian believers to remain faithful to Jesus and the message of the good news.

Chapter **13**

# Galatians

## Overview

aul is generally believed to be the author of this letter. In it, he focuses on the question, "what is the Gospel of Jesus Christ?" The title of the book is based on who he wrote the letter to: "the churches in Galatia" (Galatians 1:2). Galatia was a Roman province in Asia Minor—part of what is today the nation of Turkey.

The province of Galatia was established in 25 BC and contained the districts of Lycaonia and Isauria, as well as part of Pisidia and Phrygia. The cities of Iconium, Derbe, Lystra, and Pisidian Antioch, which Paul had reached on his first missionary journey, were part of the district, and it seems likely that it is to Christians living in these four cities that Paul is writing this letter.

**Hagar and Sarah**
*Paul compares the slave Hagar to the Law, and Abraham's wife, Sarah, to the Gospel (Galatians 4:21–27).*

## Chapter 2: **Commentary**

Jesus taught that no one should be called "father" or "rabbi" or be treated as a master (see Matthew 23:5–12, Matthew 20:25–28, Mark 10:42–45; John 13:3–17). Instead, Christians should be servants to one another. Although Christians clearly sought the advice of the apostles (see Acts 15:2), by confronting Peter for his failure to stand against encroaching legalism, Paul demonstrates that the apostles were not infallible. They could, in fact, be questioned and challenged.

**3**

Chapter **1**

Paul is amazed that the Galatians have abandoned the good news for something that isn't good news at all: legalism. Paul's message came from Jesus, not human reasoning.

**2** **3**

Chapter **2**

Paul met the apostles in Jerusalem, but what he preaches came from Jesus, not them. He once criticized Peter. If righteousness came from following the law, then why did Jesus die?

*You foolish Galatians! Who has bewitched you? Before your very eyes Jesus Christ was clearly portrayed as crucified. I would like to learn just one thing from you: Did you receive the Spirit by the works of the law, or by believing what you heard? Are you so foolish? After beginning by means of the Spirit, are you now trying to finish by means of the flesh? Have you experienced so much in vain—if it really was in vain? So again I ask, does God give you his Spirit and work miracles among you by the works of the law, or by your believing what you heard? So also Abraham "believed God, and it was credited to him as righteousness."*

**Galatians 3:1–6**

## Chapter 5: **Commentary**

The issue of circumcision had arisen when Christianity began to spread from Jews to gentiles. Some Jewish Christians taught that in order to become a Christian, a person first had to follow the Laws of Moses (see Acts 15), meaning that the gentiles had to be circumcised. Why such a stress on circumcision? Because circumcision was the proof of full conversion to Judaism. In fact, even before Christianity, many gentiles had turned to worshiping the Jewish God, but had balked at circumcision. They were called "God fearers" (see Acts 10:2, 13:16, 13:26). Circumcision had long been a source of contention between Jews and those non-Jews who were interested in Judaism. That it then became an issue for gentiles joining Christianity—then considered a Jewish sect—is not surprising. Despite the decision of the Council of Jerusalem, Paul continued to confront the issue wherever he went. He had a particular dislike for the "circumcision group" and rather colorfully denounced it (Galatians 5:12).

*But the fruit of the Spirit is love, joy, peace, forbearance, kindness, goodness, faithfulness, gentleness and self-control. Against such things there is no law. Those who belong to Christ Jesus have crucified the flesh with its passions and desires. Since we live by the Spirit, let us keep in step with the Spirit. Let us not become conceited, provoking and envying each other.*

**Galatians 5:22–26**

*May I never boast except in the cross of our Lord Jesus Christ, through which the world has been crucified to me, and I to the world.*

**Galatians 6:14**

**The Confrontation**
Paul confronted Peter for his hypocrisy and publically criticized him over his treatment of gentiles.

**③**

The Galatians have the Holy Spirit because they believed, not because they followed the law. We have been freed from the law. As children of God, we live by faith.

Chapter
3

**③**

Before you knew God, you were enslaved to false gods. Don't go back to lies. Hagar, the slave woman, represents the law. Sarah, the free woman, represents the good news.

Chapter
4

**②**    **③**    **⑩**

We have been freed from the law thanks to Jesus' sacrifice. Those old regulations don't matter. The whole law is summed up by the command to love others.

Chapter
5

**②**    **③**

Look out for one another; restore those caught in sin. Do good to everyone. Remember, circumcision doesn't matter. What matters is the new life in Jesus.

Chapter
6

# Ephesians

## Overview

The letter to the Ephesians focuses on how Christians can better relate to God and to each other. The title of the letter is taken from the name of the city, Ephesus, to which the letter seems to be addressed. The date, place of writing, and the people to whom it was written remain uncertain. Nevertheless, some scholars argue both for Paul's authorship of the letter and for it having been written to the church in Ephesus, perhaps as late as AD 63.

**3** | **12**

### Chapter 1

Paul praises God and thanks him for all the blessings he and the Church of Ephesians have in Jesus. He prays they will understand the hope and glory that Jesus has given them.

**2** | **3**

### Chapter 2

Our sins have all been forgiven thanks to what Jesus did on the cross. He brought the Jewish people and the gentiles together, making them one body in Christ.

**2** | **3**

### Chapter 3

Thanks to what Jesus did on the cross, the gentiles are able to join the nation of Israel and with Israel, become one body in Jesus. God can do more for us than we can imagine or ask.

**3** | **11**

### Chapter 4

The imprisoned Paul urges the Ephesians to be united. Jesus gives the church apostles, prophets, evangelists, pastors, and teachers. Renew your minds in Jesus and avoid evil.

**3** | **10**

### Chapter 5

There should be no bad behavior among Christians. You'll no longer be slaves to your selfish desires. Instead, submit to each other and work for the good of one another.

**3** | **12** | **15**

### Chapter 6

Put on the armor of God. Your battle is not with people, but with spiritual forces. Don't use human means in the war of ideas. Don't ever stop praying.

## Chapter 2: **Commentary**

Paul explains to the gentile Christians in Ephesus that they have become a part of the people of God—the nation of Israel—as a consequence of Jesus' sacrifice on the cross. Christians originally saw themselves as part of Judaism, with the gentile converts becoming Jewish as a consequence of their faith in Jesus. (See also Romans 11, Ephesians 2:15–16.)

## Chapter 5: **Commentary**

Paul discusses the concept of submission of Christians to one another: husbands and wives, slaves and masters, parents and children. His point is that all Christians should submit to each other (Ephesians 5:21). This is in keeping with Paul's teaching elsewhere, as well as the words of Jesus (see 1 Corinthians 9:19, Galatians 5:13, Matthew 23:5–12, Matthew 20:25–28, Mark 10:42–45, John 13:3–17). Submission is a choice that individuals make in their relationships with others, and in Paul's thinking, is simply love put into practice. As Paul wrote of Jesus: he "loved the Church and gave himself up for her" (Ephesians 5:25).

## Chapter 6: **Commentary**

At his trial, Jesus told Pilate that "My kingdom is not of this world. If it were, my servants would fight to prevent my arrest by the Jewish leaders. But now my kingdom is from another place." (John 18:36.) Elsewhere, he told the Pharisees that "The coming of the Kingdom of God is not something that can be observed, nor will people say, 'Here it is,' or 'There it is,' because the Kingdom of God is in your midst." (Luke 17:20–21.) Therefore, Paul makes it clear to the Christians in Ephesus that they are not involved in any sort of physical war or conflict with the people around them. Instead, their battle is one of ideas.

# Philippians

## Overview

The letter to the Philippians was written to Christians in Philippi to tell them about Paul's circumstances and what it means to have the mind of Christ. The title of this letter is taken from the name of the city to which it was addressed: Philippi. Scholars are generally agreed that this letter was actually written by Paul.

The letter was probably written sometime between AD 59 and 61, during Paul's first imprisonment in Rome (Acts 28:11–31). It was, to some extent, simply a thank-you letter. Epaphroditus, a member of the Philippian congregation, had carried the church's contributions to Paul to help him with his needs. Paul wrote this letter and sent it with Epaphroditus when he returned home (Philippians 2:25–30).

## Chapters 1–2: Commentary

Paul writes that in becoming human, Jesus "made himself nothing" (Philippians 2:7). Alternative translations say that Jesus "emptied himself," a more literal rendering of the underlying Greek. The word is used elsewhere by Paul, always metaphorically (Romans 4:14, 1 Corinthians 1:17, 9:15, 2 Corinthians 9:3) in the sense of "making worthless" or "emptying of significance." The point that Paul makes here is that Jesus gave up, willingly, his divine rank and became a humble servant, choosing to serve humanity. Throughout his life, Jesus served, rather than being served. Paul wants Christians to make that attitude of willing servitude—of doing for others rather than demanding others do for them—their way of living, too.

*I rejoiced greatly in the Lord that at last you renewed your concern for me. Indeed, you were concerned, but you had no opportunity to show it. I am not saying this because I am in need, for I have learned to be content whatever the circumstances. I know what it is to be in need, and I know what it is to have plenty. I have learned the secret of being content in any and every situation, whether well fed or hungry, whether living in plenty or in want. I can do all this through him who gives me strength.*

**Philippians 4:10–13**

**(3)**

Paul thanks God for the Philippians. His imprisonment has served to advance the message of the good news. He encourages them to live a life worthy of the good news.

**Chapter 1**

**(2)  (3)  (5)**

Christians should imitate Jesus. Although he was God, he chose to become human so he could die for our sins. Don't complain. God is working for his glory and purposes.

**Chapter 2**

**(2)  (3)**

Paul warns against those who believe that Christians must follow the law and get circumcised. Paul encourages Christians to follow his example.

**Chapter 3**

**(1)  (3)**

Christians should work together in unity. They should remain steadfast in their faith. They should always rejoice because they belong to Jesus forever. Paul thanks the Philippians for their help.

**Chapter 4**

# Colossians

## Overview

The Book of Colossians is a letter written to the Christians in the city of Colossae. The letter discusses the supremacy of Christ, Paul's ministry, and offers warnings against error. The title of the book is taken from the name of the city that the letter was addressed to.

Paul seems to have been prompted into writing this letter to the Colossian church because a heretical teaching had arisen there—probably a form of Gnosticism.

*The Son is the image of the invisible God, the firstborn over all creation. For in him all things were created: things in heaven and on earth, visible and invisible, whether thrones or powers or rulers or authorities; all things have been created through him and for him. He is before all things, and in him all things hold together.*

**Colossians 1:15–17**

**3**

### Chapter 1

Paul thanks God for the Christians in Colossae. Jesus is God. He is the creator of the universe. He has reconciled them to the Father by his death on the cross.

**2** **3**

### Chapter 2

Paul warns against focusing on rules and regulations. Rules are the way of the world, not the way of Christ. Righteousness comes from Jesus' death on the cross, not our behavior.

**2** **3** **10**

### Chapter 3

Since we rose with Jesus, we should set our attention on spiritual things. We've started new lives thanks to Jesus. So love each other and submit to each other.

**3** **12**

### Chapter 4

Paul encourages the Christians in Philippi to devote themselves to prayer. He thanks them for their help. He adds greetings from those who are with him.

## Chapter 2: **Commentary**

What better describes the nature of the world than rules and ever more rules? Every government that has ever existed has delighted in imposing laws and regulations. Paul argues that such legalism is the essence of worldliness. Paul points out that such worldliness seems wise, worshipful, and even properly religious. But in fact, rules do nothing to keep people from sinning. True godliness comes from being transformed through the death of Christ on the cross. Love is the focus of godliness, not rules. As Paul points out in Romans (echoing what Jesus said in Matthew 22:36–40), "The commandments, 'Do not commit adultery,' 'Do not murder,' 'Do not steal,' 'Do not covet,' and whatever other commandment there may be, are summed up in this one rule: 'Love your neighbor as yourself.' Love does no harm to its neighbor. Therefore love is the fulfillment of the law." (Romans 13:9–10; see also Galatians 5:13–14)

# I Thessalonians

## Overview

The Book of I Thessalonians is a letter to the Christians in the city of Thessalonica about living for God, about the fate of those who have died, and about the nature of the church. Paul wrote I Thessalonians in response to a question regarding Christians who had died. Apparently some of the Christians in Thessalonica were concerned about the fate of those who died before Jesus returned. The title of the letter comes from the name of the city to which it was written. It is the first of two letters that Paul wrote to the church in that city.

## Chapter 4: **Commentary**

In I Thessalonians 4:13–18 Paul reminds the recipients of his letter that just as Jesus rose from the dead, so those Christians who have died will likewise be resurrected. Because they know resurrection is coming, they need not grieve as if they were being permanently separated from their loved ones. Paul emphasizes that come the resurrection, which happens when Jesus returns, all Christians will be reunited.

*Brothers and sisters, we do not want you to be uninformed about those who sleep in death, so that you do not grieve like the rest of mankind, who have no hope. For we believe that Jesus died and rose again, and so we believe that God will bring with Jesus those who have fallen asleep in him. According to the Lord's word, we tell you that we who are still alive, who are left until the coming of the Lord, will certainly not precede those who have fallen asleep. For the Lord himself will come down from heaven, with a loud command, with the voice of the archangel and with the trumpet call of God, and the dead in Christ will rise first. After that, we who are still alive and are left will be caught up together with them in the clouds to meet the Lord in the air. And so we will be with the Lord forever. Therefore encourage one another with these words.*

**1 Thessalonians 4:13–18**

**③** Paul thanks God for the faith of the Christians in Thessalonica. They have become imitators of Paul and the Lord, becoming models for Christians in Macedonia and Achaia.

Chapter **1**

**③** Paul reminisces about his time in Thessalonica, and how its people have remained faithful to Jesus. Paul expresses how much he'd like to come back and see them again.

Chapter **2**

**③** Paul shares all the positive news that Timothy brought him about the Thessalonian believers and how encouraged he was to learn that they have remained faithful to God.

Chapter **3**

**③ ⑦ ⑩** Christians should continue living lives that please God. When Jesus returns, those who have died will be resurrected. They will live with Jesus forever.

Chapter **4**

**③ ⑦** The Day of the Lord is coming without warning. So be prepared: live lives pleasing to God instead of in debauchery. Encourage each other to love and in doing good deeds.

Chapter **5**

# 2 Thessalonians

## Overview

The Book of 2 Thessalonians is a second letter apparently written by Paul to the Christians in Thessalonica. The letter contains discussions about the Second Coming of Jesus, along with warnings and personal requests. This second letter seems to have been written to respond to those in the Church who were afraid that Jesus had already returned and that they had somehow missed it. The title of the letter comes from the name of the city to which it was written. Thessalonica was the second city in Europe where Paul had helped establish a church.

**A church in Thessalonica**
*Paul wrote to the Christian community in Thessalonica, which has thrived and endured for centuries. He helped establish a church there.*

## Chapter 2: **Commentary**

Paul tells the Christians not to believe any reports that Jesus has already come back again (cf. what Jesus himself said in Matthew 24: 4–5, 11, 23–24). He warned them that Jesus wouldn't return until "the rebellion" occurs and "the man of lawlessness" is revealed. Most commentators believe that Paul is warning about the coming of the "antichrist" and link this warning with the passages in Matthew 24, Mark 13, and Luke 21, as well as with the beast and false prophet mentioned in Revelation 13, 16, 19, and 20. Others, however, suggest that Paul is predicting the coming Jewish revolt against the Roman Empire. That revolt resulted in the destruction of Jerusalem and the Temple in 70 AD at the hands of the general Titus, the future emperor of Rome. The "man of lawlessness" is then a reference to Titus. He destroyed God's Temple, killed and enslaved many Jewish people, and referred to himself as "Lord" and was worshiped as a god.

| 3 | | 12 |
|---|---|---|
| **Chapter** **1** | Paul thanks God for the believers in Thessalonica. Wherever he goes, he tells others about their strength and perseverance during persecution. And he prays for them all the time. | |

| 3 | 7 | 13 |
|---|---|---|
| **Chapter** **2** | Jesus hasn't returned yet. Before he does, there will be a rebellion: a lawless man will exalt himself and proclaim himself to be God. So stand firm in the faith. | |

| 3 | | 12 |
|---|---|---|
| **Chapter** **3** | Paul asks Christians to pray for the rapid spread of the good news. Pray to be delivered from evil people. God will give Christians strength to endure. Keep busy and work hard. | |

*Concerning the coming of our Lord Jesus Christ and our being gathered to him, we ask you, brothers and sisters, not to become easily unsettled or alarmed by the teaching allegedly from us—whether by a prophecy or by word of mouth or by letter—asserting that the day of the Lord has already come. Don't let anyone deceive you in any way, for that day will not come until the rebellion occurs and the man of lawlessness is revealed, the man doomed to destruction. He will oppose and will exalt himself over everything that is called God or is worshiped, so that he sets himself up in God's temple, proclaiming himself to be God.*

**2 Thessalonians 2:1–4**

# 1 Timothy

## Overview

The Book of 1 Timothy is a letter from Paul to a young pastor named Timothy. Paul discusses the practical problems Timothy faced regarding deacons, elders, widows, and money. The title of the letter comes from the name of the man to whom it is addressed. It is the first of two letters written to Timothy.

---

*Here is a trustworthy saying that deserves full acceptance: Christ Jesus came into the world to save sinners—of whom I am the worst. But for that very reason I was shown mercy so that in me, the worst of sinners, Christ Jesus might display his immense patience as an example for those who would believe in him and receive eternal life.*

**1 Timothy 1:15–16**

### Chapter 3: **Commentary**

The early Christian congregations or churches were based on the model of the Jewish synagogue. Paul lays out the requirements, behaviors, and duties that would be the norm in any Jewish synagogue, giving Timothy very practical information and advice in chapters 3–5 for his particular situation. In contrast to how things normally worked in synagogues of the time, Paul thought that the elders (and pastor) should be paid for their work (see 1 Timothy 5:17–18). It was normal for rabbis of Paul's day to support themselves with outside jobs instead.

*Don't let anyone look down on you because you are young, but set an example for the believers in speech, in conduct, in love, in faith and in purity. Until I come, devote yourself to the public reading of Scripture, to preaching and to teaching. Do not neglect your gift, which was given you through prophecy when the body of elders laid their hands on you.*

**1 Timothy 4:12–14**

*The elders who direct the affairs of the church well are worthy of double honor, especially those whose work is preaching and teaching. For Scripture says, "Do not muzzle an ox while it is treading out the grain," and "The worker deserves his wages."*

**1 Timothy 5:17–18**

---

**3**

Paul encourages Timothy to oppose false teachers. Paul thanks God for giving him strength. To encourage him, Paul reminds Timothy of the prophecies given about him.

**Chapter 1**

**3** | **11**

Paul gives Timothy instructions on how to conduct worship services, including prayer, proper dress, and the role of men and women in the service.

**Chapter 2**

**3** | **5** | **11**

Paul explains the qualifications of overseers and deacons. He hopes to come and see Timothy soon, but he wanted Timothy to have this information now, in case he is delayed.

**Chapter 3**

**3**

Paul warns Timothy that there will be those who abandon the faith and instead teach odd rules and regulations. Everything God made is good. Preach the good news diligently.

**Chapter 4**

**3**

Paul tells him how to treat the people in his congregation, especially widows. Christians who work in the church deserve to be paid for their time.

**Chapter 5**

**3**

He encourages Christian slaves to respect their masters. Beware of false teachers. Do not get distracted by the pursuit of wealth. Instead, focus on God and serving him.

**Chapter 6**

# 2 Timothy

## Overview

**Paul in prison**
*Tradition has it that
Paul wrote his second
letter to Timothy while
he was in prison awaiting
his execution.*

The Book of 2 Timothy is the second of two letters written to Timothy.

On the basis of its unique vocabulary, many modern scholars believe that 2 Timothy was not written by Paul himself, but rather by one of his followers after martyrdom. However, the early patristic literature is in agreement that Paul wrote this letter. Moreover, the private and specific nature of the letter explains the vocabulary choices and makes the assumption of Paul's authorship not unreasonable.

### Chapters 2–3: **Commentary**

For Paul and Timothy, the "scripture" was what for us is the Old Testament, since the New Testament was still in the process of being written and had yet to be recognized as scripture. Paul stresses for Timothy the value of the Bible and its importance for faith and practice in the church. He argues that scripture came from God and that it provides practical help for God's people to live well. The word translated "God-breathed" appears in some translations as "inspired." The meaning is simply that the Bible has God's Spirit in it, in the same way that God breathed into Adam (Genesis 2:7) and he became a "living being" or "living soul." Though humans are made of the dust, they are alive because of God. The Bible, though written by human beings, is alive because of God.

Theologians have expended much time and effort arguing over exactly what is meant by this inspiration: is the Bible without error? Is it God's word, or does it contain God's word, or does it only become God's word when read, understood, and applied? What all agree on is that the Bible has always been considered authoritative and vitally important to Christians.

---

**3**

Chapter

**1**

Paul wishes he could visit Timothy, who must continue preaching the good news. Paul complains about those who have abandoned him, but praises those who have stuck by him.

**3**

Chapter

**2**

Paul encourages Timothy to stand firm in the faith. He explains how to deal with false teachers who quarrel about inconsequential matters that are a waste of time.

**3**

Chapter

**3**

Dark days are coming, when people will love themselves and money more than God. Paul reminds Timothy of his faithfulness to God and the good news.

**3**

Chapter

**4**

Timothy must continue preaching the good news. Paul is in prison and will be executed soon. He hopes to see Timothy before he dies. He complains about those who mistreated him.

*But as for you, continue in what you have learned and have become convinced of, because you know those from whom you learned it, and how from infancy you have known the Holy Scriptures, which are able to make you wise for salvation through faith in Christ Jesus. All Scripture is God-breathed and is useful for teaching, rebuking, correcting and training in righteousness, so that the servant of God may be thoroughly equipped for every good work.*
**2 Timothy 3:14–17**

# Titus

## Overview

The Book of Titus is a letter from Paul to Titus, warning him about false teachers and encouraging him to teach the truth. The title of the book is derived from the name of the man to whom the letter was addressed.

Titus is never mentioned by name in the Book of Acts. His name appears elsewhere in only three of Paul's other letters: 2 Corinthians (2:13, 7:6, 13, 14, 8:6, 16, 23, 12:18), Galatians (2:1, 3), and 2 Timothy (4:10). Very little is known about him. This letter, the Book of Titus, was probably written to Titus on Crete about AD 63, not long after Paul had left the island. Paul's visit to Crete probably occurred sometime after his first imprisonment in Rome (Acts 28).

*To the pure, all things are pure, but to those who are corrupted and do not believe, nothing is pure. In fact, both their minds and consciences are corrupted. They claim to know God, but by their actions they deny him. They are detestable, disobedient and unfit for doing anything good.*

**Titus 1:15–16**

## Chapter 1: **Commentary**

Paul is critical of the people of Crete, the place where the recipient of the letter, Titus, was working and living. He quotes from the Cretan author Epimenides, a sixth-century BC seer and poet–philosopher (Titus 1:12) to make his point to Titus that the Cretans will need a firm hand in order to become better people. In Paul's day, Crete was notorious as the home of liars who lived only for their bellies. Paul writes somewhat hyperbolically in order to make his point about what Titus' role should be as the pastor of the congregation of Christians on Crete.

*But when the kindness and love of God our Savior appeared, he saved us, not because of righteous things we had done, but because of his mercy. He saved us through the washing of rebirth and renewal by the Holy Spirit, whom he poured out on us generously through Jesus Christ our Savior, so that, having been justified by his grace, we might become heirs having the hope of eternal life.*

**Titus 3:4–7**

**3**   **11**

Paul describes the qualities of those who should be chosen as elders in the church. He criticizes those Christians who are rebellious and lazy.

Chapter **1**

**3**

Paul encourages Titus to teach sound doctrine. He should adapt his message to each age group, gender, and socioeconomic level of his congregation.

Chapter **2**

**3**

Christians must be obedient and respectful of those in authority. Jesus rescued them from their sins so they could do good to others, not so they could satisfy their own selfish desires.

Chapter **3**

# Philemon

## Overview

The Book of Philemon is a very short letter to a man named Philemon. Philemon was a slave owner who lived in the Lycus Valley of Asia Minor. The name of his slave was Onesimus. Paul's letter to Philemon was used in the United States and Great Britain by both proponents and opponents of slavery to bolster their positions. Even today, scholars are divided over what it is that Paul is asking Philemon to do about his slave Onesimus, though most believe that Paul expects Philemon to forgive his slave and free him.

**Hand-lettered page**
*The Book of Philemon was quickly accepted as scripture by the Christian community and was copied by hand before the invention of the printing press.*

*Perhaps the reason he was separated from you for a little while was that you might have him back forever—no longer as a slave, but better than a slave, as a dear brother. He is very dear to me but even dearer to you, both as a fellow man and as a brother in the Lord.*

*So if you consider me a partner, welcome him as you would welcome me. If he has done you any wrong or owes you anything, charge it to me. I, Paul, am writing this with my own hand. I will pay it back—not to mention that you owe me your very self. I do wish, brother, that I may have some benefit from you in the Lord; refresh my heart in Christ. Confident of your obedience, I write to you, knowing that you will do even more than I ask.*

**Philemon 1:15–21**

## Chapter 1: **Commentary**

Paul asks Philemon to forgive his runaway slave, something that was not commonly done in the Roman world of the first century. Merely freeing Onesimus would not have given him the rights and privileges of a free person. Freed slaves were often worse off than well-treated slaves. So Paul doesn't ask for Onesimus to be merely freed. He wants something much more. Paul wants Onesimus to become a full person, equal to all, treated as Philemon would treat a family member. Paul calls Philemon his brother. Then he calls Onesimus his son and brother. Paul's words would have sounded ridiculous, shocking, and even scandalous to a slave-owner in the Roman world. Paul was lifting a piece of property, a slave—and a runaway at that—to equality with both Paul and Philemon.

Chapter

**I**

Onesimus was an escaped slave that Paul converted to Christianity. Paul sends him back to his Christian owner Philemon and asks Philemon to set him free.

# Hebrews

## Overview

I   The superiority of Christ 1:1–10:18

II  Practical applications 10:19–13:25

The Book of Hebrews is an anonymous letter. It discusses the superiority of Christ, along with offering some practical applications for living as a Christian. The title is derived from the fact that the author is writing to Jewish people rather than gentiles (see Hebrews 1:1). Beyond that, the author does not identify explicitly to whom he—or she—is writing.

The author of the Book of Hebrews is unrecorded. But since Clement of Rome cites the letter around AD 95, it must have been produced prior to that time. There is no mention in the book of the destruction of the Temple in Jerusalem. Since the Temple's destruction would have been very useful to the author's point, a date before the Temple's destruction in 70 AD is probable.

**Jesus glorified**
*God told the angels of heaven to worship Jesus (Hebrews 1:6).*

---

*In the past God spoke to our ancestors through the prophets at many times and in various ways, but in these last days he has spoken to us by his Son, whom he appointed heir of all things, and through whom also he made the universe. The Son is the radiance of God's glory and the exact representation of his being, sustaining all things by his powerful word. After he had provided purification for sins, he sat down at the right hand of the Majesty in heaven. So he became as much superior to the angels as the name he has inherited is superior to theirs.*

**Hebrews 1:1–4**

## Chapter 1: **Commentary**

The author of Hebrews is reacting to questions some people had about Jesus. The author wanted to demonstrate that Jesus was more than a prophet, more than just a good man, and more than an angel. He was God himself. Therefore, he made use of a variety of texts from the Old Testament to demonstrate that conclusion.

| 3 | 5 | 15 | |
|---|---|---|---|
| Jesus is superior to everything in creation, even to the angels, because Jesus is God. Everyone in heaven and on earth must worship him. | | | Chapter 1 |

| 3 | 5 | 15 | |
|---|---|---|---|
| Jesus became a human being for a while, so he could make human beings holy. Human beings are now his brothers and sisters. Jesus suffered and was tempted like all of us. | | | Chapter 2 |

| 3 | 5 | | |
|---|---|---|---|
| Jesus is also greater than Moses. Believe today that Jesus is the Messiah. Don't reject him as the Israelites rejected God after leaving Egypt. They had to wander for 40 years. | | | Chapter 3 |

loquens patrib; in ppheus.nouif
fime dieb; iftis locutus é nobif in

**The New Covenant**
*The author of the Book of Hebrews argues that with the death, burial, and resurrection of Jesus, God has made a New Covenant with his people.*

---

**3** **5**

Chapter
**4**

Those who rejected God never entered into a place of rest with God. Today, God offers that rest in Jesus: God has rested from his work of creation. We can rest from our work.

---

**3** **5**

Chapter
**5**

Jesus is the great high priest in the order of Melchizedek. He was tempted and yet did not sin. He was obedient to God and has become the source of eternal salvation.

---

**3** **9**

Chapter
**6**

Don't fall away. It is impossible for those who fall away to ever repent again. Instead, all they have to look forward to is God's judgment. Jesus is our high priest forever.

---

**3**

Chapter
**7**

Abraham, the ancestor of the Levites, paid a tithe to Melchizedek. Thus, Melchizedek is superior to the Levites and Jesus, a priest like Melchizedek, is also superior to the Levites.

---

**2** **3** **5**

Chapter
**8**

Through Jesus, we have entered into a New Covenant with God. The covenant is written on our hearts rather than on stone tablets. This New Covenant is superior to the old one.

---

*Therefore, since we have a great high priest who has ascended into heaven, Jesus the Son of God, let us hold firmly to the faith we profess. For we do not have a high priest who is unable to empathize with our weaknesses, but we have one who has been tempted in every way, just as we are—yet he did not sin. Let us then approach God's throne of grace with confidence, so that we may receive mercy and find grace to help us in our time of need.*

**Hebrews 4:14–16**

## Chapter 5: **Commentary**

Melchizedek is mentioned only briefly in the Book of Genesis. Abraham rescues his nephew Lot who had been taken as a prisoner of war. Then he gives Melchizedek a tenth of the battle's spoils (Genesis 14:18–20). Melchizedek is then mentioned once more in the Old Testament, in Psalm 110:4. From these two brief passages, the author of Hebrews argues that Jesus, like Melchizedek, is superior to the Levitical priests descended from Aaron and that his sacrifice on the cross is likewise superior to the sacrifice of animals (Hebrews 5–7).

## Chapter 8: **Commentary**

The author of Hebrews wants to demonstrate that Jesus has changed the way that human beings are able to relate to God. The core passage that he uses is the prophecy that God would make a New Covenant with the people of Israel different from the Old Covenant of Moses. Thus, in Hebrews 8:8–12 the author of Hebrews quotes from Jeremiah 31:31–34 and argues that the New Covenant means that the first covenant is "obsolete" and "will soon disappear." (Hebrews 8:13). The author of Hebrews affirms that the New Covenant arrived with the death and resurrection of Jesus. Neither they nor the gentile converts needed anything more than the death and resurrection of Jesus to have a relationship with God.

---

*But in fact the ministry Jesus has received is as superior to theirs as the covenant of which he is mediator is superior to the old one, since the new covenant is established on better promises.*

*For if there had been nothing wrong with that first covenant, no place would have been sought for another. But God found fault with the people and said:*
*"The days are coming, declares the Lord,*
*when I will make a new covenant*
*with the people of Israel*
*and with the people of Judah."*

**Hebrews 8:6–8**

## Chapters 9–10: **Commentary**

The Temple was the center of Jewish worship until it was destroyed by the Romans in 70 AD. The entire Book of Leviticus, as well as substantial portions of the rest of the Pentateuch (Genesis–Deuteronomy), focused not only on the need for sacrifices, but the details of how and when they were to be performed. The author of Hebrews points out (Hebrews 10:1–4) that the sacrifices were merely symbols of what Jesus would accomplish with his death on the cross. While the animal sacrifices were a regular and repeated necessity, the death of Jesus was a one-time event that permanently solved the problem of sin. No more sacrifices were necessary. All that mattered now was faith, which the author of Hebrews illustrates in Hebrews 11.

## Chapter 11: **Commentary**

The life stories of the people listed in Hebrews 11 illustrate well that salvation is the consequence of what Jesus did on the cross, rather than in being good. For instance Jephtha, who is listed as a great person of faith in Hebrews 11:32, had significant flaws: he believed in the existence of other gods and he sacrificed his daughter as a burnt offering (see Judges 11–12).

*Endure hardship as discipline; God is treating you as his children. For what children are not disciplined by their father? If you are not disciplined—and everyone undergoes discipline—then you are not legitimate, not true sons and daughters at all. Moreover, we have all had human fathers who disciplined us and we respected them for it. How much more should we submit to the Father of spirits and live! They disciplined us for a little while as they thought best; but God disciplines us for our good, in order that we may share in his holiness. No discipline seems pleasant at the time, but painful. Later on, however, it produces a harvest of righteousness and peace for those who have been trained by it.*

**Hebrews 12:7–11**

*Keep your lives free from the love of money and be content with what you have, because God has said,*
   *"Never will I leave you;*
*never will I forsake you."*
*So we say with confidence,*
   *"The Lord is my helper; I will not be afraid.*
*What can mere mortals do to me?"*

**Hebrews 13:5–6**

**2** **3**

In the Temple, sacrifices must be offered regularly for sin. But the sacrifice of Jesus on the cross is a one-time sacrifice that covers all sins forever.

Chapter
**9**

**2** **3** **5**

The law is merely the shadow of what Jesus did on the cross. Do not give up. Jesus has cleansed us of sins forever, making us pure and holy. We live by faith.

Chapter
**10**

**3** **17**

Living by faith is nothing new. Look at all the people in the Old Testament who lived by faith, from Abel, Noah, and Abraham through Samuel and David.

Chapter
**11**

**2** **3** **9**

God disciplines people to make them better. Discipline is unpleasant, but ultimately beneficial. So live in hope and joy: God's kingdom is coming and you're a part of it.

Chapter
**12**

**1** **3** **10**

Keep on loving one another, submit to the authority of your leaders, and offer praise to Jesus. Pray for us and greet one another warmly.

Chapter
**13**

**Offering up Isaac**
*By faith, Abraham offered up Isaac, knowing that God could resurrect him and still fulfill his promise.*

# James
## Overview

The Book of James is a letter from James explaining that words and mere claims to faith are empty without action. The title comes from the name of the author of this letter.

The Book of James belongs to the literary genre known as wisdom literature, characterized by sayings that taught about virtue. The Book of James is largely made up of moral exhortations, making the book an example of what is called "proverbial wisdom." The book is therefore very similar to the Book of Proverbs, especially its first nine chapters.

| 3 | 18 |
|---|---|

**Chapter 1**

Don't let trouble get you down. Remember that when you are tempted it is never God who is tempting you. Listen to God and then do what he says.

| 3 | 18 |
|---|---|

**Chapter 2**

Don't show favoritism for any reason. Words are cheap. It is actions that count. If your claim to faith isn't demonstrated by your actions, then you really don't have any faith.

| 3 | 18 |
|---|---|

**Chapter 3**

The hardest thing to control is what you say. If you can control your tongue, then you really do have self-control. Wisdom is demonstrated by actions.

| 3 | 15 | 18 |
|---|---|---|

**Chapter 4**

Submit yourself to God's will. God is in control of your life and everything that happens to you. So don't be arrogant.

| 3 | 18 |
|---|---|

**Chapter 5**

Don't trust in your wealth. It won't last. If you took advantage of others, God will judge you. Suffering is hard, but God will see you through. God will answer your prayers.

*Consider it pure joy, my brothers and sisters, whenever you face trials of many kinds, because you know that the testing of your faith produces perseverance. Let perseverance finish its work so that you may be mature and complete, not lacking anything. If any of you lacks wisdom, you should ask God, who gives generously to all without finding fault, and it will be given to you. But when you ask, you must believe and not doubt, because the one who doubts is like a wave of the sea, blown and tossed by the wind. That person should not expect to receive anything from the Lord. Such a person is double-minded and unstable in all they do.*

**James 1:2–8**

## Chapter 2: **Commentary**

Some have imagined that James is contradicting Paul's insistence on salvation by grace through faith—that James is arguing that a right relationship with God is attained by good behavior and by keeping the law. However, James in fact is not talking about how people gain a right relationship with God. Instead, he is focused on the question of how Christians should live in this world, and most importantly, how they should treat the people around them.

*Now listen, you who say, "Today or tomorrow we will go to this or that city, spend a year there, carry on business and make money." Why, you do not even know what will happen tomorrow. What is your life? You are a mist that appears for a little while and then vanishes. Instead, you ought to say, "If it is the Lord's will, we will live and do this or that."*

**James 4:13–15**

# I Peter

## Overview

**I** Salutation 1:1–2

**II** Privileges and responsibilities 1:3–2:12

**III** Submission and God's honor 2:13–3:7

**IV** Suffering and persecution 3:8–5:11

**V** Conclusion 5:12–14

The Book of I Peter is a letter from Peter in which he relates the privileges and responsibilities of Christians. He encourages the letter's readers to endure suffering and persecution. The title of the letter is taken from the name of the traditional author. It is the first of two letters apparently by him.

According to I Peter 5:13, Peter wrote the letter from "Babylon," which was a common designation for Rome among first century Jews and Christians.

**The apostle Peter**
*Peter spent the years after Jesus' resurrection teaching and preaching.*

## Chapter 2: **Commentary**

Peter wrote to gentiles. He says they "were not a people" and had "not received mercy" but that now all that had changed thanks to Jesus (1:10). In I Peter 2:4–5 he tells them that they are like "living stones" being built into a "spiritual house" in order to be a "holy priesthood." And then in 2:9, he writes that they are a "chosen people, a royal priesthood, a holy nation, God's special possession." Peter recognized, thanks to his vision and interaction with the Roman centurion Cornelius (Acts 10), that God had accepted non-Jews and made them part of God's people: therefore, they had all the rights and privileges of the Israelites and together with them, served, worshiped, and belonged to God.

*Finally, all of you, be like-minded, be sympathetic, love one another, be compassionate and humble. Do not repay evil with evil or insult with insult. On the contrary, repay evil with blessing, because to this you were called so that you may inherit a blessing.*
**1 Peter 3:8–9**

| 1 | 3 | 5 |
|---|---|---|

Praise God for giving us a new birth through Jesus' resurrection. Set your hope, therefore, on the good news and the fact that you will live forever with Jesus.

**Chapter 1**

| 3 | 5 |
|---|---|

Get rid of bad behavior. Work together, live well among the nonbelievers, and give them no reason to criticize: be good obedient citizens and behave as Jesus behaved.

**Chapter 2**

| 3 | 5 | 10 |
|---|---|---|

Submit yourselves to those around you; don't give them any cause to speak badly of you. If you suffer for doing what's right, you are blessed. Keep your conscience clear.

**Chapter 3**

| 3 |
|---|

Live for God, not for yourself. The end is near, so be alert and love one another. God will be with you through suffering. Don't let trouble keep you from doing the right thing.

**Chapter 4**

| 3 | 15 |
|---|---|

Leaders should be good shepherds and watch over those that God has put into their care. Be alert and watch out for the trouble Satan might try to bring. You're not alone in suffering.

**Chapter 5**

# 2 Peter

## Overview

**I** Salutation 1:1–2

**II** Growth 1:3–11

**III** Prophets 1:12–21

**IV** False prophets 2:1–22

**V** The Second Coming 3:1–18

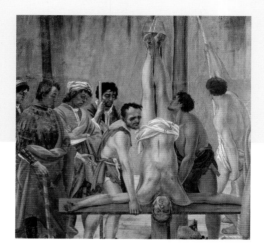

**Peter's martyrdom**
*According to tradition, Peter was crucified upside down at his request. He didn't believe he deserved to die like Jesus.*

The Book of 2 Peter is a letter from Peter warning of false prophets. He also offers encouragement about the Second Coming of Jesus. The title of the letter comes from the name of its author. It is the second of two letters claiming to have been written by Peter.

The authorship of 2 Peter has been widely questioned in scholarly circles, and the majority consensus is that the letter, though claiming to have been written by Peter, actually was not. Like the first letter, the second, if written by Peter, was probably written from Rome between AD 64 and 68. Those who reject Peter's authorship believe it was written much later, between 100 and 150 AD.

| 3 | 10 | |
|---|---|---|
| **Chapter 1** | God has given you everything you need to live for him. Pay attention to God's words from the prophets: you can depend on what God has said. | |

| 3 | 9 | 15 |
|---|---|---|
| **Chapter 2** | Just as there were false prophets in the past, so today, beware of them. They are arrogant, they don't know what they are talking about, and God will judge them. | |

| 7 | 9 | 13 |
|---|---|---|
| **Chapter 3** | The day of the Lord is coming. Just because there is a delay, doesn't mean that it isn't. So do the right thing. Live holy lives so you'll be ready when that day finally arrives. | |

## Chapter 2: **Commentary**

In 2 Peter 2:4 the author speaks about how God did not spare "angels when they sinned" but sent them to "hell." The word translated "sent them to hell" is derived from Tartarus. In Roman mythology, Tartarus was where sinners were sent. The poet Virgil describes it as an enormous place surrounded by a flaming river and guarded by a hydra. At the bottom of Tartarus were the Titans, a group of powerful gods descended from Gaia and Uranus who ruled during a golden age, until they were overthrown by the Olympians, the younger gods who then took their place and confined them to Tartarus. In the first part of the apocryphal Book of Enoch, there is a description of the fall of the Watchers, the angels who fathered the Nephalim (based on one of the possible interpretations of Genesis 6:1–4). The Book of Enoch is an ancient Jewish religious work ascribed to Enoch, an ancestor of Noah. The author of 2 Peter alludes to this story. The Book of Enoch is not accepted as scripture by either Jews or Christians.

*But do not forget this one thing, dear friends: With the Lord a day is like a thousand years, and a thousand years are like a day. The Lord is not slow in keeping his promise, as some understand slowness. Instead he is patient with you, not wanting anyone to perish, but everyone to come to repentance.*

**2 Peter 3:8–9**

# 1 John

## Overview

The title of the Book of 1 John comes from the name of the author. 1 John is the first of three letters ascribed to the apostle. The author describes God as light, righteous, and loving. He points out that those who claim to be Christians but lack love are only fooling themselves.

The author never identifies himself. Traditions that were uncontested from about the third century until the eighteenth identified the apostle John as the author. Dating 1 John is difficult and controversial. Assuming the apostle John is the author, a date between AD 85 and 90 seems probable.

---

*If we claim to be without sin, we deceive ourselves and the truth is not in us. If we confess our sins, he is faithful and just and will forgive us our sins and purify us from all unrighteousness. If we claim we have not sinned, we make him out to be a liar and his word is not in us.*

**1 John 1:8–10**

### Chapter 2: **Commentary**

The only places in the Bible that the word "antichrist" appears are in 1 John (2:18, 22, 4:3) and 2 John (1:7). The author says that "antichrist" describes those who deny that Jesus is the Messiah (1 John 2:22) and those who do not acknowledge that Jesus "came in the flesh" (2 John 1:7). 1 John 2:18 also indicates an expectation that "the antichrist" comes in "the last hour." This expectation is based on Jesus' words that many individuals would come claiming to be the Messiah (Matthew 24:5, Mark 13:6, Luke 21:8).

### Chapter 4: **Commentary**

The author of 1 John affirms that "God is love" (1 John 4:8, 16). He believed that love was the most important attribute of God, the sum of his being, and thus the clearest evidence of God's presence. Jesus argued that the entire Bible could be summed up with the two commands, "love God" and "love people." (Matthew 22:34–40, Mark 12:28–31.) Jesus also told his disciples that they would be identified on the basis of their love for each other (John 13:35). Thus, the author of 1 John emphasizes the importance of love as a way of life. It is the essence of both God and those who follow him.

---

**3**

We proclaim Jesus, a human being we knew and touched. He gives light. Those in the dark don't belong to him. Everyone sins. If you claim otherwise, you're lying.

**Chapter 1**

---

**3**   **5**   **10**

There is one old command: love each other. If you love others, you're in the light. If you don't, you're in the dark. Those who deny Jesus is the Messiah are anti-Messiahs.

**Chapter 2**

---

**2**   **3**   **10**

God has made us his children. Jesus has taken away our sins, so that we don't have to sin anymore. This is love: Jesus died for us. Jesus' commandment is to love each other.

**Chapter 3**

---

**2**   **3**   **10**

If you deny Jesus came from God and became human, then you don't know God. God is love. If we say we love God and then hate someone, we really don't love God.

**Chapter 4**

---

**2**   **3**

Whoever believes Jesus is the Messiah has eternal life. If you don't believe Jesus is the Messiah, then you don't have eternal life. We are the children of God.

**Chapter 5**

# 2 John

## Overview

**John's letters**
*The apostle John wrote letters to various churches, in addition to writing the Gospel of John and the Book of Revelation.*

The Book of 2 John is a letter that warns against deceivers and false teachers in the Church. The title of the letter comes from the name of the assumed author. 2 John is the second of three letters ascribed to the apostle John.

However, the letter does not identify its author by name. It is in fact an anonymous work, just like all the other New Testament writings attributed to John, except for the Book of Revelation. The author of 2 John is simply called "the elder." However, the style and structure of the letter seem very similar to what was seen in 1 John, and so a common author has been widely assumed until modern times.

The date of writing is impossible to place. Some have suggested a date around 90 AD, while those who reject John's authorship place it much later, in the second century AD. Part of the reason many assume such a late date is 2 John's apparent arguments against Gnosticism, a movement that most scholars believe did not become a problem for Christianity until the second century AD.

> *And now, dear lady, I am not writing you a new command but one we have had from the beginning. I ask that we love one another. And this is love: that we walk in obedience to his commands. As you have heard from the beginning, his command is that you walk in love.*
>
> **2 John 1:5–6**

## Chapter 1: **Commentary**

The "lady chosen by God" and "her children" is most likely a reference to a church and its congregation rather than to an actual woman and her offspring. Though some have suggested that the word translated "lady" could be taken as a personal name—as could the word translated "chosen"—such an understanding is very improbable. The location of the church to which "the elder" is writing is unknown, though some suggest it could be one of the churches located in Asia Minor.

**3**

**Chapter 1**
John is happy to hear that the Christian community is walking in the truth. Watch out for false teachers who deny Jesus was a human being. Anyone like that is the antichrist.

# 3 John

## Overview

The title of the Book of 3 John comes from the traditional name of the author. 3 John is the third of three letters ascribed to the apostle.

The author never identifies himself by name. He is simply called "the elder." However, the style and structure of the letter seem very similar to what was seen in 1 and 2 John.

The date of writing is hard to place. Many scholars assume a date sometime late in the first century or early second century AD. There are expressions of opposition to Gnostic and Docetic teachings in the letter, movements that were only starting to become prominent at the end of the first century or early second century. .

The author of 3 John writes to Gaius in order to encourage him. He complains about Diotrephes and his treatment of other Christians, while praising Demetrius. We have no information about any of the people named in the letter. We also do not know where Gaius or the author of the letter were at the time the letter was composed.

## Chapter 1: **Commentary**

Who is the Gaius to whom the letter is addressed? There is no certainty. Some suggest it is the Gaius of Macedonia mentioned in Acts 19:20; others, the Gaius of Corinth in Romans 16:23 and 1 Corinthians 1:14. Still others suggest he is the Gaius of Derbe, who is mentioned in Acts 20:4. Some have even suggested he is the Gaius who was the Bishop of Pergamos. Of course, it could be someone else entirely who is otherwise unknown, since the name Gaius was very common in Roman times.

**John's death**
*According to tradition, the apostle John, alone among Jesus' 12 disciples, died a peaceful death of old age.*

*Dear friend, do not imitate what is evil but what is good. Anyone who does what is good is from God. Anyone who does what is evil has not seen God.*
**3 John 1:11**

3

John hopes Gaius is well and praises him for his hospitality. He warns about Diotrephes and praises Demetrius. He'd like to write more, but he'll save it for when he sees him.

Chapter

1

# Jude
## Overview

**Jesus' half-brother**
*According to tradition, Jude was one of Jesus' half-brothers.*

The author of the Book of Jude warns about the sin of false teachers and predicts their doom. He encourages the faithful to persevere through suffering. The title of the letter comes from the name of the author. Jude is the old English equivalent of the name Judah. The spelling dates from a time when the final "e" in English was still pronounced, as it still is in German. The names Jude, Judah, and Judas are all variations of the same name: *Ioudas* in Greek or *Yehudah* in Hebrew.

Jude claims to be the brother of James (1:1). After James the son of Zebedee was martyred by Herod Agrippa I (around AD 44—see Acts 12:2), the only James well known in the early church was James of Jerusalem, whom Paul identified as "the Lord's brother" (Galatians 1:19). Therefore, the Jude of this letter is believed by some to be a half-brother of Jesus, otherwise unmentioned in the New Testament.

*These people are blemishes at your love feasts, eating with you without the slightest qualm—shepherds who feed only themselves. They are clouds without rain, blown along by the wind; autumn trees, without fruit and uprooted—twice dead. They are wild waves of the sea, foaming up their shame; wandering stars, for whom blackest darkness has been reserved forever.*

**Jude 1:12–13**

## Chapter 1: **Commentary**

Jude 1:9 describes a dispute between Michael the archangel and Satan about the body of Moses. Some commentators have understood this to be an allusion to what is described in Zechariah 3:1–2. But according to the church father Origen, the story appeared in the Assumption of Moses, an apocryphal work. Like the author of 2 Peter (see 2 Peter 2:4), the author of Jude references the Book of Enoch (see Enoch 1:14 and Jude 1:14–15). That the author of Jude uses non-biblical materials in his letter does not mean that he necessarily viewed those documents as scripture, any more than Paul thought that the Greek poets Aratus and Cleanthes that he quoted were scripture (Acts 17:28, Titus 1:12).

3    9    15

Chapter
1

Jude writes about the sin and coming doom of ungodly false teachers who reject authority. He calls upon Christians to persevere through the hard times. He praises God.

# Revelation

## Overview

The Book of Revelation is an apocalyptic series of visions about the destruction of an evil world system and the triumph of God and Christians. The title comes from the first word in the letter, *apokalypsis*, translated "revelation." It is from this Greek word that the alternative title for the book, The Apocalypse, originates.

## Chapter 1: **Commentary**

There are many examples of other books not included as scripture that are examples of the same sort of apocalyptic literary genre as the Book of Revelation, such as the Apocalypse of Baruch, the Book of Enoch, 2 Esdras, and the Assumption of Moses. Portions of other biblical books also have the characteristics of apocalyptic literature, such as Daniel, Ezekiel, Jeremiah, and Isaiah. Characteristic features of apocalyptic literature include dreams or visions, angels, mystical symbolism, and the end of the world. Apocalyptic literature is primarily the product of persecuted and oppressed religious minorities who look forward to being freed. It has some characteristics similar to the old Negro spirituals, where, for instance the "Jordan River" stood for the Ohio River, that if crossed by slaves meant freedom. Thus, for instance, "Babylon" in Jewish apocalyptic texts was common code for "Rome."

*Those whom I love I rebuke and discipline. So be earnest and repent. Here I am! I stand at the door and knock. If anyone hears my voice and opens the door, I will come in and eat with that person, and they with me.*

*To the one who is victorious, I will give the right to sit with me on my throne, just as I was victorious and sat down with my Father on his throne.*

**Revelation 3:19–21**

## Chapter 4: **Commentary**

The "living creatures" that the author of Revelation sees around God's throne are very similar to the four "living creatures" of Ezekiel 1. They match in number, they are called the same thing, their physical description is very similar, and, like Ezekiel's creatures, they are associated with God's throne. In Ezekiel 10, these "living creatures" are identified as cherubim (Ezekiel 10:20).

| 3 | | 5 | |

John writes to the seven churches in the Roman province of Asia. Like them, he has suffered and he has had a vision of Jesus who told him to write a message to the seven churches.

Chapter **1**

| 3 | | 9 | |

Ephesus must continue to perseverance. Smyrna must remain faithful during persecution. Pergamum must reject false teachings. Thyatira must endure suffering and reject immorality.

Chapter **2**

| 3 | | 9 | |

He warns Sardis to remember what they were taught. Philadelphia must hold on to what they have. Laodicea must stop depending on their wealth.

Chapter **3**

| 11 | | 13 | | 15 | |

John sees the heavenly throne room. God sits on his throne and 24 elders and four cherubs continuously praise him, the one who created the universe.

Chapter **4**

| 11 | | 13 | | 15 | |

God has a scroll sealed with seven seals. The Lamb takes the scroll. The elders and the cherubs worship the lamb, who is worthy to open the seals because he died for everyone's sins.

Chapter **5**

| 9 | | 13 | | 15 | |

The Lamb opens the seals, releasing judgments represented by horsemen: conquest, war, scarcity, famine, and death. Martyrs wait for vengeance. There is an earthquake and falling stars.

Chapter **6**

| 11 | 13 | 15 |
| --- | --- | --- |

**Chapter 7**

Four angels hold back the four winds. Another angel places a seal on the foreheads of 144,000 from the 12 tribes of Israel. A multitude in white robes praise God and the Lamb.

| 9 | 13 | 15 |
| --- | --- | --- |

**Chapter 8**

The seventh seal opens: there is a half-hour of silence. Seven angels blow trumpets: hail and fire burn the land, a burning mountain bloodies the sea, fish die, and the sun darkens.

| 9 | 13 | 15 |
| --- | --- | --- |

**Chapter 9**

The fifth trumpet: a star falls, opening the Abyss. Its smoke becomes locusts that sting those without God's seal on their foreheads. Angels from the Euphrates kill a third of humanity.

| 9 | 13 | 15 |
| --- | --- | --- |

**Chapter 10**

An angel plants his right foot on the sea and his left on the land. He shouts and seven thunders rumble. John was told to eat a little scroll. Then he was told to prophesy.

| 9 | 13 | 15 |
| --- | --- | --- |

**Chapter 11**

John measures God's Temple. The Beast of the Abyss kills the two witnesses. They rise from the dead. An earthquake devastates Jerusalem. The kingdom of the world becomes the Kingdom of God.

| 9 | 13 | 15 |
| --- | --- | --- |

**Chapter 12**

A woman bears a male child. God protects him from the dragon, Satan. Michael and his angels defeat Satan and his angels. God protects the woman from Satan, who then attacks Christians.

| 9 | 13 | 15 |
| --- | --- | --- |

**Chapter 13**

A ten-horned beast with seven heads arises, attacks God's people, rules the world, and is worshiped. A second beast forces all to take the mark of the beast on their hands or foreheads.

| 9 | 13 | 15 |
| --- | --- | --- |

**Chapter 14**

The 144,000 did not worship the beast. One angel announces judgment, a second the fall of Babylon, the third, judgment on those with the beast's mark. The beast's worshipers are destroyed.

## Chapter 8: Commentary

The disasters in the Book of Revelation are comparable to the Plagues of Egypt. The Egyptians faced ten plagues: of water turning to blood, of frogs, of gnats, of flies, of disease against the farm animals, of boils, of hail, of locusts, of darkness, and of the death of the firstborn. As the Israelites rejoiced over the destruction of Egypt (Exodus 15), so the people of God rejoice over the destruction of the Roman Empire (Revelation 7 and 19). The repetition of seven judgments (seven seals in Revelation 6–7, seven trumpets in Revelation 8, seven thunders in Revelation 10, and seven bowls in Revelation 15–16) is similar to what occurs in the Book of Leviticus. There, four sets of seven judgments are predicted against Israel for disobedience (Leviticus 26:14–45).

*And out of the smoke locusts came down on the earth and were given power like that of scorpions of the earth. They were told not to harm the grass of the earth or any plant or tree, but only those people who did not have the seal of God on their foreheads. They were not allowed to kill them but only to torture them for five months. And the agony they suffered was like that of the sting of a scorpion when it strikes. During those days people will seek death but will not find it; they will long to die, but death will elude them.*

**Revelation 9:3–6**

## Chapter 10: Commentary

In Revelation 10:9–11 John is given a small scroll to eat before being instructed to prophesy. It parallels the experience of Ezekiel, who in Ezekiel 3:1 is instructed to eat a scroll and then to prophesy. There are, throughout the Book of Revelation, many parallels and allusions to events in the Old Testament, particularly to the Pentateuch and the books of Ezekiel and Daniel.

## Chapter 13: Commentary

The number of the beast, 666 in most copies of the Greek text, is generally believed to be a reference to Nero, since the numerical value of the phrase "Caesar Nero" was 666. The idea of people being "marked" is common in the Bible. Cain is marked in Genesis 4:15 to keep people from killing him. In Deuteronomy 6, God told his people that his commands were to be symbols on their hands and foreheads (Deuteronomy 6:8; see also Exodus 13:9). In Ezekiel 9 a "man clothed in linen" placed a mark on the foreheads of those to be protected from God's judgment (Ezekiel 9:3–6). In Revelation 7, the 144,000 were "sealed" to protect them. In Revelation 13 others take the mark of the beast (Mark 14:9, 11, 16:2, 19:20, 20:4).

*Then I saw three impure spirits that looked like frogs; they came out of the mouth of the dragon, out of the mouth of the beast and out of the mouth of the false prophet. They are demonic spirits that perform signs, and they go out to the kings of the whole world, to gather them for the battle on the great day of God Almighty.*

*"Look, I come like a thief! Blessed is the one who stays awake and remains clothed, so as not to go naked and be shamefully exposed."*

*Then they gathered the kings together to the place that in Hebrew is called Armageddon.*

**Revelation 16:13–16**

## Chapter 17: Commentary

The "Whore of Babylon... sits on a scarlet beast that was covered with blasphemous names and had seven heads and ten horns." In verse 9, the author writes that "the seven heads are seven hills on which the woman sits." Then in Revelation 17:18 the woman is said to be "the great city that rules over the kings of the earth." Given that "Babylon" was commonly used by the Jewish people to describe Rome—and given that Rome famously sits on seven hills—most scholars believe that the "Whore of Babylon" is the city of Rome, while the "beast" is the Roman Empire.

## Chapter 20: Commentary

Gog and Magog first appear in Ezekiel 38 and 39, never to be mentioned again until Revelation 20:8, where they represent all the nations of the world arrayed for battle against God and his people. The battle is short and decisive. The description seems to parallel the description of events in Ezekiel, though much condensed.

## Chapter 21: Commentary

The New Jerusalem in Ezekiel 40–48 bears a striking resemblance to the description of the New Jerusalem in Revelation 20. The New Jerusalem of Revelation, however, does not appear to be a description of a physical city but rather of the Christian church—that is, all Christians—since the New Jerusalem is identified as the bride of the Lamb (see Revelation 19:7, 21:2, 21:9, 22:17).

## Chapter 22: Commentary

The river of the water of life that flows from the throne of God, on whose edges are the tree of life-bearing fruit for the healing of the nations (Revelation 22:1–5) matches Ezekiel 47:1–12 and its description of the new Jerusalem and Temple. Ezekiel 47:12 describes "fruit trees of all kinds" growing on the banks of the river and states that their fruit serves as food and their leaves for healing.

| 9 | 13 | 15 |
|---|---|---|

Seven angels come with the seven last plagues in seven bowls, the wrath of God, while those who had been faithful to God sing praises to God.

**Chapter 15**

| 9 | 13 | 15 |
|---|---|---|

God's wrath from seven bowls: festering sores, sea of blood, rivers of blood, scorching sun, darkness, and the battle at Armageddon. An earthquake devastates the city and hailstones fall.

**Chapter 16**

| 9 | 13 | 15 |
|---|---|---|

The Whore of Babylon, drunk with the blood of God's people, rides the beast with seven heads and ten horns. She is the great city that rules over the earth. She will be destroyed.

**Chapter 17**

| 9 | 13 | 15 |
|---|---|---|

A lament over the fall and destruction of Babylon. She is judged and destroyed for what she did to God's people. Though merchants mourn the loss of trade, God's people rejoice.

**Chapter 18**

| 9 | 13 | 15 |
|---|---|---|

Babylon's destruction brings rejoicing. The wedding of the Lamb arrives. Jesus defeats the beast and his armies with the sword coming from his mouth: the word of God.

**Chapter 19**

| 9 | 13 | 15 |
|---|---|---|

Satan is locked away for 1,000 years, then released. He leads an army against Jesus and God's people, but is annihilated. Satan is cast into the lake of fire and the dead are judged.

**Chapter 20**

| 13 | 15 |
|---|---|

A new heaven and new earth appear; the new Jerusalem, the Lamb's bride, descends from heaven. Only those whose names are written in the Book of Life are in it.

**Chapter 21**

| 13 | 15 |
|---|---|

A river of the water of life flows from the throne of God and the Lamb. Beside it grows the tree of life. God's people will live with him forever. Jesus is returning soon.

**Chapter 22**

# INDEX

Figures in italics indicate captions.

## Key to themes

Every chapter of the Bible is summarized briefly and color-coded according to theme. The 18 themes that have been applied to the texts will provide the reader with an overall sense of the primary point or points of each chapter. For more information about each of the themes, see pages 10–13.

|  |  |
|---|---|
| **Praise** | *1* |
| **Forgiveness** | *2* |
| **Moral teaching** | *3* |
| **Mourning** | *4* |
| **Poetry** | *5* |
| **Parables** | *6* |
| **Prophecy** | *7* |
| **Miracles** | *8* |
| **Judgment** | *9* |
| **Love** | *10* |
| **Worship** | *11* |
| **Prayer** | *12* |
| **Apocalypse** | *13* |
| **Contract** | *14* |
| **Angels and Demons** | *15* |
| **Inventory** | *16* |
| **History** | *17* |
| **Wisdom Literature** | *18* |

## FOLD-OUT FLAP

Fold out this flap to find an at-a-glance key to the color and number system used to identify the Bible themes. Keep this flap open as you use this book, or until you become familiar with the key.

**Moses**
*God appears to Moses in a burning bush and tells him to go back to Egypt.*

## CREDITS

Quarto would like to thank the following agencies for supplying images for inclusion in this book:

Alamy p.113

Bridgeman p.2, 10, 13tr, 13br, 20, 25, 27, 31, 34, 36, 37, 41, 43, 46, 48, 51, 55, 57, 59, 61, 63, 69, 71, 75, 76, 79, 81, 83, 85, 86, 87, 91, 95, 97, 101, 103, 104, 108, 109, 111, 116, 119, 121, 123, 126, 129, 134, 136, 137, 145, 147, 148, 149, 151, 152, 162, 164, 171, 179, 180, 182, 203, 207, 209, 210, 211, 221, 225, 230, 234, 236, 242, 243, 244

Dover Books p.92, 107, 110, 159, 160

Mary Evans p.77, 78, 88, 89, 90, 93, 94, 122, 124, 135, 154, 178, 186, 199, 215

The Art Archive p.6, 14, 17, 23, 24, 26, 28, 39, 42, 45, 58, 62, 64, 72, 98, 127, 130, 132, 157, 183, 185, 188, 191, 193, 194, 197, 200, 206, 212, 218, 219, 220, 223, 224, 232, 235, 237, 239, 240, 256

While every effort has been made to credit contributors, Quarto would like to apologize should there have been any omissions or errors—and would be pleased to make the appropriate correction for future editions of the book.

## About the paintings

Abbate or Abate, Niccolo dell' (c.1509–71)—p.24
Arpo, Guariento di (fl.1350–1400)—p.10bl
Bassano, Jacopo (Jacopo da Ponte) (1510–92)—p.46
Bassano, Leandro (Leandro da Ponte) (1557–1622)—p.157
Bedoli, Girolamo Mazzola (c.1500–69)—p.243
Bellini, Giovanni (1430–1516)—p.200
Bendixen, Siegfried Detler (1786–1864)—p.2, p.10tl
Blake, William (1757–1827)—p.17, p.25, p.109, opp p.256
Bonnat, Leon Joseph Florentin (1833–1922)—p.103
Borgona, Juan de (c.1470–c.1535)—p.180
Brueghel, Pieter the Elder (1525–69)—p.64
Buoninsegna, Duccio di (c.1260–1318)—p.194
Caimi, Antonio (1814–78)—p.14
Caravaggio, Michelangelo (1571–1610) (follower of)—p.57
Carrachi, Annibale (1560–1609)—p.212
Cavallino, Bernardo (1616–54)—p.69
Coli, G. (1643–81) & Gherardi, F. (1643–1704) (circle of)—p.76
Copping, Harold (1863–1932)—p.210
Claeissens, Anthuenis (1536–1613) (studio of)—p.101
Cranach, Lucas, the Elder (1472–1553)—p.149
Dutch School, (16th century)—p.91
Eeckhout, Gerbrandt van den (1621–74)—p.61
English School, (12th century) —p.121, p.129, p.135, p.236
English School, (14th century) —p.111, p.114
English School, (20th century) —p.162, p.164
Fetti or Feti, Domenico (1589–1624)—p.244
Fragonard, Jean-Honore (1732–1806)—p.71
Fredi, Bartolo di; also Manfredi de Battilori (1330–1410)—p.108
French School, (15th century) —p.20, p.182
French School, (19th century)—p.85
German School, (15th century) —p.41, p.43, p.48, p.98

German School, (19th century)—p.75
Ghirlandaio, Domenico (1449–1494)—p.235
Ghirlandaio, Ridolfo (Bigordi), Il (1483–1561)—p.225
Hermann, Franz George II (1692–1768)—p.138
Hemessen, Jan Sanders van (c.1504–66)—p.209
Hole, William Brassey (1846–1917) —p.27, p.79, p.81, p.83, p.97, p. 147
Italian School, (15th century)—p.234
Jordaens, Jacob (1593–1678)—p.207
Jordan, L. (20th century) (after)—p.37
Kronberg, Julius (1850–1921)—p.63
Letin, Jacques de (1597–1661)—p.45
Leyden, Lucas van (1494–1533)—p.197
Martin, John (1789–1854)—p.130
Moreau, Gustave (1826–98)—p.145
Murillo, Bartolome Esteban (1618–82)—p.206
Orsel, Victor (1795–1850)—p.224
Raphael (Raffaello Sanzio of Urbino) (1483–1520) (after)—p.86
Rembrandt, Harmenszoon van Rijn (1606–69)—p.31, p.232
Romanian School, (17th century)—p.126
Rubens, Peter Paul (1577–1640)—p.137
Sassoferato (1609–1685)—p.220
Scheits, Matthias (c.1630–c.1700)—p.119
Scorel, Jan van (1495–1562) (follower of)—p.59
Serra, Pedro (fl 1375–1408)—p.239
Shields, Frederic James (1833–1911)—p.179
Simpson, William "Crimea" (1823–99)—p.87
Solimena, Francesco (1657–1747)—p.55
Spanish School, (12th century)—p.151
Surikov, Vasilij Ivanovic (1848–1916)—p.123
Texier, Charles Felix Marie (1802–71) (after)—p.230
Tiepolo, Giambattista (1696–1770)—p.237
Tissot, James (1836–1902)—p.26, p.39, p.42, p.62, p.132, p.185, p.188, p.191
Tito, Santi di (1536–1603)—p.211
Trevisani, Francesco (1656–1746)—p.221
Vincent, Francois Andre (1746–1816)—p.104
Wet or Wett, Jacob Willemsz de (c.1610–72)—p.28, p.203,
Zurbaran, Francisco de (1598–1664) (follower of)—p.242